Water and man: The conne(... block of our existence, it accou(... drink it. We bathe in it. Some swim in it. (I won't! I don't! I can't! More on that later.) Best of all, many of us fish its varied forms: creeks, rivers, ponds, reservoirs, lakes, and oceans. With water covering approximately 75% of Earth's surface, an outback sage postulated that man should allocate three-quarters of his time to fishing and one-quarter to working. Oh, to be so lucky.

Why fish? For food? To commune with nature? To fulfill a primal urge, the thrill of the hunt, matching wits with an unseen foe? When in a boat, to experience the anti-gravitational sensation of floating, and when gently rocking in the waves, reverting to the soothing rhythm of the cradle? To enjoy time away from the rat race with family and friends? The answer could be any or all of the above.

The U.S. Fish & Wildlife Service National Survey (most recent completed in 2011) reported that 41.6 million Americans fished. By my count, that's "a lot." I'm happy to say I'm one of those. Like multi-colored braid line through the eyelets of a rod, fishing has threaded its way through my life's trolling run.

Both on the water and off, I've sailed many Cs: a Chicago childhood; conversations at Crystal Creek; catching carp, catfish, and crappies from the Chain O' Lakes; consuming *czarnina* (Polish duck blood soup); making calls from corporate cubicles; college and its collage of characters; the Chicago Cubs (curses!); the chagrin of constipation and colonoscopies; and casting captivating Canadian waters in the quest to catch the fish of a lifetime. With those experiences (many highlighting the "fun" in "dysfunction") tucked in this Baby Boomer's creel, "now" was the time to document them.

All the occurrences herein took place, more or less, and have been recorded to the best of my recollection. Some names, places, and incidental details have been changed. With regard to certain individuals, the changes protect their right to deny they ever knew me. Not having carried a recording device, much of the dialog has been created, but I feel it captures the spirit of our conversations and is true to the personalities of those who have appeared in one or more of my life's vignettes. Several small pieces of this work were originally published, in slightly altered form, in *Musky Hunter Magazine*.

Table of Contents

Page 3	Part 1	Growing Up Chicago – The Guppy Years
Page 51	Part 2	"There's Hair Down There!" – The Testicle Takeover Years
Page 124	Part 3	Post College – Out of the Aquarium, Into the Ocean
Page 205	Part 4	Fishing? Seriously? – Fishing Seriously
Page 381	Part 5	Favorite Things
Page 390	Part 6	Dad
Page 413	Part 7	Fishing for the Meaning of Life
Page 431	Part 8	Sunset and Another Dawn – Fishing for Serenity

The two best times to fish is when it's raining and when it ain't.
—Patrick F. McManus

Heavy overcast, a positive in musky hunting, blankets the sky as we move to Twin Falls Bay. During that brief ride, a bald eagle, white head and tail feathers alight against the gray sky, wings overhead. With a lifelong affinity for eagles, I silently hope that the sight of the majestic raptor is a sign of good things to come.

Moments later, we begin our routine, flinging casts in various directions. I rocket the Giant Jackpot toward the outlet where the falls cascade into Big Vermilion. The retrieve ensues, uneventful. With the topwater lure some fifteen feet from the boat, I pause, reaching down to make an adjustment to the trolling motor while also taking a peek at the depth contours for this area on the lake map resting atop the small platform next to my seat.

Upon looking up, a sizeable shadow suspends several feet behind and below the motionless bait. I alert Larry and Art, who hold their casts. With little room to work the lure in its normal manner, I contemplate the next move. Intensively focused on my musky fishing "first," I slowly reel in the small amount of slack line that curves from my rod tip to the lure, hoping to leave the Jackpot undisturbed until I decide if a subtle or exaggerated movement might up the odds of enticing this lion of the lake to strike. The last turn of the reel handle causes a barely perceptible twitch of the Jackpot's nose. The fish rises to within inches of the lure: curious, perhaps hungry, menacing. It's big— bigger than the one Larry landed a few short hours ago.

Indecision be gone, I think, it's time to do something. A short, quick jerk of the rod propels the lure several inches forward. As if shot out of a canon, the musky breaches the surface and with alligator, tooth-lined jaw agape, engulfs the lure.

"Holy crap!" Art yells, as all hell breaks loose.

The drag on my reel completely tightened down, there's nowhere for the fish to go; it's a wild steer at the end of a lasso. Both hands gripping the rod, I'm hanging on for dear life. The frenzied fish, seesawing the surface at boatside, showers us with lake water. In spite of the chaos, Larry manages to grab the net. As the musky powers from stern to bow, he corrals it. Sort of ...

~ ~ ~ ~ ~

Part One
Growing Up Chicago -- The Guppy Years

Born to Fish?

In his 1653 work *THE COMPLEAT ANGLER, Or, the Contemplative Man's Recreation,* Izaak Walton states, "... as no man is born an artist, so no man is born an angler...." Though I can't say for certain, I'm not aware of any comments on this subject from the likes of Rembrandt, Shakespeare, Mozart or any of their virtuoso brethren. From a personal perspective, with all due respect, Izzy, I choose to disagree. Feeling destined to fish from the beginning, I can't help but see the world through an angler's eyes.

There's Something Fishy Going on Today

Late on Easter Sunday, in the spring of 1952, the annual smelt run peaks for hearty nighttime anglers as they ply their pastime in mid-30 degree temperatures, casting and retrieving weighted nets with hopes of snagging the silvery, sardine-size fish that congregate near shore in the cold waters of Lake Michigan along Chicago's lakefront. Two miles to the west, inside St. Mary of Nazareth Hospital, another endeavor, significantly nobler, unfolds.

Mom labors through the dark of night, transacting one of nature's most painful yet rewarding processes, the miracle of childbirth. Her unwavering focus further one-ups the fishermen, the night of pain and stress prolonged beyond the hours of dawn and sunrise, and further to her credit, negotiated without the numbing properties of a flask filled with rye whiskey, flavored brandy, or peppermint schnapps that often makes its way from the pockets of nocturnal anglers to their lips.

Afloat for nine months in Mom's hatchery tank, the warm, soothing waters swaddle me like a bedding bass in Lincoln Park Lagoon. Quite content floating in carefree comfort, although blissfully unaware that my watery surroundings are becoming increasingly cramped by the day, must all good things come to an end?

The next morning, at 7:53 a.m., the bubble bursts. What the hell? Splish ... splash ... slip ... slide ... flip ... flop. Like a fish out of water, I'm hand-landed by Dr. Casimir Przypyszny. (Yes, that's his real name. Yes, it's very Polish. And, no, I can't pronounce it either.) Grasped by the ankles, "Dr. Casey" hoists me high into the air in a move similar to fishing legends Roland Martin or Jimmy Houston triumphantly presenting the winning entry in a Bass Masters

Classic tournament to an adoring crowd. Though my coming-out party plays to a limited audience of doctor, nurse, and Mom, at 7-pounds, 1¾-ounces, and 21¾-inches, I weigh and tape at the size of a nice largemouth bass that most anglers would be proud to catch. My eyes, the blue-gray of a glacial stream, gush a whitewater rapid of tears as I wail the call of a forlorn loon. The delivery room lights reflect off a tuft of my hair, shimmering a metallic glow like the scales of a golden shiner minnow in morning's first light. And so my terrestrial journey begins.

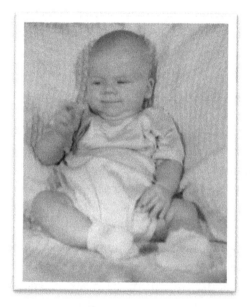

Mmmm ... Something to nibble on!

What's in a Name?

I'm named after my father, Edward. My childhood nickname, "Eddie," carries some aqua-fishing connections:

> In the world of water and fish, an "eddy" forms when a natural or wind-induced current flows in a circular pattern around and behind a structural element such as a point of land, a reef, or a fallen tree. Slack water created in its center provides a favorite ambush point where predatory fish lie in wait for an easy meal as unsuspecting prey whirlpool to their dinner table by the swiftly flowing waters.

In addition to me, the 1950s also spawns the Original Eddie's Bait, a large, gliding, wooden bait in the shape of a billy-club that replaced the casting of harnessed live suckers when fishing for muskellunge and pike.

Years later, the company expands its line of lures to include the Surfin' Ed, Jointed Ed, Steady Eddie, Little Eddie, Curly Ed and Squirrelly Ed.

In early childhood, many family members referred to me as "Little Eddie" and at times in later life, "Steady Eddie." Ocean-absent, "surfin'" was never part of the Midwest scene. With straight locks, "Curly Ed" didn't apply. Although a strong case could be advanced for tagging me with the "squirrelly" moniker, that one never surfaced. With the passing of years, I'd become the aching-Jointed Ed. Whatever those descriptions, I'd always be the "Fishing Eddie."

I don't recall, nor did my parents or relatives advise me of any significant occurrences between my birth and age four or five. I filled those early years with the usual baby stuff: a little bit of cute offset by bouts of crying, whining, and crapping my pants. At some point later in that timeframe, in addition to enjoying the card game Go Fish, I developed the manual dexterity necessary to successfully grip and maneuver a bamboo fishing pole that allowed me to actually "go fish."

Some Background
(More "Ground" than Water)

Home Town

Numerous nicknames tag Chicago: "The City That Works" (assuming you know whose palms to grease), "The Second City" (ask any New Yorker), and "The Windy City" (not because of any weather-related phenomenon but rather due to the hot air bellowed by its politicians). It's "The City of Big Shoulders" and "Hog Butcher to the World," as Carl Sandburg describes it in his aptly titled poem *Chicago*.

Deriving its name from the Indian *chicagoua*, the meaning of the word among the local Miami, Potawatomi, Algonquin, and Illinois tribes includes garlic plant, stinkweed, wild onion, and skunk. The goats n skunks n onions n garlic n stinkweed n stockyards define a city with distinctively "aromatic" days of yore.

Despite its odiferous beginning, Chicago *did* make a silk purse out of that butchered sow's ear, evolving into a world-class city whose impressive skyline reflects on the cool, aquamarine waters of Lake Michigan. Even the lake, however, isn't shy about providing reminders of the etymology of the city's name. In the mid-1960s, she regurgitated several billion dead alewives onto the metro area's beaches. "I have no recollection, Senator, in spite of the oppressively pungent fumes, of pleading with Dad to take me to the lakeshore to scoop up some of the silvery finned fish for bait, in anticipation of our next angling outing." But I'm getting ahead of myself.

House

In 1951, the year preceding my birth, my parents purchased the house at 2212 West Dickens Avenue on the city's northwest side. From there, I toddled Bucktown during my childhood years. (*Chicago [That Toddlin' Town]*, published in 1922, was written by Fred Fisher. Fred "Fisher"—just another coincidence?) The major thoroughfares of Western, Armitage, Fullerton, and Damen Avenues bounded our Bucktown neighborhood, also sliced on the diagonal by the Kennedy Expressway (completed in 1960 when I turned eight years of age) on the northeast and Milwaukee Avenue on the southwest.

Populated primarily by Polish and German immigrants in the early 1800s, the Bucktown moniker originated from the settlers' penchant for raising goats, the male of the species known as a buck. I might have been prouder if my neighborhood had taken its "buck" nickname from a male deer, like those with impressive multi-point racks, rather than a bearded, garbage-eating ruminant, but I guess I can take solace that my ancestral inhabitants didn't keep donkeys, or Asstown may have been the sight of my juvenility.

My parent's acquisition of the all-brick house, constructed in the years either side of the turn of the 20th century, necessitated a staggering $12,500 mortgage. The majority of the tightly packed neighborhood houses, separated by narrow gangways, were multi-family, built or modified to contain several living spaces referred to as "flats" for use by extended family, or to rent. Although many of these structures rose to two or three levels, ours spanned a modest one-and-one-half stories with flats front and back, and a dormered, attic apartment. The street-side flat, years ago converted from a candy store, was fronted by an oxblood-color brick façade that abutted the sidewalk. All the other homes on the block featured setbacks that allowed for postage-stamp-size front yards, or stairways leading to porches or front doors. A row of low-cut hedges along the entire length of our block, as most others, separated the front sidewalk from the street.

The side and rear of our house adjoined alleys (Chicago is also known as "The Alley Capital of America"), which allowed access to the garage and backyard. In the concrete-paved alleys, rusty 55-gallon drums stood behind each property. Residents dumped their household refuse and food waste, unbagged, into these large metal garbage cans. City sanitation trucks, manned by crews of three, emptied them on a weekly basis. Compounding the putrid funk from the loose-lidded cans, the alleys also served as an outdoor latrine for neighborhood pets and strays, as well as the urinal for over-served patrons of The Corner Tavern, a nearby drinking establishment on the southwest corner of Leavitt and Charleston Avenues. A robust population of flies found the alley environment delightfully agreeable for their April through October lifestyle. In later years, the alley side of our house, which included the unattached garage, served as the canvas for spray-painted gang symbols.

The opposite side of our abode boasted a rare double-width gangway, five steps down from street level. A short length of four-foot-high cyclone fence and an adjoining gate, strung with a metal "Beware of Dog" sign, guarded the gangway entrance. (We didn't own a dog, the notice meant to deter would-be up-to-no-gooders.) Halfway to the back apartment, a wooden stairway rose to a small platform and door leading to the attic flat.

Behind that door, a dimly lit stairway ascended to a set of rooms configured in a straight line, front to back: a living room, kitchen, bathroom (commode and sink only), and two bedrooms. The angled walls matched the pitch of the roof, further constricting the feel of the small rooms and low ceilings. The bedrooms, with ominous trap doors at the base of the walls, were divided by the landing of another creaky stairway leading down to a bedroom of the back flat.

Unoccupied by renters or family, a boogeyman lived in the attic, the diabolic presence always *just* out of sight: at the top or bottom of the stairways; in the next room; in a shadowed corner. The morphing combination of Frankenstein, Dracula, the Werewolf, Cyclops, the Mummy, and the Creature from the Black Lagoon (a coincidence that movies with these fiends appeared on WGN's Saturday Night *Creature Features*?) prowled every nook and cranny.

Affixed to the back of the house, a gray, wood-sided enclosed porch served as the rear flat's only point of entry and exit. Immediately inside were two sets of stairs, each with a half dozen steps: to the left, wooden ones leading up to another door (its lock accessed with a skeleton key) allowing entry to the flat; and down, concrete steps constructed in a quarter-turn arriving at the mud-colored basement door. A boogeyman, likely one and the same commuting from the attic via the trap doors, slinked about the dark recesses of the basement. Without exception, my heart raced in the frightful moments each time I unlatched and opened the basement door. "Jesus, Mary, Joseph," I'd whisper, racing the ten feet (that seemed the length of a football field) to pull the string that turned on the light that would keep the many-faced faceless beast at bay. My fear gradually eased under the illumination, though my vigilance remained steadfast during every moment in the subterranean space.

The basement's low ceiling of exposed joists cocooned a cool, musty area that included a slop sink, a Maytag wringer washing machine, a workbench, boiler, and an imposing black metal storage tank for heating oil. On the gangway side, a pair of small windows constructed of glass blocks allowed minimal amounts of filtered daylight into the underground space. A three-foot metal standpipe rose from the center of the cement floor. When removed, it exposed a drain that doubled as a makeshift urinal when the intensity of play did not allow time for a trip to the upstairs bathroom. Spiders and "not a fish" insects known as silverfish also scurried about this dank space. For several years we dealt with "flying ants," until the pest control folks properly identified them as termites and implemented their exterminating magic.

Shelving units that Dad crafted from 2 x 4s lined two of the basement walls. Important groupings of my possessions occupied space on the lower levels. One shelf held models of World War I and World War II planes assembled from Revell and Aurora kits. The collection included the Red Baron's Fokker triplane, a British Sopwith Camel, American P-40 Flying Tiger, German Messerschmitt ME-109, and a Japanese Mitsubishi Zero. A plane gripped in each hand, dogfights played out with the sway of arms and the imitated hum of roaring engines and bursts of machine gun fire. The Allies always won.

A second shelf contained a wide array of board games, among them Monopoly, Life, Clue, Sorry, Stratego, Battleship, checkers, and my no-doubt-about-it favorite, a table hockey game. Controlled by rods pushed, pulled, and twirled, the metal players glided and pivoted as they defended and shot the magnetized puck, winging it around the rink with hopes of winning the miniature replica of the Stanley Cup. The basement also served as the rink for two-on-two games of hockey played with a Ping-pong ball puck.

Baseball gloves, league and rubber balls, 16-inch softballs in various states of wear, a football, and a pair of badminton racquets pancaking rubber-tipped shuttlecocks filled a third shelf. Baseball bats and hockey sticks stood upright in a kitchen-size garbage can. Ready for action at a moment's notice, our fishing rods, their tips coming together like the supports of a tipi, rested in the corner closest to the basement door.

The rear flat housed our family of four: my dad and me (the two Eds), my mom, Virginia, and sister, Nancy. Our rear flat living space spanned less than 1,000 square feet. The turn-of-the-century rooms, baseboards and windows trimmed in wide, dark wood, included a small kitchen, a small living room, a small bathroom and two small bedrooms. The house was old and, well, small.

Red and white linoleum tiles checkered the kitchen floor, and an intricately designed stamped-metal ceiling matched the floor's bold red. One of two doors in the kitchen led to a pantry that housed another boogeyman. The second door provided access to a bathroom with a cast iron claw-foot tub and another door leading to a small walk-in linen closet. A boogeyman lurked in there, too.

During the heat of summer, box fans in several of the windows "cooled" our flat by replacing the hot air inside the house with hot air from the outside. In winter, hot water heat flowed through floor-standing cast iron radiators. Dark brown, ornately crafted metal radiator covers encased the ones in the living room and kitchen. Hinged tops opened to reveal a rectangular pan spanning the length of these radiators, which when filled with water, served as primitive humidifiers. On numerous occasions, I resisted the urge to turn them into my personal aquariums by adding goldfish. A good choice, this averted a rancid lesson in the physics of heat, evaporation, and decomposition.

Mom's Uncle Stanley and my godmother, Aunt Frances, lived in the front flat, those rooms roughly matching ours in number and size. My childless great-uncle and great-aunt filled an important role in my life as "second parents." No sweeter or gentler a person to be found, Auntie Fran, bespectacled with always-permed, short, curly red hair, babysat me in my early years as both Mom and Dad worked to make ends meet. She prepared my breakfasts and lunches. I always enjoyed the sweet, Polish treat known as *nalesniki,* a homemade, jelly-filled crepe, rolled into the shape of one of Uncle Stanley's cigars.

On evenings that featured television "wrestling" matches (as Uncle Stanley called them), we'd enjoy hot dogs—the mouth-watering fully trimmed delights were served on a steamed bun, surrounded by a generous portion of French fries, all tucked in a tin foil wrap. These aroma-beckoning treats were purchased from "Sam, Sam, the hot dog man," his walk-up stand located on Armitage Avenue just steps east of Western Avenue.

Uncle Stanley, *Stashu,* as adult relatives called him, juxtaposed a stoic nature with an imposing, barrel-chested physique. He toiled as a trolley conductor for several decades until the streetcar traveled the route to extinction in 1947, at which time he transitioned to driving a bus for the newly formed Chicago Transit Authority.

Neighborhood friends and I often joined him for three- or four-handed games of pinochle, "pigs knuckles" as he called it. On the occasions when "Franya" was away at church or out shopping, he'd relent to our pestering requests to take a puff of his Dutch Masters cigar, snuggly tucked into a holder swirled in amber tones. His wily eyes peering from behind wire rim bifocals, a half smile surrounded by the silver stubble of a day-old beard left little doubt he expected us to turn some shade of upset-stomach green. Tough little *Polaks,* we surprised him, handling the stogie like seasoned pros.

Although I never fished with Uncle Stanley or Auntie Fran, the enjoyment of unwinding in a fishing cabin with a cigar, and engaging in a game of pinochle with my fishing partners after a long day on the water, recapture those enjoyable and carefree childhood times.

2212 W. Dickens ... showing off her big alley.

~ ~ ~ ~ ~

Humboldt Park Lagoon

A Rose of Sharon bush that produced baseball-sized, papery lavender blossoms in late summer, a smattering of less-than-lush grass, and a row of four o'clock plants edged the 12-foot-square backyard separating our Dickens

Avenue house from the garage. This small plot of soil served an important purpose in my youth: free bait. On evenings following a rainstorm, the air thick with moisture and musk, I'd venture out, flashlight in hand, to gather night crawlers surfacing for a drink of air from the water-logged earth.

Capture required a stealth approach, lightning quickness, and pinpoint accuracy. Anything less than perfection, on any count, resulted in retraction into their holes faster than I could say, "Stinking earthworm!" After a properly executed stab-grab, a tug-of-war ensued. A favorable outcome required applying the right amount of pressure to accomplish the extraction: pulling too fast or too hard would result in an undesirable break off; too loose allowed the slimy hermaphrodite to slip away to the freedom of its home hole. I stored the successfully plucked *lumbricus terrestris* in a blue Maxwell House three-pound coffee can half-filled with moistened dirt and topped with a handful of grass clippings. I monitored the booty daily, awaiting the next time Dad would take me (or us, Nancy joining on occasion) to the Lincoln Park or Humboldt Park lagoons.

Tucked near the center of the Chicago metropolitan area that houses approximately three million inhabitants, Humboldt Park, an oasis of woods and water in the concrete and asphalt urban landscape, provided an agreeable "out in the country" feel. Upon arriving at the park after a ten-minute car ride, we would set up and cast hooks baited with my hand-harvested night crawlers, the lines releasing from the spools of old Pflueger bait-casting reels attached to whippy fiberglass rods. Split shot affixed inches above the hook pulled the bait to the lagoon's muddy bottom.

Whiskered yellow bullheads, less than a foot in length, scavenged the offerings. When removing the hook, they often "talked" to us with guttural groans and squeaks, bullhead-speak I interpreted as, "Hurry up and put me back in the water, jerk!" We always worked with haste to accommodate their request, though handling them required special care. Sharp spines at the base of their dorsal and pectoral fins could easily pierce a hand, leaving a not-so-pleasant reminder of an otherwise pleasant outing.

~ ~ ~ ~ ~

Soon after our 6 p.m. arrival on this mid-May Friday, I observe two boys on the far shore scurrying about as they wrap up their after-school fishing excursion. Probably ten- and thirteen-years-old, the taller of the two attaches the no-longer-baited hooks to the rod eyelets, drawing the lines tight with turns of the reel handles. A tinny "clang" announces the closing of a metal tackle box the size of a cigar box. His younger partner drags in a stringer clipped with three bullheads. The sun, still above the treeline, illuminates their distinctive yellow bellies that contrast with dark brown sides. He holds them, arm outstretched, at shoulder height. Admiring the fruits of their angling effort that slowly twirls in the afternoon breeze, lagoon water mixes with slime from their scaleless sides, the stringy mixture flicked about by flapping tails.

The older boy, holding the tackle box in one hand, grabs the handlebars of his bicycle with the other and lifts it from its prone position. After settling onto the driver's seat, his friend, with the rods and stringer of fish in tow, hops onto the handle bars to begin their departure for home.

Just as they begin picking up speed, two youths emerge from the brush several yards ahead. Side by side, with legs spread and arms crossed, they block the path. As the bike approaches, the taller of the two, black hair slicked back, steps forward. No doubt a high-schooler by size and dress, his white sleeveless T-shirt tucked into blue jeans with rolled cuffs, he raises his right hand, palm forward and fingers toward the sky like a policeman stopping traffic at a busy intersection. A well-defined triceps muscle ripples across his upper arm as he extends it. As the bike skids to a stop, the handle-bar rider jumps off and the driver dismounts, slowly releasing his grip to guide the bike to a gentle landing on the gravel path. Outside of our earshot, an animated conversation ensues between the older boys as the "traffic cop," who towers a head taller, moves closer while emphatically pointing to the bicycle.

The fisherman does not back down as the tough approaches, now but a foot or two away. Momentarily turning their heads in the direction of their smaller companions and waving them back, the youth with thievery in his heart uses his other hand to deliver a sucker-punch to the bike owner's stomach. Stunned by the unexpected blow, he stumbles backwards, doubled over in pain.

Dad jumps to his feet, shouting, "Hey, what the hell are you doing? Knock it off!" and hastily departs in their direction. The distance, however, will not allow immediate intervention. I hope his emphatic words will bring the menacing situation to a quick end.

Unaware of our observation and distracted by Dad's words, the bully glances across the water in our direction. At that instant, the punch victim bolts forward, exploding his shoulder into his attacker's mid-section, lifting and driving forward several steps before slamming him to the ground in a move reminiscent of a Dick Butkus highlight-reel tackle. The unexpected turn of events continues as the smaller combatant, straddling the chest of the startled ruffian, delivers a series of right-hand headshots strongly laced with vengeance.

With the robbery plot going awry, the younger partner-in-crime scurries toward his partner to lend assistance. The young fisherman, by far the smallest in stature of the four, races behind him, swinging the stringer of bullheads above his head like a spiked-ball-on-a-chain flail used in medieval combat. In an "I can't believe what I'm seeing moment," he whips the collection of fish-turned-weapon toward the unsuspecting hooligan, one of the bony lances concealed in the fins of each fish impaling him in a macabre game of pin the bullhead on the bully's back.

"Yeowwwwwww!" His piercing cry brings a pause to the beating being wrought upon his friend, allowing him to free himself from the pummeling. The human dartboard's arms and hands wildly waving above his head, his partner pulls the stringered fish free and throws them to the ground before the bloodied pair hightail it to the shelter of the woods.

Over as quickly as it began, Dad returns. Seldom at a loss for words, he quips, "Bullheads—good little fighters in and out of the water."

I don't remember what we caught that day but will always remember how a trio of little brown fish delivered a big dose of street justice.

A Troll through the Neighborhood

The city of Chicago houses the largest population of people of Polish descent outside of Poland's capital, Warsaw. The Bucktown neighborhood reflected this strong ethnic presence. Our house stood across from Pulaski Elementary School, a three-story, yellow-brick building and its surrounding grounds that occupy an entire square block bounded by Dickens, Leavitt, McLean, and Oakley Streets. The school was named in honor of Kazimierz Michał Władysław Wiktor (we know him as "Casimir") Pulaski, the Warsaw-born Brigadier General, "Father of the American Cavalry," who fought and died for America's independence during the Revolutionary War. History lesson concluded.

In spite of our close proximity to Pulaski School, I attended St. Hedwig, the Catholic grade school located six blocks from our house. (My sister, Nancy, five years my senior, attended and graduated from Pulaski School. Deprived of the Catholic elementary schooling I received, she was likewise "deprived" of the permanent mental scars inflicted by the reign of terror wrought by some of the nuns—uncomfortable details to follow.) Kindergarten bypassed, my academic career began with first grade.

My daily route to and from school took me past a number of mom-and-pop storefronts embedded among the residences of the neighborhood side streets.

The eclectic sprinkling included three taverns, Dolozinski's Bakery, (Mom worked the 5 a.m. to noon shift at Krusinski's Bakery, two blocks south on Armitage Avenue), Krause's Shoe Repair, Okonski's Drug Store, Antoinette's Pizzeria, and Wojciechowski's Funeral Home (never walk in front, *always* cross the street!).

Any non-solo trek, whether to school, a park, or shopping, included participation in the game Stinkfish, the label attached to the individual who unwittingly stepped in any sidewalk square that included the few-inches-in-size maker's mark imprinted in the corner of the concrete.

Halfway between school and home, Chippy's (note: not Chip*ski's*) Candy Store was a frequent stop-off point. The owner, an ornery, gray-haired fart wearing black horn rim glasses with lenses as thick as Coke bottle bottoms, lacked patience when dealing with neighborhood kids. Magazines and comic books lined the back wall of the cramped store. When he was occupied behind the counter, I'd page through *Sgt. Rock* or *Superman* comic books. More often than not, he'd catch me.

"This ain't a library, kid. If you're not buying it, put it back," he'd bark.

Most of the neighborhood kids agonized over the choices of penny candies that called out from behind the angled glass of the oak-trimmed display case. With only a handful of copper Lincolns to spend on any particular visit, the number of sweet confections, their colors, textures, and tastes, overwhelmed: flying saucers, dots (rows of three candy buttons attached to a strip of paper the width of an adding machine tape), gold-foil-wrapped "lipstick," Bazooka bubble gum, candy cigarettes, pink and white candy-coated licorice Good & Plenty, pumpkin seeds in a box bearing the image of an Indian chief, Twizzlers, wax lips, bullseyes, Mary Janes, Bit-O-Honey, Lik-M-Aid, chocolate gold-foil-wrapped "coins," wax syrup sticks and bottles, jawbreakers, Snaps, and nonpareils.

"Sometime today, kid, before I get old," he'd growl with a scowl.

A high-end confectionery (I only window-shopped the store, never able to afford its pricey delights) located at the intersection of Western and Armitage Avenues, Margie's Candies purveyed homemade candies, ice cream and toppings. A neighborhood institution, in business under that name since 1933, its bold yellow and red scripted marquee, neon lit at night, drew locals as well as celebrities and sports figures of worldwide prominence. The Beatles satisfied their sweet tooth at Margie's after their 1965 Comiskey Park concert. Years later, the Rolling Stones did likewise, requesting the same booth that seated the Fab Four.

No accommodations to eat lunch at St. Hedwig necessitated an additional trip to and from school each day. The trek left 15- to 20-minutes to scarf down a bread, butter, and jelly sandwich or bowl of soup, the midday break made more enjoyable by viewing *Bozo's Circus* on our 19-inch Zenith black and white television. After school I'd race home attempting to catch the last few innings of the Cubs games, then head outside to play in the Pulaski schoolyard until dinner. Weather not permitting or friends unable to join me (calling from the sidewalk outside their homes, "Yo, Jim-my!" "Yo, Jo-ey!" "Yo-o Greg!"), I'd view WGN-TV's *Garfield Goose and Friends* and *The Three Stooges* shorts hosted by Andy Starr, the elderly caretaker of the every-neighborhood Odeon Theatre.

I enjoyed the benefit of living across from a schoolyard that provided a steady revenue stream, minimal as it was, for my purchases. "Older kids," teenagers who played ball at Pulaski, would leave their empty soda bottles strewn about the schoolyard. I scooped them up on an almost-daily basis; their litter was my gain. I'd return them for a deposit of two cents each, converting the coins to candy treats or ten-cent rubber balls (solid, in a size slightly smaller than a tennis ball, coated white and embossed with seams imitating a league ball) used in games of fast-pitch against the school building bricks chalked with boxes delineating the strike zones. The most frequent location for our games, however, played out against a perfectly sized square coal chute, the distinctive *thunk!* of pitched ball hitting metal leaving no doubt or disagreement about whether the pitch was a ball or strike.

Like many of the neighborhood businesses, it seemed as if the surnames of every other kid in my St. Hedwig classes ended in "ski." Seats assigned by student height, Ronald Brynski and I alternated the one-two position as the perennial shortest boys in class, occupying the front desk in any given year. Each of two classrooms per grade, crammed to the brink like a Polish *kielbasa* sausage, averaged over forty students. It's no wonder most of the Sisters of the Holy Family of Nazareth (same order that operated the hospital of my birth) often displayed short fuses when meting out discipline. Other factors may have also contributed to their often less-than-congenial "attitude":

> A cloistered life confined to one square block of real estate.
>
> "Designer" garb: black, floor-length habits that kept them warm in the winter and "hot under the (high buttoned) collar" in summer. Old film footage of their movements from convent to church to school may have inspired the movie, *March of the Penguins.*

Large, arched and starched black headgear, lined in white across the front hairline. Though veiled to mid-back in the rear, I was certain the material possessed see-through qualities, allowing a clear field of vision for the eyes in the back of their heads.

Attached at the belt, mega rosaries with beads the size of my Cat's Eye marbles, cascaded to ankle length. The image impressed the strange marriage of religion and armament.

Rimless glasses for one and all. Mother Superior, the penguin captain, probably negotiated a quantity discount with the local optometrist, Dr. Dubinsky. Never able to confirm if each wore a second pair for the eyes in back of their heads, that likelihood laid the groundwork for future "buy one, get one free" optical promotions.

Early on, I believed that nuns, strange creatures in dress, mannerisms, speech, and behavior, were of alien origin. When the folly of that notion dissipated, I next surmised they were neither male nor female but rather a third, neuter gender. Some of my nuns were kind, almost grandmotherly: Sister Raphael in second grade, Sister Neri in sixth, and Sister Seraphia in eighth. On the flipside, stories heard about some Catholic school nuns using attack weaponry such as pointers, rulers, chalk, erasers, paddles, belts, and in the absence of those, the bare forehand and backhand, ring as true as St. Hedwig's bell towers calling parishioners to daily mass. Sister Sarastine in third grade and Sister Eugenia in seventh answered that bell, like boxers being called to center ring.

~ ~ ~ ~ ~

A day like most others, Sister Sarastine rides herd over our unfortunate group of eight-year-olds, iron fists flying with each misfire of her synapses. With vocabulary the last topic of each school day, today's exercise practices the understanding of words by using them in sentences. I haven't been called on yet. From my front desk, I'm unable to see the monolith in black that slowly paces the aisles behind me.

The confident voice of Elizabeth Ivanowski answers, "Transportation … We use my daddy's car as transportation." Know-it-all little bitch.

Staring into my workbook, eyes wide in disbelief, I don't know the meaning of a couple of the words. I *knew* I should have studied the list instead of watching *The Untouchables* last night, but I couldn't take a chance on missing the episode where Eliot Ness might finally catch up with Al Capone somewhere in the streets of Chicago.

God help me, it could get ugly if Sister Sarastine calls on me. Should I slink in my seat, turtling to make a less obvious target? No, the motion might draw attention. Take short breaths. Freeze. Pray.

Before I can plead my case heavenward, I pick up the flowery scent of Cashmere Bouquet soap. I'm familiar with it as the brand used by Auntie Fran. But here, now, it invades the space around me, hovering like the plague, the scent of death.

"*Pyuh-trrruv-ski...*" The thick voice, neither male nor female, calls out my last name in the proper Polish pronunciation. Fear overflowing my core, oozing out of every pore, I turn my head to the right. At first, eye to eye with the jumbo rosary backed by the black curtain of her habit, I slowly tilt my head upward, following the beads with the deliberation and anxiety of a prisoner on the gallows peeking at the noose that will soon take him to his Maker.

A hundred stories above me her face comes into view. In a permanent frown, washboard wrinkles line her forehead. Behind her rounded rimless spectacles, crow's feet brand the outer edge of each eye and brown bags droop beneath them. Her cheeks and mouth purse as if she's just sucked on a lemon.

I gulp out a timid acknowledgement. "Yes, sister?"

"Use *homely* in a sentence."

Homely ... homely ... homely .... Paralyzed, the word reverberates in the spatial void of my skull, the area formerly occupied by my brain. It slows and echoes with each bounce ... homely ... homely ... homely; I'm clueless as to its meaning. Is there time for divine intervention? Will it be held against me that just a minute ago I thought Elizabeth a bitch? Why couldn't I have been sick today?

"Homely. Use it in a sentence," the gatekeeper barks with more urgency.

Hands clammy, I pray for my immediate conveyance to another galaxy. In a failed attempt to connect the dots, I trickle the words, "When a person stays at home ... they are homely."

Whack! An open hand contacts the area between my shoulder blades.

Stunned, another silent plea follows, this one more urgent: "St. Edward, St. Hedwig, *anybody* up there listening—help me!" I blurt out another set of words: "The Sisters in the convent are homely."

Whack! Whack!

"Sister Sarastine is very homely!"

Whack! Whack! Whack!

At that moment, from several desks back, the distinctive snicker of the class clown, George Malkowski, slices the tension-filled air. I'm not sure if he's taking joy in my knucklehead answers, the crazed response to them, or a combination of both. It doesn't matter—he's the answer to my prayer. With the eyes in the back of her head identifying the source, Sister Sarastine twirls and rockets to his desk like a missile fired from Cape Canaveral. Whack! Whack! Whack! Whack! ... Whack! Thankful for the diversion, I've always admired George's ability to take his beatings with a smirk or a smile, this one no different from any of the many others he's received. Seconds later the bell sounds, signaling the end of the school day. Scared and scarred, I'll pray extra hard tonight that our teacher-tormentor will have a short memory. I'll also put in some extra time with my A.C. Gilbert chemistry kit, concocting a potion that can make me disappear. Or, better yet, Sister Sarastine.

~ ~ ~ ~ ~

Year after year, first desk proximity to the nun played out as a squirmingly uncomfortable proposition. On the plus side, however, sitting close to the blackboard benefited my advancing nearsightedness. By fifth grade, the condition worsened to the point that glasses became necessary. Fitted with corrective lenses, Mom handpicked a pair of oversized gray plastic frames from the "dorky" collection. Add "four eyes" to this short, skinny kid's monikers that included "Mr. Ed," television's talking horse from a series of the same name, and "Eddie Munster," (from TV's *The Munsters)*, a "normal" grade-schooler with the exception of his pointed ears and exaggerated widow's peak (his genetic makeup included werewolf and vampire genes), and Fauntleroy suit. My nickname also easily translated into creative, childhood poetry: "Eddie spaghetti wets his beddie." Oddly enough, no one ever combined my beloved hobby with my heritage by referring to me as a "fishing Pole."

The small St. Hedwig schoolyard, tucked in the center of the building complex, provided the site for the annual summer carnival that occurred on consecutive weekends and in the evenings of the week sandwiched between them. The nuns never attended these festive gatherings. I surmised that among the sacred vows taken before departing the spaceship, they agreed to forego any activities involving earthly enjoyment. Their fun forbidden, I sensed our merriment came under their watch, with multiple sets of eyes gandering our every move from behind the drapes hung on the convent windows, making sure *we* weren't having too much fun. Or was it just my imagination? Or not. Or was it? Ah, paranoia, another parochial school endowment.

Crammed into the small venue, the carnival bombarded the senses, though in a pleasant way: yellow and white blinking lights lining booths and rides; the merry-go-round's horses gently galloping to the tunes of the calliope; the swirling aroma of popcorn, hot dogs, peanuts, and tobacco smoke from cigars and cigarettes; the gravity defying spins of the Tilt-a-Whirl; puffs of pink cotton candy on rolled paper "sticks"; the Ferris wheel, on its circular tour cresting above the school's third story, offering views of neighborhood rooftops; and refreshing, shaved-ice snow cones, flooded with syrup flavors in blue raspberry and cherry.

Many patrons engaged in assorted games of chance, perhaps better referred to in the world of carnies as "no chance." Children generally easy marks, the slick hucksters met their match when I toed the line for one particular game. I couldn't believe my good fortune the first time my eyes set sight on a contest seemingly made for me: Ping-pong ball fishing.

A short distance behind a waist-high rope strung across metal poles, small circular bowls the size of a Magic 8-Ball rested atop a long rectangular table. Placed several inches apart, each bowl, its water dyed a color of the rainbow, contained a goldfish. A nickel per ball or three for a dime entitled the player to make tosses toward the colorful maze. If the tiny white celluloid sphere did not "swish" into one of the bowls it bounced helter-skelter, each contact with the glass surfaces emitting a hollow "click." Sometimes it ricocheted its way into one of the bowls—a winner! During carnival week, I reallocated my bottle deposit money originally targeted for the purchase of 5-cent packages of Topps baseball cards, 10-cent rubber balls, or penny candies to the pursuit of these fish. Fairly good at the game, I'm not sure Mom shared my delight when I'd walk through the door with another bowl or two, cupped hands carefully presenting the objects of my success.

Of course the carnies always had the last laugh, their cost of my "winnings" covered the first night I raced up to the rope and emptied the change in my pockets. They don't lose even when you win. True of Ping-pong ball fishing as well as the more conventional methods of the pursuit of fish, it's the thrill of the hunt. You can always go to the market and plunk down a couple of bucks for some fillets, but how much fun is that?

Fishing for a Vocation

As a child, I realized that short of hosting a television program like *The Virgil Ward Championship Fishing Show*, where Virgil makes a living being filmed catching fish, one at a time, the odds of making a living by fishing were remote at best. With the founding of the Bass Anglers Sportsman Society (B.A.S.S.) in the 1960s, professional tournaments followed soon thereafter. In subsequent decades, the Bassmaster, Professional Walleye, and Professional Musky Tournament Trails arrived and prospered, the annual increases in popularity and prize money dramatic. Success on the Bassmaster Tour could net the winning angler tens to hundreds of thousands of dollars in a given year. Lack of a "Bullhead Tour" forced my career aspirations in other directions.

As most young boys, I dreamed of becoming a professional athlete. For baseball and football, we'd latch onto and emulate a favorite player, with the expectation of following in their footsteps on the hallowed ground of Wrigley Field where both the Cubs and Bears played in the early 1960s, before the Bears moved on to Soldier Field. Although these Chicago teams boasted the likes of such greats as Ernie Banks, Dick Butkus, and Gale Sayers, my lower sights lived and died with the performances of Cubs outfielder Walt "Moose" Moryn and Bears hard-nosed but certainly less than spectacular fullback Ronnie Bull. The Cubs and Bears employed a "Moose" and a "Bull," but odd to the story at hand, no player sported a fish moniker onto which I could hook my hopes.

In spite of always graphing at the lower end of the growth chart, quick reflexes, reasonable coordination, and good foot speed compensated for my lack of size, enabling above average sandlot performance for Pulaski schoolyard games. Hockey an exception, never having learned to ice skate (Holstein Park, four blocks to the north and west was flooded as an ice rink each winter) put a damper on thoughts of a career in the NHL. The deceptive stickhandling of Stan Mikita and hard slapshot of Bobby Hull played out on the black asphalt in games of street hockey. On the chance the Cubs or Bears would not avail themselves of my athletic skills, I covered my bases by exploring other vocations and careers.

In an effort to keep their species from becoming extinct, St. Hedwig's nuns and priests periodically delivered a pitch about joining the religious order; a "calling," they called it. Young, impressionable, God-fearing, nun-fearing, and a captive audience, we listened because, well, because we had to.

Tired of waiting for the "call" to come to our home number over the Illinois Bell Telephone lines, I grabbed the habit by the horns with a solemn declaration that would set my career path *and* buy me some slack in the bizarre world of often-demented discipline endemic to parochial education. Confident about scoring extra credit holy points with parish management (goodness knows, my classmates and I *must* be in good stead with the Man upstairs, our ledger of accumulated credits sufficient to move us from hell to purgatory or purgatory to heaven), I proudly declared my intention to Sister Eugenia: "When I grow up I want to be a monk." In a magical moment, the only time I ever saw a smile light her face, she commented, "Oh, that's *wonderful!*"

Perhaps I should have thought it through a little better. What made me think that wearing a mud-brown hooded habit while claustrophobically cloistered 24 hours per day, kneeling and praying for forgiveness for the sins of the world, might be a good idea? Maybe the "Jesus fish" symbol or the phrase "Holy mackerel" caught my fancy.

Before signing a non-binding letter of intent to turn my life into a permanent "mea culpa," I soon discovered that committing sins, albeit in the name of vocational search, seemed a better fit. The Catholic Church deems seven years of age, "or thereabout," as the "age of reason," the age of moral responsibility. Being a slow study, it was at about that age that I confused moral responsibility with moral irresponsibility. For eternal damnation purposes, I'll hang my hat on the "or thereabout" clause as it pertained to age. Heck, at age seven, these were my three biggest concerns:

> Having any Cubs player appear after ripping open a five-cent pack of Topps baseball cards.
>
> Avoid slicing my tongue when taking the first couple of chews on the rock-hard sliver of pink gum with the sweet powder coating found inside the Topps package that I had just ripped open.
>
> Living happily ever after with Lizzy Rosinski.

Guppy Love

Three doors down from our house on Dickens stood a gray frame house, the basement flat occupied by the Rosinski family. Mr. and Mrs. Rosinski had five children: somebody, somebody, somebody, somebody, and Lizzy. With long silken locks the color of spun gold and eyes the deep blue of Pacific waters kissing the shores of Tahiti, sweet, beautiful Lizzy captured my heart as my first love.

At age seven, my relationship with Lizzy started on a strictly professional level when she agreed to assist in my search of a vocational choice as an alternative to monkdom. In those decades-ago days, this noble effort was known as "playing doctor." I set up shop in a coat closet in the small foyer just inside the Rosinski's front door. A clearance of several feet between the bottom of the hanging coats and the floor created the "exam room." Tucked back several more feet, a small frosted window that adjoined the gangway provided a perfect combination of light and privacy. Unbeknownst to me, had a shingle hung on the door it would have described my medical practice as "Specializing in Gynecology."

On a third or fourth follow-up visit (perhaps my career was headed in a chiropractic direction?), we heard Mrs. Rosinski's voice: "Lizzy, where are you?"

Hastily concluding the exam, Lizzy answered, "We're in the closet."

With a noticeable increase in volume and urgency, Mrs. Rosinski queried, "What are you doing in there?"

"We're ... playing house." Good answer, Lizzy! Not too far from the truth, her innocent reply bespoke her ability to think quickly on her back. The answer did not, however, play too well with Mrs. Rosinski.

"Come out here right now. And stay out of there!"

With a wholesome fear of nuns, priests, parents, and adults in general, the tone of her voice led to the shuttering of the main closet office. Not wanting to completely shut down the practice just yet, I opened an alternate location in the basement of our house. Caution to the wind, I risked encounters with the boogeyman for the greater good of my clientele. Lizzy, however, sufficiently freaked, believed it to be in her best interest to *not* schedule visits at my new office.

With this unfortunate turn of events, I attempted to expand my patient base by making a cold call to the Podgornik's, whose dwelling stood two doors beyond the Rosinski's. The Podgorniks had three children: somebody, somebody, and Christine. A year older and a couple of inches taller than me, Christine had shoulder length brown hair, wore glasses, and was slightly pigeon-toed. Had I played my cards right, I would have approached her as an optometrist or podiatrist. Instead, with unpolished salesmanship skills, I sputtered an offer: "Wanna come over to my house so I can give you a full doctor exam?" The last word barely off my lips, a resounding "NO!" sent my career path into limbo.

At least she didn't tell her mother. Or mine. Or Lizzy.

But in the grand scheme of Catholicism and conscience, a price would have to be paid.

Few events in life rival the trauma of the Sacrament of Confession. Prior to these most recent escapades, my indiscretions typically included the following, nervously whispered to the holy presence behind the screen in the confessional booth:

"I lied five times."

"I disobeyed my parents, uh … five times" (Doh! Change up the number, idiot, or he'll know you didn't do a good "examination of conscience.")

The going rate for a small collection of these "venial" or "slight" sins usually garnered penance of three Our Fathers and three Hail Marys. When it came time to face the music regarding my recent job search, I figured there would be some additional consequences, perhaps something as torturesome as ten each of the traditional Catholic prayers.

Magnified by going in with a borderline "mortal" sin brought a new level of clamminess to my hands and beads of perspiration to my brow. Upon entering and kneeling down, my anxiety increased as I heard the muffled voice of Father Zabrowski laying a tongue-lashing on George Malkowski, who had just spilled his guts to the Pastor in the other compartment of the two-sided booth.

My mind raced—there was still time to bolt—no, too late…. The murmur ended and the small door behind the screen slid open, exposing the omnipotent shadow of my confessor. An aroma combining incense, aftershave, and freshly laundered sacred garments came rushing into the coffin-size confessional. As my heart thumped with trepidation, I blurted out, "Bless me Father, for I have sinned. I don't think I'm gonna be a monk, a doctor, or a salesman…."

~ ~ ~ ~ ~

Smoked carp tastes just as good as smoked salmon when you ain't got no smoked salmon.
—Patrick F. McManus

Childhood Cuisine - Guppy Food

My fascination with fish included consumption of same at the dinner table. I'd venture to say the depth and breathe of my tastes ranged well beyond most kids my age, and probably a fair number of adults, as well. Sardines, breaded smelts ("schmelts," as they are referred to by the phonetically challenged immigrant-descendants of our fair city), and smoked chubs all received the "thumbs up."

The early 1960s introduced the hippest fish in the school, the raspy voiced beret-and-sunglass-wearing Charlie the Tuna. Charlie attempted to convince the StarKist folks that he possessed a high level of class and sophistication worthy of their product. Continuously rejected with a "Sorry Charlie!" sign floated down on a fish hook, StarKist didn't want tuna with good taste—they wanted tuna that tasted good. I received the message as an advertiser's dream, frequently sneaking a can or two into our cart when grocery shopping with Mom.

On the non-fish front, no peanut butter and jelly for me: too mainstream. I preferred my white bread and jelly combined with either Philadelphia Cream Cheese or butter.

Soups topped my preferred food list, a staple of my childhood diet. In addition to the standard Lipton's chicken noodle and Campbell's tomato, my maternal grandmother, Victoria—*Busia,* the Americanized Polish word for grandmother—provided a steady flow of gems. Her hearty soups, accompanied by thinly cut homemade *kluski* (noodles), included beet (*borscht*), tomato, sauerkraut, carrot and pea, and *czarnina,* my favorite.

Czarnina, its main ingredient duck's blood, wears the unappetizing dark brown color of a bullhead. Stewed raisins the size of half-ounce split shot and one-inch diameter bobber-size prunes suspend in the coagulating liquid. Many people, including most family members, couldn't get past the color. Or the ingredients. Or the consistency. Too bad. More for me.

As a four-year-old (give or take a year), I recall shopping trips to the National Tea and A&P grocery stores. From my perch in the shopping cart, I'd reach into the meat case and poke my fingers through the cellophane wrap and into the ground meat—it felt squishy-good. I'm sure the butchers and customers following us had a different take.

When preparing hamburgers for dinner, Mom would give me a small bowl of the raw ground beef. Mixed with chopped onions, salt, pepper, and catsup, I devoured the treat with gusto. Years down the road I contemplated a possible connection between this "steak tartar" appetizer and my appendectomy at age eight, as it has been conjectured that the useless appendage known as the appendix may have functioned to digest raw meat in prehistoric man. Okay, not likely, so let's move on to other examples of my young and indiscriminating palate.

Kiszka, Polish blood sausage, is another food I enjoyed as a youth. Animal intestines encased ingredients of beef blood, barley, pork snouts, pork tongue, and pork skins seasoned with a dash of salt and a pinch of pepper. Boiled and served, I'd mash it up and douse it with catsup before diving in. Strange but true, the dish has been immortalized in song. For those who have yet to experience a Polish wedding, the polka favorite *"Who Stole the Kiszka?"* awaits. Perhaps Vlad the Impaler stole it. The hematological connection of *czarnina* and *kiszka* makes me wonder if perhaps a peculiar historical link exists between Poland and Transylvania.

Our family rarely dined at restaurants during my childhood. A meager household budget did not allow for such extravagance. Most of the meals Mom served were mainstream American, but on occasion she or Busia presented an offering with an ingredient at the core of eastern European cuisine: cabbage. At ten cents a pound, it's no wonder some prepared form of the leafy green bowling ball often appeared on the dinner table.

Pierogi, fried or boiled dumplings (Polish ravioli, one might say), are stuffed with meat, cheese, or *cabbage*. *Golabki* (yes, the English phonetic makes it sound like the yellow-green goop that runs from nose when affected by a head cold, but the Polish pronunciation is roughly "go-WOOMP-kee) ingredients include ground beef, rice, and chopped onions, boiled in rolled *cabbage* leaves. A frequently served side dish, coleslaw, contains *cabbage* flavored with vinegar, sugar, and garlic. Polish sausage is typically served on a bed of sauerkraut, that side dish defined as finely sliced *cabbage* fermented by various lactic acid bacteria including Leuconostoc, Lactobacillus, and Pediococcus. Mmm, Mmmh! Sounds like VD and the antibiotic right there on your dinner plate. Man, that's some good eatin'!

Dad, me, Mom, Nancy ~
And a plate of sausage & sauerkraut ... front and center.

~ ~ ~ ~ ~

Simon Peter went up and drew the net to land, full of large fish, 153 of them.
—The Bible, John 21:11

Stat-man

A bachelor into his early 40s, Mom's younger brother, my Uncle Rich, found great joy in viewing sporting events, baseball a particular favorite. When unable to attend games in person, he watched them on the blond-wood RCA console color television (one of the early models of the mid-1950s and an extraordinary luxury on his modest salary) in the small living room of the second floor apartment on Noble Street that he shared with Busia. A zigzag pattern afghan covered a vinyl upholstered rocker, his "box seat" angled in the room's corner. Atop an end table beside him were a circular glass ashtray, his pack of Salem cigarettes, and a cocktail glass filled with ice cubes and a couple of olives soaking in vodka with a splash of dry vermouth.

As a child, an injury to his right shoulder severely limited his ability to participate in sports. To fill that void, while staying connected with his neighborhood buddies who played in park league games, he became well-versed on the intricacies of official scorekeeping. On the occasions when his nieces and nephews joined him at Wrigley Field or Comiskey Park, he willingly tutored those of us who had an interest in learning the notations and documenting the nuances of the game we all loved.

Those early lessons in "national pastime" accounting sparked a personal fascination with record keeping. In addition to the major league games, I began tracking batting averages, homeruns, runs-batted-in, and earned run average for summertime dawn-to-dusk games of fast-pitch at Pulaski School; similar statistics for Strat-O-Matic Baseball; running and passing yardage for Foto-Electric Football; and tallying goals from the metal players firing the magnetic puck past the goalie in table-hockey contests. My cousin Larry and I also devised a point system for the distance traveled by homemade paper airplanes as we launched them down the alley (fighting for airspace with flies in flight) behind the house on Dickens Avenue. Oh, and this statistical bent flowed into my fishing world, too.

One might ask, "What's the point of keeping track of fish caught? Isn't fishing to be enjoyed as an innocent leisure, a respite from the day-to-day routine, a getaway allowing the spirit to commune with nature? Okay. All that. But go play a round of golf or bowl three lines without keeping score, then come talk to me.

Everyone should believe in something. I believe I'll go fishing.
—Henry David Thoreau

Childhood Places of Worship

On many weekend days, when we weren't fishing or attending a ball game, Dad would drive us to one of a variety of cultural and educational attractions located near downtown Chicago, most accessed via picturesque Lakeshore Drive. Navy Pier, Lincoln Park Zoo, and Buckingham Fountain among them, our destination more frequently included one of the buildings along Lake Michigan's shore, those in the style of classic Greek architecture rising like ancient temples of the Acropolis of Athens. These structures housed the Museum of Science and Industry, the Field Museum of Natural History, the Adler Planetarium, and the John G. Shedd Aquarium.

For many individuals, certain venues breed special feelings, some combination of comfort, reverence, and wonderment. In my childhood world, these places included the Shedd, St. Hedwig Church, and Wrigley Field. (And, of course, any fish-bearing body of water.)

The Shedd Aquarium

I eagerly begin my quasi-religious experience, flying with the speed of Mercury's winged feet up the broad stone staircase and beyond the towering Doric columns. As I wait for Dad and Nancy to catch up, my eyes dart about, taking in the detail of the carved marble door-surround and stout bronze doors, both bold with aquatic themes that include shells, coral, eels, crabs, seahorses, starfish, and jellyfish.

Inside, the foyer exudes the look of a Roman basilica, the opaque ceiling panels of the rotunda diffusing soft light around polished slabs of marble and granite tiles swirled in shades of brown, white, and gray. Marine life and nautical designs abound: bronze sconces in the form of devil rays; circular and octagonal ceiling lights with octopi arms draped over the art-glass fixtures; an ornate bronze and glass clock hung from the ceiling, its backlit panels illuminating, in lieu of numerals, the images of turtles, crayfish, frogs, and fish.

Archways line the rotunda's perimeter leading to dark, humid corridors, catacombs saturated with the soothing hum of aerators and a subtle glow from the tanks, much like votive candlelight in a church. I move methodically from display to display, gallery to gallery. Dad understands my obsession and Nancy tolerates it, allowing me to worship in my own way, at my own pace. After all, ours is a country of religious freedom.

Maps adjacent to the tanks highlight the world region in which each species resides. Fishes by continent and fishes of the oceans provide the warm-up: docile nurse sharks swimming low and slow; a jutting-jawed silver-scaled tarpon; elegant stingrays in effortless glide; brown- and white-striped lionfish with elaborate spikes and feathery fins, costumed like Las Vegas showgirls; a lime green moray eel threading through a rock formation's holes; an aged, air-breathing lungfish, motionless in a shallow pool of water, a resident of the Shedd since 1933; and a school of glitter-sided, orange-throated piranhas, beautiful but deadly with the ability to "...rip a man to shreds in a matter of minutes..." as Dad would describe on each visit.

My viewing of these exotic species complete, I always save the best for last—the freshwater fishes of the Great Lakes region. Upon entering that gallery, my pace slows further as I absorb the fine details of shapes, markings, colors, and movements of the fish that roam our local lakes. We catch these with some regularity, though the Shedd's specimens appear to be twice the size of the ones we pull from the lakes and ponds. Must be the aquarium glass creating an illusion.

Whiskered and without scales, catfish and bullheads scavenge their tank bottom. Panfish of the sunfish family share a thin body with a profile in the shape of the palm of a hand. The bluegill is easily identified by the dark "blue" spot behind its "gill." The pumpkinseed, lighter in color, displays vibrant speckles of orange, yellow, green, and blue. The silvery sides of white crappies are speckled with black; black crappies are dotted with silvery white. Largemouth and smallmouth bass, the larger and longer members of the sunfish family, share tank space with their smaller relatives, who keep a respectful distance in the confined space.

Perch, also a panfish though elongated in shape, flash green-yellow sides with vertical stripes that narrow toward an orange belly. They share Shedd living quarters with their larger relative, the walleye, its mottled olive-gray-gold color punctuated by a white spot on the bottom edge of its tail.

If bass and walleye whet my appetite for bigger and better, imagine the hopes and dreams created by the fearsome northern pike and its bigger cousin, the mighty muskellunge. Both toothy species occupy a double-width tank. Oval yellow spots freckle the green sides of the pike. The muskellunge, brown to silver, is painted with muted vertical stripes, some of which break into spots. Streamlined, with flat heads and fins set back on the body, these cousins are killing torpedoes, built for bursts of speed.

What will it feel like to have one of these leviathans on the other end of my line? What strain on my equipment, on my body? How long the fight? I yearn for the day, "when I get older," to experience the answers to these questions. For now, I can only study the objects of my fascination as they swim, glide, and suspend. I meditate the rhythmic opening and closing of gills and the gentle sway of spellbinding fins.

Each visit concludes with a stop at the Aquarium's gift shop. I marvel at detailed pewter shark castings, the blown-glass angelfish, and sculpted mahogany whales. Gray ceramic porpoises suspend in mid-air above curling, acrylic aquamarine waves. All these works of fine art bear price tags well beyond our means. Glass cases present fine women's jewelry—gold and silver necklaces, earrings, and pendants in the form of shells, whale tails, and seahorses. Rotating racks of postcards adjoin inexpensive, marine theme souvenir items, most under a dollar, including key chains, decks of playing cards, and plastic fishes. Rows of shelves display books with vibrant color photographs of the seas' many and varied inhabitants.

I've had my eye on one of the books for a while now: *FISHES*, a soft cover, pocket-size, 160-page "Golden Nature Guide from the Golden Press." I make it a point to paw it on every visit, this "Guide to Familiar American Species" featuring 278 species "in full color." Eleven of them swim across the glossy cover's blue background. On this visit, Dad disturbs my ritual by snatching the book from the shelf just as I was reaching for it. He hands it to the grandmotherly volunteer attending the cash register. "A bible for my son," he proclaims with a smile.

St. Hedwig Church

Built in 1888, at the corner of Hoyne and Webster Avenues, this impressive edifice anchors the religious campus occupying the square block that also includes the school, rectory, and convent. The Polish cathedral architectural form boasts staunch, two-story slabs of white limestone that bookend a colonnade of four massive, gray granite columns. Above the portico, three arches frame stained glass windows ascending two additional stories, and a pair of copper-dome bell tower spires flank them, resting atop the building's front corners. Architects refer to the building's façade as combining Renaissance and Romanesque styles. To those of us not-in-the-know, what all this means is that your jaw might drop when you look at it.

From ground level, up five stairs and behind the columns, three sets of heavy, ornate wooden double doors open to the vestibule. A few steps further, a second set of doors, with lead crystal inserts, gateway to art and architectural beauty one would never expect to find in a lunch pail community such as ours. Stories-high gray-green polished marble columns boast the strength of the Almighty, the gold-painted scrolls and leaves of their Corinthian caps providing a decorative base for the rib-vaulted dome ceiling sections arching skyward. Murals of cloud-floating angels and saints adorn them, funneling prayers of the faithful toward the heavens. A larger-than-life statue of Jesus on the cross, his crown-of-thorns-capped countenance replete with agony and acceptance, rests against the granite pillar closest to the right side of the altar.

Dark, intricately carved wood flows throughout the church: two-door confessionals in the back corners; pews with a capacity for 1,500 faithful; Stations of the Cross on side walls between the windows; and a Baroque, two-story roofed pulpit to the left of the altar. Bavarian stained glass windows, pietistic mosaics in ruby, emerald, sapphire, citrine, and amethyst, backlit by the sun, radiate warmth and divinity. These luminescent works of art also back the balcony and ring the semi-circular wall behind the massive, white marble altar. Statues honoring various saints, Mary, and Joseph stand in niches built into the altar and in alcoves adjacent to it. To the right of the pulpit a stand of votive candles flicker inside red glass holders. Above the vestibule a full balcony includes a seating area for the choir and a pipe organ, its gold-tone metal pipes stepping skyward.

Every Sunday morning Mom delivers a wake-up nudge to Nancy and me so we can attend the 7:30 a.m. mass with her. There's that matter of the Third Commandment: "Remember thou keep holy the Sabbath day." In addition to the Rule being handed down directly from God, any statement with a "thou" in it must be important. Further, a Monday morning inquisition by the nuns regarding the specific mass attended strikes more fear than the consequence of eternal damnation for a mortal sin acquired for failing to honor the Commandment. That as it is, Dad usually sleeps in, appreciative of Mom's dispensation that allows *him* a "day of rest."

Between the daily masses during the school year, Sunday services, Stations of the Cross, and Holy Days of Obligation, by age nine I've cracked the 1,000 visit mark to St. Hedwig Church. Yes, God's house exudes awe and spirituality, but c'mon—between prayers at bedtime, penance after Confession, and an occasional rosary in the classroom, all in addition to the prayers said in church, there's only so much praying a kid can do. Am I wrong to spend a few minutes contemplating my Cubs lineup for the after-school game of fast pitch? Or where we'll next fish? Or what baseball cards to trade? I'm certain my prayers have sufficiently interceded for lost souls, made sure God knows Dad works hard all week and needs his shuteye, and paved the way to heaven for me and the rest of the family a dozen times over.

Mandatory weekday masses at 7 a.m. precede the start of each school day. First graders sit in the pews closest to the altar, followed in order by the other grades. The boys fill the pews on one side, the main aisle separating them from the girls on the other. We're uniformed like novitiates, the boys in blue slacks, black shoes, white shirts, and blue ties, some of us facing the embarrassment of having the clip-on variety, easily and frequently tugged from its tenuous attachment by a mischievous classmate. The girls' attire consists of gray and blue plaid pleated skirts and white blouses. It wasn't until years later that I would learn of the missed opportunity provided by their black patent leather shoes (mirrored instruments for my gynecology practice?), the nuns schooling them to always be on guard that their footwear "reflects up." About the time I learned of this subtle yet significant nuance, the ship had sailed—black patent leather was no longer in vogue.

During mass, the nuns sit in the last boy's row for each class, the close quarters allowing them an unobstructed view of the candidates most likely to disturb the sacred goings-on. Because of my lack of height, I always find myself with a few pews of separation from the habited sheriff.

After surviving third grade and psycho Sister Sarastine, I'm thrilled with my fourth grade teacher, the school's first non-nun, Miss Collette. The principal tells us this is her first job after graduating from college. With reddish-brown hair that's usually pinned up but sometimes tied in a ponytail, she's thin and not much taller than Danny Rybarkiewicz, the giant of our class who, year after year, towers above the rest of us.

Miss Collette is kind. Her voice is light and sweet and pleasant, like Fizzies bubbles tickling the tongue. I pray to grow taller, in a hurry, so I can sit next to Miss Collette during the daily mass. I've got a crush on her. But I also know she won't be able to wait for me to get older so we can marry.

Across the aisle, closer yet somehow just as far away, another distraction to prayerful meditation causes me to ache, though strangely in what feels to be a good way. Since the first day of the school year, thoughts of Penny Wenczyk have dominated my mind's wanderings during the hour-long masses bloated with chanted, Latin gobbledygook. Short, like me, she sits and stands and kneels in the first pew of the fourth grade girls. She is pretty, with short blonde hair—blonde hair like Lizzy Rosinski's. I've moved on from Lizzy, my first love. Just a youngster, she's only in third grade—and attends Pulaski School. I don't want to be viewed as a cradle robber, or marrying someone whose soul might be in jeopardy because her parents sent her to the public school.

I use all sorts of secretive methods with the hope of catching an across-the-aisle glimpse of Penny: rubbing my hand across my forehead; faking a sneeze; dropping my prayer book into the aisle. I can't marry Miss Collette, but there's no reason I can't marry Penny. Other than her not wanting to, that is. I don't think she's noticed me, but maybe I'll say a prayer so that she does. And then we'll be on our way to happily ever after.

This short-distance relationship will only live until graduation from eighth grade, when I'll leave the neighborhood. With our family's relocation to the suburbs, my prayers will remain somewhere in the clouded murals of St. Hedwig's vaulted ceiling.

The difference between wishes and hopes and prayers sometimes confuses me. And like the thought of marrying Penny, I'm not sure when any of those might involve a miracle. Like catching a really big fish. Or being at Wrigley for the game that clinches the World Series. Or at least being there for a no-hitter.

Despite my wandering mind and sometimes self-serving prayers, the venue of St. Hedwig's, bathed in soft lighting and warmed by the scent of glowing candles and incense, solemn and awe-inspiring, cavernous yet intimate, delivers a message without speaking a word. I've never seen Him, but if there is a God, he lives here. And the boogeyman doesn't.

Wrigley Field

Two major league baseball teams wear jerseys bearing the name "Chicago," although based on their play decade after decade, describing them as "major league" might be a stretch. The White Sox won the World Series in 1917. Two years later, eight team members were banned from the game for life when they conspired to intentionally lose the 1919 Series in the infamous Black Sox Scandal. The team's next almost-success occurred in 1959 when they captured the American League pennant before falling to the Dodgers in the Fall Classic.

An anomaly in this metropolitan area, our family roots for both teams, though our allegiance leans toward the Cubs, largely a function of our closer proximity to Wrigley Field and their all-day-game schedule. Our Cubs lose more than they win. A lot more. They last hoisted a world championship banner in 1908. Their last National League pennant flew in 1945, when the bulk of healthy major leaguers were overseas wrapping up the war effort. As a personal benefit of the "north-siders" ongoing futility, Wrigley typically fills to less than half capacity, so finding a good seat isn't a problem and ticket prices remain reasonable and affordable.

The talented and affable "Mr. Cub," Ernie Banks, coined Wrigley Field as "The Friendly Confines," and frequently gushes the familiar phrase, "It's a beautiful day for a ballgame. Let's play two!" Hope flows eternal, and I'm conditioned to "Wait 'til next year."

Friday, May 13, 1960. As I look across the dinner table this evening, Dad looks especially tired. A wrinkle or two creasing his otherwise smooth forehead and dark circles under his eyes tell of another long day of another long week at Wheeler Protective Apparel. The task of cutting asbestos for the manufacture of fire rescue suits is physically demanding and tedious, all the more so in a cramped factory environment that lacks air conditioning.

On some Friday evenings, we head over to Humboldt Park Lagoon with the hope of catching bullheads. With no expectations for this evening, I anticipate he'll want to hunker down on the slip-covered rocker-recliner and take in the Gillette Cavalcade of Sports. Our meatless Friday dinner of spaghetti completed, Dad surprises me with, "Do you want to go outside and play catch?"

Not needing to hear his question twice, I bolt from my chair and head to the basement to grab our baseball gloves and ball. Dad's mitt is a Joe Gordon model. The league ball, worn to an almost glossy finish, has faded from white to tan with years of use. It also bears a few scuffs from the pebbled concrete sidewalk as a result of an occasional errant throw or missed catch.

I'm still breaking in my glove, a Don Cardwell autograph model. I received it last month as an eighth birthday gift from my godfather, Uncle Lenny. Daily use helps loosen it up. And Dad bought me a small can of neatsfoot oil that I've been working into the leather to soften it. Each night I tuck the ball into the pocket to deepen it, tightly tying the glove closed with a pair of old shoestrings.

After a couple of lobs, Dad says, "I was listening to WGN radio on the way home from work today. Did you hear about the trade the Cubs made?"

Play stops. Fearful one of my favorite players may have been shipped out of town, I grind the ball into the pocket of my glove, the neatsfoot oil turning the sphere another shade darker. If the trade doesn't involve Moose Moryn (my favorite player, partly, I think, because he swings from the left side, just like Dad) or Ernie Banks, I'll be okay with it. "No ... who?"

"Cal Neeman and Tony Taylor to the Phillies for Ed Bouchee and Don Cardwell."

A smile lights my face. I look into the palm of my glove, my index finger tracing the imprinted autograph scrolled across the length of the little finger:

Don Cardwell. "I thought you'd like that," Dad calls out. He continues, "They said he'll pitch in one of the doubleheader games against St. Louis on Sunday. Do you want to go?"

An even wider smile provides the answer.

Sunday, May 15, 1960. With the ballpark located in a residential neighborhood, finding a parking space on the days we attend often presents a challenge. Today is one of those days, with the hated Cardinals in town for a twin-bill. Our '54 Mercury Monterey rolls through the side streets, Nancy and I keeping our eyes peeled for a break in the line of parked cars that might fit our burly behemoth, its forest green roof topping a mint green body. Just up ahead, "There's one!" I shout, excited as a child discovering the object of quest on an Easter egg hunt. My perception of the available space shrinking as we approach it, my tone turns somber. "Never mind ... it's too small."

Without speaking a word, Dad pulls up beside the car at the front of the opening and within an arm's length of it. He shifts into high concentration mode, right arm across the top of the front passenger's seat, head turning to analyze the angles for the parallel parking attempt. The lack of power steering and power brakes ratchets up the difficulty factor. After a series of multiple gearshifts, herky-jerky stops and starts between forward and reverse, and swift hand-over-hand muscling of the steering wheel in alternating directions, Dad completes the masterpiece, successfully shoehorning the Merc with little more than the width of a baseball separating us from the vehicles front and back.

Whether parked two blocks from the ballpark or twelve, the walk always looms long with the anticipation of seeing my baseball heroes in the flesh. The number of street vendors increases as we near Wrigley. From makeshift tents, some sell baseball caps, T-shirts, and pennants. Others, with portable carts, offer popcorn, peanuts, or hot dogs. The number of fans marching the sidewalks and crossing the streets swells as we approach the main entrance at the intersection of Clark and Addison.

My heart races as the iconic, art deco marquee in Cubby blue (there is talk of changing its color to red) "Wrigley Field Home of Chicago Cubs," comes into view above the ticket windows. Although the backless benches of the bleachers best fit the family budget at 75 cents per, their distance from the pitcher, catcher, and infield action, along with hours of viewing time under the broiling sun makes the shaded, $1.25 stadium chairs of the grandstand the location of choice. Unlike the assigned box seats, pricey at $2.50 (for the upper deck) and up, the grandstands fill on a first-come, first-served basis.

After passing through the turnstile, we hear the call of a vendor, outfitted in a navy blue butcher's apron, preaching his sermon from behind a wooden pulpit stacked with his wares: "Scorecards, getchyur scorecards here!" Dad hands me a pair of dimes, the tithe that will allow me to score both games as well as identify today's opposing players by their numbers (all Cubs jersey numbers already committed to memory). I always bring a yellow, hexagonal #2 pencil from home, saving the unnecessary expense of purchasing one. I do admit, however, to coveting the smooth, glossy white one stamped with "Chicago Cubs" and the circular team logo in red and blue sold by the scorecard vendor.

The faithful mill about as vendors hawk food and baseball-related merchandise, higher priced as compared to similar items available outside the park. In the dank passageway of the concourse, gray painted beams and girders support the stands above. An eclectic blend of odors lingers: Old Style beer, freshly poured from 12-ounce bottles into wax-coated paper cups, the liquid's foamy head magically stopping at the brim; smoke, mostly cigarette with a hint of cigar; freshly popped popcorn; "red hots"—hot dogs on steamed buns nestled in tinfoil wrappers; and steamy urine wafting from the men's rooms, same-color-in, same-color-out Old Style, pungent, bubbly gold rivers flowing down the lengths of stainless steel trough urinals.

The crowd continues to build as we snake our way to the third base side, the one with the Cubs dugout. We carry brown paper bags that transport homemade lunchmeat sandwiches. A picnic jug with iced lemonade will wash them down.

Up a dozen concrete stairs to the walkway separating the box seats from the grandstand, a burst of refreshing mid-May air accompanies the first view of the field, a magical moment of glorious sunlight illuminating the revered ground where men play a child's game at its highest level. If heavenly choirs of angels can sing, this is their moment. The infield and outfield grass, crisply mowed, creates a subtle, checkerboard pattern in vivid, emerald tones. Recently budded leaves sprout on the ivy vines, cushioning the outfield wall. Yellow numerals painted on red bricks, spotted at intervals from the left field foul line to the right, "355," "368," "400," "368," and "353," peek out from openings in the vines, marking the distances from home plate. The walls contain subtle curves in left- and right-center field, shortening the distance to the "power alleys" before resuming their path to the deepest part of center field. Wooden benches line the bleachers, pews rising skyward as they approach center field in ascent to the grand altar, the manually operated rectangular scoreboard. A blue sky and puffs of white clouds background the edged-in-white, jade-color shrine topped with a circular clock. Poles strung with team pennants, arranged in the order of their league standings, rise along both sides of the clock. Above them all, the American flag billows in today's southwest breeze that could push a long fly ball into the stands, or completely out of the park onto Waveland or Sheffield Avenues.

Our early arrival, in addition to allowing a first glimpse of the players as they jog across the outfield and groove their swings in the oversize batting cage surrounding home plate, also enables us to secure seats in our preferred location between third base and home plate. We opt for and are generally successful in claiming seats behind the railing of a down stairway that ensures our view will be unobstructed by passersby. Today, however, with an unusually large crowd, we're forced into seats halfway down the left field line in the middle of the grandstand.

As the 1 p.m. start time approaches, the grounds crew springs into action. Like a group of highly focused worker bees, they smooth the brown dirt of the pitcher's mound and infield, install fresh, pillowy white bases, and line the batter's boxes with chalk tapped from the bottom of rectangular wooden frames. Concurrently, public address announcer Pat Pieper calls the starting lineups, as he has for every game since 1916. His staccato delivery reverberates through the stadium: "...'tention ... attention please! Have your pencils ... and scorecards ready ... and I will give you the correct lineup ... for today's ballgame." A smattering of claps follows the announcement of each Cub. One exception draws a hearty ovation, the National League's Most Valuable Player in 1958 and 1959: "Number 14 ... Ernie Banks ... shortstop."

Soon thereafter, another round of applause, combined with the rhythmic clanking of a cowbell, signals the appearance of the Cub starters sprinting from the dugout to assume their fielding positions. In the world of long-suffering Cub fans, this excitement frequently represents the day's high-water mark, the moment when anticipation kisses optimism. Disappointment not a stranger, indeed more a close family member, it's often downhill from here. Game one follows this pattern.

Cardinal leadoff man Ken Boyer walks and steals second. Cub leadoff man Richie Ashburn walks and gets picked off first. Cardinal pitcher Larry Jackson triples in the top of the fifth, and is homered in by Boyer. In the sixth, Jackson strokes a two-run single to center. Boyer homers again in the ninth. Jackson pitches a complete game, 6-1, 4-hit victory over Cub starter Dick Drott and three relievers. Ernie goes 0-for-4 but on the bright side, Moose Moryn goes 2-for-2 and steals a base.

Recalibrating hope, I look forward to Don Cardwell's start. Pat Pieper announces the newest Cub will be wearing jersey number 43. The grounds crew smooths the infield dirt and freshens up the baselines and batters boxes. Dad springs for treats, lifting thumb and index finger to mouth, ripping a shrill whistle to gain the vendors' attention, followed by, "Yo, Cracker Jack!" and "Hey, Frosty Malt!" I've consumed them both before Cardwell's first fastball *smmmacks!* the catcher's glove to start the game a few minutes after 4 p.m.

Cardinal leadoff man Joe Cunningham grounds out to Ernie Banks, short to first. Good start. Next up, shortstop Alex Grammas draws a walk. "So much for the perfect game," I grumble, marking my scorecard with the "BB" notation for "base on balls" in the first inning square next to Grammas's name. Of course, I know I'll be happy with a win, regardless of how imperfect, and am pleased the inning ends with no damage as the remaining batters go down in order. The teams trade scoreless at-bats until the bottom of the fifth when the Cubs break through for a run on a fielder's choice.

In the bottom of the sixth Richie Ashburn draws a leadoff walk. Two outs later, Ernie enters the batter's box. As with every at-bat, his routine plays out slow and methodical. He smooths the dirt with the spikes of his left foot and then, like a dog pawing dirt when unearthing a bone, digs a foothold into the back of the box with his right. Into his upright stance, he leans slightly forward at the waist and then lowers the bat in practice swings swaying the deliberate rhythm of a pendulum. As he readies for the pitch he raises the bat to perfect vertical, fingers twiddling the handle like a saxophone player limbering up for a concert. Eyes trained on the pitcher, his aura transforms from seeming nonchalance to concentrated intensity. On the first pitch, the unmistakable *crrrack!* of pitched ball meeting "sweet spot" rings out from Ernie's thirty-some-ounce, thirty-some-inch Louisville Slugger, driving Redbird starter Lindy McDaniel's pitch deep into the left field bleachers. The congregation rises, their outstretched arms reaching heavenward in hopes of grabbing Chicago's baseball version of the Holy Grail.

The Cardinals go down in order and the Cubs add another run in the seventh as Ashburn drives in Jerry Kindall with a two-out double, increasing the lead to 4-0. At this point, I notice the string of zeroes on the bottom of the inning-by-inning Cardinal portion of my scorecard. A double-take confirms my first view: 0 runs, 0 hits! Cardwell's winging a no-hitter!

Well aware of the superstition that the mention of those words could derail history in the making and not wanting to bear the shame and responsibility for ruining same, I shove my elbows left and right to gain the attention of my father and sister who sit on either side of me, pointing out the row of goose eggs.

Nancy reacts immediately, "Oh my gosh! A no-..."

I cut her off in the nick of time: "Don't say it!"

Dad smiles with a "Noooooo kidding!"

I sense an energy that tells me most of today's patrons have likewise become aware of a miracle in the making. Excitement builds as each Cardinal enters the batter's box. Swinging from the left side, Daryl Spencer rockets a ground ball to second baseman Jerry Kindall's right. Catlike, he stabs it on a tricky hop and retires Spencer with an on-the-money throw to first. High-shrilled whistles and cheers recognize the defensive gem.

With the buzz of the last play still in the air, the next batter, Leon Wagner, swings at the first pitch and hits a hard but routine two-hopper to first baseman Ed Bouchee. He waves off Cardwell as he outraces Wagner to the bag, making the putout unassisted.

Background noise thickens, matching the increasing level of tension. I slide forward to the edge of my seat as jersey number "6" leaves the on-deck circle. Pat Pieper announces the pinch-hitter for Curt Flood.

No-doubt-about-it future Hall of Famer Stan Musial approaches the left-hand batter's box. Despite being a lifetime Cardinal, I like "Stan the Man." Probably something to do with Dad's frequent reminders about *Stashu*, "One of the game's best hitters—ever—*and* he's a *Polak*, just like us." Two years ago, on another May afternoon at Wrigley, Musial stroked his 3,000th hit, a pinch double. But not having started either game today, five long hours in the dugout leave Musial uncharacteristically overmatched, unable to catch up with Cardwell's fastballs. Lunging at pitches as he uncoils from his crouched stance he strikes out swinging, failing to even foul one off. The crowd erupts in satisfied delight.

The Cubs go down in order in the bottom of the eighth. It's onto the nerve-wracking ninth. With the clock nearing 6 p.m., the late afternoon sun and the upper deck create a shadow, cast over most of the infield parallel to the left field line and extending to the bleachers in left-center field. The center and right fielders will have to battle not only the wind and the low-hanging sun as they track down any balls hit in their direction; they will also have less time to react to batted balls as they emerge from the shade.

Cards manager Solly Hemus continues to play the percentages against Cardwell's right-hand offerings, pinch-hitting lefty Carl Sawatski for Hal Smith. Breaking my concentration, Dad puts his hand on my shoulder, leans over, and in a voice loud enough for me to hear above the boisterous crowd says, "Another *Polak*—and he's number 1," a reference to his jersey number. I shake my head, roll my eyes, and zero back in on the adversaries at either end of the 60 feet, 6 inches that separate them. I hold my breath with every Cardwell windup. On the 1-2 delivery, the stocky, bespectacled Sawatski gets full extension of his arms, the swing making solid contact. That's trouble! Every muscle in my body tightens. Driven high and deep to right field, I lose sight of the ball (as is the case from our grandstand seats with any ball hit above the overhang of the upper deck). I hone in on the reactions and movements of the fielders to gain a sense of the direction and depth of the ball's flight. Already playing deep in respect of Sawatski's power, Cub right fielder George Altman backpedals to the warning track.

"It's over," I think to myself. A flash of sunlight reflects off Altman's sunglasses, his distance to the wall narrowing. "Damn *Polak*," I whisper, cursing Sawatski. In my world, home team love always trumps heritage. Still retreating toward the wall and inches from it, Altman reaches up and grabs the ball. Turned to the outfield, Cardwell raises his glove to eye level and slaps his hand into it in a gesture of "Amen!" Head bowed, he places his hands on his hips, the body language acknowledging, "I just dodged a bullet...." I can *feel* sighs of relief lacing the crowd's thunderous ovation.

One out. Next up, Hemus pinch-hits lefty George Crowe for pitcher McDaniel. I cringe with the announcement of his name, recalling a story from my *Big-Time Baseball* book about spoiled no-hitters. Crowe was such a villain in a May 1955 game between the Cubs and Braves in Milwaukee's County Stadium. *Just like today*, with one out in the ninth inning, *just like today* Crowe pinch-hit for the pitcher and ruined Cub hurler Warren Hacker's bid for baseball immortality by cracking a solo home run. Eerie and unsettling, I hope to ward off the demon of repetitive circumstance. "Pinch-hit? Pinch-*out*!" I scream.

One of 33,000-plus on the manic rollercoaster, I squirm with every pitch. Cardwell, still shaken by Sawatski's blast, overthrows the first two fastballs, badly missing high and outside. In an effort to settle him down, catcher Del Rice asks the ump for timeout and walks toward the mound. Cardwell, in slow, measured steps, meets him halfway. Rice extends his catcher's mitt to the small of Cardwell's back as he offers words of encouragement. A tap of glove to the pitcher's butt sends him back to the mound. Settled by the impromptu conference, he winds and fires a knee-high strike. The crowd shrieks its approval. On the next pitch, Crowe, like Sawatski, makes solid contact. "Noooooo!" Altman and center fielder Ashburn, "on their horses," race to deep right-center field. Altman veers away as Ashburn slows, raises his glove, and makes the catch. "Yessssss!" Two outs.

Leadoff man Joe Cunningham remains the only obstacle between Cardwell and his date with destiny. Although Cardwell's had his number all day by inducing ground balls to short, second, and the pitcher, I know he's a dangerous hitter, remembering his .345 average from last year when he finished second to Hank Aaron. He's due. He's overdue. I've got a vise-grip on my scorecard, now rolled in the form of a miniature Louisville Slugger.

Number 15 enters the left-hand batter's box. As if contemplating the significance of the at-bat, Cunningham, head down, momentarily pauses, draws a deep breath, extends his right foot to smooth the dirt then tugs at the side of his belt. He assumes his batting stance, wide and "closed," his front foot extending closer to the plate than the back one. He chokes up an inch on the bat handle, the bat over his shoulder and readied at the classic 45-degree angle. As he finishes his second practice swing Cardwell goes into his windup. With the stadium atmosphere charged electric, the first pitch fastball races low and outside. 1-0.

The ball quickly returned from Rice, Cardwell toes the rubber and gets the sign. Cunningham, looking more aggressive and intense, levels his war club across the plate several more times. The pitch on its way, he unleashes a vicious cut. Bat strikes ball ... Ohs, oohs, and aahs.... It's fouled back to the screen ... out of play. 1-1.

Cunningham swipes his right hand across his pant leg to dry his palm. I do the same, trying to calm the heebie-jeebies that are snowballing with each passing moment. Cunningham steps to the back of the box. Understandably on edge, he again touches the side of his uniform at the belt, adjusts his helmet, switches the bat from one hand to the other and slides the barrel through the palm of his left hand. Back in position, he lays off the next pitch that arrives low and inside. The clamor of the wired crowd amplifies. 2-1.

Cardwell, not pleased with himself, takes the return toss from Rice and initiates an animated routine of his own: hand to cap; toe smoothing dirt around rubber; fingers to mouth; hand to rosin bag; adjust front and side of belt; fingers to brim of cap. The actions do not have the desired calming effect. A high, inside fastball sends Cunningham twisting out of the box. A disquieting howl fills the park as his momentum carries him in the direction of the on-deck circle. A few steps further he picks up the floppy, off-white rosin bag. Smoke-like puffs rise as he tosses it between his palms and taps it against the bat handle, drying stress-created moisture to secure a good grip. The classic confrontation nears its climax. 3-1.

The count now in the batter's favor, Cardwell removes his glove, tucks it into his left armpit, and rubs the ball with both hands. When Cunningham returns to the box, the Cub hurler is ready to go and delivers without delay. Low and inside, similar in location to the third pitch, Cunningham, certain he has taken ball four, takes two steps toward first when the umpire bellows, "Steeerike two!" Incensed, the Redbird right fielder does an about-face and bellies up to the ump, jawing in animated disagreement. A fight he can't win, he steps back into the box, reaches down to grab a fistful of dirt, and tosses it behind him in willful disgust. Whoops and hollers laud the questionable but favorable call, and moreso the angry reaction of the archenemy seeking to play the role of spoiler. Full count: 3-2.

At only 24 years of age, Cardwell's baseball immortality teeters on the outcome of a single pitch—the next one. His deliberate mannerisms strike me as amazingly calm in the squall of pressure, now spinning to a fever pitch. All eyes upon him in the eye of the storm, he picks the ball out of his mitt and tosses it back in, blows on his pitching hand, then lifts his cap slightly off his head before repositioning it with a final tug. His arms hang limply at his sides as he leans forward for the sign.

Cunningham levels the bat over the plate once ... twice.... With the third, Cardwell's arms swing back, then rise over his head. The ball concealed in his glove, his body turns, right foot against the pitching rubber, left leg curled upward. His right hand emerges, tightly gripping the ball. As he pushes off the rubber, the forward movement of his right arm uncoils the rest of his body with the release and follow-through. The red-laced, cowhide-covered orb lasers toward home plate on its less-than-one-second journey.

My heart pounds, like a jackhammer to concrete, as Cunningham reaches across the plate with a wicked cut, slicing a line drive to left field. Screams and squeals pierce the stadium air. Not sure if my vocal cords are working ... "Jesus!" ... the trajectory of the ball's flight just high enough to be taken out of sight by the upper deck above us, my eyes lock on burly left fielder Moose Moryn galloping in ... "Mary!" ... lowering his glove just above his shoe tops while in full stride ... "Joseph!" ... the ball hitting the heel of his glove, hopping ever-so-slightly forward toward the pocket and webbing, squeezed as he lifts it triumphantly skyward to a deafening *rrrroar!* ... "Moooose!" Fans jump with delirious joy, the concrete beneath my feet rocking with the force of an earthquake's seismic waves.

Cub players bolt from the dugout as fans swarm the field, flush with 50-plus years of pent-up enthusiasm. A limited number of blue uniformed Andy Frain ushers are swallowed by the masses steeped in pandemonium that encircles Cardwell. On my feet with the rest of the crowd still in the stands, I'm trying to shuffle past Nancy when a healthy tug on the back of my shirt halts my progress. Through the commotion, Dad shouts, "Where do you think you're going?"

Annoyed by the delay, I reply, "On the field ... C'mon, let's go!"

"Hold on, mister. Too many nuts down there. We'll enjoy it from up here."

And we did. And on the ride home, too, with the fanfare continuing on WGN radio. I'm not sure the Merc's tires ever touched the pavement. We'd just witnessed sports history with a personal touch: the epicenter being my baseball glove's namesake, accomplished against *the* despised rival, with the saving catch by my favorite player, all in the cathedral of Wrigley Field. A marvel. A masterpiece. A miracle, to be savored for a lifetime.

Grayslake

My mom and dad did a nice job coordinating the development of our family with that of her younger sister, Irene, and her husband, Ben. Nancy and Cousin Jim were born within two years of each other, and Cousin Larry preceded my birth by nine months. Aunt Irene and Uncle Ben had three more children: Peggy, Rich, and Ben. Not being able to improve upon perfection, my parents stopped with me, and yes, that *was* a fish that just flew by.

Larry and I were like brothers, or as close as brothers could be living 40 miles apart. My cousin's white frame, blue-roofed Cape Cod-style house stood on an acre of land some 15 miles south of the Wisconsin border, in the rural community of Grayslake. Yes, there is a lake in Grayslake. That lake is Grays Lake and no, I don't have a clue why the town and the lake have different spellings.

During weekend visits or a summer vacation weeklong stay, our days brimmed with activity, fishing usually at the top of the list. On some of those days, however, some form of the national pastime occupied us on the acre plot of land, which viewed through childhood eyes, rivaled the expanses of Wrigley Field.

In-depth reviews of Major League box scores, posted in the daily newspaper, helped us form the line-ups for our wiffle-ball games. Dirt depressions in the grass on either side of home plate (a circular cast iron sewer cover stamped with a waffle pattern and the words Neenah Foundry, Neenah Wisconsin) formed the batter's box. Our at-bats emulated the batting stances or some nuance of each player. Recalling a few, the coiled crouch of left-handed swinging "Stan the Man" Musial; the rolled up T-shirt sleeves exposing the massive upper arms of Cincinnati Reds slugger "Big Klu," Ted Kluszewski; and the Milwaukee Braves' Hank Aaron, wrists nonchalantly flicking the bat across the plate as if it weighed ounces instead of pounds.

Behind home plate, a shallow pit containing incinerated garbage and yard waste served as the "catcher." Like the batters' boxes, years of play created dirt depressions for first and second base, the grass sprouting in them each spring quickly worn away with the first games of the new season. A gnarly-branched crab apple tree represented third base. It stood in front of a row of stately elms that marked the property border with his uncle's neighboring farm. As the season progressed, rows of tall corn stalks swallowed foul balls hit in that direction.

Jim often participated in these games, contested long and hard under a stifling summer sun. Occasional breaks found us wiping sweaty brows with our T-shirt sleeves and quenching parched throats with cold well water sipped from cupped hands beneath the hose bib affixed to the side of the house. The conclusion of the "official" ballgames did not end our day. The competitive juices continued to flow with contests of "infield practice," "running bases," or "home run derby."

In home run derby, we assumed the identity of big league sluggers such as Banks, Maris, Aaron, Mantle, Mays, McCovey, Matthews, Killebrew, or Clemente. The game required a robust poke to straight-away center field, past the four-foot cyclone fence that defined the yard extending from the back of the house. Just inside the fence, next to the free-standing one-car garage, loomed the Grayslake version of Fenway's Green Monster. The large elm knocked down many a monstrous clout, causing the ball to descend plinko-like through the tree's branches, often dropping harmlessly into the glove of the outfielder propped against the fence beneath it. A half-inning consisted of as many home runs as you could muster, with three non-home run swings concluding your turn at bat.

The carefree joy of youth suddenly turned bleak if one of our swats took the sphere to right field, landing in Uncle Ben's extensive vegetable patch, referred to simply as "The Garden." At first frozen with fear, winds calmed and sunny skies clouded as the rotating Earth screeched to a halt. Batter, pitcher, and fielder, fierce competitors moments earlier, bonded as teammates with gazes locked, tensed muscles constricting speechless vocal chords. As we melted back to reality and approached Uncle Ben's mecca, we hoped against hope that the ball was visible (not hidden beneath some leafy green) and lay close enough to the edge to be drawn out with a bat or rake.

The reason for equal parts anxiety and caution involved Uncle Ben's daily ritual of checking his plot upon returning from his job as a welder of huge farming and construction machines at the International Harvester factory in nearby Libertyville. The physically taxing job, magnified by his torch's flame and the protective clothing and helmet-mask he wore, combined to magnify the oppressive summer heat and make his after-workday mood understandably edgy.

Sometimes the gods would smile upon us with a smooth, straightforward retrieval. Less fortunate circumstances necessitated a perilous search and rescue mission. Jim or Larry always took the lead, traversing the rows as if on a balance beam, careful not to disturb the plants. After finding the ball, they covered their tracks, smoothing their footprints on the same-way-in, same-way-out path. If a hint of intrusion remained or a plant showed evidence of damage, sparks could fly, like those thrown by my uncle's welding torch.

A summer Saturday or Sunday would find a calmer, cooler Uncle Ben and Dad taking Larry and me on a day trip to any one of a number of small lakes carved by the retreat of the glaciers of the last Ice Age. Most of these lakes within a half-hour drive of Grayslake, they included Deep, Third, Sand, Cedar, Fish (based on results should have been named No-Fish), and, of course, Grays Lake.

*Dad, Larry, and me ~
Savoring a summer stringer.*

~ ~ ~ ~ ~

Grays Lake

In my pre-documentation fishing era, lasting until 1964, three catches from Grays Lake forever emblazon my memory:

> Larry, me, and our dads racked up a prolific one-day catch of 96 fish that included perch, crappie, bullhead, and bluegill.

> The only time my sister Nancy joined us, she landed a brute nearly twice the size of any fish that I had ever caught. I can still hear her scream (more of fright than joy, I believe) as she swung the slimy, whiskered, mud-brown 15-inch catfish onto

the dock. Not proud to admit, I wished the fish would have chosen my worm instead of hers. "Bless me father, for I have sinned. I've invested a lot of time and allowance money to catch fish which, for the most part, fit in the palm of my hand. Then, my sister comes along and with beginners luck scores a whale, so I'm guilty of whatever that 'coveting' commandment is, I guess, coveting the fish my sister caught..."

In a furious hour of dock fishing, 44 kamikaze bluegills inhaled our scantily baited hooks, the feeding frenzy occurring as the sky blackened with the approach of a thunderstorm. As our supply of earthworms dwindled, the fish continued to bite on the tiniest bits of worm covering the hook points. When our supply of bait finally exhausted, they continued to strike bare hooks. (If only it were always that simple.)

~ ~ ~ ~ ~

Poets talk about "spots of time," but it is really fishermen who experience eternity compressed into a moment. No one can tell what a spot of time is until suddenly the whole world is a fish, and the fish is gone.
—Norman McLean

A Life Lesson
(There is an "I" in "Life")

    The sun's rays softened in a silky haze on a midsummer Saturday morning when Dad, Larry, I (six or seven years old at the time) and cigar-chomping Uncle Ben fished Grays Lake. We drove to a cottage on the lake's east shore, the one with a hand-painted sign on the front lawn advertising "Boats for Rent." After Dad paid a minimal fee, Uncle Ben picked the best of the worst from a collection of a half dozen wooden boats that sported multiple layers of gray paint, blistered and peeling from age and exposure to the elements. He lifted the bow, the leverage allowing him to push the craft across the solidly packed sand, stopping when the back half floated free in the shallow water. Our fishing gear in tow, we four fellows crammed into the narrow-beamed skiff better suited to accommodate two or three and shoved off for the day's outing.
    Uncle Ben rowed us toward the center of the lake, gliding to a stop over what was likely the deepest water, some 15- to 20-feet. Dad, in a "subtlety be damned" maneuver, tossed the anchor overboard. The block of concrete, attached to a weather-beaten length of frayed rope, hit the water like a detonating hand grenade. Larry and I

exchanged a cringing glance, fearful the commotion would cause any nearby fish to scatter.

Anxious to get the fish catching underway, my cousin and I energetically prepared our offerings. We threaded lengths of worm through our hooks multiple times, the bait dug last night from the edge of the cornfield adjoining their Grayslake homestead. We'd learned from previous outings that the worm needed to fully cover the hook's point and barb to enhance the chances of success. With split shot pinched a few inches above the baited hooks, we released the line until it went slack, signaling contact with the lake bottom. Several turns of the reel handle then raised the bait a few inches off the lake's floor. Ready for action, we held tight awaiting the first nibble. The air, thick with clouds of anticipation and hope swirled about us—or was that Uncle Ben's cigar smoke? Likely both…

On days when the fish cooperated, our creel included an assortment of panfish, most measuring five to eight inches. On this day, the deep-water bite was not "on," or the annoyed fish *had* vacated the area as a result of the anchor dropping explosion, so we moved to a weedbed along the shore opposite the boat rental. The shallower water called for, and received, a gentler drop of the anchor.

At our new location, more time passed without a bite. "There ain't no fish in here," Larry remarked. He and I often used this phrase as a verbal talisman to change our luck. The words working their magic, not a minute passed before my rod jerked down with a violent strike, then froze in a horseshoe-shaped bend. Try as I might, the reel handle would not turn under the weight of the unseen monster. (There is an "I" in "weakling.") My heart raced. Never having battled any finned creature of such considerable proportion, I discounted the possibility I had hooked the water boogeyman, who, common knowledge, lives in much deeper water.

Being on the losing side in the early stages of the tug-o-war, I sounded a call for reinforcements. (There is an "I" in "panic.") In fear of losing the submerged goliath, I made an urgent request to my uncle seated in front of me. "Uncle Ben, take my rod!" (There is an "I" in "wimp.")

He instantaneously replied in his no-nonsense voice that laced silk and gravel: "No, no, that's your fish!" An instant after the words registered, my rod sprang upward, the tension on the line gone. The unseen behemoth had regained its freedom. (There is an "I" in "dammit.")

I remember the disappointment of losing what had to be the largest fish of my life, in retrospect probably a 2- or 3-pound bass or northern pike. But I also recall not being upset or angry with Uncle Ben. Even at that tender age, his words made sense: it *was* my fish, to land or lose.

Fishing and Statistics

Recorded history began with a 9- by 6-inch spiral-top steno pad, its brown cover penciled with the words *"Fishing Log of E.P."* The entry on the first page read as follows:

"On the 24th of June, 1965, 2 bullheads were caught at Crystal Creek, Grayslake, Illinois. By E.P."

A sketch of a bullhead followed, beneath it the script:
"Length 5½ - 6½ inches."

A second entry on the same page read:

"On the 24th of June, 1965, 5 carp were caught at Crystal Creek, Grayslake, Illinois. By E.P."

Then, a drawing of a carp, followed by:

"Length 5 - 5 - 5½ - 5½ - 6 inches."

Same day, same place—not sure why I found it necessary (perhaps the artwork?) to write separate entries. Subsequent pages recorded other catches from local lakes: sunfish from Lake Potawatomi; crappies from Deep Lake; a single bluegill from Sand Lake; and mixed bags of panfish from Grays Lake and the Chain O' Lakes. The majority of the entries, however, like the first, occurred at Crystal Creek, where fish swam and water, conversation, and dreams flowed.

~ ~ ~ ~ ~

They are greatly in error who suppose that all there is of fishing is to fish.
—George Dawson

Crystal Creek

A slow-flowing rill bounded the south end of Uncle Ben and Aunt Irene's property, as well as the adjacent acreage owned by Uncle Ben's brother, Edwin. Irony not lost on Larry and me even at an early age, we named the lazy-flowing, *czarnina*-colored body of water "Crystal Creek."

Edged by rows of tall cornstalks, most of the tiny waterway didn't exceed a 10-foot width during normal pool. Some 50 yards from our baseball field, however, the murky water deepened and expanded, its banks widening to span perhaps 25-feet before narrowing to continue its journey west.

Small in size but huge in memories, our secluded Utopia offered a sanctuary not only where bullhead, carp, or sunfish would offer at our baits but also the perfect setting for conversation on important matters of the day—important as seen through the eyes of two young boys.

Beyond the Chicago sports scene (normally bleak but a '61 Blackhawks Stanley Cup and '63 Bears NFL championship still fresh) the 1960s overflowed with topics providing ample fodder for discussion: a young, vibrant, (and first Catholic!) President John F. Kennedy; the "Space Race" between the US and the USSR; UFO's, "flying saucers" manned by grotesque, alien boogeymen bent on destroying the world; nightmares courtesy of chilling episodes of the television shows *The Twilight Zone*, *The Outer Limits*, and *One Step Beyond*; the Cuban Missile Crisis and "The Cold War," the threat of atomic bombs and nuclear annihilation woven into our consciousness via weekly "duck and cover" air raid drills at school: single file into the hallway, kneel down, hands behind head, head between legs and kiss your ass goodbye. And the non-threatening "British Invasion" of rock 'n roll music from "across the pond," spearheaded by The Beatles.

Golf hit its stride on the national scene with televised duels between "The King" Arnold Palmer, and the "Golden Bear" Jack Nicklaus. More spectacle than sport, "Pro" Wrestling roped us in with the likes of Dick the Bruiser, The Crusher, "Mad Dog" Vachon, Vern Gagne, The Assassins, Doctor 'X', Pretty Boy Bobby Heenan, Baron Von Raschke, Yukon Moose Cholak, Bobo Brazil, Nick Bockwinkel, and The Sheik. (How is it that I can remember this collection of entertaining characters when I can't recall today's breakfast?) And, of course, we practiced some of these wrestling "greats" signature holds including "The Claw," "The Sleeper," and "The Figure-Four Leg Lock."

Up a notch from professional wrestlers' choreographed dances, we also imitated the physical, comedic antics of The Three Stooges. Roller Derby, a must-see on the weekly viewing agenda, featured star skater Joanie Weston, the "Blonde Bomber," elbowing her way around the competition on the banked track. Other popular television shows of the day found us assuming the identities of various characters: recreating World War II battles across France as Lieutenant Gil Hanley and Sergeant Chip Saunders from *Combat*; fighting the evil forces of T.H.R.U.S.H. (Technological Hierarchy for the Removal of Undesirables and the Subjugation of Humanity) as Napoleon Solo and Illya Kuryakin of *The Man From U.N.C.L.E.* (United Network Command for Law and Enforcement); and, on the wrong side of the law, underworld figures Dutch Schultz and Frank Nitti, wreaking havoc on the streets of Chicago in the Roaring Twenties, matching wits and firepower with Federal Agent Eliot Ness in

The Untouchables. On the big screen, we admired James Bond, 007, his heroic struggles against diabolic henchmen only exceeded by his dominating antics in the boudoir.

A Conversation at Crystal Creek in the Summer of '66

Upon arriving at our favorite fishing hole, baiting hooks, and setting our rods, I had some important information to convey to my older cousin. "Well, kiss grade school good-bye. Another school year come and gone, like a fart in a high wind. We finished it off with a field trip to Springfield week before last."

Innocent enough, to which my cousin replied, "Ours was last year. Did you bring home a lot of cheesy 'Land of Lincoln' souvenirs?"

"Yeah, but there was one special souvenir I have to tell you about, and it involves one Miss Penny Wenczyk."

Larry shifted his position to face me, perked up by the name I often mentioned when the subject of our conversations turned to girls, which was early and often. His questions came rapid-fire: "*THE* Penny Wenczyk, the cutest blonde in the school? Your top love interest since you sent Lizzy Rosinski packing? We talkin' bunt single or grand slam?"

"You be the official scorer," I replied.

"Lay it on me."

"On the ride home, I managed to get her to sit next to me on the backseat of the bus."

"Major League! So…?"

"So, we're heading back after a long day on the tourist trail. It's dark outside, the bus driver doesn't have any inside lights on, and there I am next to doll-face making small talk. Before I freeze up, I figure I better make my move."

"So…?" Larry asks, his voice hinting curiosity and urgency, interest further piquing.

"So I take hold of her hand."

"And…"

"And … she doesn't pull back."

"*And…*"

"And with things moving along nicely I figure it's time to go for the whole ball of wax. The small talk becomes no talk and I'm afraid my hand might turn cold and clammy, like one of our refrigerated crappie fillets, so I give her hand a little squeeze, look her in the eye, and say, 'Would it be alright if I give you a kiss?' Was I James Bond or what?"

"Oh, you were *something* alright. Other than the fact that Bond wouldn't have asked, you're doing a hell of a job."

"She nods her head yes, closes her eyes and leans toward me. I do the same and it's the fireworks display at Comiskey after a Sox homer. I tell ya, time stood still for those three glorious seconds. Peel me off the ceiling and light me a Dunhill."

"And what about an encore, 007? Did you keep your Thunderballs under control?" Goldfinger make an appearance? Did you go for more and have her turn into Dr. No?"

I always marveled at my cousin's quick, connect-the-dots wit.

"Nah, that was it," I replied, matter-of-factly.

"Alright, not bad. I'll give you a ground rule double."

"There's more to the story."

"Uh oh. Did the nuns catch you and turn your Rudolph-Valentino-ass into a bus-ridin' pinball?"

"No, the rest of the ride home was cool. Over the weekend I'm still on 'Cloud Nine.' Back at school on Monday though, Penny gives me the cold shoulder."

"Maybe she wanted more."

"I wish. I find out that big-mouth George Malkowski told her the only reason I did it was because I bet him I could."

"Why'd the jerk do that?"

"Uh, because I did. But I didn't think he was going to tell her. I think I screwed up."

"What did she say when she found out?"

"He said she called me an effin' son of a bitch."

"Ouch!"

"Yeah. I didn't know words like that could come out of such a soft, sweet, Barbie doll mouth."

"As official scorer, I'm changing your at-bat. You cranked one over the fence but it hooked foul. On the next pitch you struck out. And boy, you really did 'kiss' eighth grade goodbye."

As my cousin spoke those words, one of the red-bottomed, white-topped bobbers began its subtle dance, concentric circles rippling along the surface of Crystal Creek. Scrambling to grab the pole, the angst recanted moments earlier faded away with the anticipation of setting the hook, our friend the creek providing a soothing tonic to comfort the wound of young love lost.

Part Two
"There's Hair Down There!" -- The Testicle Takeover Years

Ah, the teenage years, that tumultuous time of life that begins bridge-building from the innocence of childhood to the responsibilities of adulthood. Nurtured and fledged, we prepare to take flight from the comfort of the nest. Boundaries exist solely to be tested.

Toes are dipped, at first with care and caution, into an ocean of seemingly endless possibilities. It feels good. Feeling braver, we take the next steps. Courage begets confidence. Further emboldened, we head deeper still—the water boogeyman be damned.

This period of growth and discovery propagates unfettered thoughts that jettison the spirit, often prompting actions that sail us into uncharted waters, perhaps to swim with the sharks. Some navigate them with the grace worthy of an Olympic "10." Others, ahem, struggle with the non-elegance of a whirling dervish.

In late 1963, we moved from the bowels of the inner city to a new residence some 15 miles away in the suburb of Niles. The blond brick, ranch-style home, located on Milwaukee Avenue, stood kitty-corner from Maryhill Cemetery. Dad, with a hint of a wry smile frequently quipped, "People are dyin' to get in." Milwaukee Avenue, one of the metropolitan area's busiest thoroughfares, tracks diagonally through Chicago (our house on Dickens Avenue was only four blocks from it) into the northwest suburbs and through the rural countryside, terminating before reaching the Wisconsin border, oddly enough not quite making it to Milwaukee.

Dad and Mom agonized over the budget-stretching decision, finally pulling the trigger on a $23,000 purchase price. With a one-car garage, three bedrooms, and one bath (a tub, with a showerhead—what's that?!), Dad finished the full basement himself with blond faux-wood paneling and red floor tiles reminiscent of the kitchen on Dickens Avenue.

The move to suburbia tripled Dad's commute time to his job at Wheeler Protective Apparel. Nancy and I drove with him the first two years, she finishing her junior and senior years at St. Stanislaus Kostka High School (one block from Busia's Noble Street apartment where she spent time before and after school) and I wrapping up seventh and eighth grade at St. Hedwig, with Uncle Stanley and Auntie Fran's flat at the Dickens house the drop-off and pick-up point.

Schooling Young Love

Two miles from our Niles home, the Golf-Mill Shopping Center, one of the earliest outdoor malls in the Chicago metropolitan area, opened its doors to the public in 1960. My mother gained part-time employment in the customer service department at Sears, Roebuck and Company, the anchor store of the retail complex. As an employee, she received a 10% discount on all store and catalog purchases. Benefitting from advertised sales, in addition to the employee discount, Sears became our family's retailer of choice for household items, guaranteed-for-life Craftsman tools, Kenmore appliances, and clothing.

After hanging up his spikes, one of baseball's greatest players, Ted Williams, signed a huge endorsement deal with Sears in the early '60s. His name smothered a vast array of sports-related items carried by the store: baseballs, bats, gloves, tents, lanterns, sleeping bags, rain suits, bicycles, shotguns, gun cabinets, rods, reels, and motors. Dad and I bought "field-tested-Ted-approved" fishing gear, including spinning and baitcasting rods and reels, and a portable, transom mount, battery-powered trolling motor. On Christmas day of my freshman year of high school, Santa delivered the one item on my wish list: a Ted Williams Signature barbell and dumbbell set.

Only a three-block walk from our Milwaukee Avenue home, Notre Dame High School for Boys was governed by the Holy Cross Brothers, their black cassocks and no-nonsense demeanor triggering flashbacks to the Sisters of Nazareth clan at St. Hedwig. Multiplying my anxiety as a small fish in a big, unfamiliar pond, I enrolled as an elfin, 5-foot tall, 89-pound young Mickey Rooney look-alike. Beefing up in the interest of self-preservation and improved self-confidence scored high on my list of New Year's resolutions. The weightlifting set, outweighing me at 110 pounds, consisted of interlocking 5-, 10-, and 20-pound discs covered in bronze-color plastic (also stamped with Ted's name, of course), capable of arrangements in varying weight configurations depending on the exercise and strength level of the user. The "certified and approved by Ted Williams for active Americans" instruction booklet offered the following encouraging words from Ted:

"Keep fit … exercise! A strong, healthy body is a man's most valuable asset."

Yeah, baby. Work out and gorge on loaves of Wonder Bread "to build strong bodies 12 ways." It shouldn't take long to tack on swells of Charles Atlas-like muscle mass. That, along with another foot of height, should send a boatload of chicks beating a path to my door.

Unlike the artificially enhanced goons of baseball's recent "Steroid Era," I chose to do it the old fashioned way—no, not the cigarettes, cigars, and-or alcohol consumption of Ruth, Cobb, Mantle, et al.—but rather through hard work and perseverance, even avoiding the temptation to ingest the mix-it-with-milk muscle-building-miracle DynaPower supplement hawked by wrestling great Vern Gagne. Doing it my way, in less than a year, I worked my way up from an 89-pound weakling to a 98-pound weakling, achieving notable goals: a chest size larger than my waist, biceps bigger than my wrists, and thighs bulkier than my calves. My perspiration-soaked body, straining to eke out the last reps of a given set (in spite of more weight disks littering the floor than attached to the barbell), my forehead-vein-popping basement workouts took on a religious fervor, invoking a higher power; "Jesus Christ, I can't lift another ounce!" and "Goddamn, this thing is heavy!"

In addition to the scrawny reflection staring back at me in the mirror, other hurdles (likely more perceived than real, but hey, I'll hang my hat on any good excuse) stood in the way of winning the race for female companionship. With a healthy dose of testosterone backing its name, the guys from Marmion Military Academy seemed to have a built in edge in attracting the ladies. Compare to Notre Dame High School for Boys (for *Boys*!—years later changed to Notre Dame College Prep), with the school nickname "Dons," Spanish gentlemen. Bullfighter bullcrap. Give me something I can use.

Is there an upside to a school without females? Certainly freedom from dealing with, on a daily basis, the paranoia fed by the "-ness" twins: "shy" and "awkward." A second burden avoided, which I heard from friends attending co-ed public schools, is the embarrassing warrior erection that can occur anywhere, anytime. (Is that what that good feeling was when I peered at Penny Wenczyk across the aisle in St. Hedwig church during mass?) Virtually uncontrollable, its unwelcome appearance results from the male teen sensing, like a stag in continuous rut, the pheromones unknowingly emitted by the female gender as they sit in classrooms, walk the halls, or run the track surrounding the football field, even though said track is hundreds of yards away.

Mimicking the phobia that occurs when I enter a body of water, my general approach to girls during the high school years reflected an innocent and cowardly mixture of awe, apprehension, consternation, and fear. Munchkin stature and an "all boys" school impeding the development of social etiquette and courting skills, I treaded lightly in the high school dating pool.

As a sophomore, I secured a date to join me, along with a number of classmates and their dates, in the wholesome, all-American activity of building a float for the homecoming parade. Not yet having acquired my driver's license, I believe she was less than impressed when my dad and I picked her up in our turquoise, '64 Rambler American. Her calendar seemed to fill up after that outing, being "busy" the next time or two I asked her out.

Time healed the wounds of my early teen awkwardness, or at least its physical aspect. As the clock tick-tocked, growth spurts tacked on several inches of height and 10 to 15 pounds of weight through each year of high school. A number of future female encounters, facilitated by friends and like-age relatives, found me dating friends of relatives and relatives of friends. Of those winsome forays, I'd win some, and lose some. Stay tuned.

A Jewel of a Job and a Friend for Life

After raising some spending money by mowing a few of our new Niles neighbors' lawns, I officially entered the working world during the summer between my freshman and sophomore years, at age 16, at a newly opened Jewel Tea food store located in the adjoining town of Park Ridge. Hung in the grocery stockroom in the back of the store, the weekly work schedule contained the hand-written names and work hours for each employee. Scrawled in the left column of the bottom two lines were the names "Chuck" and "Ed."

I met Chuck at a pre-opening store meeting. Both of us similar in physical stature, the grocery manager likely surmised the scrawny, blond-hair kids probably couldn't handle the rigors associated with the duties of a stock boy. Requiring a bit of seasoning, we began our employment as "bottle boys."

"What in the world," you may ask, "was a bottle boy?" The bottle boy represented the lowest form of life in the grocery store labor hierarchy. Back in the Middle Ages of soda packaging, 12- and 16-ounce glass bottles were sold in cardboard cartons containing quantities of six or eight. With recycling on a mass scale in its infancy, stores collected two to five cents per bottle as a deposit, refunded upon their return. The bottle boy transported the bottles from the service desk at the front of the store to the stockroom in the back, where they were sorted by manufacturer and placed in wooden crates. The challenge of the work was to stay awake while performing it. (The position ultimately traveled the occupational path of the wagon wheel repairman, dodo bird breeder, and door-to-door vacuum cleaner salesman.)

Aside from working the grand opening weekend in tandem, future scheduling did not require both of us to be present on any given day or evening. My first non-work related conversation with Chuck occurred when I received a telephone call from him, imploring that I work his upcoming Saturday night hours, as he had secured tickets to a rock concert that he hoped to parlay into a long-term relationship with a high school heartthrob who worked at Jewel as a cashier. Sensitive to the fragility of the male-female dating process and the urgency and importance lacing his words, I agreed to pick up his hours, and as an unexpected but welcomed byproduct, acquired a friend for life.

Chuck attended the public high school, Maine East, located less than a mile from both his Park Ridge home and Jewel. Though only two months older than me, his early start placed him a year ahead in the educational system.

Common ground surfaced as our friendship grew. Before our families moved to suburbia, the streets of Chicago rooted our childhoods. Our Eastern European ancestors, living in Czechoslovakia and Poland, shared a mutual border. As a *Bohunk* and a *Polak*, Chuck and I cherished every nickel we earned, squeezing ol' Tom Jefferson until his head hurt. In both our worlds, interests included fishing, playing chess, pinochle, board games, and writing bad poetry (mine notably worse than his) that spilled teenage angst on topics of love and war (Vietnam). Report card grades indicated above average success in our studies so we occasionally presented as pseudo-intellectuals, in those instances closer to "Nonsensa" than "Mensa" with a layer of dry wit encasing most of what we spewed. We cheered on our beloved Chicago sports teams and starred as intensely competitive, well-coordinated top-of-the-line sandlot athletes in our respective childhood neighborhoods.

On the flip side, though both introverts, my stoically bent demeanor provided a blunt contrast to Chuck's expressions of assertiveness that surfaced on occasion. Concern of being named a defendant in a lawsuit deters me from using terms such as cocky, brash, crude, defiant, abrasive, and obnoxious to describe Chuck. Sometimes I viewed his actions with disdain. Sometimes I secretly admired the devil-may-care attitude he exuded. Sometimes I wished I could push myself to walk the edgy tightrope he frequently negotiated with success. Most of all, I wished I had access to "wheels" like the one available to him and his older brothers, a 1963 sky-blue Buick Wildcat convertible. A cruise in that sweet ride sure beat a jaunt in our stodgy Rambler sedan.

Okay, enough about Chuck; let's get back to me. As previously noted, I tacked on some height and weight during each of my high school years. That, along with my ability to recognize soda labels *and* properly sort them sufficiently impressed my boss to the point of being awarded a promotion to the prestigious position of stock boy. How difficult could it be? The job title included "boy," as it did for the bottle-toting-sorting position. In spite of that nuance, lost on most of the pimple-faced high school working force, the baggers and parking-lot-shopping-cart-gatherers could still look my way in awe hoping that, someday, they too would reach this "promised land" of the part-time grocery store employee pecking order. (Though it pains me to say it, Chuck won the first of our countless competitions, becoming a stock boy months before I.)

The position entailed many strenuous duties. The first required the "boy" to push and pull a hand-operated pallet jack, typically loaded five to eight feet high with varying size boxes of "stock," in total weighing hundreds of pounds, from the stockroom at the back of the store to the appropriate aisle. These loads often swayed precariously during the course of negotiating turns and slaloming shoppers. A tumble could result in, at a minimum, a messy cleanup or, in the worst case, a messy lawsuit.

The actual task of "stocking" the shelves demanded a significant level of manual dexterity, starting with the use of a box cutter. To ensure personal safety and maintain the store's profit margin required a delicate balance of applying just the right amount of pressure and speed to cut through the tops or sides of the corrugated cardboard boxes, typically containing quantities of 12 to 24 grocery items. Carelessness with the razor-sharp instrument could result in a self-inflicted wound or terrible injury to beloved brand icons such as the matronly Mrs. Butterworth, the bald-headed "I'm a Stud" Mr. Clean, or the high-talking, pudgy Pillsbury Doughboy. When lack of care in the cereal aisle resulted in Tony the Tiger bleeding sugar-coated frosted flakes, it could have been Tony or me uttering with frustrated disgust, "Oh, Grrrrrrrrrrrrrrrreat!"

In the pre-UPC code days of yore, each can, bottle, or boxed grocery product required pricing. Another manual process, a hand-gripped, ink-stamp or labeling gun flew across the tops of cans, bottles, and boxes with lightning quickness. Next, onto the shelves, two, four, six pieces at a time depending on their size, rotating labels forward in one continuous, fluid motion, and lastly hand-ripping the emptied boxes until folded flat. Then, onto the next product, and the next, and the next, on and on, through the end of my senior year of high school.

Jewel Tea management felt good enough about my performance that they saw fit to hire me back during the summer following my first year of college. A new store policy, however, required stocking after hours via a night shift crew. This served the dual purpose of maximizing shopper safety while minimizing their inconvenience. The adjustment to working nights did "a number" on my social life and fishing outings (that number close to zero), but having a relatively well-paying full-time job to replenish the educational expense coffers overrode that negative.

Working the 11 p.m. to 7 a.m. graveyard shift in a shopper-less store provided the side benefit of successfully addressing hunger pangs frequently arising in the 2 a.m. to 3 a.m. timeframe. Like fishing, there was something to be said for being in the right place at the right time. For instance, the urge to gorge intensified when working the cookie aisle, my stomach begging for sustenance as the aroma of sweet confections swirled about. The colorful and creative packaging further enticed the senses, delivering a strong message of want and need created by the marketing geniuses at Nabisco, Keebler, and others.

On a lucky night I'd find an opened package, often tucked near the back of the shelf. Perhaps a daytime customer needed a sample. Perhaps the stock boy who worked the aisle the evening before miscalculated with the box cutter. Perhaps ... no matter; by refusing to allow the sugary love-disks to go to waste, I provided an honorable service to the men and women who worked so hard to produce, package, and deliver their fine product, or so I told myself. The difficult-to-control urge to ravage like a nocturnal buzzard on classics such as Oreos, Chips Ahoy, and Nutter Butters kicked sugar in the face of a weary conscience that struggled to say "no." Satisfy or die. On rare occasions of desperation, the Keebler Elf pooped cookies as he found himself cowering to the blade of my box cutter when the overwhelming impulse of the sweet tooth took my insatiable culinary craving to a side darker than chocolate chips.

One particular night found me in the *wrong* place (aisle) at the *wrong* time when my stomach began ringing the snack-time bell. Perusing the shelves before me, a colorful array of labels with familiar brands came into focus: Friskees, Alpo, Gaines Burgers, and Chuck Wagon, packaged in containers of varying size and shape: hockey puck-size cans, 10-pound bags, soup-size cans, 20-pound bags. My out-of-whack craving radar honed in on a small, white package, approximately the size of an Animal Crackers cookie box. A cartoon drawing of a smiling beagle stood next to bold black letters: LIV-A-SNAPS.

Yes I did.

Well, a Ritz or a Triscuit it wasn't. Sympathies to your pallets, my four-legged friends, though likely your thoughts would be the same for me if you munched on an offering from the "1,001 Ways to Prepare Cabbage" cookbook.

Though not a result of my gastronomical indiscretion, I did not return to Jewel the next summer, and just as well. It might have saved the embarrassment of having the grocery supervisor show up at my parent's door in the wee hours of the morning: "I'm sorry Mr. and Mrs. Piotrowski, we found him unconscious on the floor in the paper goods aisle with his stomach grotesquely bloated and only three sheets of a thousand-sheet roll of Scott toilet tissue dangling from his mouth...."

~ ~ ~ ~ ~

Give a man a fish, and he can eat for a day. But teach a man how to fish, and he'll be dead of mercury poisoning inside of three years.
—Charles Haas

Chain O' Lakes

By the 1960s, many bodies of water across the United States flowed "sludgingly" down the path toward becoming aqua-graveyards as a result of decades of industrial and other manmade forms of pollution. One of the five Great Lakes, Lake Erie, became the poster-child for environmental disrespect. Fed by the Detroit River and Cleveland's Cuyahoga River, phosphorus and nitrogen levels led to severe algae blooms and eutrophication. To the fish population, eutrophication of a body of water is the equivalent of tying a plastic bag around your head, which, by the way, is the headgear I wore as a child when imitating scuba diver Mike Nelson, played by Lloyd Bridges, in the 1958-1961 television series, *Sea Hunt.* (Fighting imaginary villains and imaginary man-eating sharks in imaginary knife wielding hand-to-hand combat in the imaginary sea, I always managed to "pop to the surface" moments before the oxygen supply in my air tank became fully depleted, or in this case, fully replaced by carbon dioxide. This playtime activity may explain a number of my future behaviors to family and friends.)

On June 22, 1969, the oil-slickened, debris-filled Cuyahoga River actually caught fire. On August 1, 1969, *Time* magazine said of the Cuyahoga:

> Some River! Chocolate-brown, oily, bubbling with subsurface gases, it oozes rather than flows.... The Federal Water Pollution Control Administration dryly notes: "The lower Cuyahoga has no visible signs of life, not even low forms such as leeches and sludge worms that usually thrive on wastes." It is also—literally—a fire hazard.

Lacking in formal scientific training, it is my uneducated belief that "no visible signs of life" likely made for some tough angling.

Closer to home, northern Illinois' Chain O' Lakes comprises eleven interconnected bodies of water created by the flow of the 202-mile-long Fox River on its journey from southeast Wisconsin to Ottawa, Illinois. Lakes of the

Fox Chain include Spring, Fox, Nippersink, Grass, Redhead, Pistakee, Petite, Bluff, Marie, Channel, and Catherine. Though also environmentally challenged in the 1960s, "The Chain" teemed with fish. Unfortunately, the plentitude took the form of "rough fish"—scavenger carp proliferated. A sludge quotient also existed in "The Chain," but unlike her sister waterway in Ohio, she had not yet accumulated enough toxic waste to become combustible. I know this to be true having seen Uncle Ben, on numerous occasions, flick a glowing ember from his White Owl cigar into the water. Rather than a Hindenburg-like explosion and fire, only a subtle sizzle could be heard as water, or whatever liquefied chemical compound the water had become, extinguished the hot ash.

Relative to the small, "stand alone" lakes we typically fished, "The Chain" represented "big water." Each outing afforded the opportunity to connect with a big fish. It also provided the possibility of doing battle with a number of other equally large but less desirable objects. "Structure," defined in a fishing context, is a change in bottom contour as a result of an irregular feature. Fish often congregate in these areas, which, depending on their characteristics, are further defined as humps, bars, reefs, saddles, or ledges. Each lake of "The Chain," in addition to its natural contours, possessed other ever-changing and growing "structure" elements. A bottom-bumping lure could dredge up a steering wheel, hubcap, or hood ornament from a DeSoto, Studebaker, Edsel, or some other "quality" vehicle conceived and produced by the folks in Detroit. On other hook-ups, the challenge centered on trying to determine if the pull on your line resulted from a snagged carp or a rusted Schlitz, Blatz, or Pabst Blue Ribbon beer can. (Milwaukee, "Brew City," is within an hour's drive of "The Chain.")

"Admiring" my catch from The Chain.

The Fox River Chain O' Lakes holds the dubious distinction, per acre, as America's busiest inland recreational waterway. This taught us valuable lessons about living harmoniously with our fellow man, in this instance, non-fishermen who also sought the recreational opportunities provided by this significant expanse of water. The main lesson learned? We, in our anchored, 14-foot rowboat, *would* share the 14 feet of shoreline we fished with boats ranging in size from destroyers to battleships, every one of them choosing not to utilize the majority of the other 14,000 acres of available open water. These joy riders, in return, shared their exuberance by shouting, laughing, and waving one-fingered salutes in our direction as they headed toward us, not veering off until we could identify the charm on the gold chains hanging from their necks and smell the Coppertone lathered on their bronze-basted bodies. Sometimes, in the true spirit of fellowship, they would offer us a beverage by winging a beer can in our direction, though it often missed the mark as we hung on for dear life, tossed about like a cork in the wake of their enthusiasm.

By mid-morning on any summer day, directionless three- to four-foot waves stirred the lakes to the color of a Bosco-mixed glass of milk. Not the result of the wind, these waves rose courtesy of the armada of powerful "cigar boats" and cabin cruisers. Fishermen foolhardy enough to stand while casting assumed the appearance of high-wire acrobats attempting to maintain their balance on a delicate walk across a tightrope.

In later years, trolling with the Ted Williams portable electronic motor allowed us to fish the turbulent seas while seated, though even seasoned anglers were sometimes roiled to the brink of seasickness by the tsunamis wrought by the maritime revelers. As we trolled, water skiers would sometimes slalom the fishing lines trailing behind our boat. Our fishing success slowed on those occasions, and fortunately (unfortunately?) our catch never included the vainglorious species known as the "water-walking jackass."

When we reached our limit of fast-pace "fun," we'd tuck into one of the many channels connecting the various lakes. Though these relatively narrow no-wake corridors provided respite from the dizzying seas, the gray haze of exhaust fumes from the slow and unending parade of mammoth vessels shrouded us. We hugged the shoreline in our tiny craft as the imposing hulls of the titanic cruisers passed. Though we despised them, we still marveled at the captains' skill in negotiating the narrow passageways from lake to lake.

With the passing of years, we learned to be selective when choosing times to fish "The Chain." On summer weekends, we'd start pre-dawn and end by 10 a.m. Weekdays extended fishable hours, and any day before Memorial Day or after Labor Day (and the further out the better) generally ensured a more pleasant fishing experience.

In spite of the obstacles, we routinely caught fish on "The Chain." Spinning rods and reels spooled with 6- or 8-pound monofilament line pulled silver, gold, or copper #2 Mepps spinners, the blade the size of a Jefferson nickel stretched to an oval. White- and yellow-striped bass, five- to ten-inches in length, fiercely attacked the offerings, their strikes deceptively strong considering their diminutive proportion. Infrequently, largemouth bass, crappie, perch, channel catfish, walleye, and northern pike also mistook the shiny, whirling metal blades for an easy meal.

Despite almost exclusive use of the Mepps trolling method, boat members deadpanned inane questions or comments that took on a life of their own, spewed like clockwork with a bend of the rod or after landing a fish: "What were you using?"; "How deep were you fishing?"; "Did you cross its eyes?" (Setting the hook with vigor.); "Tap, tap, bam!" (Setting the hook after a nibble.); "Fish or foul?" (Is the "strike" a fish or a weed?); "You're in the (penalty) box!" (When a strike purported to be a fish turn out to be a weed.); "Fish 'em low, fish 'em slow"; "Where there's perch, there's walleye."

We'd heard rumors that muskellunge once roamed these waters but disappeared with the deterioration of the water quality from manufacturing and recreational pollution. That never stopped us, however, from dreaming that a leviathan or two might still remain and perhaps one day take a liking to one of our shiny little spinners. Better yet, how about the fishing experience of a young lifetime where we're sure the big ones swim, in pristine waters.

Chuck with a "Chain" first -- a turtle. Turning the unusual catch competitively positive, he commented, "Bet you never caught one."

It seems the further north you go, the more nature rules—the lakes and trees seem endless, the only way to savor it, to find a shoreline or bay and watch and wait and fish. Fishing breaks the mystery of water with a thin filament line—a telegraph wire between one world and another.
—Larry Starzec

Oh, Canada

"From far and wide, O Canada," telling words from the Canadian National Anthem. Second only to Russia in land area, this vast and majestic country adjoins three of the world's five oceans: the Atlantic, Pacific, and Arctic. With three territories and ten provinces it claims sovereignty of the North Pole and, to the south, an international border with the U.S. that is the world's longest between two countries. Natural wonders abound from Rocky Mountains grandeur to the splendor of Niagara Falls.

Too numerous to count, 60% of the *world's* lakes glisten within its boundaries. The province of Ontario's second largest lake, Lake of the Woods, spans 70 miles with 65,000 miles of shoreline and 14,500 islands. Unobtrusive among the thousands is 11-acre Kipling Island, where a lodge and seven rustic cabins sit in a wooded alcove, providing a retreat for fishermen who want to test their skill and luck in these fertile waters.

Employed as a foreman at the A. Finkl and Sons steel foundry on Chicago's north side, my Uncle Bill earned a salary commensurate with the high level of stress accompanying the position. He rewarded himself in several ways: a rec-room bar lined with top-shelf liquor, a new Buick every three years, and an annual fishing vacation to Lake of the Woods. At family get-togethers he regaled us with stories of stringers full of superb-tasting walleye, ferocious northern pike savagely striking lures cast their way, and his impassioned quest to capture the king of freshwater predators, the "fish of 10,000 casts," the mighty muskellunge.

In the late 1960s, Uncle Ben, Larry, Dad, and I joined my cousin Billy, Uncle Bill, and his co-worker Caravello (I'm sure he had a first name but Uncle Bill referred to him only by his surname) on one of these late June adventures. A new world of opportunity dawned enabling the pursuit of game fish in sizes (or species) not available in local lakes. With my Fishing Log only containing entries of bullhead, carp, and panfish, the prospect of catching walleye, smallmouth bass, northern pike, and muskellunge evoked an artistic stir as I practiced pencil drawings, hopeful of adding these "exotic" species to my piscatorial journal.

The night before our departure, burgeoning excitement resulted in tossing and turning that overruled any chance of peaceful slumber. Frequent peeks at the Baby Ben Westclox alarm clock seemed to slow the movement of its glow-in-the-dark hands. Though planning to leave at dawn, our inability to sleep put us on the road at 3 a.m. Luggage and fishing equipment packed the evening before, Uncle Ben, Larry, and I slid onto the vinyl and cloth seats as Dad fired up our "roll down the windows if you want to be cooled off" '64 AMC Rambler American 220 sedan. An open-air, wooden car-top carrier that Dad specifically built for this long distance expedition hugged the roof, with four suction cups the size of saucers holding it in place along with makeshift straps and metal clasps jerry-rigged to the roof trim.

Seasoned by previous trips, Uncle Bill, Billy, and Caravello likely enjoyed a few good hours of shuteye before departing at first light from their rendezvous point. The leather upholstered, white-as-first-snow air-conditioned LeSabre, boasting a powerful V-8 engine and cavernous trunk, easily accommodated their baggage and gear; it could also have swallowed up the contents squeezed into (and onto) our scramblin', ramblin' Rambler. In spite of our head start, a gamblin' man makes easy money placing a bet on the Buick to win the unofficial race to the Canadian border.

Crossing into Wisconsin within the first hour, we pass numerous billboards advertising sundry products. Two are particularly prominent. The first, with block yellow lettering against a red background reads, "CHEESE AND FIREWORKS THIS EXIT." The second, with block red lettering against a yellow background informs, "GUNS, LIQUOR, AND TOBACCO THIS EXIT."

The signs conjure up images of chunks of cheddar rocketing through the air on the Fourth of July, happy holiday revelers catching them in their mouths in a chum-like frenzy, or skeet shooting them out of the sky with a hunting rifle in one hand and a bottle of Pabst Blue Ribbon and a cigarette in the other.

We cruise the next eight hours through the state of cheese, fireworks, guns, liquor, and tobacco, a major portion of it on two-lane U.S. Route 53. The true vacation feeling begins kicking in as we motor through small Wisconsin towns with names embodying a pleasant Northwood's feel, among them: Black River Falls, Chippewa Falls, Rice Lake, Spooner, and Solon Springs.

At the western tip of Lake Superior, we pass through the "Twin Ports" cities of Superior, Wisconsin, and Duluth, Minnesota. Also known as "The City on the Hill," many of Duluth's bluff-built businesses and residential areas overlook the greatest Great Lake. Our views of the harbor impress with postcard-like quality. On this sunny summer day, sailboats skitter across the bays, while docked freighters and barges take on loads of ore transported via rail hopper from Minnesota's northern mining region.

The remaining three-plus hours of the first day's travel continues on Route 53 through the northeastern section of the state, referred to as the "Minnesota Arrowhead." We observe exit signs: Eveleth, soon-to-be home of the U.S. Hockey Hall of Fame; Virginia (Mom's name!); and Hibbing, childhood home of Robert Zimmerman, aka Bob Dylan. Further north, past the small towns of Cook and Orr, the latter the home of Pelican Lake and the giant Billy Bluegill on the town welcome sign, the pines and birches grow thick and closer to the highway. With only one more hour to go, we'll bed down in International Falls after a long day on the road.

A Letter to Mom from International Falls, Minnesota

I can imagine Mom's delight upon receiving my letter. Making such a significant impression, she tucked it away in the envelope containing my birth and baptismal certificates. Perhaps she saved it as evidence, should the need ever arise, to have her nut-ball kid institutionalized. The single sheet of motel stationery contains an embossed header in red ink:

TEE PEE MOTEL (There is a picture of a tipi here.)
INTERNATIONAL FALLS, MN 56649 HWY 53 PHONE 283-8494

In the upper right hand corner I had written:

This is official Tee Pee Motel Stationery
Friday

Then, the letter. The first paragraph proceeds innocently enough prior to some sort of travel delirium setting in.

Dear Mother,

We arrived at International Falls about 5 this afternoon. The weather is clear, though it is a little cool. Uncle Bill, Billy, and Caravello were already here, even though they left later than we did. They caught and passed us near Eau Claire, but we cruised past them in Minong, as they were stopped by one of Wisconsin's finest who apparently didn't appreciate the urgency of the journey or the powerful LeSabre's impressive top speed. Uncle Bill made up the lost time in Minnesota, the blur of his white Buick rocketing past us on the outskirts of Duluth. The Minnesota troopers must have "gone fishin'."

It only took me 15 minutes to take my right contact lens out tonight. Please dust my new bookends twice a day. Make sure the doors are locked and the gas jets on the stove are off. Don't go out to eat with your friend Marie. Stay home and protect the house, but it's okay to take out the garbage. Wish us luck. Thank you.

Love,
Ed & Dad

Full Speed Ahead

After a solid night's sleep, it's up for breakfast, followed by the agony of "hurry up and wait" to get across the border. Lines of vehicles, most towing boats, stretch for blocks in both directions. Bright-eyed while engaging in enthusiastic conversation about giant fish awaiting our arrival, we exchange glances with fishermen whose vacations are ending, their droopy eyes peering at us through bug-splattered windshields. Week-old beards dress faces displaying suntans, melancholy, and a hint of envy as they know our time on the water is yet to begin. The only redeeming feature of their slow-moving line back to the U.S. is the ability to make a vice-of-your-choice purchase at the duty free shop, teenage runners hustling bags to your vehicle just yards before crossing the Fort Frances-International Falls International Bridge.

The road and rail bridge, its riveted steel girders painted midsummer algae green, spans 750-yards of the Rainy River. Privately and jointly owned by Boise Cascade and Abitibi Consolidated, the companies operate paper mills on the U.S. and Canadian sides of the river, respectively. These corporate entities equally share responsibility for the byproduct of their manufacturing processes, formally referred to in scientific environmental studies as "stench." As we approach the bridge in a queue of vehicles moving at the pace of an injured Galapagos turtle, the offensive odor simulating a combination of rotten eggs and week-old fish entrails, sprinkled with a pinch of sawdust, accosts and overwhelms the olfactory sense. Mouth breathe or die.

Regardless of the direction traveled, the border guards from both countries inspire a healthy dose of uneasiness. The omnipotent pecking order goes something like this: Father, Son, Holy Spirit, Border Guard. Impeccable uniforms sport polished brass rank insignias on epaulettes and crisply starched collars, multi-colored, embroidered flags and agency patches, two-way radios, and holstered firearms.

Several cars ahead of us, Uncle Bill successfully passes through the checkpoint and zips out of sight. After snailing across the metal-grate bridge, the Rambler inches to a stop at the red traffic signal. We're next.

Dad and Uncle Benny in the front seat, Larry and I in the back, I could sense that even our "Greatest Generation," tough-as-nails, cigar-chomping fathers, whose life experiences included childhoods during the Great Depression and combat engagements during World War II, feel humble to a level of minor uneasiness. They also want to engrain within us their respect for men in uniform. Uncle Ben growls instructions, "Sit up straight, look him right in the eye, and answer anything he asks you."

Green light. We cross the double set of rail tracks and roll to a stop at the guard booth. A robotic, steely-eye stare greets us, an expressionless face filling the driver's side window. His gaze penetrates the soul, capable of bringing even the likes of a saintly Mother Teresa to her knees— "Yes, I'm guilty, whatever it is: I did it!" Even with nothing to hide, you're made to feel as if you do. And if you do, watch out. Rumored to still be shoveling peat moss in a Yukon Gulag are the unfortunate souls whose last words were: "No sir, it's not live bait. Those 18-inch suckers are our pets. They'd die of loneliness if we left them alone at home. And the 12-dozen leeches—those are condiments for our bratwurst."

Fighting the fidget-urge, we must remain calm and cool under a tricky round of prosecutorial questioning that seeks to expose us as murderers or international spies, when in fact all we've done is unknowingly pack a few pounds of illegal potatoes. I am certain they know of my entry into the dark underbelly of the criminal world, when past the "age of reason" as a hardened eight-year-old, I pocketed a pack of Juicy Fruit gum from the local grocery store. Please, please let the Border Guards' omniscient records reflect my guilt-ridden return to the store later that afternoon, righting the wrong by leaving six cents (a nickel for the gum and a penny interest) near one of the cash registers. I squirm in my seat, wondering if my failed gynecology practice with patient Lizzy Rosinski also inks their permanent record.

The Canadian border officer's icy stare moves in a calculated fashion among the car's occupants, locking on me. My memory is cloudy here. I think the interrogation went something like this:

"What's your name, son?"

"Uh, I don't know."

"What's the purpose of your visit to Canada?"

"Uh, I don't know."

"Is this your father?"

"Uh, I don't know."

"Where and how long will you be staying?"

"Uh, somewhere ... I don't know."

I must have done better than I thought. We get the nod to proceed, breathing a collective sigh of relief. Critical until driving out of sight, a demur demeanor *must* be maintained. With our overly active imaginations working overtime, Larry and I telepathically understand any celebratory facial expressions will be picked up by their 10,000x optical zoom cross-hair sights and misinterpreted as "we sure pulled one over on them," resulting in a Bonnie and Clyde ending wrought by Gatling guns, grenade launchers, and howitzers camouflaged on the roof of the border building.

On through the town of Fort Frances, then reaching the open road, the anticipation of a weeklong sojourn in fishing Valhalla slows each turn of the car's odometer during the final four-hour drive through the Canadian wilderness. For all the good feelings triggered by the anticipation of a fishing trip, this eagerness also jumps to the forefront as the culprit making the ride to any lake significantly longer than the return from it.

Chiseled gray slate rock outcroppings, pristine lakes with lily pads and rows of reeds along shorelines, and meandering creeks all nestle up to the road with greater frequency. At random intervals along our route, small piles of rocks in assorted sizes balance in varying configurations. An aura of mystery surrounds those we see, giving rise to Stonehenge-like questions. Who built them? When? What is their message? A worldwide phenomenon, cairns date back thousands of years with many potential purposes. Are the contemporary architects pointing the way to fertile hunting or fishing grounds? Warning of danger? Tutoring astronomy? Marking a location of spiritual significance? We surmise local teenagers construct them for their amusement and tourist bemusement, displaying their rudimentary engineering skills after practicing their alcohol consumption skills on boring Saturday nights.

After yesterday's full day in the car, the remaining three hours of drive time feel more like another thirteen. We finally arrive at the north shore of Lake of the Woods, a lacquered wooden sign held by timber posts coming into view: "Welcome to Kenora." We make a brief stop at McLeod Park, taking in the wonder of Husky the Muskie, a 40-foot sculpture of a skyward-leaping muskellunge. At a small visitor's kiosk, I grab a brochure containing interesting historical nuggets: the Kenora Thistles victorious as 1907 Stanley Cup Champions, and the city's previous name, Rat Portage. Now there's quite a visual.

Uncle Bill and company, having arrived ahead of us despite another lead-foot incident (this one an encounter with the Ontario Provincial Police), meet us at the public landing. After logging over 800 miles and 16 hours on the road over two days, we're ready for the next phase of our adventure. Our host for the upcoming week, camp owner Doug Weston, greets us.

With a rugged look, an athletic build, and reddish-blond hair cropped in a crew-cut, Mr. Weston stands a few inches taller than Dad and Uncle Ben, putting his height at about 6-feet. I'd guess he's also about the same age as our dads, though the Canadian summers have chiseled more wrinkles into his weathered, tanned face. Many outdoor repairs task a lodge owner, including those on camp dwellings and outbuildings, docks, and a fleet of fishing boats and motors. Uncle Bill had also told us that, on occasion, Mr. Weston guides guests to some of the better fishing haunts. After loading our gear into his boat, a 25-minute ferry transports us to our accommodations on Kipling Island.

We motor across large tracts of open water, through channels, and in and around islands, all appearing one-and-the-same to me. I wonder how Mr. Weston finds his way, GPS technology not yet available to the general public. My untrained eye fails to recognize natural waypoints that solve the maze. Bald rock, beaver huts, the outline of distant treetops, an eagle's nest, a fallen birch, and many others, no doubt, guide the camp proprietor.

I marvel at the seemingly limitless expanse of woods and water, in awe that this short ride is but a glimpse of one million surface-acres of water that comprise Lake of the Woods. Apprehensive about getting lost when we will be out on our own, a second concern also surfaces. How will we ever find any fish in all this water?

When catching does not go as anticipated, the community of fisher-people can call upon any number of excuses: unstable weather, too hot, too cold, too windy, too calm, too sunny, too stormy, water level too high, water level too low, mayfly hatch, wrong moon phase, high pressure, low pressure, too much fishing pressure, lake in turn-over phase, pre-spawn skittishness, post-spawn recovery, inadequate water oxygenation, ph levels (water acidity) too high, ph levels too low, bad water clarity, too much weed growth, not enough weed growth, wrong kind of weed growth. If the week in Canada ends as a bust, I prepare to break new ground with a "too much water, too many places for the fish to hide" hypothesis.

Upon arriving at the camp, Mr. Weston directs us to the two *rustic* cabins that will house us in the same combination as the carpool pairings. The *rustic* cabins' gray shingle roofs, splotched with chunks of velvety green moss, sit atop red-painted plywood exteriors. The *rustic*, knotty pine interior walls house

Spartan furnishings that include a metal-leg, gray and white swirl Formica-top kitchen table, and an eclectic collection of wood-frame chairs and beds. In Canada, *rustic* also means we will be sharing the cabin with a family of mice.

Between the dock and our cabin, a five-by-five-foot outhouse emits a scent reminiscent of the drive through Fort Frances, with a good dose of methane added. When seated to carry out nature's calling, I cringe with the knowledge and ever-present fear that the grotesque combination of a python, tarantula, and scorpion, with pincers the size of a first-baseman's mitt, lies in wait near the top of the hole, ready to latch onto my private parts. The Canadian boogeyman, lurking in the forest surrounding the cabin, calls this rare, sewage-dwelling creature his beloved pet.

The "mostly dining room" main lodge also houses a small office area. Several taxidermist works of art ornament one of the knotty pine walls. On the left, a metal stringer holds three vertically mounted walleye, the clear-coat varnish causing their scales to shimmer, giving the appearance they've just been pulled from the lake. Affixed to the right, a thick-belly northern pike looks upward, emerging from beneath a piece of driftwood, ready to attack two unsuspecting perch on a branch above. Between the walleyes and the pike, decoupaged to a square piece of dark-stained mahogany, a yellowed parchment with burnt edges reads:

Fisherman's Lament

Let me gather my tackle and fishing gear
And go down to the water's edge
Let me catch the big one that got away
As I fished from the rocky ledge;

I cast my line in a likely spot
It becomes entangled and entwined
But I pull and tug to set it free
For I'm not the quitting kind;

I break my line and I lose my lure
And the boat springs a leak or two
The sun wreaks vengeance; mosquitoes bite
Before the day is through;

I've had enough to drive me mad
Just fisherman's luck I suppose
But I'll be back another day
To see how the fishing goes.

—H. McCormick

Mom and Dad never told me I had a long-lost brother.

As I continue to scan the room, my eyes lock on the huge head of a muskellunge hung at eye level on an adjacent wall. Larger in size than any single fish I've ever caught, a menacing scowl frames piercing eyes that follow me as I approach it. Face-to-face, I peer into its alligator-like mouth, top and bottom lined with mini-mountain ranges of jagged teeth. I curl the fingers of my hands into their respective palms and raise both fists toward the mouth, satisfied they would easily fit into the cavernous opening with room to spare. The head exudes the essence of a freshwater Tyrannosaurus Rex, perfectly defining the mystique of the elusive, fearsome predator. This close-up and personal encounter convinces me that the muskellunge can indeed spawn nightmares. No doubt the Canadian boogeyman keeps one in his aquarium.

Next to the mount, a black and white photo displays the catch, its length nearly matching the height of the fisherman laboring under its weight. Right hand slipped inside the gill plate, left hand tightly gripping the right wrist for additional support, his pursed lips and furrowed brow evidence his struggle to keep the tail of the mammoth muskellunge off the ground.

The diminutive fellow holding the fish bears a strong facial resemblance to a gracefully aged George Burns. Circular, wire-rim glasses askew, a flattened yacht cap inscribed "Captain" rests awkwardly atop his head, tilted at an angle opposite that of his glasses. The photo allows a glimpse at the remainder of his Burns-like attire. An embroidered wreath encircling an anchor adorns the pocket of a dark, double-breasted blazer. A diamond-pattern ascot rises above the collar tucked beneath his chin. Ankle length trousers allow a peek at light color socks and boat shoes. Adding to the intrigue, the gentleman struggling to hold up the fish is soaked from head to toe, as if doused by a storm without the protection of raingear. A caption beneath the photo announces the fish, a 47-pounder, as the camp record. Curious about the details of the catch, Mr. Weston fills in the blanks for me.

"Ol' Doc Watson caught that monster a couple of years ago near Billy Goat Island. Doc is a surgeon, traveling here solo from Toronto. He always reserves the middle two weeks of July. He's a real nice fella, eh? but his bungling nature pretty much matches Sherlock Holmes' sidekick with the same name. Thank goodness he takes a guide every day, else he'd for sure get lost if he went out on his own. The guides could tell you a ton of stories. They put him 'on' fish, but the loveable ol' cluck usually manages to screw it up—fingers slipping off the reel handle and having line fly off the spool in a tangled mess, losing the fish *and* his lure with a bad knot, using bargain-basement fishing line that looks like used surgical thread that kinks and breaks. It's a wonder he ever lands anything, eh?"

I smile and shake my head, though with no experience on the big water, I'm thinking the Doc and I may not be that far apart in our fishing acumen.

Mr. Weston continues, "The planets lined up for Doc on the day he caught the big one. It struck a tiny #2 Mepps spinner with no leader. He thought he was hooked on a log, so the guide rowed toward it. Doc wasn't reeling in fast enough to keep up so the line goes slack—the fish should have gotten off but didn't. Right over the 'snag,' with his rod doubled over and rod tip in the water, he's straining to lift what he thought was a big piece of timber. As the load got within a few feet of the surface, the fish bolted out of the water, scarin' the bejesus out of Doc and the guide. Picture the weight of three bowling balls tied together as they hit the water on the way down, eh? The explosion gave 'em a shower as the guide scrambled for the net. Doc hung on for dear life as the fish made some powerful bursts along the surface, throwin' more water as it shook its big, ugly head. Then it made some deep runs, twistin' and turning' as it fought. The line got wrapped around its mouth, gills, and half its body. It came to the surface looking like a mummy as Doc reeled it to the boat. With a better look, the guide knows it's not going to fit in the net, so he grabbed King MuskiTut near the tail with one hand and slid his other near the gill, lifting it toward the boat. Lopsided with the guide and heavy fish, the boat tipped and started taking on water before he hoisted it over the side. The guide wasn't sure if hysterical Doc was screaming with joy 'cause of the fish or fear of being swamped. Fish in hand, the guide tried to stand up but lost his balance, the tail whacking Doc across his chops. His arms windmill as *he* gets knocked off balance and ends up falling backwards into the drink. Luckily, the fish landed inside the boat. The guide helped Doc back in, clubbed the musky that was thrashin' aboot, and they made a beeline for camp. As soon as they got in we took some photos, then he dragged it into the fish-cleaning hut. Sure as heck Doc could have afforded to have it mounted but he preferred to fill the freezer with fillets with some on-site surgery. He's gruntin' and groanin' as he's hacking away—blood's splatterin' all over the screens. I'll tell you what, eh? If I ever need surgery, I'm not goin' to Toronto! When he finished up I asked if we could keep the head to display with the photo, and there it is, in all its beastly glory." The account of the event complete I smile again, now confident there's hope for any of us.

The "American Plan" we purchased provides all meals during our stay, with breakfasts and dinners served at the main lodge. Though closed for lunch, each morning the cook assembles your choice of two take-in-the-boat lunches, enabling guests to maximize their fishing time by not having to return to the camp at midday. The first option consists of sandwiches, potato chips, cans of soda, and cookies. The second, more elaborate alternative involves a large, rope-handle wooden box containing the fixings and tools for the glorious meal known as the shore lunch. The fully loaded crate includes cornmeal and a couple of eggs, cans of lard and baked beans, onions, potatoes, and all the necessary cooking and eating utensils. This luncheon choice requires the fishermen catch their entrée. For the first couple of days we play it safe with sandwiches, selecting tuna salad versus chicken salad in keeping with the theme of a fishing vacation.

Each morning, the cast iron church bell affixed to the exterior wall of the lodge clangs at 8:30, calling all guests to breakfast. Various combinations of eggs, pancakes, waffles, potatoes, toast, and muffins provide stick-to-your-ribs heartiness before taking to the water.

Beyond the food, these morning gatherings brim with significance by virtue of the presence of two individuals. The first, a barrel-chested, bearded Pavarotti look-alike, the gregarious and fishing savvy Caravello mentors us on casting and trolling techniques, use of spinning and bait-casting equipment, and best lures to entice strikes in various situations and locations, the lessons equally taught with words and exaggerated hand gestures. The other, polite and unpretentious with Scandinavian features and blonde hair, petite but well-endowed, Elin is a high school lass who waits and buses tables. Before the week ends perhaps Caravello can mentor us on situations and locations in which to cast forth Cupid's arrow in an attempt to lure the fair maiden. Her blue eyes, high cheek bones, thin lips, and the absence of makeup complete a package that exudes a simple beauty, no doubt soon to be stunning. She is another of Canada's many natural wonders. More on her later.

Although Uncle Bill, Billy, and Caravello will fish together (as in years past) for most of the week, Caravello spends the early portion of the first day in Uncle Ben and Larry's boat, and later joins Dad and me in ours. This allows hands-on tutoring of the angling lessons taught at breakfast. Familiar with better areas to fish and the only one among us able to translate the island-filled lake map to our actual location, Caravello hopes we will become familiar with navigating the hodgepodge of islands that splatter the map like unconnected parts of a 1000-piece jigsaw puzzle. Without his guidance, our dads' comfort zone (with our small lake Illinois fishing experience always keeping us within sight of a shoreline) would likely have only encompassed fishing locations within sight of Kipling Island. Envision flying to Paris (I can't, but work with me here) and feeling as though your viewing horizon must always include the airport; you'd miss the Eiffel Tower, the Louvre, and the Arc de Triomphe, to name a few.

On Monday, Uncle Bill, Billy, and Caravello bolt immediately after breakfast, hot on the trail of a huge musky rumored to be working the area around Town Island. Dad and I, Larry and Uncle Ben will travel in tandem for the remainder of the week: "safety in numbers," hopefully not "misery loves company." On the first day without Caravello, our dads, not comfortable with their recall of Caravello's lake topography tutelage (and less comfortable with the map reading skills of my cousin and me), decide to spend the morning "circling the Paris airport."

Our merry-go-round pattern and lack of success not going unnoticed, Mr. Weston takes a break from the repair of a Johnson outboard affixed to a makeshift sawhorse and waves us in. He walks down to the dock as we tie up, offering to take us to one of his favorite fishing spots, Indian Bay. "I guarantee we'll get some fish there. So sure, in fact, I'll get the shore lunch box and we'll have a great meal too, eh?" Our dads give him the "Nah, that's okay, you've got work to do," and "We don't want you to go to any trouble." I glance at Larry. Eyebrows raised, our eyes widen and roll. I give my father the low volume ventriloquist bit through gritted teeth, "Dad, let him take us..." Not sure if he heard my Charlie McCarthy imitation, Mr. Weston says "I insist—won't take 'no' for an answer. I'll meet you back down here in aboot ten minutes."

Right on time and whistling the "Canadian National Anthem," Mr. Weston bounds down the grassy knoll atop which the lodge sits. Based on the ease with which he carries the heavy crate it might as well be filled with feathers. He strides onto the dock and swings the oversize lunch war-chest into the middle of Uncle Ben's boat. Smiling, he comments, "Make sure you've still got room for your fishin' equipment. We need to catch the meat that goes with the potatoes." He heads back to his storage shed, returning with a battle-scarred spinning outfit in one hand, and in the other, a tiny metal utility box that can't hold more than a half-dozen small lures. He has Dad shift over to the middle seat, hops onto the driver's bench, and we're off, Uncle Ben and Larry right behind.

To discern the proper path to Indian Bay, Mr. Weston points out unique land and water features, like the ones he uses to navigate from Kenora to Kipling. I follow our course on the lake map, making notes that will allow us to make future trips without him. It takes forever, that 20-minute ride in the small boats with the small motors, but we finally arrive, ready to start the pleasant task of "working" for our lunch.

Mr. Weston puts the motor in neutral and points out to Uncle Ben the area we will be fishing. Shouting above the din of the two idling motors, he indicates we will use a technique called back-trolling. Reverse gear allows the boat to move at a much slower speed versus forward, giving occupants of the same boat the option to either cast or troll. Not having experienced it with Caravello, we look forward to expanding our repertoire.

As Mr. Weston opens his mini-box, I crane my neck around Dad attempting to behold the magic lures that guarantee fish. I'm hopeful at least one item in my eight-tray, 64-compartment Old Pal tackle box matches something in Mr. Weston's. I catch a glimpse of his little chest's treasures, a simple collection of worn and weathered warriors: a four-inch gold spoon with hammered finish; a lead-head jig painted yellow with a matching tuft of hair covering the shank of the hook; a medium size silver blade in-line spinner with a black bucktail partially covering a single treble hook; and a couple of June-bug spinners, a live-bait rig consisting of a small spinner blade with red beads above and below it, the wire shaft attached to a long-shank hook baited with either a night crawler, leech, or minnow.

As he holds up the small, round-head yellow jig, Mr. Weston asks, "You fellas got anything that looks like this?" I begin rifling through my Old Pal, knowing jigs were not on the suggested list of lures provided by Uncle Bill before the trip. The closest thing I find is a heavier jig with a flat-bottom head called a stand-up, this one with orange and green hair whose color, I suppose, is to imitate a perch. As I raise it for Mr. Weston to see, he hesitates a second before replying, "Close enough; hook on a minnow and give 'er a try, eh?"

With Dad generally preferring to fish with live bait, his inventory of lures comes nowhere close to my massive accumulation. As he examines the inventory in his simple, two-tray tackle box, nothing fits the bill. An old hula popper and plastic frog, both of which float on the surface, aren't going to cut it. My recollection of the 100-piece fishing set he bought from Sears in the late 1950s contained two small crescent-shaped flatfish, one half-yellow and half-orange, and the other orange with black spots. The remaining 98 pieces seemed to be an assortment of various size swivels, sinkers, and hooks. Mr. Weston hands him one of the June-bug spinners.

Shifting out of neutral into reverse, Mr. Weston and I cast our jigs toward a stand of reeds lining a point that defines one of the entrances to the large bay. Before I engage my reel he shouts, "Got one!" As I look in his direction, the taut line streaming from his rod tip cuts through and out of the water as a hefty smallmouth bass takes flight. With a confident air that says "I've done this hundreds of times," the camp owner tactfully battles his burly competitor, raising and lowering his rod tip as he works to control the fish that fights with the power of a diesel locomotive. As Dad nets and hoists it into the boat, I am in awe of its length and meaty girth, as well as Mr. Weston's knack for locating and catching the feisty fish on cast number one. Regal bronze in color, the sun highlights the lustrous, honey-gold edges of its scales, further dazzling. By far the largest bass (largemouth or smallmouth) I have ever seen in the flesh, I ask, "How much do you think she weighs?"

"Five pounds give or take. I think we've got a good start for lunch, eh?"

The magic continues. Within the next ten casts, he bags two more beefy smallmouths. Not as large as the first, but using it as a reference point, the next two likely tip the scale between three and four pounds. Perhaps feeling sorry for us he lays down his rod and lights up a Player cigarette. "We'll be coming up on another good stretch in just a little bit." Thirty seconds after his comment, Dad, trolling the June-bug baited with a minnow, bags a 17-inch walleye.

As they pass the same spot a minute later, Larry and Uncle Ben, who are back-trolling behind us, experience a simultaneous strike. Rods doubled over as they focus on the task at hand, their faces move from tense excitement to happy relief as Uncle Ben directs his walleye to the net, and with the fish still in it, scoops Larry's to complete the successful double.

Not pleased I haven't yet made a contribution to the luncheon menu, I make a mental note of a moss-covered rock the size of a two-man tent that juts into the lake from a nearby shoreline. That marker could be important to the success of future visits to Indian Bay. (Work with me here, too; I'm trying to make myself useful.)

As I survey the shoreline, I hear the tinny ring of metal-on-metal in the bottom of the boat, near my feet. Seeing a June-bug spinner I look up at Mr. Weston, who flashes me a wink. I immediately tie it on and bait it with a minnow as our boat turns back in the direction of the bewitching spot. As we pass the rock marker, my spinning rod pulls and pulses, a 19-inch northern pike engulfing the offering and coming to net. The significance of the different species not lost on Mr. Weston, he says, "Lunch time! When a pike or musky comes a callin' on a school of walleye they scatter, and before long the buffet shuts down. Besides, we've got enough fish to dine like kings, eh?"

We motor a short distance to a small island, not more than an acre or two, tucked in a bend of the shoreline we had just fished. After sliding the front half of both boats onto smooth shale slabs that gently slope toward the water, Larry and I remove the anchors from our respective boats, tying the anchor ropes around a birch tree located several yards further up the incline. Obviously a shore lunch stopping point known by locals and guides, a circular set of rocks serving as the fire pit encompass remnants of charred wood scattered among small piles of gray ashes.

Our stomachs in the solid grasp of hunger, a flurry of activity begins. Larry and I gather kindling and break dead branches to a size useable for the fire, then start peeling and cutting potatoes. (I am overjoyed when I complete the task without drawing blood.) Dad and Uncle Ben get the fire started, set up the grate, ready the pots and pans, and fill the coffee pot with lake water while Mr. Weston fillets the fish.

An epiphanous revelation follows. The preparation and consumption of food can elicit an orgiastic, borderline orgasmic response. Crackling wood stirs orange flames that tickle the bottom and sides of skillets and pots; intense heat bubbles baking beans as onions and potatoes fry with a not-so-subtle sizzle; percolating coffee pops as it dances against the hollowed glass knob at the top of the aluminum pot; cornmeal coated fillets smack like bumper cars in the rumbling boil of melted lard, plated when golden crisp on the outside ensuring melt-in-your-mouth flaky on the inside. The senses—sight, smell, sound, taste, and touch—all are kissed by the ambrosial swirl mixed by a cool lake breeze under a warm summer sun.

Several items minimally detract from an otherwise perfect culinary-outdoor experience. First and foremost, the eye-candy lodge waitress is not present. Next, as my ravenous appetite becomes satisfied and non-stop consumption slows, I catch, out of the corner of my eye, the discarded skin, entrails, and skeletal remains of our unfortunate prey. Not having died in vain, I whisper a "thank you" for the daily bread, the nourishment of the "it doesn't get any fresher than this" delectable meal of fresh fish. I remind myself of the food chain hierarchy, the natural order, which helps soothe my gluttonous guilt. Even the remnants, not fit for human ingestion, will not go to waste, providing food for scavenging sea gulls. Lastly, when the lake breeze stills, black flies the size of pecans targets us as the main course for their *en plein air* feast. During those brief windless interludes, every other bite of our mouthwatering meal is interrupted by a bite of their own. Land and bite ... swat and eat ... land and swat ... swat and eat.... Materializing out of nowhere, the dumber ones, staying near the torso (and the plate of food), are more easily dispatched. The smarter, stealth bloodsuckers dine heartily on filet mignon ankles. Annoying, irritating bastards!

Belly full, I have little recollection of the remainder of the afternoon. Larry and I may have asked Mr. Weston for a Player—I don't know. (Doesn't a cigarette "hit the spot" after a fine meal, too?) The fatted calves, my cousin and I may have reclined for a minute, (or two, or ten) against the trunks of a couple of aspens, the shade a blanket to soothe heavy eyelids—I don't know. Fathers may have mustered their siesta-thinking sons to clean and pack up—I don't know. We may have traveled directly to Kipling Island to allow our gracious host to return to the task of his motor repair—I don't know. We may have spent part of the afternoon still-fishing off the dock when we got back—I don't know. Euphoria: what a damn pleasant mania. The only thing I know for certain?—I don't know. Actually, I do. Today's shore lunch vaults to the top of my "best meals ever consumed" list.

Our plan for tomorrow will take us back (surprise!) to Indian Bay. Uncle Bill, Billy, and Caravello will return to Town Island, not yet having raised the big musky. After a solid night's sleep and another hearty breakfast, Mr. Weston comes down to the dock before we depart. "Keep an eye to the sky, eh?" Pointing to the east, a rosy glow provides the backdrop for some low-hanging clouds. "Red sky in the morning, sailors take warning. The forecast calls for some nasty storms to come sweeping in later this afternoon." Thanking him for the "red flag," we depart for our new found fertile fishing grounds with the confidence of Columbus on his second voyage to the new world.

Map in hand I am the navigator, using exaggerated hand signals as if waving a 707 to its gate, directing Dad left, right, or steady as she goes. Uncle Ben and Larry ride the smooth water directly behind us, avoiding the waves of the wake that symmetrically spread from the rear of our boat in an ever-expanding "V." I breathe a sigh of relief as we approach the point with the reeds where Mr. Weston bagged the smallmouth bass, confirming our successful arrival and likely soothing the unspoken uneasiness of our father-drivers.

We begin to back-troll, using the June-bug spinners gifted by Mr. Weston. Like clockwork, someone in the group connects with a walleye each time we pass the rock marker. They're not huge, but good "eaters" in the 14- to 20-inch range. Blessed be our host. A high old time is being had by all. So busy with the hooking, landing, stringing, and baiting, no one notices (or, perhaps because of the great fishing, has chosen to ignore) the change in wind speed and direction, as well as the dark clouds creeping threateningly close.

The first to become aware of the nasty weather arriving ahead of schedule, Uncle Ben motors toward us. A short conference confirms it will be in our best interest to hightail it back to Kipling. We close down our fishing gear, put on our ponchos, and streak toward home. Uncle Ben leads the way as Larry provides the directional hand signals to steer us in the proper path. All goes well through the maze of islands until we arrive at a final stretch of open water, a distance of about a mile that stands between us and the camp. The skies open, releasing a monsoon of cold rain. Exposed as we lose the protection of the islands, the wind begins blowing a gale.

Uncle Ben and Dad cut back on the throttle post-haste, as three- to four-foot waves heave us about. As the boats reach a crest and begin the slap-down into a trough, the motors sputter as the props lift out of the water. I'm not sure if seeing Uncle Ben and Larry's boat is a negative (tossing about like a cork in a whirlpool) or a positive (still upright, as thoughtfully engineered and manufactured). In the bow, I hold on for dear life. Like a cowboy on a bucking bronco, I'm unnerved yet invigorated by the wild ride that includes the pelting rain and spray of lake water as the boat undulates and pounds with each wave. As I look back at Dad, he's not sharing my enthusiasm. Concentration and determination fill his eyes. Although each minute seems like five, slow and steady progress closes the distance until we safely dock. Only then do we share smiles dripping with exhilarated relief, our facial expressions mirroring that of Tilt-A-Whirl riders stepping out of the cars after completing their inaugural twirl.

This analogy gains strength if the carnival riders perspired and peed on themselves, as a good portion of our clothing displays massive patches of moisture. Our 99-cent K-Mart ponchos, whose clinging properties and thickness match a sheet of Saran Wrap, can claim responsibility for the lion's share of the unwelcome baptism. A mental note made, I'll be asking Santa to outfit me with a set of quality raingear endorsed by Ted Williams.

The storm clears out overnight. A strong, cool northwest breeze brings a chill to the morning air under high pressure and bluebird skies. Such post-frontal conditions are the bane of fishermen, every fish in the lake seemingly going on strike by refusing to strike. I prepare to roll out excuses 4, 6, and 12 to explain our inability to catch fish should the catching not go as hoped.

And roll them out I do. Joined by Uncle Bill's party we "go to the well" once too often, drawing a blank at Indian Bay. The Nina, Pinta, and Santa Maria travel back to some of Caravello's spots. As we troll Lunny Island, Larry's arm is nearly ripped from its socket by a vicious strike. Early in the fight his no-name reel (another K-Mart purchase), like a Wiley Coyote procurement from the Acme Corporation, literally falls apart in his hand, making a bad day "reely" worse. Other than a few stragglers picked up by Uncle Bill's crew, the fish lock-jaw epidemic continues.

I have fished through fishless days that I remember happily without regret.
—Roderick Haig Brown

A Conversation at "Crystal Creek North - Canada Bay"

After bugging our dads for the better part of the week, Larry and I finally get the okay to venture out on our own after dinner. We interpret this as a major rite of passage. It also does not escape us that our dads will better enjoy their evening relaxing with a therapeutic mixture of Early Times (during the 1920-1933 alcohol prohibition era in the United States, this was one of only five manufacturers that were exempt from the law, having been designated as "medicinal whiskey") mixed over ice with a splash of seltzer. Larry and I submit a mandatory "flight plan" detailing our fishing destinations and time of return. Before departing, our dads strongly suggest steady, stable, and safe behavior, summarized with an emphatic, "Don't do anything stupid!"

Our actions adhere to the directive, with one minor exception. As soon as our boat rounds the corner of Kipling Island and escapes sight of the dock, I join Larry on the rear bench seat. The additional weight raises the front half of the boat off the water, the erroneous belief being that we could squeeze more speed out of the 20-horse motor, expediting our arrival at our preferred fishing grounds to enable a few more casts. Years would pass before we would learn that our physics-flawed thinking actually slowed our speed (though it was still pretty cool seeing the bow of the boat galloping along at eye level.)

We motor across a stretch of open water to a lily pad-studded five-acre bay, discreetly tucked behind a narrow opening on a long stretch of featureless shoreline. During those last hours of daylight, this hidden gem became our Canadian "Crystal Creek." Larry provided his recollection of "our" bay in a journal entry some years later:

> *I only now, as a conservative parent, know how great the permission was granted by our fathers to allow us to fish the bay. And we enjoyed it, casting, joking, and catching fish, wishing for fish, imagining the peace. That little bay was a special place, secluded, serene, and protected from the big water. It didn't hold the big fish we imagined it did, but held us in a beautiful place to fish. The big rock at the opening, on the other side an ample dome of wood branches where a beaver had made its home. Vintage, mature, wild Northwoods, pines growing up the bluffs on the other three sides, and our boat the only one on the water there. The water could be clear and mirror-like, reflecting the colors of the sky and trees, the*

silence broken by the sizzle of line flying out from our reels as we cast Dardevles, Mepps, and silver spoons, catching pike. They weren't big, but they were fun. It was fun. It was beautiful.

Turning off the motor as we coast into the bay, Larry picks up his rod and reel, releases the lure hooked in one of the eyelets, then stands and steadies himself as the backwash of the boat's wake gives us a final push forward. He drops a long cast within inches of the shoreline, his #3 Mepps spinner coming to life, its silver blade dashing, flashing, reflecting the more-orange-than-yellow sun soon to give up her light behind a row of pines on the distant horizon.

His question breaks the evening silence. "Have you noticed Elin?"

The answer will have to wait. My outfit already in hand before sliding through the narrow opening to our secret sanctuary, I step onto the bench seat in the bow, the extra foot of height allowing me to survey the many nuances of the weeds, lily pads, and rocks that dot our sheltered harbor. I select a prime spot where those three pieces of structure converge and launch a cast, my Dardevle spoon slapping the water with a distinctive "splat," its barber pole red and white stripes fluttering downward before a turn of the reel handle initiates its exaggerated wobble back to the boat. That task successfully underway let the conversation begin.

"What—*am I blind?*"

Larry continues, "Every time we're in the lodge dining room, my mind is undressing her. It's hard to even concentrate on eating."

"Oh, it's hard alright," I reply. "Sounds like the fresh melons on the breakfast menu have taken on a whole new meaning for you. Smitten by the luscious, Canadian kitten, eh?"

"Fucklucious is more like it. When she comes around taking the order for our meal, I'd like to roll out a 'What I want is *not* on the menu.'"

"Sounds like you've got a textbook case of raging uncontrollable teenage hormonal lust, which, if my geographic calculations are correct, will soon be turning into a case of *long distance* raging uncontrollable teenage hormonal *unrequited* lust."

"Like that's something new?"

"With the Lizzy Rosinski and Penny Wenczyk fiascos, you know I'm no expert on girls. Of course I'm hopeful I can still knock one out of the park with Donna Muscala—I've got a good feeling about her."

"Hey, if you don't mind, weren't we talking about me?"

"Yeah, sorry. Not to take the wind out of your sails, but I think the odds of you and Miss Maple Leaf Melons connecting are as likely as me catching a sturgeon using a horse's head for bait."

"What the hell are you talking about?"

"I mentioned to Mr. Weston how I'd like to tie into a big sturgeon, and he … oh, never mind. So, what's the plan?"

Our lures, inches below the water's glassy surface, dart and flicker in enticing dance but arrive at the boat without provoking a strike. As we fire off another set of casts, conversation flows like the line effortlessly releasing from our reel spools.

"I don't know. I've been thinking about it for a couple of days. It's tough. There are always people around when she's working, and I'm not really comfortable tapping on her cabin door in the dead of night, though her shadow behind the shade does create some interesting images."

"Do we need to add voyeurism to your list of favorite activities?"

"Not that I have to explain, but I was having a hard time falling asleep last night so I went out to see if I could get lucky with a northern lights show. I got lucky all right—but the show was the fair maiden's shadow against that flimsy curtain, brushing her long hair that we only see tied up in that daytime proletariat ponytail."

"Geez, this is more serious than I thought. I'll see if I can get the Kenora Fire Department to make an island call to hose you down with some cold lake water."

"I know this whole thing is probably going nowhere, but…"

"You took to the pen again, didn't you?"

"Yeah, when in doubt, I write it out."

"Whaddaya got, Shakespeare?"

As our next fishless casts near the boat, Larry pulls his lure from the water and in one swift motion rockets another cast. The pace of the retrieve proceeds in rhythm with the soliloquy, the pauses between lines enabling me to digest the words:

> *"Me thinks if I should wonder*
> *For ages of uncertain bliss,*
> *The silent thoughts I ponder,*
> *A face of which I'll miss.*
> *But if perchance I see you,*
> *And God, I know not when,*
> *I'll look into your wondrous eyes*
> *And ponder once again"*

"Wow. Heavy duty. That'll need the extra-strength Charmin. You may want to try shoveling that load face-to-face. Take her to the bluff on the far side of the island and lay that on her as you're taking in one of those unbelievable sunsets. Juliet could melt in your arms, like a carp dough-ball in a rain-swelled creek. I wish you'd have written that a couple of years ago. I could have used it to try and re-stoke the flames in Penny's love furnace."

I fling another cast as Larry sits down, removing his black, horn-rimmed glasses before resting elbows on his knees. Head down, it's as if he's contemplating the bottom of the boat trying to divine an answer to a seemingly no-win situation. "I'm thinking I'll just slip it under her door the morning we leave. No chance of rejection that way."

"No, no, you've gotta come up with something better than that. You're not catching anything if your lure's not in the water. Kinda like now. Time's running short. Let me think…"

My retrieve complete, I cast again: lure, then words. "Okay, here's some Bard of Avon of my own for you: 'Um … parting is such sweet sorrow, and … uh … there's little time left from which you can borrow, and … and … you'll never see her again after today and tomorrow.'"

Fittingly unimpressed, Larry comments, "Stick to Shakespeare rods and reels," referencing the longtime tackle manufacturer.

My Dardevle still some distance from the boat, a large northern pike raises from the weeds. "There's one!" It follows the lure for a short distance before darting away. In a singular motion, Larry rises, grabs his rig, and propels a cast in the direction the fish had turned. Immediately upon splashdown the fish reappears, apparently more interested in glimmer and shimmer than blood and white.

Twice the length of the fare we typically encounter in our bay, the fish, expending little energy with effortless sways of its tail, keeps pace behind the steady retrieve of the lure. Attempting to coax a strike, Larry reels faster. The large pike bursts forward, closing the distance in the blink of an eye. It opens its mouth and flares its gills preparing for the final lunge. As the lure skirts the edge of a group of lily pads, the treble hook snags the shaft of a pad that had not yet emerged. The forward movement of the lure and its spinning blade abruptly stops. In reaction to the unnatural turn of events, the pike closes its mouth and arcs downward, fading into the forest of weeds.

"Son of a fucking bitch," Larry moans, his voice laced with exasperation and disappointment.

I attempt to cover the wound, fresh and raw, with a humorous bandage. "Hey, *hey,* we're guests here in a foreign land. A little decorum, eh?"

Recognizing the attempt to heal, Larry replies "Sorry. Son of an effin' bitch, eh?" Acrimony surfacing, a violent pull of the rod frees the lure, whizzing back toward him. Within inches of his face he bats it away, as if swatting at an annoying fly, fortunate to avoid contact with the treble hook. He dejectedly offers, "Man, if that isn't a perfect metaphor I don't know what is."

"What's a metaphor?" I ask. "Is that the fiber powder stuff you mix that helps you take a good crap?"

"That's Metamucil. Jesus Christ—try and stay awake in your English classes."

He slumps onto the bench seat and tosses down his rod, which comes to rest at a 45-degree angle against the gunnel. The silver spinner blade dangles over the edge of the boat like a teardrop.

In matters of our quests to land fish and females, my well-read cousin had often quoted lines from a poem by John Greenleaf Whittier. Those words seemed apropos to this evening's conversation and events.

For of all sad words of tongue or pen,
The saddest are these: 'It might have been!'

~ ~ ~ ~ ~

The Kipling Island Tally

The entry in the *"Fishing Log of E.P.,"* resplendent with recent pencil drawings of walleye, northern pike, and smallmouth bass, bears witness to that first glorious week north of the border:

Sunday, June 23, 1968
Walleye – 18 inches

Monday, June 24, 1968
Smallmouth Bass – 12, 9 inches
Northern Pike – 19 inches
Perch – 10, 10, 9½, 4 inches
Rock bass – 8, 8, 8½, 9 inches
Walleye – 10 inches

Tuesday, June 25, 1968
Walleye – 14, 20, 12 inches
Perch – 10½, 9 inches
Northern Pike – 14 inches
Smallmouth Bass – 13 inches

Wednesday, June 26, 1968
Walleye – 18 inches
Perch – 8, 8½, 10, 10½ inches

Thursday, June 27, 1968
Perch – 8, 9, 9, 8½ inches
Walleye – 11, 13, 14, 16, 16, 19 inches
Northern Pike – 32 inches, 6 pounds

This record reflects several items of particular interest:

It is not until this very moment that I take note and wonder, "Hmmm, why did I find it necessary to write the year for each consecutive day and date in the same week?" to which I reply, "I, well, I don't know." (Perhaps the subconscious anticipation of the display of my archives at the *Freshwater Fishing Hall of Fame* caused the anal preciseness.)

Excluding Wednesday, June 26, 1968 (in case of any doubt about what year it was), each day resulted in my personal best largest fish:

Sunday: 18-inch walleye
Monday: 19-inch northern pike
Tuesday: 20-inch walleye
Thursday: 32-inch northern pike

The perch and rock bass, one-half of the total quantity of fish listed, were caught "still-fishing" off the dock. So much for the concern about where to find fish in all that water.

No entry exists for Friday, June 28, 1968. That is because no fish were caught that day. No fish were caught that day because we departed for home one day early. We departed for home one day early because our dads were getting homesick and/or their supply of liquor had run out. Early departures from subsequent weeklong fishing trips with our dads emerged as a disturbing and recurring certainty, this in spite of our pleas, falling on deaf and sometimes "hung-over" ears, that they err on the side of either overstocking their refreshments of choice or level-loading their intake pattern to ensure "the well" would not run dry before the end of the week.

*Larry (r) and me (l) ~
Catching some fish ... but girls remain elusive.*

~ ~ ~ ~ ~

Uncle Bill never hooked a muskellunge, the fish of his dreams. He wasn't alone. No one in our group landed one during the Kipling Island years. We collectively defied the odds, coming up empty while likely pitching more than the requisite 10,000 casts.

We knew they were out there because of Doc Watson and another fisherman who based at Kipling Island during one of our stays. Hailing from Mississippi, "Tex" (we couldn't figure that one out, either), a bassin' man, spent his week in pursuit of smallmouth bass. One day, we and other camp patrons gathered at the dock to admire a mid-30-inch musky he brought in. Tex told the story in his melodically lulling southern drawl.

"I casted out my floatin' Repeler (understood-interpreted as a "Rapala") near some reeds n chunk rock. I let it set there till all them circles inside a circles wint away, then I waited another 30 seconds. I always count 'em out like this: 'wun Mis-sis-sip-pi ... two Mis-sis-sip-pi ... three Mis-sis-sip-pi...' It reminds me a home when I count like that. Then I gave that there Repeler a little twitch, and Bam! The big ol' gal thought that injured minna was a easy meal. Instead she got a jawful a steel."

Anxious for more details, Dad asked, "Where'd you get her?"

Tex paused and smiled, pointing as he replied "Why, out thar, in the lake."

Larry and I looked at each other, our thoughts in sync. We know that fishermen fall into any of three categories: those who share information about lures and locations, those who don't, and the lowest of the low who purposely provide misinformation. With his smart-alecky reply, Tex placed himself solidly in category two. He ruptured our rapture, lowering our view of him from lauded hero to borderline jerk.

"Jag-off," Larry muttered under his breath.

Concluding the brief sidebar, I whispered back, "Yeah ... How do you think that good ol' boy would look with a three-foot musky shoved up his Tex-ass?"

If Doc and Tex caught one, to what can we chalk up our group's combined failure? Lack of proper equipment? Early on, sure. Lack of technique? Little doubt, still shedding the "still-fishing" syndrome. Lack of knowledge of lake, fish habits, and habitat? Students in training, learning as we go. Lack of luck? The "Lady" certainly did not shine upon us. But damn, with all that time and all that water someone should have landed one, even if by accident.

Cousin Billy was the only one among us to hook one, a big one. Exactly how big we'll never know. On their second day fishing at Town Island it engulfed his Johnson Silver Minnow spoon at mid-retrieve, battling some ten minutes before freeing itself. The aura of the monster that got away would stay with us, appear in dreams, bury itself in our subconscious, and, later in life, resurface and drive some to higher levels of fishing obsession.

The fishing week ended with my last (and largest-ever, to that point in my life) fish, a 32-inch pike, duped by my favorite red and white Dardevle in the final minutes of the last evening as Larry and I fished "our" bay. A blank page in my log book remains reserved for a yet-to-be-caught muskellunge. On another note of unfinished business, Larry didn't slip his poem under Elin's door before we departed on Friday morning.

The camp on Kipling Island, sold to a private concern, closed its doors to the general public in the early 1970s. Lake of the Woods—home to countless quantities of fish and dotted with many resorts (that employ many waitresses)—is but one of a quarter of a million lakes in Ontario. I'm not sure if this weeklong peephole glimpse at the colossus of Canada tips the odds for or against ever connecting with lunkers—and ladies.

In the grand scheme, with these as our most pressing concerns, life was good. Just over the horizon, however, issues far more ominous loomed.

~ ~ ~ ~ ~

...for look how it begins to rain, and by the clouds, if I mistake not, we shall presently have a smoking showre; and therefore sit close, this sycamore tree will shelter us...." (Piscator to Viator)
—Izaak Walton
THE COMPLEAT ANGLER
Or, The Contemplative Man's Recreation - 1653

Dark Clouds

America's continuing involvement in the Vietnam War casts a long, distressing shadow. An undercurrent of uneasiness permeates the nation. A groundswell of opposition builds with fervor on most college campuses. Beginning with military advisors in the 1950s, the conflict escalates through the 1960s with the first combat units deploying in 1965. By the late 1960s, the evening news broadcasts *weekly* U.S. death totals in the hundreds. If merciless Vietcong combatants don't maim, capture or kill U.S. soldiers, many fall victim to poisonous snakes, malaria, typhus, dysentery, or heat prostration. Forty thousand of the U.S. war dead perish at 22 years of age or less. College age. Anti-war sentiment increases with each passing year, reaching a fever pitch on

May 4, 1970, when National Guard troops kill four unarmed student protestors at Kent State University in Ohio.

The revival of conscription uproots men not far removed from boyhood, hurling them to the other side of the world to fight in the hell of jungles, rice paddies, heat, and monsoons. Annual draft lotteries from 1969 through 1972 decide the order, based on birth dates, in which men born from 1946 to 1952 will be called to serve, or not. College attendees, however, receive a "2-S" student deferment, delaying the call-up until the completion of a four-year degree or reaching the age of 24, whichever comes first.

Darker Clouds

Sunday, July 5, 1970. Four days ago, the Selective Service System tumbled the fate of hundreds of thousands of young men in a rotating drum, dates and numbers yanked in a high-stakes, life-altering, potentially life-ending lottery. Larry involuntarily participates in this year's federally sponsored game of Russian roulette. I don't face the ugly barrel until next year. In spite of Larry sharing his birth date with the birthday of our country's independence, the 4th of July draws number 59. With call-ups anticipated through number 125, the future does not bode well for him upon completion of his student deferment. That evening I phone him to commiserate on Lady Luck's desertion. Neither of us big on telephone conversations, he inquires about my availability for a day on the lake. He wants to talk. Our history says we do that well with fishing poles in our hands.

The grind of another week of stocking shelves on the graveyard shift at Jewel completed, I pick him up early Sunday morning. We agree to avoid the noisy whirlpool created by speedboats on the Chain O' Lakes. With many others from which to choose, I'm not sure how or why we decide to fish Crooked Lake. One of the few lakes in northern Illinois we never fished as children, perhaps our subconscious recognizes that "crooked" provides an accurate description of our nation's fractured outlook. The war continues to polarize, and an Arab oil embargo and a severe recession lurk to further cripple an already distraught country.

After arriving at the boat rental, we load our gear into a small wooden craft. Larry mans the oars and I push us off, hopping into the bow as the boat glides across the lake's morning calm. A few strokes into our journey Larry releases the oars, points both arms toward me, and wiggles his fingers as if performing some sort of hokey magic trick.

Not sure where his thoughts are headed, I comment, "If you're trying to make me disappear you'll have better luck if you just toss me overboard."

"Do you see these? These are my fingers. And I still have them all." He grabs the oars, continues rowing, and embarks on a monologue.

"Not to diminish the difficulty or manual dexterity of your job tossing cans of cream corn on the shelves at the grocery store, but working the Number 5 press at Titan Moulder over the past couple of summers I've learned that the rhythm of manual labor can cause your mind to wander throughout the day—not the safest thing when working a machine that can lop off a finger or flatten your hand like a flounder.

"The shop radio is always tuned to WGN because of the Cubs home day games. Last Wednesday they're in St. Louis playing a night game, so the World's Greatest Network broadcasts the draft lottery instead. When they get to July my heart starts pounding like it's going to fly out of my chest. Just as they're announcing the number for the 4th, I shut down my press but the shop noise cranks up, so I'm not sure if they said 69 or 59. Either way I'm hosed, but the 59 is more appropriate 'cause it's a one-way screw job. Nice guy—Uncle Sam lays it to me on his own birthday. No one hears the 'son of a bitch' I blurt out but that's just as well because someone might have been distracted into thinking I left a couple of fingers on the table.

"My mind starts racing. I wonder if our dads will take us on one more trip to Kipling Island, and I'll see if I can stay and work there as a hired hand for Mr. Weston ... and maybe a certain waitress might still be working there ... and finding pure and true love, we marry and have a boatload of kids. The cherry on top of the happiness-and-personal-fulfillment sundae completes during the winters when I preside as the resident philosopher of Kenora.

"Then, the stateside fantasy relationships kick in for the soldier-in-waiting scenario: Diane Carlson and Carrie Scott on the Grayslake home front, and half the coeds at NIU who I've never had the guts to talk to, let alone ask out. This one a better option, I ditch the Canadian escape idea and decide to ride out the educational deferment and not worry about the looming number—the same way I've always detached from the idea of death.

"In spite of the radio-delivered kick in the balls, I make it through my shift with all digits intact, but the story doesn't end there. Dad didn't let me take the Chevelle to work that day. The friggin' two-mile drive to the factory was *way* too risky, and besides, my mom might need both cars, parked safely at home during the course of the day, in case the gas evaporates out of one she'll have the second to drive to the A&P to cash in if there's a sale on ketchup.

"Anyway, on the walk home on the gravel shoulder of Washington Street, where dirtbag drivers toss their beer cans and other garbage, I spot what looks like a 45 RPM record. It's covered in mud and grit, and I brush it off well enough to read 'ALL YOU NEED IS LOVE' and 'THE BEATLES' across the top and bottom of the yellow and orange swirl on the 'Capitol' label. I remember thinking, 'So this is what happens to peace and love, and any poor sap that's looking for it.'"

His discourse complete, I'm at a loss for words, at least ones that will offer appropriate insight or comfort. Concern for my cousin's plight foremost, I also cast a thought to my own luck-of-the-draw future. "Damn…" I mutter.

The hours that follow, burdened by the lottery results and the cumulative physical strain of our summer jobs, limits our typically lively conversation. We fish a number of different spots, but the fish are missing in action at all of them. Presently at the south end of the lake, we're a long row from the boat rental in the northeast corner. With the sun and humidity squeezing every last ounce of sweat from our pores and the fish in an uncooperative mood, I sense we're about ready to call it a day. This "intuition" manifests itself when I snap out of a trance fixating on a motionless bobber to find Larry in a prone position atop his bench seat, eyes closed and head resting on the gunnel, legs crossed at the ankles, and feet hanging over the other edge of the boat. Arms outstretched in a crucifixion pose, his right hand loosely clutches the handle of his rod and reel combo.

Turning an eye to the sky, I catch a glimpse of an apocalyptic line of gray-black clouds pluming over the southwest treeline, uncoiling and expanding with a speed I have never before seen, the devil himself exhaling a giant puff of smoke from the eternal fires raging in the depths of hell. This soul-rattling sight could make a man without religion reexamine his belief system.

"Holy shit!" The verbal alarm startles my cousin, the fishing rod dropping out of his hand to the bottom of the boat as he bolts to an upright position.

"What the hell…?"

I point over his shoulder and reply, "Exactly!"

A wordless flurry of activity ensues: reeling in and dismantling fishing gear, pulling in the anchor, tackle boxes slamming shut, and unfolding then sliding the hooded, semitransparent plastic ponchos over our heads. I grab the oars, slip the oarlocks into their sockets, and begin rowing, urgency permeating each exaggerated pull. The oars slice into the dark water that now reflects the blackened sky. Aware the swiftly moving "black death" will not allow us to make it back to the boat rental, our course tracks to the nearest shore. The distance closes rapidly. As the bow slides onto the sandy shore, Larry hops out, then drags the front half of our skiff out of the water. At that moment, the crack of lightning and rumble of thunder commence the deluge.

Lightning-related safety issues race through my mind: don't stay near water; don't be the tallest object in an open space; don't stand under a tree. We're screwed. With no time to evaluate, we choose the least of the evils, scrambling to a stand of smaller hickories a short distance from several towering oaks. After catching our breath, we turn toward the lake to see the silvery-gray sheets of rain swirling helter-skelter. The trees' canopies provide only partial protection as leaves and branches sway like an out-of-control seesaw. Gusts of wind continue to whip the watery curtain in our direction, pelting our ponchos. The rapid-fire raindrops disintegrate with dull splats before re-forming and rolling downward, soaking our lower legs and gym shoe-clad feet. Mother Nature, angry and sad, funnels her tempestuous energy in a barrage of thunderbolts surrounded by waterfalls of tears.

Larry turns away from the moisture-spewing gale and hunches his shoulders, reaching beneath his poncho. Digging into his shirt pocket, he pulls out two cigarettes. Head bowed to keep them dry, he lights them simultaneously before handing one to me. Forefinger and thumb squeezing the filter, I cradle it in my left hand, tightly curled fingers forming a makeshift hangar to protect the precious cargo.

We draw hard on the Winstons. Exaggerated exhales follow long, deep drags, each intense puff glowing the vermilion tips bright then dull in the rhythm of fireflies at dusk. Still-warm ashes tumble, raindrops intercepting them as they parachute toward the wet turf, dying with a muted fizz. Our surroundings, this weather, drenched somber like the subject of today's discourse, lead Larry to an ominous comment: "Just think, in a few years we could be in Vietnam doing this..."

~ ~ ~ ~ ~

Scholars have long known that fishing eventually turns men into philosophers. Unfortunately, it is almost impossible to buy decent tackle on a philosopher's salary.
—Patrick McManus

College:
Fishing for an Education and Learning the Game of Life

Many variables can factor into the process of evaluating institutions of higher learning. When deciding which to attend, location and distance from home, net cost after scholarships and financial aid packages, academic requirements, and desired areas of study matched to the strengths of each school come into play. My choice? Northern Illinois University, 65 miles west of Chicago. Why? Because Larry and Chuck go there.

They sail as freshman for the 1969-70 school year while I, one year behind, toil to complete my senior year of high school. I anxiously await their letters (snail-mail in these pre-email, pre-texting, pre-Facebook, pre-tweeting, pre-Skype, pre-cellphone, pre-computer days) and stories told during breaks and vacations, all magnifying my "still in port" status. Dropping anchor in DeKalb can't arrive too soon.

That late August day finally arrives. The streets and drop-off driveways surrounding the dorms bustle like a train station during rush hour. Students, their siblings, and parents scurry about toting boxes and a sundry array of items. As cars depart after shedding their cargo, others wait to replace them in the unpacking parade.

Our turn. Dad swings the Rambler into a vacated space outside Stevenson South residence hall, one of eight chalky white monoliths on the far west side of the campus that sprout next to cornfields stretching to the horizon. As we exit the car, Mom grabs the loops of black wire hangers that hold an abbreviated selection of my shirts and pants. Her other hand grips a brown bag containing personally selected snacks: Salerno Butter cookies, a box of Ritz crackers, Snickers candy bars, and several cans of sardines. Dad and I each hoist a box from the trunk, one with other clothes and bedding items, and the second containing the remainder of my significant (non-fishing) worldly possessions. For 18 years on this earth, it's a short list: flesh-tone onyx fish-head bookends (you remember, the ones I asked Mom to dust twice daily in my letter from International Falls); a Zenith clock-radio; the Hermann Hesse paperbacks *Siddhartha, Demian,* and *Steppenwolf;* the hardcover 1,336-page *The Wise Fishermen's Encyclopedia* and Sir Arthur Conan Doyle's *The Complete*

Sherlock Holmes; a Cubs calendar, a Blackhawks pennant, a Bears schedule, and a deck of pinochle cards.

Up the steps, through the door, and into the lobby, we pass a massive bank of steel-gray mailboxes before stalling in a queue to catch one of two elevators that will transport us to the 11th floor, one short of the "penthouse." Then it's on to room 1146, where my roommate has yet to arrive. Just as well. The three of us can barely turn in this Spartan, cozy cube, each side a mirror image of the other: closet, bed, desk, chair, and bookshelf. A large window frames blue sky that touches the sea of green cornstalks.

A quick unpack leads to a hug and a kiss for Mom and a handshake for Dad, sending them on their way back to Niles. Alone in my new micro residence with the door closed, fleeting thoughts and emotions flash, though not in the cause and effect that one might expect. No car, no television, no refrigerator ... no melancholy, no misery, no problem. Head bowed and arms outstretched skyward, the corners of my mouth edge upward as I inhale a big dose of freedom.

How might the college years be best described? Advice columnist Carolyn Hax summarizes them as follows:

> *Your college years are a one-time convergence of youth, unprecedented independence, lowered barriers to varied opportunities, an atmosphere that encourages discovery, a hand-picked abundance of peers, and quantities of unstructured time that you've never seen before and will probably never see again, if not the pinnacle of your existence, at least it deserves recognition as a rare and fleeting opportunity for profound personal growth.*

As the college experience unfolds, I acclimate well and confirm with a resounding, "Yeah, what she said!"

Roommate and residence hall selection not an option, Larry, Chuck, and I reside in different dormitories during my freshman year: Larry in Grant, Chuck in Douglas, and me in Stevenson. The only reason I mention the names of the buildings (Grant the Civil War General and President of the U.S., Douglas and Stevenson politicians of note, all three hailing from Illinois) is that a member of the Stevenson family will intersect with my fishing world a couple of decades down the road.

Educational opportunities both in and outside the classroom abound during the inaugural year at my new home away from home.

I learn…

...the dormitory elevator aids and frustrates as friend and foe. As an ally it negates the need to trudge up and down 11 flights of stairs. On the downside, precious time slips away on every trip to and from classes, meals, sporting competitions, and social events. The claustrophobic carriage creeps at its own drowsy pace. Waiting begets hating ... deliberate doors ... multiple stops ... weekend vertical vomitoreum.

...to share less than 200 square feet of living space with a complete stranger, establishing a congenial relationship with my first roommate, a sophomore. Aside from his body clock mixing up days and nights, he seems like a fairly normal guy. As a result of his nocturnality, he apprises me of several entertaining "talk in my sleep" narratives, jokingly threatening to reveal them only if he "has to."

...that although Niles is only an hour and a half from DeKalb, the only time I need to visit the old homestead is during extended breaks and vacations when the university formally closes.

...to never schedule a class before 10 a.m. This a function of never turning in before midnight.

...the proper juggling of study and play time, negotiating the minefield of distractions and temptations littering campus life, though "proper juggling" often translates to "cramming" into the early hours of the morning on the day of a quiz or test.

...the prudent allocation of clothing to minimize laundry duty. In my first solo effort with the Maytag, I debate whether the red jersey with the white collar should go with the colors or whites. The coin flip betrays me as I end up with a load of pink underwear.

...to (generally) reserve partying for Friday and Saturday nights.

...through (sometimes gut-wrenching) trial and error, my consumption limits of various attitude-adjusting beverages, including "Old Kishwaukee," the affectionate, student-given moniker for Old Milwaukee beer (the value-priced, entry-level brand of the Schlitz Brewing Company whose taste and appearance draw unflattering parallels to the nearby Kishwaukee River), and Boone's Farm Strawberry Hill wine, the economy inebriant from the vineyards of Ernest and Julio Gallo (need I say more?).

Note to close family members: <u>Do not</u> read the next paragraph.

...that marijuana and me don't mix, meaning that, yes, I gave it the ol' college try. (Hey, so did Kennedy, Carter, Clinton, G.W. Bush, and Obama.) I find no positives in a stupor that causes my head to expand to the size of a beluga whale while my body freezes with the rigor mortis of day-old road kill.

Note to close family members that just read the above paragraph—Shame on you!

In addition to sharing an occasional meal and participating in pick-up games of touch football or basketball, Larry, Chuck, and I begin a tradition we name the "Symposium." Several times each year, an evening meeting convenes in one of our dorm rooms. Over a bottle of Ruby Port, we engage in lively verbal jousts on any number of esoteric topics, words crafting abstract concepts that flow freely about the candlelit room. Our mental gymnastics seek to uncover hidden truths and solve scholarly riddles through pure thought.

Although these pre-scheduled noble endeavors do not result (as many believe) from dateless Saturday nights where we collectively drown our sorrows by consuming a bottle of cheap wine while smoking cigarettes and puffing on pipes, by coincidence, we do consume cheap wine, smoke cigarettes, and puff on pipes on certain Saturday nights that lack female companionship. Our trio, friends and cerebral combatants, contemplate philosophical and metaphysical questions of the ages, hoping to unravel puzzling pansophic mysteries and attack erudite questions unanswered by the greatest minds of multiple millennia, perhaps similar to those posed centuries B.C. to the Oracle at Delphi. There is no truth to suggestions that inquisition and debate center on questions such as, "Why can't you tickle yourself?" or "If a pope shits in the woods and a hard-of-smelling bear does not notice the foul odor, does the odor exist, and further, if the bear is also blind and knocks over a tree but the pope does not hear it because he is deaf, does the falling tree make a sound, and further, if the falling tree strikes the pope, who would otherwise scream in agony but cannot because he is also mute, should the bear, if he could talk (though the deaf pope would not hear), apologize on general principle for his clumsiness?" More on Symposiums later.

Undecided on major and minor fields of study, most of my freshman classes gear toward fulfilling general education requirements: Psychology, Sociology, Astronomy, Economics, Philosophy, Political Science, Art History, Physical Education, English something or other ... you get the picture. Larry pursues a major in philosophy and I have thoughts of doing the same, that potential choice fed by the (wine-enhanced) intellectual exhilaration of the Symposiums.

I submit my first Philosophy 110 class assignment, "How Plato Differentiates Between Rhetoric and Philosophy in the Phaedrus, and a Discussion on Philosophy in that Light as the 'Fourth Sort of Madness,' or Love," with great pride and anticipation. I'm confident I nailed it.

Half right. Professor Walton nailed *me*. He returns it with the following comments:

There is no coherence in your treatment of your material. You misconstrue the major concepts involved. You need to improve on your writing of your ideas into sentences, to express clear thoughts in every statement. 'D.'

Up yours, Doc. How's that for clarity?

Just having squeaked into the top 10% of my high school graduation class at number 37 of 400 with a 3.47 out of 4.0 grade point average and an Illinois State Scholarship worth a couple hundred bucks, I'm smart enough to realize there are a lot of people, 36 at Notre Dame alone, smarter than me. So it goes with most of life, increasingly evident as I move to each next level. In spite of what Mom thinks, there's always someone more intelligent, more athletic, bigger, stronger, harder working, better looking, better-than-you-name-it. Stunned and deflated by the philosophy paper that tells me I'm more an intellectual pretender than contender, I acknowledge the likelihood that my scholastic aptitude more closely approximates a 75-watt bulb than a 100-. There, I've built a case to justify the upper end of mediocrity. Just as well. I've never seen a want ad for a philosopher. Welcome to the School of Business.

A Conversation at Crystal Creek in the Summer of '71

Although kindred spirits and close as brothers, no one would link us as relatives, let alone brothers, based on physical appearance. Larry's features sourced from our mothers' side of the family—shorter and slighter of build. Mine drew more heavily from my dad's. While also on the slim side, my height leveled at a half-head taller than Larry. My blond hair contrasted with his dark brown. Though we both wore glasses in grammar school, I traded mine for contact lenses in high school. As most teenagers, we both dealt with the scourge of complexion issues. Some minor blemishes, unwelcome souvenirs from the dermatological onslaught remained, as did a few psychological scars from the growing up process.

Aside from the Canadian fishing adventure Larry and I shared, the demands of summer jobs during our high school and college years limited fishing and talk time during the school year hiatuses. Upon completion of my freshman year at NIU, a late June day found our schedules allowing a get together for an afternoon of fishing, and hopefully, catching. If the fish don't cooperate at least we'd do some "catching up" on recent life events. Though we had seen each other often on campus during the school year, several years had passed since we last connected in the solitude provided by the treasured waters of Crystal Creek.

As we cross the acre site of our old ball field on the walk to the creek, it strikes me how visual perspectives change as we grow older. The gargantuan poke required for a childhood home-run could now be attained with a swing resulting in little more than a bat-handle popup. So, too, has the vista of Crystal Creek transformed. The meandering waterway and its widened pool where we wet a line likewise diminished in physical dimension. Intangibly, however, this venue for dialog will always retain its importance for sharing the steps and missteps of our ever-expanding worldly experiences.

We arrive at the water's edge where two partially exposed boulders lay a couple of strides apart. I sit on the ground, back propped against one as Larry perches atop the other, his elevated position appropriate to many of the conversations in which he serves as my mentor and confessor.

He opens his tackle box and reaches in, grabbing a pack of Winston cigarettes. After removing the cellophane wrapper and peeling away the silver foil, he gives it a few quick taps against the curled index finger of his left hand. Several of the light brown filters jut from the opening, uneven yet orderly, like the pillars of St. Hedwig's pipe organ. As he raises the pack to his mouth, his pursed lips pull out the one that had risen above the others. With a flick of his wrist he tosses the red and white banded package in my direction, coming to rest beside me on a mat of thick grass. He strikes a match and touches the flame to the tip of the "thinking stick," a wisp of smoke hovering in the stagnant summer air. A deep drag inhaled, he closes the plain, white cover of the matchbook and flips it toward me. It lands atop the pack, covering the "W" in "Winston." After an exaggerated exhale, Larry comments, "Ah, noth*in*' as satisfy*in*' as an *in*ston … *in*ston tastes good, like a cigarette should."

I reach over and pluck one, replying, "Are you done?"

"Yeah, go ahead."

Words imbedded in the gray haze of freshly tendered smoke, I begin. "I think I had a dream…"

Cut off in mid-sentence, Larry interrupts: "You *think?* You *think* you had a dream? How many brain cells have you and the boys on Stevenson 11 killed that you wouldn't know a dream from reality?"

"I think I hope it was a dream," I reply.

"You killed them all. They're all dead," Larry says, slowly moving his head from side to side, not pleased with the continuing lack of clarity.

"It should become clear as the mud in Crystal Creek. Freud and friends would have a field day with this. So real this dream, my ego suffered severe damage—it got stomped as the middleman in the tug-o-war between the id and superego."

"Well, well, well, look who paid attention in his Psych 101 class. I'm proud of you. Dream away."

"Do you remember my grade school friend, Jimmy Muscala? Or, more to the point, do you remember his younger sister, Donna?"

"If you had to change the sheets the morning after this dream, I don't want to hear about it."

I look skyward, then lob an exhaustive glance my cousin's way. Properly interpreted as my want to get on with the recollection, Larry continues, "Donna? Of course. Bella donna, 'beautiful woman,' though I believe your quest began when the little darlin' hadn't yet emerged from the pupae stage on her way to spreading her … er … wings, a beautiful butterfly yet to be. If memory serves me correctly, she was on the cusp of her high school career when you, the worldly high school junior, took her to the Cubs opener at Wrigley in '69."

"Nothing escapes you, does it, professor?" I ask rhetorically, amazed at my cousin's memory.

"1969," he continues, "Memorable, unforgettable: The music and free love at Woodstock; man walks on the moon; I register with the Selective Service and receive my draft card; and for you, my friend, an exciting afternoon in the third base grandstand with Donna Muscala. I can picture your mutual joy as Ernie cranked two home runs, and the unbridled ecstasy when Willie Smith deposited that pinch-hit two-run homer into the right field bleachers in the bottom of the 11th securing a 7-6 victory over the Phillies, launching the most emotion-filled season in Cubs history. Your original commentary to me about the day's events seemed oddly heavy with game details but pretty sketchy regarding your interaction with Madam Pre-Butterfly."

"Nothing to tell—pretty much a one and done. We had an okay time, but she *was* kinda young. I don't even know why Mr. Muscala let me take her out."

"He knew you were harmless, more aw-shucks Beaver Cleaver than Eddie Haskell, more Timmy from *Lassie* than Dennis the Menace."

"And he knew Jimmy would beat the crap out of me if I tried anything funny with her."

"So, you're saying your "69" experience left a bad taste in your mouth, wasn't as satisfying or fulfilling as it might have been?"

I toss the Winstons and matchbook back to Larry. "Grab a couple, then chuck 'em back over here. We're both going to need them for the main event, dreamin' Donna Muscala, the sequel."

As his cigarette burns down near the filter, he brings a fresh one to his lips and lights it from the first, speaking as it dangles from his lips. "So, the Donna Muscala saga continues, with perhaps a twist on a Chicago tradition, a combo sandwich where Italian Beef meets Polish sausage? Excellent!"

"A week after our finals I went into the city to visit Jimmy and compare notes on our freshman experiences at NIU and SIU. Donna comes bouncing into their living room—she just finished her sophomore year at St. Stanislaus Kostka High. She's looking good, blossoming nicely, if you know what I mean."

"Same school your sister Nancy went to, right?"

"Yeah, it could have been a conversation starter, but I was preoccupied loading up my eyeballs."

"Which balls?"

"Her hair was real short two years ago. Now it's long and straight, well past her shoulders. She's wearing round, wire-frame glasses. The whole package is schoolgirl innocent and *really* cute."

"Sounds like her hairstyle and glasses are the Yoko Ono look, without the ugly. That reminds me of one of the many witty gems your dad passed along to us to lighten things up when we're in the boat and the bite has slowed: 'Never make passes at lasses with glasses—unless they've got a nice frame.'"

"As she's passing through the room she gives her head a quick turn, bringing her hand up to brush one side of her long locks from the front of her shoulder to the back. I get a friendly 'Hi, how are you? Long time no see!' She's meeting some girlfriends to go shopping, so there's not much small talk. As she's leaving she repeats that flirtatious little move with her hair and says 'Bye, hope to see you soon.' Jimmy tells me she's been on a couple of dates and overheard her and her friends giggling about getting to second base. At first I'm disgusted. Then intrigued. Then encouraged."

"So, you're ready to step in and round the bases with your Willie Smith imitation?"

"Our brother-sister-like outing at Wrigley notwithstanding, I give her a call the following week, and she agrees to a date at the movies."

"1969: One small step for man. 1971: One giant leap for your one-eye walleye?"

"Dad's letting me take the Rambler, so I get it all cleaned up and ready to go. No power steering, no power brakes, no a/c or 8-track, and I cover the hole in the passenger-side floorboard with a piece of plywood and old carpeting. It's rough, but it still beats the CTA bus we took to the Cubs game.

"It's the hottest damn day of the year, humid, mid-90s. I finish my shower and the box fan in the window is working overtime to help evaporate the beads of perspiration popping up as fast as I can towel them off. Then it's dealing with the all-important 'What to wear?' question. I settle on white Levi's and a baby blue shirt."

"I'm sure the Beach Boys appreciate it, but this level of detail is important, *why*? Did you forgo the underwear option? I'm sure you're planning on finding out if Donna did."

"Those questions will be answered in due time, my friend, all in due time. I'm in front of the medicine cabinet mirror, combing my hair and wailing to Led Zeppelin's 'Communication Breakdown' that's spinning on the turntable and cranked up full blast. I'm psyched."

"'Psycho' is more like it. I'll send along your apologies to Robert Plant and Jimmy Page."

"I finish up with a splash of cool, icy blue Aqua Velva, and I'm ready to go."

"Ah, you foresee your date needing to regulate her output of passion in the throes of midsummer's night heat, seeking relief by licking the fragrant coolness from your face? By the way, do you still get by shaving only once a week?"

"My facial hair is blond. You just can't see it; that's my story, and I'm sticking to it."

Momentarily sidetracked, a deep drag from the Winston returns me to my tale. "I've got some time, but the anticipation is killing me and I don't want to be late, so I take off. It's a half-hour ride to her house, and I get there a half-hour too early, so I'm killing the extra time riding around in the non-air conditioned car the sun has been pounding into all day. The heat's doing a number on my armpits; I peek down, realizing the light color shirt is a *big* mistake. Damn it! I hide it as best I can and head up to the front door, ringing the doorbell while keeping my upper arms tight against my sides so the sweat ring stays hidden."

"Time to pony-up the extra couple of pennies for the Right Guard labeled 'antiperspirant.'"

"Donna comes to the door and greets me with a smiling 'Hi!' Sweet as a perfectly ripened peach, she's wearing an orange top, white miniskirt, and white moccasins."

"Orange and white, a dreamsicle come true."

"We walk down the driveway and I open the car door for her. She slides her sweet cheeks onto the seat, then swings her legs (tanned nicely, by the way, and making a great statement against the white miniskirt) up and in. As I'm closing the door, I glance heavenward and whisper, 'Thank you!'"

"After twelve years of Catholic schooling, I thought you went atheist during your first year in college."

"Agnostic—I'm still hedging my bet. I thought you knew I became a Golden Rule guy. Plus, I've got a ton of indulgences in reserve, built up from daily mass during the eight years at St. Hedwig. Anyway, things look promising. Donna's crossing the bridge from newbie to nubile, still impressionable for the James Bond cosmopolitan swagger I'm feeling. Except for my sweaty pits, I'm holding all the trump cards. I've got the world by the ass with a year of college tucked under my belt: intramural multi-sport jock, a perfect streak of not getting to bed before midnight the entire school year, and acing my Intro to Psych and Sociology classes. I can toss out a few nuggets on Art History and Philosophy, too, even though Doc Walton gave me a 'D' in Classic Greek Philosophy. I kept getting Aristotle, Plato, and Socrates mixed up."

"Not to worry. I'm sure the only philosophic doctrine you're hoping to experience before the evening ends is hedonism."

"Call it Epicurean delight—see, I did study a little. Anyway, I get in the car feeling *real* good, and though I can't offer her a 007 shaken-not-stirred martini, I reach into my shirt pocket and toss a pack of Winston's on the dashboard. Before I can tell her to help herself, she hits me with a condescending 'Oh, you smoke?'"

"Didn't take long for the 'dream' to melt out of the dreamsicle, did it?"

"Yeah, an upbeat 'Oh, you smoke, *too!*' would have been nice. Not a good start. We're on our way to the movie and she's not impressed with my minutia about R. Buckminster Fuller's geodesic domes or Pavlov's dogs. Aristotle and his buddies are as Greek to her as they are to me. All my 'big man' college crap is going nowhere. There are these long, awkward chunks of silence as that hairball of useless sophistication gets caught in my throat. It seems like we've got nothing in common. My brain is racing to come up with something. I mention Jimmy and things get on track a little bit. I tell her the story of when we were in third grade playing auto mechanic and he got his fingers stuck in the tailpipe of their dad's '55 Chevy. She starts laughing. I keep going with the story, looking her way, great eye contact. We're feeding off each other's laughter."

Larry nods, lighting another cigarette. "Other than a bottle of Boone's Farm, there's nothing like laughter to help undress one's inhibitions."

"All of sudden horns start blaring. We're near the junction of Elston and Milwaukee, you know, where the road has that subtle curve. I swivel my head to find we're in the oncoming lane of traffic with an 18-wheeler bearing down on us. I stiff-arm the steering wheel and hit the brake pedal with a force that would do Freddy Flintstone proud. I'm not sure if she heard the 'SHIT!' I screamed through the high pitched squeal of the tire tread I'm leaving on the asphalt. The ass end of the car swings out, and we T-bone to a stop inches from the Peterbilt. Its grill is staring down into my driver's side window like a set of jail bars. At that moment I'd have preferred to be anywhere else in the world, including behind the pipes in a maximum security cell at Joliet."

"Sounds like this may have caused some 'Peter-wilt?'"

"I ask her if she's alright and she says 'I think so.' After that there's dead silence till we get to the show."

"A light-hearted comedy will get things back on track. What did you see?"

"*Shaft.*"

"I asked what movie you saw, not what the day is dealing you, or the surprise you may have planted for her in the box of popcorn on your lap."

"I have no clue what the movie's about. I've got my eyeballs glued to her thighs, but I can't even put my arm around her because the air conditioning is really cranking, and it feels like I'm growing icicles in my armpits. I need a Plan 'B' to salvage some dignity. I promise myself that before the evening ends I'm gonna get my lips on her if it kills me."

"You had some fine practice on the drive to the theatre, the almost getting killed part, that is."

"The movie ends and I ask if she'd like to go for a bite to eat so I can tell her about my career plan of becoming a Hollywood stunt man. She hesitates a moment. I hold my breath. She replies 'nnn ... ooo ... kay.'"

"She must have been *super* hungry."

"We agree on Giuseppe's, home of 'the grease makes it great' pizza. On the drive there I'm concentrating on the road, but I'm doing a satire of myself with a play-by-play, like a Driver's Ed teacher giving verbal instructions every step of the way: 'And you never want to take your eyes off the road, son, or you might end up as the hood ornament of a Mack truck....' She chuckles. Slow but sure, the auger is making its way through the layers of ice that have been building since I picked her up."

"That's some phallic imagery, young man."

"For chrissakes, professor, are you sure your folks didn't name you after Larry *Flynt*? ... I get a great parking space near the door. We go in, get seated, and check out the menu. I'm hoping she's good with anchovies. Little known fact going back to ancient Rome: The mini-fishes are an aphrodisiac."

"The perfect combination of your passions, Caligula, fish and sex. And I think I've listed them in the proper order."

"No luck on the question of the briny topping I floated out there. Cheese and sausage it is. Things are getting back to normal as she gives me the lowdown of high school life at St. Stans."

"Out-*stan*-ding."

"The more she talks, the better. Less chance of me tripping over my tongue. As she breaks for a sip of Coke, they bring the pizza, so I scoop a couple of pieces on each of our plates and before she puts her glass down, I'm digging in."

"007 would have waited for Pussy Galore before beginning the masticating ritual."

"I take a bite and the goddamn thing is so hot it burns my tongue and the roof of my mouth. As I fling it back toward my plate, a piece of sausage rebounds off the greasy cheese onto the napkin-less lap of my white Levis."

Mid-inhale of a fresh Winston, my cousin is caught in an intense combination of coughing and laughing, rendering him temporarily speechless. This provides an opportunity for me to light another cigarette, surveying the oddity of how my misfortune could bring such amusement. He gradually regains his composure, wiping tears from beneath his glasses with the back of his hand. My tale of a dream going awry continues.

"As I'm digging for the sausage ball I mumble 'Careful, that's one hot pizza.' Like she hasn't figured it out. With an affirming 'I guess...' I fear she may be starting to feel sorry for me."

"You never want that."

"Tell me about it. Now I have to figure out how to deal with the red, tomato sauce bull's-eye on my crotch."

Another laughing jag ensues, this one of shorter duration. "So you didn't feel it appropriate to ask for Donna's help in the search and clean-up mission? It may have provided a perfect segue to the rest of your evening."

"I toss the offending meat-stuffed animal intestine onto my plate and give my pants a dab or two with my napkin, but I know I won't be able to do anything about the stain so I decide to ignore it and just make sure Donna is always in front of me as we make the final trips to and from the car under cover of darkness. Conversation slows down again—big surprise. It gives me lots of time to roll my tongue across the blistered bubble of flesh on the roof of my mouth."

"Poor Mr. Tongue. Not at all what he had in mind as the day began."

"The dining fiasco completed, we make our way back to the car. I follow through on my plan to walk behind Donna to avoid any more embarrassment the unsightly stain will cause. She opens the car door herself as I walk around the back to enter the driver's side. I turn the key to start the engine, flip on the headlights, put my foot on the brake, move the gear shift lever, and bring my right hand to the top edge of her seat as I turn my head to back out of the space. I hit the accelerator and the car lurches forward. She screams, I hit the brakes, and the front end comes to rest in a bunch of thick evergreen bushes under Giuseppe's front windows."

"Holy hedges, Batman! (Muffled chuckle.) You poor son of a bitch—now *I'm* feeling sorry for you. At this point she probably doubts that you know the difference between 'D' and 'R.' Are you starting to wonder if this day is some sort of divine payback for your agnosticism?"

"Everybody in the restaurant comes racing to the windows, some with serious looks on their faces, some pointing, others laughing. I'm not getting out of the car to check for damage and give them more to chortle about with the target on my crotch. I jam it in reverse and get the hell out of there. On the drive back to her house, it's like we're riding in a hearse. I give it my best shot to bring her out of her zombie gaze. 'It was awful inconsiderate of my dad not to tell me about the transmission recall.' Silence. 'Maybe the car needed to go to the bathroom before we left.' Dead silence. 'Ya know, if I'm 60 years older, nobody gives this a second thought.' She turns my way with a hint of a smile, brings her hand up to my cheek, and gives it a couple of gentle pats."

"Uh oh. Sounds like she's anointed you with the sacrament of Last Rights, the laying of the 'you-sorry-ass-loser' hands, dating's death knell."

"I wasn't sure what to make of it. We pull into her driveway and I'm still hoping to get my lips on her."

"You'll be Broadway Joe Namath upsetting the Colts in Super Bowl III if you do."

"I put the car in park with a little more play by play: 'Let's see … 'P' is for park … turn the key counterclockwise to shut off the engine…'" Then, I understate the obvious. "Well, here we are."

"Smooth."

"She comes back with—are you ready for this— 'Yeah, here we are.' She's still looking straight ahead as I lean toward her, closing my eyes, hoping to again feel those soft fingers caressing my cheek as our lips meet."

"Was Zeppelin's 'Dazed and Confused' playing in your head?"

"I'm not even sure she saw me angling toward her when my eyelids lift at the sound of the car door opening as she bolts out. She takes a couple of steps toward the house then stops to wait for me as I scramble out of the car."

"Maybe she waited so she could kick you in the nuts."

"When I get to where she's standing, she turns to move in stride with me toward the house. I put my hand on her upper back and make some short, gentle strokes up and down her long hair, stopping at the small of her back as we head up the porch stairs. Not repulsed by my touch, I'm thinking I've got one last shot at glory."

"You've got stones of steel and shit for brains."

"We stop at the top of the landing. The moonlight is dancing through her auburn hair. I lead with 'Beautiful full moon tonight.' Silent for a few seconds, she replies 'Yeah ... that could explain a lot.' Knowing the shot clock is running down, it's now or never to nibble a neck and snag a kiss."

"I wonder," Larry muses, "if a 50-pound carp slapped upside your head would have knocked some sense into you."

"I move off the post, reaching my hand toward her shoulder when 10,000 watts of light go on. I hear the deadbolt unlock and I see her old lady in the door sidelight as she crows 'Donna, is that you?' Son of a bitch. Donna spins toward the door with a 'Yes, mother,' opening it while turning her head back toward me. She's got a weird expression on her face; the kind of look you might have between the time a dentist gives you the laughing gas and rips out your tooth. 'Sorry, I better go' precedes the obligatory, 'Thanks for everything,' as she steps into the house and closes the door in one continuous motion. I'm not even down the steps when the porch lights turn off."

"You just lived the Cubs '69 season in one day," Larry says.

I nod in affirmation and take four Winstons out of the pack, put them between my lips, and light them all.

"What the hell are you doing?"

"I'm showing you how many cigarettes I smoked between the time I got in the car and pulled out of her driveway."

"You're insane, but no court in the land would say it's not without good cause. Dream? You call that a dream? I call it a nightmare."

Our bobberless fishing lines, obligingly stationary during the telling of my surreal anecdote, remain motionless through the minutes that follow. More than ready for a diversion, I break the silence. "There ain't no fish in here."

As in many days past, action begins shortly after uttering the words that had become our personal fish-catching abracadabra. Both lines begin moving, ever so slightly, in the direction opposite the creek's flow, signaling a take. We grasp our rigs in tandem as we rise, fully focused on the task at hand.

Upon feeling a hint of weight, I set the hook with a quick upward motion and reel in a 12-inch carp. Larry, however, comes up empty as his line goes slack after the attempted hookset, his nibbler retaining its freedom. After unhooking my catch, I examine both sides, as most fishermen unexplainably do. I'm not sure what it is we're looking for. Maybe we're taking a mental snapshot for inclusion in the "fishing life flashing before your eyes" deathbed highlight reel. Or perhaps it's as simple as spending a few more seconds to admire our conquest, savoring the moment. Sunlight glistening off its golden brown scales and a reddish hue tinting the edges of its fins and tail, the combination reminds me of the color of Donna's hair.

About to release the fish, I crouch at the water's edge. Larry stands beside me, hunched over with hands on knees. He offers the simple words, "Sometimes we catch 'em, sometimes we don't."

In the final ritual prior to release, I present the fish toward my cousin with outstretched arm. With a reassuring pat on the back, he comments, "Nice one."

~ ~ ~ ~ ~

Back to NIU for Year Two - and Beyond

My sophomore year I move to five-story Douglas Hall, D-wing, my second floor room number 285, two doors away from Chuck. Larry also relocates to Douglas on the fourth floor of C-wing. Other than lacking the air-conditioning present in the Stevenson dorm rooms, the positives outweigh the negatives. Kiss elevator waiting good-bye. The location of Douglas, a couple of blocks closer to the university's central core, also saves time and steps to and from classes multiple times per day. That looms large during winter when the howling winds and snow whip across the open fields, the sub-zero wind chills capable of literally taking your breath away.

Many friendships develop among our diverse group of D-2 cohabitants, the floor inheriting the name "Wacos TMF" (the "T" standing for "tough"), the moniker retained from a gone but not forgotten cast of characters from years past. Most of the current residents call towns in Illinois their home, with many from the metropolitan Chicago area. Political correctness not yet invented, nicknames of D-2ers include Gook, the Latin Beat, Rice, Super Jew, Farmer, Tike, Hose Nose, Reb, Rat, Gabby, L.F. (the "L" standing for "Little"), Jolly,

Gomer, Wetz, Snuggy, Huk, and Hawk. Sweet "P," that's me, the tag not assigned in honor of my April birth month flower, nor a reference to my urine, but rather the first letter of my last name combined with the recognition of smooth moves and effortless jump-shots displayed on the basketball court. Pity more of them didn't translate into baskets.

The four hallways and study (but don't count on doing any in there) of our dorm floor buzzes with activity on many evenings and most weekends. Good-natured foul-mouthed utterances lace virtually every sentence on D-2, female visitation hours the exception when decorum kicks in and obscenities sprinkle only every *other* sentence. Music from The Beatles, Crosby, Stills, Nash, and Young, The Rolling Stones, Ten Years After, The Who, Janis Joplin, Led Zeppelin, The Doors, Jimi Hendrix, and other top rock artists of the day explodes from speakers connected to turntables spinning the 33-rpm vinyl albums in rooms whose open doors welcome visitors. Inside those claustrophobic TV-less rooms, groups of two, three, or four engage in card games of pinochle, hearts, or spades. Board games might also provide the diversion of choice: chess to demonstrate intellectual superiority; commanding world supremacy in Risk; Super Bowl victories via Sports Illustrated Football; or financial dominance in Stock Market.

Although the Kishwaukee River flows near the campus and some of the Wacos possess the "I love to fish" gene, the demands of the school year and the lack of storage for fishing equipment in our Lilliputian rooms work against wetting a line. The river's color and consistency, similar to the regurgitated combination of Boone's Farm and pizza one might find in or around the toilet stalls on a Saturday night, further relegates our hallowed hobby to summertime outings at local lakes, those arranged around limiting work schedules. Two of my D-2 floor-mates, Terry and Art (Burnie and Slim, respectively) would become friends for life by virtue of our common interest in fishing.

A year ahead of me like Larry and Chuck, Terry hails from south suburban Burbank. His physical features embody an interesting juxtaposition. Lumbering through the halls at an imposing 6' 6", his straight blond hair that drops below his ears crowns a bespectacled, contemplative countenance that befits a mathematics-studying egghead. His intellect a dichotomy, he possesses the ability to unravel and understand abstract concepts on a broad range of subjects, yet on occasion struggles with the simple addition of two dice as we engage in board game competitions. He is also the S.O.B. who set the curve with the highest grade in the introductory Planetary and Space Science general education elective class, leaving the rest of us (400-plus, taught in a lecture hall) to fend for scraps of Bs and Cs.

Art, a number's savant from suburban Streamwood, studies accounting, his frame and stature shouting "linebacker" rather than "bean counter." Ah, but how looks can deceive. Reverberating through the halls, the call "Market's going up!" draws participants for the Stock Market game, Art usually among them. The players appreciate his commanding presence, amazed by the "human calculator" as he mentally processes all transactions ("Let's see ... 54 shares of Woolworth ... at $134 per share ... that's $7,236) with speed and accuracy that could threaten calculator manufacturer Texas Instruments.

The hallways themselves also serve as a venue for a range of athletic competitions:

Tin Can: Rolling a tennis ball down of one of the 50-foot hallways, contestants attempt to knock over an empty 12-ounce aluminum can. A bowling-like contest with one "pin," the "gutter-less" hall walls keep the ball in play. Tin Can exemplifies a reserved and gentlemanly game of skill.

Nerf Hoops with "Tips": This contest uses a spongy Nerf ball the size and color of a large navel orange. A first player shoots a free-throw toward a miniature basketball hoop affixed to the hall wall with a suction-cup. One point for each shot made, a second player stationed next to the hoop takes up to three tries to tip-in any missed shot, receiving a point for a rebound attempt successfully dropping through the hoop. After three free-throw misses, the players change positions. This is another tame game that combines concentration and manual dexterity.

Ping-pong Baseball: A pitcher and catcher, standing some 20-feet apart, work to strike out a batter armed with a rolled-up copy of NIU's daily newspaper, *The Northern Star*. The "baseball" is a Ping-pong ball, whipped at hyper-speed or flung in wicked curves. The challenge of the game magnifies as pitches (or successful swings cracking the small sphere back toward the pitcher) rapidly change direction as the ball whacks the narrow hall walls, picking up speed and "English" as it spins away at crazy angles. Mandatory skills to participate include lightning reflexes and above average hand-eye coordination.

Killer Frisbee: At either end of a hallway they stand, one and the same: gunslinger and goalie. The innocuous, molded-plastic, pie-tin-shape saucer, a joy to innocently float across a verdant field on a summer day, morphs into a sinister missile that may leave a calling card that reads "decapitation." One gladiator will fling it down the hall with a violent snap of the wrist, sending the disk on the wild ride of a runaway roller coaster, picking up speed as it bounds against the narrow walls and doors, bouncing off the linoleum-square floor, scraping the panels of the eight-foot ceiling and the light fixtures that hang from it, wildly changing directions with each touch, spinning crazily, the objective to pass the unprotected defender at the other end, or, should he have the wherewithal to stop it, hit him in a spot that will render his future childless.

In the more formal sporting domain, intramural activities and dormitory tournaments include basketball, touch-football, and 16-inch softball. (No-mitt, 16-inch, slow pitch softball, a decidedly Chicago sport, has experienced continuing popularity in the area both in leagues and casual play since its inception prior to the turn of the 20th century.) Although most of the Wacos never participated in formal team sports at the high school level, our talented collection of well-coordinated sandlot athletes score many second place finishes for D-2.

Comfortable and thriving in the social atmosphere provided by dorm living, most of us decline the apartment option, instead choosing to continue on in the residence hall through our graduation year.

Huskie Hardcourt – A Year to Remember

The 1971-72 NIU basketball Huskies create a buzz like no other team in school history. In their fifth game of the season, the talented hoopsters defeat Bobby Knight's fifth-ranked Indiana Hoosiers 85-71 in DeKalb. The Chick Evans Fieldhouse bursts at the seams for that and every other home game, 6,000-plus rabid fans whipped into a frenzy by the up-tempo style of play that nets, pre-three-point line, 95.2 points per game, third best in the nation. The fever rages on as they crack into the Top 20 national rankings at number 18. (Chuck suffers a "too close for comfort" brush with the dark side of delirium when a couple of non-student thugs from Chicago accost him in his room a few hours before tip-off of a mid-winter game, put a knife to his throat, and relieve him of his tickets.) In spite of a 21-4 final record, the NCAA committee selecting 25 teams for its tournament snubs NIU. The rejection notwithstanding, NBA and ABA (later to merge with the NBA) teams would recognize the special talents of the players by drafting four of the team's starters: Jim Bradley, Billy "The Kid" Harris, Jerry "Z" Zielinski, and Larry Jackson.

~ ~ ~ ~ ~

Okay, back to business. Time to decide on a major. My history as a fish-documenting statistician points toward the numbers-heavy disciplines of finance or accounting as potential fits. After taking the introductory classes, however, I find them too dry, too black and white. (Okay to read as "too hard.") I take a liking to marketing, nice and gray with a sprinkle of creativity. Let's go with that. Sweet "P" will concentrate on the four P's of marketing: Product, Price, Promotion, and Place. And an economics minor, bartender, as a paper umbrella to dress up the resumé.

Neither a Monk, Ballplayer, Gynecologist, Stock Boy nor an Assembler Be

In the remaining summers of my college years, I bounced among several employers. The longest tenure, lasting an entire summer, found me drawing a paycheck from a newly opened store, Memco. Short for "Membership Company," the retailer was an early example of the consumer membership business model. (What a concept—shoppers pay an annual fee for the privilege of purchasing your wares.) Memco offered a diverse inventory, its feel more department store than warehouse. It included a grocery section where I stocked shelves during the nightshift. At $4.99, it paid a buck an hour better than Jewel, and I exhibited an improved level of restraint when my stomach begged for caloric reinforcement.

The summer prior to graduation, I procured employment stocking the dairy cases at Jerry's Fruit Market. *Borrrrring.* Not enough variety: eggs, milk, cheese, butter, margarine, sour cream, and cottage cheese. The lack of challenge approximated the old bottle boy days, the only significant difference being a chillin' cold dairy stockroom. Limited items to stock also created a bad news/good news scenario: no dog food—but no cookies, either. Out of code milk and cheeses did not tempt me.

Two weeks into the new job stint, I advised my manager of the need for a week off, a previously planned fishing excursion to Lake of the Woods in the offing. Upon returning from the trip, I went to the store to check the work schedule for the upcoming week. Not finding my name on the list (and slow on the uptake), I tracked down my boss and told him of the omission.

"So, what do you think that means?" was his dryly delivered straight-faced reply.

Okay, I get it. May your cumquats shrivel to the size of raisins, and oh, by the way, did the dates on all those perishable items I stocked mean anything?

The summer before my final year at NIU, Chuck tracked down a couple of jobs for us, their connection to the fishing industry most apropos. Housed in an enlarged garage-like space, the small "factory" sited the assembly, one at a time, of Li'l Dude boat trailers. Our arrival on the first day of work doubled the company's labor force. This work environment didn't seem to be a particularly good fit for us. We didn't sport any tattoos and we didn't smoke non-filtered Camel cigarettes that we didn't carry in the rolled up sleeves of white T-shirts we weren't wearing. My mechanical acumen rating solidly in the range between "highly suspect" and "all thumbs" left much to be desired. Asked for a flathead, I looked around for a catfish. The difference between a hex nut and a hazel nut perplexed me. Told to take care with the hammerhead, I wondered where they kept the shark.

Chuck and I assembled one trailer that day. If you happened to be the folks with the broken down boat and trailer on Route 53 just north of Duluth in the summer of '73, I'm sorry. At the end of our first day on the job, the owner handed us each a paycheck. Though not very proficient at putting together a trailer, I had no problem putting two and two together this time. Having learned the lesson at Jerry's Fruit Market, I didn't have to ask a question that would again elicit the response, "So what do you think that means?"

Clear Skies

Dame Fortune bestows her graces upon Terry, Art, Chuck, and I with regard to the draft lottery, as we draw respective numbers of 153, 229, 233, and 248. Actual numbers called for those eligible without deferments peaks at number 125 for 1970, then decreases to 95 for both 1971 and 1972. Fortunately for all, but foremost Larry, these numbers would soon be of no consequence. The war and conscription end in 1973, and the nation institutes an all-volunteer army.

~ ~ ~ ~ ~

When you fish for love, bait with your heart, not your brain.
—Mark Twain

Still, Fishing for Love

"Flower children" and "free love" do well on the coasts at Haight-Ashbury and Berkley in California, and Woodstock in New York. In the cornfields of DeKalb, Illinois, however, well, not so much. Still stuck in the prudish Stone Age with regard to co-ed living arrangements, entire dorm wings or towers remain segregated by gender with conservative hours of visitation rigidly enforced. Early each fall semester, some of the dormitories break the ice by linking up "brother and sister" floors via social gatherings. Although these dashes for lasses and the resulting relationships work well (with the "brother and sister" misnomer many of these hook-ups could soon be referred to as incestuous) for many of my Waco compatriots, my quest for female companionship originates from a different source.

Terry inquires as to my potential interest in a date with his girlfriend Vicky's former roommate, who plans a visit for the upcoming weekend. She left NIU the previous year to pursue a nursing degree through the less costly junior college route. With my alternative for a non-Symposium Saturday night likely finding me at the gaming tables on D-2 while quaffing "Old Kish" with other dateless saps, what have I got to lose? Unless she's Quasimodo's twin sister, nothing. Terry assures me I will not be disappointed. Upon returning from an afternoon class, a scribbled note taped to my door reads: "You have a date. But she doesn't do it! Terry." He secures six tickets for the NIU production of *Cat on a Hot Tin Roof.*

A day before her arrival, Terry delivers good and bad news. The bad: She maintains a relationship with an NIU-met boyfriend. The good: He recently bolted to a university in Florida to "get his head together." All's fair in love and war, and a thousand-mile buffer zone with a competitor who's working on a cranial jigsaw puzzle can't hurt.

Saturday evening, October 21, 1972. I'm decked out in a baby blue V-neck sweater, dark blue T-shirt visible in the "V," light blue Levi Nuvo Flare bell bottoms, and gray suede Converse gym shoes with black stars n stripes ablazin'. Blond locks at mid-60s-Beatle-length and ocean blue contacts complete the "I must think blue is cool" ensemble. In retrospect, perhaps the mid-summer Beach Boys look wasn't the best selection for late October in northern Illinois. And wasn't that the same color I wore on my ill-fated date with Donna Muscala (oops!)? Or perhaps, on short notice, these may be the only clothes that haven't yet found the inside of my dirty laundry sack, or turned some ungodly color through my moronic laundering.

On the short walk to Terry's room, each step increases adrenaline output that accompanies the nervousness, excitement, and anticipation of any first date, particularly the "blind" one. I pause outside his door and take a deep breath. Three rapid knocks halt the muted conversation inside. The door opens and the skyscraping Terry peers down to greet me.

"Welcome, Sweet 'P'!" followed by an obvious reference to my attire, "Surf's up! Let's grab our boards and head down to the Kish!"

In a whisper only he can hear, I reply, "Asshole."

Upon entering the room, my eyes lock in on my companion for the evening. Before Terry's introduction, my mind processes, at warp speed, a thorough work-up of the object occupying my field of vision. And what to my wondering eyes did appear? Allow me to quote the "eloquent" and "descriptive" words recorded in my (short-lived) journal, jotted at 4:30 a.m. on Sunday morning immediately following the date:

> *The young lady in question is named Jo Ann.*
> *Her facial features entice and she possesses an extremely desirable body.*

Ah, young lust.

She sits in the corner, right arm resting the desk. The alluring package includes the facial features of a Mediterranean beauty, true to her Sicilian heritage. A pair of circular, wire-frame glasses rest atop her head. Hair, the color of *café noir*, flows beyond the shoulders. Light gray slacks compliment a slightly darker gray sweater. A thin gold chain trickles from the turtleneck, a cross resting near the valley created by nicely rounded twin mounds. She's Donna Muscala—only better—more grown up ... the next level of sexy, intriguing, luscious. Hey Terry, you done good.

The importance of first impressions should not be underestimated. It's love at first sight for me, but I'm not picking up a reciprocal vibe. We're clothed in the colors of Civil War combatants, our blue and gray. Also recall she has a boyfriend, though he has to be an idiot to leave this sweet young thing to fend for herself against opportunistic vultures, of which I hope to become the lead scavenger.

On the walk to the theatre, the bulk of the conversation bounces, uninterrupted, between Jo Ann and Vicky. Just as well. I make mental notes of life details overheard—younger sister Jackie, '66 Mustang, Triton Junior College—in the event a later evening lull in our conversation requires rekindling. Chuck and his date, Judy, join us at the venue. After taking our seats, Jo Ann turns to me and says, "So, tell me about yourself." Shit. I hadn't prepared for a job interview.

"Well ... it all began in a log cabin it the spring of '52." Doh! Converse meets glossa. Slowly turning my head toward the stage I close my eyes for a moment—a moment that approaches eternity. Stupid! Senses finely tuned following the verbal fumble, I think I can *hear* her eyes rolling in her head.

Maybe not. As our eyes reconnect, she smiles. Maybe she found it endearing. Whatever. Over the next couple of minutes, I monologue a *Cliff Notes* version of the first two decades of my life. I wrap it up as the lights dim and the curtain rises, "And after having enrolled, imagine my disappointment to learn that NIU doesn't offer a major in fishing." Although it elicits another smile, this one hints "Cute, but corny."

As the play unfolds, the thespians do not distract me from strategizing potential moves. After successful small talk during the intermission, and with my confidence building, I'm ready to roll Cupid's cubes, believing they're loaded in my favor. Minutes into the third and final act, I ease my lower leg in her direction, making ever-so-slight contact at the outside edge of our calves. Holding my breath, she does not rebuff the bold yet gentle gambit. Assuming she even felt it. With no thought given to potential blood circulation impairment, I strain to maintain the position, motionless, frozen like a tongue to a metal flagpole on an icy winter day.

That mission successfully executed until the play concludes, our group discusses restaurant options. Permanently scarred by the Giuseppe's dream date disaster, a haunting flashback prompts me to cast the only dissenting vote against popular Pizza Villa. My companions, unaware of my life-altering experience, express surprise at my poo-poo of the to-do of dining on the best pizza in DeKalb. Chuck jabs that my nonsensical aversion may center on a deep-rooted psychological issue with the creepy mechanical clown perched on the mantle of the two story fireplace on the east wall of the dining area.

I chuckle his suggestion away, but silently take pause as I recall the eerie image. The three-foot harlequin, costumed in yellow with poofy red buttons, dangles limp and lifeless. Arms, stretched overhead, grip a metal bar. Head tilted forward as if hanging from the gallows, a face heavy with ashen pallor flaunts blood-red triangle eyes, eyes that see all, painted above an unnerving, twisted smile. The incubus lives. S…l…o…w…l…y pushing forward then s…l…o…w…l…y pulling up, the awkwardly angled arms contort unnaturally behind the soulless body. Reaching the top, the spineless mass bends backwards, headfirst slithering over the bar, body spilling as it follows, jellyfish legs thrashing opposite the torso. The freakish tumble concludes as the boneless bag of clown suit wobbles to a stop. Motionless for seconds that disturb, a nudge from Mephistopheles sets the nightmare in motion anew. A toy of the boogeyman's offspring, I'm certain the ghoulish little bastard joins the parade of the undead in the dark of night. I guess there are *several* reasons I prefer to skip Pizza Villa.

Outvoted five to one, I'm forced to make the best of it. I nibble with care on two small, adequately cooled pieces of cheese-only, completing that stressful task without incident. And addressing the other, I'm seated in a chair at a corner table where the clown can't see me.

The six of us return to my room in Douglas, the cramped quarters not disturbing the ebb and flow of conversation and laughter enjoyed between sips of sloe gin fizz. Our voices compete with tunes from Grand Funk Railroad and

The Moody Blues. As the Yes album *Fragile* drops onto the turntable and the stereo's arm and needle move to the "Roundabout" track, Terry entertains by placing a rubber band around the back of his head and between his nose and upper lip in the front, contorting his face in an attempt to move the elastic band past the bottom of his chin. Chuck and Judy depart (coincidence?) and minutes later Vicky advises the improv entertainer that she is ready to have him walk her back to her Douglas B-wing room. To my surprise, Jo Ann does not mention returning with Vicky to call it an evening. The unexpected bonus time produces a titillating line of thought: stay with me, lay with me, sway with me, play with me, have your way with me....

"Wanna go for a walk?" My carnal thought process takes a detour from brain to mouth. With the return time of my roommate Huk unknown, we embark on a midnight stroll around the campus. She carries the conversation as we pass the Lincoln and Neptune dormitories, through the courtyard adjoining the Holmes Student Center, and the corridor between Altgeld and the library. Minutes later we arrive at the tree-lined lagoon located at the eastern edge of the campus.

A chilly mist pervades the late night air, minute iridescent crystals of moisture brought to life by the full moon hovering atop the leafless branches of towering sycamores. The shimmering specks of light collectively return the favor, providing a luminescent glow that feathers the edges of the golden orb into the night sky. The soft light reflects off the lagoon's still water, creating a warmth that also wells up within. Our footsteps and conversation stop to absorb the magic. This is it—the perfect setting for that perfect moment of virginal enchantment when our lips touch for the first time.

"Wanna stop by Neptune so I can introduce you to my cousin Larry? He works as a door guard overnight on weekends." Doh! The evening continues to succeed in spite of recurring episodes of bunching underwear followed by verbal doltishness. A nod of her head accompanying a "sure" sends us on our way, the all-girl dorm conveniently on our return path.

Seated at a small desk inside double sets of glass doors, Larry rises to greet us. He follows my introduction with a congenial line of elementary questions directed to my date: Where do you live? What's your major? What did you do tonight? Not having seen the play but familiar with the works of Tennessee Williams, he carries on a brief discussion with Jo Ann about tonight's production. Shifting my weight from leg to leg, I do not participate and hope they will not draw me into a conversation that will expose my lack of attentiveness during the performance. Preoccupied and distracted then and now, my mind continues to drift, dart, evaluate, plot. I snap back to the moment upon hearing Larry ask, "My cousin didn't eat much pizza tonight, did he?"

"As a matter of fact, he didn't," she replies.

"I'll have to tell you about that sometime, but there's only eight years to the end of the decade, and I don't think that allows enough time to adequately cover it."

"Interesting. He had plenty of time on our walk to and from the lagoon, but he never got around to it."

"Oh, you went to the lagoon?"

Answering with the intonation of a question, Jo Ann replies, "Yes…?"

"Did you fish?"

"No…"

Reaching out his hand and taking hers in a delicate handshake, Larry comments, "Congratulations, Jo Ann. I believe you are the first person to accompany my cousin within casting distance of a body of water without him insisting he have a fishing pole in his hand."

Several young ladies, still immersed in the revelry of a college Saturday night (Sunday morning, actually), stumble into the lobby. Cackling as they rummage through purses and jean pockets for their IDs, Larry resumes coverage of his post and smiles as we bid him farewell. As we exit, I turn to wave a final goodbye. He points his right arm toward me, clenched fist fronting a "thumbs up," then smoothly morphing to the "number one" by raising his index finger while exaggeratedly mouthing the words last heard at Crystal Creek when congratulating me on another good catch: "Nice one!"

That encouragement provides the stimulus for my next move. Few words spoken as we amble the final two blocks down Lucinda Avenue back to Douglas, I take hold of her hand. Hope realized, her small, soft fingers respond with a gentle squeeze as they grip the outside edge of my palm. We enter the lobby. The clock reads 2:45. I do not want this date to end. Ever.

Reality dictating otherwise, we make our way to the entrance to Vicky's floor. Parting is such sweet sorrow … will I see her again after today and tomorrow? "Will I see you tomorrow before you leave? Maybe we can have a bite in the cafeteria in the morning."

"I *do* remember the dorm food, you know. Are you trying to poison me?"

"If it means you'll have to stay…"

"I wish I could…"

The urchin that does all the strategizing in the back of my mind shouts, "It's now or never, numskull!" as he races down to my heart and begins pounding it with a sledgehammer. Hyperventilation, red-face, and cold sweats poised and ready to wreak havoc, I lean forward, eyes closing with the engagement of her cool-warm-soft lips. Paradise found! Gentle movement. Angelic! Amorous pressure proffered, acknowledged, reciprocated. Delectation! Oh, tender lips, fragile guardian and portal to sweet nectar delivered with the tender touches of tongues, be forever this boundless bliss!

Consumed by the emotional whirlwind, I'm certain the soles of my shoes never touch the ground in the early strides of the return to my room; the stars affixed to the sides of my Converse float with those in the heavens. Then, halfway across the lobby, a heavy heart grounds me as my thoughts turn to her impending departure and prospects for the future unknown. As I enter D-2, the only sign of life in the dark hallway is a trapezoid of light illuminating the gray tile floor outside Terry's room. I stop in his doorway to find the southpaw striking, rapid-fire, chalk to a blackboard that leans against the window curtains. Numbers, lines, and mathematical notations jumble about, scribbled with the verve of an alchemist on the verge of turning silly putty to gold. I reflect how Larry might comment that the scene before me is a metaphor for the date I just experienced.

Not wanting to disturb my friend, whose intensity likely centers on the geometry of moving the rubber band from lips to neck, I step back ready to continue on to my room. Before escaping unnoticed, Terry commands, "Get your ass in here, blue boy." As I enter the room, he continues, "Are your balls blue, too, or did you do it?"

"Hey, knock it off—that's the girl I'm going to marry!" After a momentary pause, I continue, "And if you want to get back in my good graces after that untowardly comment, you'll get in touch with Vicky and arrange for the four of us to have breakfast tomorrow morning, and further, have a bouquet of flowers ready for me to present to her. I need to make sure she doesn't focus on the last words I said tonight."

"This should be good..." Patiently waiting with no response forthcoming, he follows up more emphatically, "*Well?*"

"Maybe we can go fishing sometime." Doh!

Me: Seemingly more "in spite of" than "because of," our relationship blossoms over the weeks and months that follow. Long distance telephone calls too expensive, letters affixed with 8-cent stamps minimize the emotional and physical distance from her Melrose Park home, 55 miles east of DeKalb. Corresponding via the written word allows me to draft, review, edit, and carefully craft thoughts to words, not having to face the brain to mouth shortcut that often short-circuits. Also more budget friendly than store bought cards, notes spiced with hand-drawn characters provide a personal "missing you" touch that not even Hallmark can match. The affectionate creations transform the Florida boyfriend to a persona non grata. As the school year progresses, all these communiqués help bridge the gap between weekend visits that gradually increase in frequency.

My neighbors on D-2 cringe at an annoying trend arising from my long-distance, weekday yearning. Hard-rock-not! tunes by The Association, thick and sweet, ooze from my room into the hallway like a broken, thousand-pound jar of honey. Google the lyrics and gag: "Cherish," "Everything that Touches You," "Never My Love," "We Love," and "Windy" (for those blustery afternoon and evening weekend walks to and from the Burger King on Lincoln Highway, "our place"). Floor mates also poke fun at my late Friday afternoon regimen of weightlifting on the machines tucked in the bowels of the football stadium, "pumping up" before Jo Ann's arrival on most Friday evenings.

A Fishy Proposal
(She's a Keeper)

In the whirlwind between October of 1972 and the following summer, I'm quite certain my parting comment on our first date, as later relayed to Terry, was indeed a premonition. In August, Jo Ann's Aunt Marcy invites us, along with some other relatives, for a weekend visit to her cottage located one block from southern Wisconsin's Lake Como. "I suppose we can go, if you want to," is my poorly veiled response, spoken as I toss fishing gear into the trunk of the car with one hand while rifling through my wallet with the other, making sure it holds a Wisconsin fishing license. Both tasks complete, I query, "Are you ready to go? You know it wouldn't be polite to keep your aunt waiting—she *is* so looking forward to seeing you."

We enjoy the afternoon portion of the family gathering on the water with Jo Ann's younger stepbrother Tony and stepsister Nancy. I do a lot of rowing, the kids do a little fishing, but the fish don't do any biting. Cross off "fishing guide" from my list of occupational possibilities. If NIU offered it as a major, I'd be on academic probation.

The sun an hour past dipping below the horizon, Jo Ann and I return to the lake's shore to absorb the beauty and serenity provided by the moonlit night, a night made for lovers. And fishing. Spinning rods in hand, I bait them with night crawlers, attach bobbers, and cast the lines into the tranquil water.

Unlike the smooth, white-top, red-bottom bobbers that define the age-old standard, the ones in use tonight sport royal blue bottoms and faceted, mirror-like tops. The purchase of the goofy floats, their look reminiscent of the reflective globes hung from dance hall ceilings in the Roaring 20s and making a comeback with the 1970s disco genre, begs the question, "What could I have been thinking when I bought these?"

(Speaking of disco, I don't like it. If you do, don't take offense. I'm an equal opportunity music moron. Simply stated, if it's not rock n roll, I don't like it. I'm lyrically challenged, with two tin ears. When forced to the dance floor, my sole goal is to keep my two left feet untangled. And now, back to our story...)

Not long after making a cast, one of the silver globes begins dancing like Travolta before disappearing from view. I set the hook and land an eight-inch bullhead. A few minutes later, the next contestant in this fishing version of *Saturday Night Fever* swims to center stage, the disco ball swaying hither and yon before sounding to the depths. Caught and release—a second bullhead, identical in size to the first.

Now past midnight, the fish dance hall has shut down. I hope to make one more catch, the catch of a lifetime, before calling it a night. Summoning more courage than it took to unhook slimy bullheads by moonlight at midnight, I turn to Jo Ann. Our eyes meet. With the muculent aroma of night crawlers and whiskered scavengers wafting about, I utter some form of the following words with the eloquence of a lobotomized Shakespeare: "I love you. Will you marry me?"

Her contemplative gaze cradles my fragile heart like the fine mesh of a landing net just slid beneath a delicate yearling rainbow trout. Choosing her words carefully, as Juliet to Romeo, she replies, "Are you talking to me or the bullheads?"

Stunned, my expression says, "Huh? Oh-damn-what-do-I-do-or-say-now?"

Without delay she smiles, caresses me with a hug, and whispers, "I love you too. Of course I will.... Can we go in now?"

Senior Year

A few weeks into the final school year, I receive a piece of mail, the envelope postmarked, "Sep 10 1973." Often finding a letter or card from Jo Ann, this one bears a return address label with Steve Piotrowski as the sender. Never having received any correspondence from my brother-in-law of seven years, this arrival piques my interest. Still in the dorm lobby, I use my index finger as a makeshift letter opener (not drawing blood, by the way—good for me), and remove a greeting card. The front, displaying a neat arrangement of white and purple flowers interspersed with some greenery, also contains the words "In Deepest Sympathy." Curious.

Inside, the verse:

> Words alone can only tell
> The very smallest part
> Of all the thoughts of sympathy
> This brings you from the heart

Handwritten below, in blue ink, the "explanation":
Congratulations on your engagement!
Steve

~ ~ ~ ~ ~

Smitten and betrothed, my final two semesters fly by. The revelry associated with the first three years in the dormitory droops in a decided downturn. Larry and Chuck, having graduated last spring, vault to the next phase of their lives, leaving a void in the weekday camaraderie that was facilitated by our close proximity on the university campus. Before their departure, we vow to keep the venerable tradition of the Symposiums alive, formalizing a process to retain open lines of communication. Beginning late in the inaugural year of 1973, we agree to compose and send a letter annually, each member to the others. A gathering to discuss the written offerings would follow a short time thereafter, to occur in an insular venue reminiscent of the original meetings. (Terry, also graduating a year ahead of me, joined our Symposium group in 1977.)

Larry accepts a graduate assistant position in the philosophy department at the University of Georgia in Athens. (What better city name in which to study philosophy?) Chuck, undergrad reporter, editorial writer, and night editor for *The Northern Star* continues at NIU to pursue a master's degree in journalism. As a result of his job responsibilities and intensified studies, he relocates to off-campus housing. After a full year search for employment, Terry begins his career as a math teacher at Zion-Benton High School.

A lost pup without my core group, I allocate free time to a triumphant run (unopposed likely contributing to my victory) for the dorm floor presidency, my drive and desire to serve only outweighed by the value of adding the successful undertaking to my otherwise nondescript resumé. Other than attending the monthly dorm council meetings, my main contribution as

"President Ulterior Motive" involves designing and painting, with the help of Terry's girlfriend, Vicky, the wall adjoining the interior door that allows entrance to our floor. Our scripted *"D-Two"* design jumps off the wall in eye-popping orange, a beacon for late night library returnees. Ahem.

Art, I, and a handful of others composing the "old guard" fight to keep traditions alive but fail in our attempt to pass the Waco baton as the new wave of underclassmen that outnumber us rip out our hearts by changing the floor name to Bush Dwellers. The quiet D-2 halls disquiet with the ghosts of good times past. Those of us remaining refuse to surrender the Waco heritage and form WIO, Waco Independent Organization. We relocate our intramural athletic artistry from the dormitory to the highly competitive independent division, which includes fraternities and other more skilled teams. This move provides the opportunity to have some of the *"older* guard" join us—Chuck, and through the use of a borrowed ID card, Terry.

On the basketball court, one might think Terry's height, at the midpoint between six and seven feet tall, would be an asset. Alas, he possesses many talents; unfortunately, basketball does not rank near the top. Boasting a vertical leap of three inches, give or take, and thus often outrebounded by players topping out at the height of his armpits, makes us question whether his sneakers had been dipped in cement. The big man, however, is not alone. Chuck, a tireless and annoying defender, fouls out of every game. Art coughs up turnovers at a rate that would do Pepperidge Farm proud. I retract like a turtle in my 6-foot frame, never blocking a shot. Huk makes a frigid 5% of his field goal attempts. Maybe our five shots of Tvarscki vodka in the "pre-" pre-game warm-up wasn't such a good idea, though my "while partially pickled" lifetime 53.3% free-throw percentage still topped NBA greats Wilt Chamberlain (51.1%) and Shaquille O'Neal (52.7%). Our most inspiring effort, a 23-17 defeat, highlighted a winless season that also included losses of 69-10, 84-25, 127-26, and 84-12.

In another dismal example of "things ain't what they used to be," my roommate Huk and I engage in a housefly-kill competition. A chalkboard tally tracks the red and black splotches that dot the walls, door, and windows of our room, the weapon of extermination a tattered-edge, rolled up copy of *The Northern Star*.

On the brighter side, Jo Ann and I settle into a routine of comfortable weekend visits that include attendance at football and basketball games (the glory years gone, the fieldhouse at half capacity for a hardcourt team finishing 8-17), theatre productions, trips to the library (brief as they are), and lengthy walks to discuss plans for our upcoming marriage and life together. She sticks with me in spite of my eclectic sandwich of choice, made possible by the minifridge Huk and I rent that enables me to store the fixins: butter, liverwurst, and American cheese, dressed with ketchup and a slice of raw onion, self-served between slices of white bread.

During spring break, Chuck and I ramble down to Athens, the road trip to visit Larry revitalizing our triadic friendship temporarily thinned by the span of distance and the unrelenting march of time. The welcome reunion, trailblazing the first off-NIU-campus Symposium, convenes in Larry's room in the graduate dorm at the University of Georgia. Weeks after our return, my graduation times with the blooming lilacs of spring, the terrestrial signal that bass are on their beds, spawning life anew.

Sweet "P" on the NIU intramural hardcourt
(leaping inches off the floor!) while launching a 20-foot jumper.

The Graduate

St. Hedwig

Notre Dame H.S.

Northern Illinois University
(It's from a photo booth, not a mug shot!)

Part Three
Post-College – Out of the Aquarium, Into the Ocean

Amid the distractions of college life, I and the remaining group in my 1974 year-class manage to squeeze in the needed amount of study and graduate in four years. Our inability to devise any dorm-friendly fishing games looms as our most significant failing. Pomp, circumstance, and recognition unimportant to me (though Mom's disappointment lasts to this day), I choose not to attend the graduation ceremony. Maybe it's a subliminal payback for when she threw out my baseball cards (although in fairness, I seem to recall giving the okay).

Toeing the inconsequential line between the high end of average and the low end of above average, my final grade point of 3.13 out of 4.0 stations me as a frontrunner of the pedestrian pack. That performance should demonstrate the well-roundedness of my collegiate experience to potential employers. Surely self-evident and common knowledge, all study and no play makes Sweet "P" a dull boy. Add it to the growing stack of youthful miscalculations.

A fine time to think about it, but exactly what type of job do I intend to pursue with a marketing major? Perhaps something in sales? My temperament, personality, skills, and desires (except for the "lust" part of desires) better fits the profile of a monk than the career of a "go-getter" who pounds the pavement needing to exceed a sales quota. Bent more to the background and research side of marketing, those few and far between positions generally require an advanced degree. With marriage on the horizon and feeling "schooled out," it's time to move on, murky as those waters may be. With no plan in place, I'm as close to landing a job as I am to catching my first musky.

Blind mailings of my resumé garner an array of rejection letters on beautifully colored and embossed stationery from some of the most respected companies in the nation at the time: A.B. Dick (yes there was!), Alberto Culver, Allied Van Lines, Avon, Burroughs, Caterpillar Tractor, Chicago Milwaukee St. Paul and Pacific Railroad, Ford, IBM, Maytag (no mention made of their product as an accessory in tinting my underwear pink), and Teletype. Perhaps an independent proofread of my resumé would benefit. Possible suggestions for improvement? A broader selection of hobbies instead of Fishing, Fishing, and Fishing, and personal references other than Super Jew, Gebfart, and the Latin Beat.

Cold calls on local companies like Illinois Tool Works and A.C. Nielsen gain an audience and introductory interviews with personnel managers. These are the same professionals who would later manage "human resources," and eventually gain the title of "corporate grim reaper."

"So, Mr. Piotrowski, in what type of position do you have an interest?"

"Anything." My self-marketing also leaves much to be desired.

With no prospects in sight, I respond to a help wanted ad for a "note teller" at the Golf Mill State Bank. Passing notes among the tellers seems kind of school-girlish to me, but I refrain from asking the question until the interviewing bank officer explains that the job entails the administration of small commercial loans in addition to regular teller duties. Apparently the most qualified among the desperate, they offer and I accept the job at a starting wage of $138.50 per week. Low entry level pay a hallmark of the banking industry, this salary computes to a dollar per hour less than my job stocking shelves at Memco two years earlier. But stockboy is a job and banking is a profession, I tell myself, and you have to start somewhere. Besides, it's a short commute, and with Sears at the other end of the mall (they rejected me too), I can keep close tabs on when Ted Williams Signature outdoor goodies go on sale.

The Best, Man

After one year of separation and solitude in the Deep South, Larry abandons philosophy in Athens following the spring 1973 semester, trading in Nietzsche, Kierkegaard, and Heidegger for Ed, Chuck, and Terry. He returns home and follows my lead by taking a job as a teller at the Lakehurst Bank in suburban Waukegan. How confounding, the shuffle from Descartes to dollars, Sartre to cents. Actually, he attributes his career veer to my sage advice. As he's out of school, out of work, and desperate for a job in the middle of a summer heat wave I tell him, "Try banking, it's air-conditioned." He would later declare this insight as the only good reason to become a banker. Funny (not so), the direction a life can take, must take, when driven by the need for a paycheck—and less sweaty armpits.

On a late August morning, Larry and I venture out to troll the Chain's Channel Lake for anything that will bite. Permanently tucked in our subconscious lurks the image of the massive 47-pound musky landed by Doc Watson on a #2 Mepps at Lake of the Woods. Although muskies haven't roamed The Chain for decades, their close relative, the northern pike still do. With that knowledge we remain vigilant, gripping our rod handles in a stranglehold of hope. Oh, that the next vicious pull produces the muskies' equally ornery cousin, perhaps a fat-body specimen whose weight tips the scale in double digits. Hope never realized, promising strikes disappoint or fool when either a foul-hooked carp or rusted beer can comes into view, or worse, when the heart-stopping jolt results from the trolling motor's propeller grabbing the line and spinning it around the shaft in a tangle of gargantuan misfortune.

The early morning hours of today's outing harvests the standard fare, a half-dozen "fighting whites" each. By mid-morning a southwest wind begins blowing a gale, the underpowered electric motor and weakening battery no match for the roll of bulldozing waves that push us to the area farthest from the boat rental docks. Unlike the beastly day on Crooked Lake, the sun shines brightly today, but a beaching looms without swift, evasive action.

We take up positions beside each other on the center bench seat, each choking one of the oars in a two-hand death-grip. Our arms labor in unison as we begin the intense undertaking of returning to our home base. We occasionally lose synchronization that causes the boat to turn sideways, sunlit whitecaps pounding the aluminum hull like a bass drum. The spray leaping over the gunnels provides a refreshing shower in the heat of our aerobic workout. Over the tumult of the wailing wind, whipping waves, and squawking seagulls that hover above us as if we're today's entrée, Larry begins bellowing the lyrics to The Beatles "Octopus's Garden."

As we regain some semblance of control, I interrupt his solo and shout above the din, "Hold on, Ringo. I've got a question for you. Will you be my best man?"

Without missing a beat, his trumpet-tongued vocal shifts tunes to another Fab Four title, "She Loves You." Upon completing a few bars and with an emphatic pull of the oar, he concludes, "Hell yes!'"

Back to concentrating and coordinating the task at hand, we struggle mightily, our progress slow but steady. Just a few yards from shore, the oarlock on Larry's side breaks, leaving me to complete the final frantic pulls that brings our latest aquatic adventure to a close. The nose of our craft cuts a "V" into the moistened sand of the wave-swept beach. Drenched with lake water and the sweat of our effort, each heavy breath exclaims exhaustion and relief.

My cousin, blessed and cursed with a mind that never rests, comments, "Thank God he didn't find us any sooner."

My furrowed brow precedes the question, "Who?"

"Why, the oarlock warlock, of course."

Larry answers my negative nod and wry grin with a smile of his own, as he extends his hand. Unsure if the gesture represents congratulations for our successful battle with the elements or my upcoming marriage, his words encompass a combination of both. "Good sailing, my friend."

~ ~ ~ ~ ~

Several weeks in advance of our nuptials, Jo Ann and I rode the "L," Chicago's elevated rail transit system (that turns "subway" as it approaches downtown) for a day in the city. Joining us as planned, we met Larry at the Sears Tower (now the Willis Tower), at the time the tallest building in the world. Union Station, two blocks west and across the Chicago River, was Larry's arrival point via commuter train from Grayslake.

Our leisurely yet full day in the "Loop" and areas adjacent included points of interest such as the untitled (perhaps he didn't know what it is, either?) Picasso sculpture, the Art Institute, and Buckingham Fountain. Jo Ann did not object when Larry and I, the pipe smoking cousins, detoured to peruse the wares of Iwan Ries & Company and the Cellini Pipe Shop. In between, we lunched at Plato's Place, the restaurant choice an easy one based on Larry's former formal philosophical studies. Although swept up by the attractions and distractions of the city, we did not lose sight of the trip's purpose. Before departing for home, we secured our marriage license from the office of the Cook County Clerk.

The Best Catch

The air crisp and cool, Jo Ann and I wed on a sunny, 60-degree Saturday in early November 1974. Family and friends attend the morning ceremony followed by a reception at the Broadview VFW hall. I continue the unfortunate streak of disappointing my mother by failing to enlist the services of a band to provide music for the oxymoron of a subdued, early afternoon Polish-Italian wedding banquet.

We honeymoon for three days at Lake of the Ozarks (boat rentals shut down for the season so no fishing, damn!) in central Missouri. On our return home, we take a 200-mile detour to Kansas City, Kansas, for the sole purpose of purchasing a case of iconic Coors beer. Brewed in Colorado, its distribution only stretches as far east as Kansas in the mid-1970s. Though a quality beverage, the time and expense of the side trip fails to match the legendary hype. Another post-school lesson learned.

Two blocks from Milwaukee Avenue and Niles, in the northwest corner of Chicago, we sign a lease on a one-bedroom garden apartment on Harlem Avenue. Jo Ann secures a nursing position at Resurrection Hospital, several miles to the south. We settle into a comfortable routine as happy newlyweds.

The catch of a lifetime.

~ ~ ~ ~ ~

Nibbling for a New Job

Six months in their employ and apparently pleased with my performance, the Golf Mill State Bank prepares to boost my salary to $150.00 per week. About that time, my sister Nancy's husband, Steve, a salesman for Motorola Communications and Electronics, facilitates an interview for me with a credit manager from his company.

Nepotism, eminently prevalent in Chicago business and politics be damned, I *will* be hired, or not, based on my own merit. So what, that we have the same last name. What? Yes, Steve Piotrowski married my sister, Nancy Piotrowski. (Her driver's license photo must have been a good one, her not wanting to give it up, and all. How fortunate she wisely foregoes the Nancy Piotrowski-Piotrowski surname, the hyphenated retention of the maiden name coming into vogue with the burgeoning women's liberation movement.)

Learning from past experiences, I research the company and go to the interview well prepared. The credit analyst's job of approving contracts and collecting the receivables for equipment and service orders resides under the finance umbrella, so I underplay my marketing major. The hiring manager (also named Ed—I take this as a good sign) does not seem concerned. My response to questions asked hints at a level of some intelligence, as do questions of my own. The meeting going well and comfortable with each other as the session nears its conclusion, I query, "What are the normal work hours? Not that it matters, of course, as I'll be putting in whatever amount of time it takes to get the job done..." Now only a thought, but not many months ago I may have blurted out, "How soon can I blow out of this joint every day? I've got fishing shows to watch, lures to buy, hooks to sharpen!"

The last dam that can block my upstream career move is a psychological exam given to all (or so they tell me) potential hires slated for the company's professional ranks. I endure a daylong battery of rigorous and intriguing timed (how well do you work under pressure, blue boy?) tests and interviews administered by the psychologists of a company named Psychometric Affiliates. Concerned with what they may (or may not) find, the results of the exam could torpedo a significant job upgrade paying $175.00 per week.

A two-page work-up by W.A. Kerr includes a qualitative summary as well as a numeric rating on a scale of 1-minus-minus to 4-plus-plus in four categories:

> General ability: Intellectually keen, his *** I.Q. *(Ed note: Holy crap, a healthy, three-digit I.Q.! Maybe I should have stuck with philosophy.)* places him above 99% of employed men, 88% of factory promotion candidates, 84% of service representatives, 78% of salesmen, 82% of middle management men, 76% of sales managers, and 65% of graduate engineers.
>
> Fairly good in his empathic knowledge of other people, he outdistances 72% of men, 56% of general business people, 41% of lower management men, 36% of salesmen, 24% of sales managers, and 32% of upper management men. *(Man,*

was I right about myself not being a salesman ... and on another note, I wonder how I stack up against the women in management positions. Oops, shame on 1970s Motorola.)

Quite good in general ability level and fair in attention balance *(What?)*, he is quite good in abstract and fairly good in consultative strategy tendencies.

Rating: 4

<u>Aptitudes</u>: Superior at simple arithmetic and incidental memory *(by golly, I <u>can</u> remember the location of every fish I've ever caught, <u>and</u> accurately record the tally)*, excellent in simple judgment speed, and strong at layout work, Mr. Piotrowski is good on complex numerical operations and fair on written workups. *(I guess Doc Walton was right after all.)* He is a competent performer of diverse supportive tasks, particularly the technical. *(I assume Dr. Kerr isn't the unlucky individual who purchased the Li'l Dude Trailer that Chuck and I "assembled.")*

Rating: 3++ to 4- -

<u>Motivation</u>: Devoted to altruistic service goals, he reacts very well also to religious-philosophical matters *(And I never mentioned the Symposiums!)* and technology *(Wrong!)*, mildly to aesthetic gratifications and monetary incentives *(Damn, I probably cost myself an extra ten bucks a week)*, and little to personal recognition incentives. Likes the outdoors *(Yes!)*, and technical detail *(No!)*, but may tend to slightly neglect people *(Only if they're jerks.)*

High in basic energy level, Mr. Piotrowski has good achievement and competitive drives, releasing energy most readily into service-accented technology, quite compatible with credit analyst performance.

Rating (for credit analyst position): 3+ to 3++

<u>Temperament</u>: Notably quiet and humble *(Aw, shucks!)*, Mr. Piotrowski is emotionally cool, shy, and sensitive. A bit cautious about others' motives (*Why'd he say that ... WHY?)*, his outlook seems to be much more analytically critical than traditional. Keenly alert and highly independently resourceful, he is inwardly self-assured and he has strong self-discipline. Youthfully anxious, fairly solemn, and somewhat original, he tends to be quite overtly conventional, simple in tastes

(*Winstons taste good, like a cigarette should...*), and yet somewhat nonconforming in social perceptions *(That was Terry performing the rubber band trick, not me.)*, with fair tenacity in goal pursuits.

Rating (for credit analyst position): 4

Recommendation: Mr. Piotrowski needs coaching on basic economics *(so much for the econ minor)*, expressiveness, and if he goes toward human relations, attending more to people.

Rating: 4-

~~~~~

Joining the Motorola Family

I'm hired.

What a great company. And like me, I'm proud to say, born in Chicago. From the first car radio in the 1930s, to the World War II "Walkie-talkie," to the car radiotelephone, to consumer radios, televisions, and pagers, to automotive 8-track players, to relaying television signals and Neil Armstrong's first words from the moon, to manufacturing semiconductors, to the nation's first cellular system and first commercial portable cellular phone, and on and on and on, a peerless innovator in electronics. Best of all, its offices are air-conditioned.

Over the decades, thousands of Chicagoans draw paychecks from the company, many having worked at 4545 West Augusta Boulevard, which served as its headquarters and manufacturing facility from 1937 until the mid-1960s when west suburban Schaumburg became its new home. As employment balloons to tens of thousands worldwide, Motorola continues to foster an employee-friendly work environment. Upon achieving a decade of employment with the firm, automatic induction into the 10-Year Service Club ensures continued employment if performance standards are met; loyal employees look forward to being "Galvanized," a takeoff on the name of the founder, Paul Galvin, and his son, Bob, the current CEO. Dismissal papers of any tenured employee require review by the CEO's office. The company hosts an annual picnic for employees and their families each summer, supplying food and beverage, and sponsoring games, pony rides, and a fishing contest for the kids, held at ponds spread about the many acres of the Schaumburg campus. Yes, it's my kind of company.

Mature trees and strategically placed flower plantings dot a manicured landscape that contains a half-dozen two-story-or-less buildings that house manufacturing, office space, and parking lots for the company's varied electronics-based businesses. Also set among the buildings, two sets of basketball hoops rise from the edges of an asphalt court, the space easily converting to volleyball when a pair of tall nets stretch across it. In another area, a cyclone fence backstop calls 16-inch softball players for company league games. An open field receives the footsteps of friendly competitors in contests of Frisbee football. During most lunch hours and after work, the sports fields are alive with workers exercising their physical skills and competitive wills.

The corporate tower, visible to travelers on Interstate 90, anchors the campus. The geometrically square structure, 12 stories high with equal sides of 12 smoke-colored windows per floor, resembles a colorless Rubik's Cube. The configuration and façade eerily similar to the Stevenson and Grant residence halls at NIU, its roof sprouts communication antennas like an unsightly cowlick. The architecturally bland headquarters, conservative, humdrum, and stodgy, fails to match the company's impressive legacy of life-enhancing innovation. Well, look at me—maybe I should have applied for a critic's position at *Architectural Digest* magazine.

Not needing to travel the 17 miles from our Harlem Avenue apartment to Schaumburg, the tasks of my first job assignment will unfold at a location less than half that distance. The corporation rents a modest, three-story building for its Midwestern territory sales, service, and support employees in Elk Grove Village.

December 2, 1974. A gray sky machine-guns sleet pellets, pinging my '67 Chevy with the speed of an IBM Selectric typeball striking letters to paper at 60 words-per-minute. The dicey driving conditions and excitement (okay to read as sphincter-puckering anxiety) of the first day at a new job combine to cause my Trix cereal breakfast to churn tricks in my stomach as the car slides across the half-inch of winter white layering the parking lot at 700 Nicholas Boulevard. The Chevelle, a beast without power-steering that handles like a Sherman tank, skids to a stop near the rear bumper of a Ford Pinto, one of a dozen cars diagonally parked near the building's back entrance. Reminded of the controversy regarding a potentially explosive flaw in the Pinto's fuel system design, I sigh in relief that my first day on the job won't go up in flames, at least not literally. With the bulk of the parking lot still empty, I muse that the later arrivals are likely salespeople, and perhaps that career choice merited more serious consideration.

I pull in next to a red Plymouth Fury, its roof and trunk displaying an impressive collection of long and short antennas which, no doubt, allow two-way communication with office management, key customers, and alien beings in far-away galaxies. The icy bullets rifling from the sky just moments ago ease to a softer form of precipitation. Feathery snowflakes the size of nickels begin fluttering earthward with the gentle sway of a rowboat in one-foot waves. I turn off the engine, and in a matter of moments, the serene snow globe scene fades under a blanket of white. The totally obscured view induces a deep, anti-claustrophobic breath. I feel as if I'm shrouded by a Polish *pieszina*, a thick, fluffy, goose down comforter. I grab the window handle and make a couple of quick cranks, inhaling a rush of cold air.

About ready to confront the inevitable, I push back the layers of clothing covering my left wrist—the sleeves of a navy blue overcoat, a gray, three-piece suit from Sears (Mom still gets the employee discount), and a yellow shirt—glancing at the circular face of my Timex watch. The big hand touches the twelve, the small the eight. With one-half hour until my official starting time, the imp in my left ear suggests I turn the key to the "accessory" notch and relax to a few tunes and the daily wisecracking from the Steve Dahl show on WDAI-FM. In my other ear, wedging unsolicited advice into my life with increased frequency, the pragmatic buzz-kill whispers, "You're married and supposed to be a responsible adult now," and jogs the memory of my interview commitment, "I'll be putting in whatever amount of hours it takes to get the job done...."

Buzz-kill wins. I exit the car and tread with care. My indestructible, black rubber, four-buckle, "over the shoe" boots remain at home, standing at attention on the mat inside our front door. Only the slow and rhythmic crunch of my Wingtip Oxfords, compressing the carpet of fresh December snow, interrupts the morning silence. I'd like to make an impression my first day on the job but not in the form of a snow angel writhing in pain as a result of an ankle-snapping, elbow-cracking, hip-breaking tumble; a scene made all the more painful by health insurance that hasn't yet been activated.

I pause for a moment to capture a mental photo of the building. On either side of a pair of stair railings leading down, masonry rows and columns separate windows in horizontal and vertical sets of three, giving the appearance of two large tic-tac-toe boards. Will my workspace offer a view through one of them? A whimsical wish places an "X" on one, and "O" on another, both on the third floor, to which I've been told to report. Back in motion and successfully completing the remainder of the short walk without incident, a descent of five stairs leads to a set of double glass doors. I push forward into a narrow, dimly lit hall, where immediately before me stands a single elevator.

The button with the up arrow lights as I touch it. The numerals above the door slowly illuminate in descending sequence, ……3……2……1……, as if just wakening from their weekend slumber. The wait kindles a flashback to my days in Stevenson South. Oh, to be beamed back to those carefree days when a wait such as this (or for what disgusting weekend leftover might be found inside) reigned as life's only annoyance. The doors open, presenting a space empty and clean, save a few melting chunks of slush in zig-zag treads from the galoshes of early arrivers. My eyes move to the doors' metal threshold. I contemplate it as the boundary delineating a point of no return. Words again echo in my head, "You're married and supposed to be a responsible adult now…" Onward and upward. I enter, take a deep breath, and push the "3."

The doors slide and close, fitted jaws clenched in a tight seal with the finality of a casket cover closing on the day of interment. The hint of a previous rider's sweet perfume lingers, incense of the burial rite. No window to open, I tug at the knot of my yellow and gray striped tie, hoping the gesture will allow for an increased flow of oxygen to help deal with the stifling crypt. Inhale. Exhale. Inhale. Exhale. Inhale. Exhale. Not so fast … not so fast. Hyperventilation, be gone! It's cold outside and discernibly cool in here. Then why are beads of perspiration beginning to bubble on my exposed flesh? Are these faux-wood walls creeping closer? Why are these faux-wood walls creeping closer? Were there stairs in the entryway? Certainly there were stairs. Damn it, why didn't I look for a stairway? Or, go back to the car—am I certain I turned off the headlights? The chamber's ascent begins with a jolt. The mechanized whir of motors and cables and pulleys chirps like my distressed innards.

Eyes closed, my heart races as the confining booth rises. Deep breath. I make a conscious effort to recompose versus decompose. Deep breath. Upward movement ends with a muffled thump and a dull "ding." Another deep breath. My eyes open in sync with the elevator doors, revealing a small reception area bright with wattage powered by Commonwealth Edison and the smile of a gray-haired, bespectacled secretary seated at a neatly organized, semi-circular mahogany desk. On the wall behind her, a large, metalwork, powder blue "M-batwings" logo, followed by *MOTOROLA* in slightly smaller lettering, proudly heralds the company. She offers a cheerful "Good morning!" that will segue into a blur of a day swirling with activity: new-hire paperwork, facility familiarization, introductions, smiles, handshakes, and small talk.

My boss, Ed, facilitates a tour. The collage of co-workers varies widely in age, experience, and background: silver-haired, pipe-smoking Dutch, "everyone's grandpa"; Vietnam war vets Tom and John; Hope and Thelma, with thick southern drawls; "a hint of liquor on my breath" Peter; first time papa Mark; "I have a cute nickname for everyone" Carol; "numbers are our lives" Dean and Ben; mild-mannered, "everyone's uncle" Al; "the word 'fair' does not exist in my dictionary" (it's blacked out, he would later show me) Jim; Sharon "Boom-Boom," the blonde bombshell; "sports is my life" Rich; Mary, Rich's stepmother (the nepotism connection!); and gruff, tough, chain-smoking Ada among them.

As we shuttle from department to department, I can't help but notice the values of gray present in *every* piece of office furniture: four- and six-foot divider panels; cloth-covered push-pin boards; composite desktops and locking, overhead storage compartments; metal shelves; two- and four-drawer file cabinets; and armless chairs on rollers. The carpet is gray, too, much like the ashen color of my skin on the elevator ride up. The office décor falls under the design category known as "modular," deriving from the Greek for "maze seeking to confine, confuse, and demoralize mice, rats, and corporate dwelling mammals." The only exception to the drab color palette hovers overhead in the form of unsightly drop-ceiling panels, stained brownish-yellow from the tar and nicotine of cigarette smoke that freely wafts about.

Our tour ends in a small bullpen area away from the windows (so much for the unrealized hope of the imaginary "Xs" and "Os"), with desks at the four corners. Two of them are occupied, one by 19-year-old Judy "with the long blonde hair," and the other by 22-year-old Nancy "with the short blonde hair." Ed introduces me as their new supervisor and explains they will be responsible for training me. Well, well—won't *that* be comfortable?

They set me up at one of the two remaining work areas, the desk naked with the exception of a beige, push-button phone and a thick-as-a-bible but twice as wide "run" of accounts receivable. Organized by state, the fanfold, perforated, green-bar paper contains customer names, addresses, invoices and payments, aged in columns labeled 30 Days, 60 Days, 90 Days, and Prior. Like a kindly kindergarten teacher schooling the ABCs to a wide-eyed child on the first day of school, Judy explains the job as making telephone calls to collect the unpaid invoices, starting with items in the Prior column, then working back as far as possible through the 90 and 60 until the end of the month, at which time the cycle begins anew with the arrival of the next month's report. And don't forget to pencil-in notes of the calls on the green-bar report. Training completed. Simple enough. Four years of college to be a bill collector.

Like the word "fair" blacked out in Jim's dictionary, consider doing the same with the word "privacy." In this environment, none will be found among the open bullpen areas and thin dividers that separate the workers. Clicking typewriters, ringing telephones, and business and personal conversations that bounce about the walls and non-opening windows create an annoying cacophony that filters through every crevice of the close quarters.

Unsure of whether to consider it coincidence or karma, even a fish swims its way into my wintery, whirlwind first day on the job. Our Midwestern territory, designated by our Communications and Electronics division as "Area B," boasts an aggressive moniker that portrays the competitive nature of a sales-driven organization. The wall outside the vice-president's office (one of the half-dozen hard-wall offices for various department managers of sales, service, engineering, and finance) boasts a silver, black, and sea-blue embroidered totem depicting a fierce, gape-mouthed fish curled to strike, with lettering reading "Mighty 'B' Barracudas."

Judy and Nancy call it a day at 5:01 p.m. As their supervisor, I feel obligated to stay beyond the time of their departure. Under the cover of winter darkness, I exit the building at 5:03 p.m.

Upon arriving home a half hour later, I find Jo Ann, having completed her work day at the hospital, moving about the kitchen as she prepares dinner. Steam curls from a pot of boiling spaghetti, mingling with the aroma of her homemade sauce (gravy, as it's known to those of Italian heritage, as I soon learned) and slices of garlic bread warming in the oven. The multi-sensory homespun vignette ferries me from the stresses of the first day on a new job.

The delight of dining on the simple feast matches the glorious anticipation. Unable to master (it's not all that complicated, but I gave up anyway) the Italian method of eating spaghetti—twirling the pasta around fork tines while pressing them against the bowl of a tablespoon, layering the strings to the size of an edible ball—I continue to employ my own "Polish" method of devouring my new favorite food. I rapidly cut a checkerboard of horizontal and vertical slices into my plate of pasta smothered in rich red "gravy" (see, I'm a quick study) flavored with pork, and seasoned with garlic, oregano, and a host of other flavorful family-secret ingredients, the recipe lovingly handed down from grandmother to granddaughter. My method of upfront time expended pays back immediate dividends, allowing a continuous consumption flow. Between mouthfuls, we converse.

Jo Ann begins, "So ... how did it go today?"

"It started on an exciting note," I replied. "I slid into the parking lot and skidded to a stop just before exploding into the rear end of a Pinto."

"Well that's a good news, could-have-been bad news beginning."

"And it carried into the elevator."

"How so?"

"It didn't get stuck between floors, but the space was terribly cramped. Smothering, suffocating, you might say."

"So the ride gave you an early opportunity to meet some of your new co-workers?"

"No, I was alone." Met with a quizzical look, I explain, "First day on the job jitters."

Her line of questioning continues. "How's the office?"

"Tight. And gray. Like your slacks and sweater on our first date."

"Should I take that as a complim…?"

Not waiting to swallow a mouthful of equal parts spaghetti and bread, I garble out an "*Oooooh*, yeah."

"How did you like your boss?"

"Confirmed my impression from the interview. Ed seems to be a good guy, easy going. All the folks I met were real friendly."

"And the job itself?"

After a deliberate pause that includes scooping a healthy portion of seconds onto my plate, I reply, "You know, if you keep feeding me like this, you better still like me when I'm 300 pounds."

"Uh oh. You didn't like it?"

"*Mi amore,* your spaghett is *magnifico*."

"The job … do you think you made a mistake leaving the bank?"

"Nah. Short of hooking myself with a treble, there's nothing I'd prefer doing." I smile, then take a sip from a can of Coke. "It'll be fine. I have to start somewhere, and that bump in the paycheck helps. And not having to work a half day on Saturdays will free up some fishing time."

Jo Ann nods and smiles. "So, anything special on tap for tomorrow?"

"Yeah. I'm going to begin planning my retirement."

My early career moves ahead slow and steady with carefully measured steps, like tight-roping from the back to the front of a canoe. I earn two small promotions from 1974 to 1979. During these formative years, I conclude that supervisory responsibility, oh, how shall I say this (insert the sound of clucking chickens here…), "pretty much sucks," and that I will attempt to navigate the remainder of my career avoiding it. Toward that end, and also with no interest in relocating, I turn down a promotion opportunity to a management position in Houston. Of course, I can't share either of these reasons with my boss.

How about blaming it on Jo Ann? Yes, that'll work. "My wife has a very close-knit family, and to leave them would be terribly troubling for her. Though it pains me professionally to turn down such a wonderful opportunity, with the corporate office and many of our growing businesses in the metropolitan Chicago area, I'm certain that future advancement prospects will be available locally." Gag me with an antenna.

Satisfied with my decision for a self-directed career path limited to positions within a 50-mile radius of the town of my birth, workday habits settle into a predictable pattern. I become lunch buddies with a co-worker who administers returned and reconditioned equipment. Five years my senior, Rich is pleasantly unpolished around the edges. His "born and raised in Chicago" and Italian heritage blend into a personality that defines the consummate "nice guy." Long on street smarts and longer on insight into the world of sports, empty your wallet when Rich offers a recommendation for a sporting event winner. And stay on the sidelines or plan to lose your wager when Rich enters any sports-related office pool.

With modest paychecks and frugal upbringing, we both realize the benefit of the money saved by brown-bagging our lunches while also acknowledging the mental relief provided by a midday break from the confines of the office. Bags in hand, we depart promptly at 11:25 for the five-minute ride to an informal sandwich eatery known in the Chicago metro area as a "beef stand." Frankie's Two, whose owner of Italian ancestry is a longtime *goombah* of Rich, does not frown on our "carry *in*" practice, as we supplement our lunchmeat sandwiches with the purchase of a bowl of chili, crinkle cut fries, or a hot tamale. Between mouthfuls as we chow down, discussions always center on news from the world of sports.

On Fridays, we splurge as full-pay patrons, springing for a basket meal that includes fries, a pop, and one of a variety of mouth-watering "entrees": a Vienna beef "Chicago-style" hot dog on a steamed poppy seed bun, "dragged through the garden" in a multi-texture concoction including relish, onions, tomato wedges, a dill pickle spear, mustard (ask for ketchup and they'll kick your ass out), and hot, sport peppers, the entire package sprinkled with celery salt; an Italian beef sandwich—thin slices of seasoned roast beef, dripping with meat juices that soak into the top and bottom of 8-inches of Italian-style bread, finished with either sautéed green "sweet " peppers, or colorful, crunchy, mouth-tingling *giardiniera*; a cheeseburger with all the fixins—American cheese, lettuce, pickle slices, tomato, and raw onion, with ketchup and mustard optional to taste; and for those Lenten, meatless Fridays, a pepper and egg sandwich—green peppers roasted in garlic and olive oil, fried with eggs, seasoned with salt, pepper, and Romano cheese, served on French bread. Damn, I'm hungry.

Back to work. In a support function, I interface on a regular basis with Motorola sales managers, most exuding the corporate culture of "work hard, play hard." Accounts receivables "scrubs," the review of outstanding invoices with the sales team to enlist their support with the resolution of problems impeding collection efforts, occur periodically. I participate at meetings in various "exotic" locations, among them Des Moines, Indianapolis, Madison, Omaha, and Springfield.

The gatherings typically take place in meeting rooms at the regional offices that house the sales and service representatives for the defined geography. The regional manager gathers his troops quarterly or semi-annually. The agenda covers multiple topics that could include area office guests from the disciplines of marketing, engineering, and finance. Anywhere from eight to fifteen individuals gather at conference tables set up in a u-shape, with an overhead projector on a wheeled metal cart available for presentations. Q&A at any of these "dog and pony shows" would typically include some form of this give and take:

"What have you got to bring to the table?"

"If we think outside the box and employ best practices to benchmark and institutionalize the value-added paradigm shift, the synergies from leveraging our bandwidth should provide transparency for a seamless mission-critical transition."

"What's the ROI if we reach out to pluck the low-hanging fruit?"

"A drill down will allow us to ballpark it and right-size it. Then we touch base before running it up the flagpole."

"In the big picture, are our ducks in a row for a win-win?"

"Not a problem. At the end of the day, we're empowered to minimize windshield time and maximize face time to pro-actively optimize total customer satisfaction."

While these sales-led meetings are generally upbeat, my portion of the program brings them down, diving into the world of deadbeats and customer complaints. It involves a review of the hard-copy, green-bar receivable "run" that identifies accounts whose payments are delinquent 60 days or more, and determining the course of action and "to do's" for both myself and the sales reps. The long meeting day includes a lunch break of ordered-in sandwiches, and concludes with a group dinner at a nice restaurant, often followed by an optional nightcap (or two, or three…) at the bar.

Back in Illinois, during the casual "get to know" component at the conclusion of frequent business telephone conversations, I learn that Ron, the manager working out of our Minneapolis office, ranks as an accomplished muskellunge angler. His passion for the sport includes membership in Muskies, Inc., an organization dedicated to the practices of catch and release, proper handling procedures, and the promotion and enjoyment of musky fishing. As he becomes aware of my love to wet a line, he asks me to join him and his "number two in command," Tom, for an abbreviated receivable scrub on the shores of the Class "A" (Department of Natural Resources designated "premier") musky waters of Bone Lake in northwest Wisconsin.

~~~~~

I have laid aside business, and gone a-fishing.
—Izaak Walton

A Musky Encounter

I fly to Minneapolis mid-morning, joining my hosts for the one and one-half hour drive to the lake. Time passes quickly, our brief conversations on business issues quickly turning to more extensive discussions on a variety of fishing topics. We turn off the asphalt of the lightly traveled County Road GG, pulling onto a gravel driveway leading to our simple accommodations. Set back from the lakeshore the distance of an easy cast, the dirt-brown, clapboard-sided cottage, with a shingled roof the green-blue color of a blue spruce, stands in a clearing edged on both sides by clusters of white-bark birches.

The interior shouts classic "cabin," much like most others I've experienced on fishing trips to the Northwood's: knotty pine walls and a hodgepodge of furniture. The main space is "open concept," a fancy term from the world of interior design meaning "one room." A sink, 1940s vintage Tappan stove and Frigidaire refrigerator, both in white, line one wall. A "full of character" (nicked and scratched) wooden table, with four mismatched chairs, separates and bridges the kitchen and living room areas.

I place my belongings in the smallest of three bedrooms. Upon returning to the not-so "great room," I sink into the cushions of a tattered though still serviceable couch. The color of a Hershey's chocolate bar, it has the feel of pliable plastic and emits the subtle scent of a PVC fishing rainsuit. Familiar with the composite vinyl fabric as leather-imitating naugahyde, the living room sofa of my childhood home on Dickens Avenue was upholstered with the same material, though in a turquoise color popular for the period. The distinctive sensation of touch and smell triggers a recall of the humorous marketing campaign that featured the Nauga, a squat, horned monster with a toothy grin stretching between its pointed ears. Unlike other animals that must be killed to obtain their hides, the "so ugly they're cute" Naugas have the ability to shed their "hydes" without harming themselves, the fictional creatures evolving into an urban legend with the help of the product ad label: The Cruelty Free Fabric.

Above the couch on the back wall, a picture window flanked by yellow and green plaid curtains frames a lake view. Thumbtacked to the right, a laminated map of the long and relatively narrow lake, which stretches from northwest to southeast, details depth contours with lines marking ten-foot increments, each progressive band colored in a darker shade of blue. An "x" at 43-feet marks the deepest hole. The map legend lists Bone Lake's surface acreage at 1,781, almost twice the combined size of Marie, Catherine, and Channel lakes, the three northernmost waters of the Chain O' Lakes that I regularly fish.

Pleasantly transacted over several hours in the relaxing atmosphere provided by the cottage (versus a stuffy conference room), the work portion of the meeting concludes. It's time for R&R and my introduction to the world of hardcore angling that specifically targets the king of freshwater fish. Our boat, tied to a dock at the bottom of a slow tapering incline from the cottage, is replete with creature comforts never experienced in my years of fishing from bare-bones wooden or aluminum rental boats.

The 17-footer, a floating mansion by my standards, features a carpeted interior (gray, to simulate the feel of an afternoon in the office), front casting deck, center console with windshield, high-back folding seats (covered in naugahyde?), and an imposing, 75-horsepower outboard motor.

The engine growls as we pull away from the dock, then purrs after reaching plane, the well-balanced craft soothing and smoothing the chop of two-foot waves beget by the southerly summer breeze of a late June day. The cushioned seats provide additional comfort to the ride that speeds us to the fishing destination planned to receive our first casts. I think I'm going to like musky fishing.

Ron shuts down the boat near the center of the lake between two large islands, Chaffee and Bald Eagle, and provides a quick primer on the equipment, lures, and methods for today's outing, all of which serve as eye-openers. In spite of extensive fishing experience, this new frontier intimidates. Stout fishing rods, with long handles that extend at least a foot behind the reels, carry three times the weight and thickness of the limber rods I wield for "anything that will bite." Likewise a far cry from my lightweight spinning reels filled with thin-diameter monofilament, large baitcasters affixed to the heavy-duty rods are spooled with black, threadlike, 50-pound test Dacron line. Even this line, however, provides no match for a mouth filled with musky incisors. A one-foot, taut wire leader spans the distance from line to lure. An "Original Eddie's Bait," a wooden, 8-inch lure in the shape of a miniature police baton, solid black, dangles from the leader. The retrieve of this lure requires a downward pull of the rod to impart side-to-side gliding action simulating an injured baitfish, the slack line reeled in cadence with the rod's upward movement.

Ron directs me to the front casting deck, the section of the boat which, for multiple reasons, holds the best odds for encountering a fish: first cast to virgin water; the ability to fan-cast 180 degrees of open water; the increased elevation allowing improved viewing of submerged rock and weed structures, the goal to place casts near these areas the musky may be using as ambush points; and the unencumbered capability to perform the "figure-8" maneuver, swirling the rod and lure at boatside at the end of each cast to entice a following fish to strike.

At appropriate times, as a golf instructor to a struggling but eager student, Ron offers pointers: "Keep your eye on the spot where you want your lure to land"; "Thumb the spool near the end of each cast to slow it down to avoid a backlash"; "Always watch for a follow, and make sure you do a figure-8 after each cast whether you see one or not." My prime casting location notwithstanding, the lack of familiarity with the heavy duty equipment prompts embarrassing ineptitude with casts and retrieves, at least in the early going. I mumble an occasional "dammit," to which Ron always replies, "The frustrations of fishing are proportional to the size of the fish sought." As things start clicking for me, I welcome his words of encouragement: "Nice cast"; "Good rhythm with the Eddie, Eddie"; "Beautiful figure-8."

Tom, not an avid fisherman but accompanying Ron on occasional outings, chucks lures from the middle of the boat for half an hour before deciding to kick back. He slumps into one of the seats and tilts his baseball cap to cover his face, a prelude to drifting off to dreamland. Ron, from his position in the back of the boat, pitches what looks like a one-ounce black jighead dressed with a same-color, six-inch "Reaper" tail, a thin, soft plastic bait in the shape of a willow leaf. Fishing it requires the finesse of non-rhythmic hops and drags along the lake bottom, the Reaper tail in a stand-up position as it jumps and slides through the water. During pauses in the retrieve, Ron controls our course with periodic hand adjustments to the trolling motor.

Protected from the brunt of the wind, we thoroughly fish the areas around and between the islands, and a weedy bay and point that adjoin them. Totally immersed in the experience and anxiously awaiting a jolt from the finned goliath of our quest, hours pass. As nightfall overtakes dusk, we return to the cottage, follow-less and fishless. Maybe Tom had the right idea.

While acknowledging that a few hours on the water does not constitute a fair test, a hint of doubt enters my mind. I question the effort-reward ratio for this strenuous fishing method that uses stout gear to launch crazy-long casts of heavy, oddly shaped lures followed by slow, tedious retrieves that only snag weeds and push dead water. Further, a nagging soreness radiates from my solar plexus. The intense concentration of casting, retrieving, and watching for a following fish obscures the fact that I had been driving the butt of the long rod handle into my midsection with each stroke of the lure retrieve. An early start tomorrow morning for more of the same does not excite me. Maybe musky fishing *isn't* for me. A few ounces of Crown Royal Canadian Whisky soothe me to sleep.

I wake the next morning, stupid-sore, but prepare to go through the motions so as to not disappoint my gracious host, whose thoughtfulness has extended to outfitting me with a lure bearing my name. I head down to the boat with noticeably less spring in my step than exhibited the previous afternoon. Foggy pockets, created by the calm of cool night air contacting the warm water, shroud areas protected from the warmth of the morning sun and the gradually building breeze. We motor to a bay at the far northwest corner of the lake, stopping short of the edge of a field of lily pads.

I catapult the morning's first cast with the thought, "This is bull … oney." On the second downward stroke, I feel resistance similar to the grab of weeds on Original Eddie's treble hooks that occurred numerous times yesterday. Pulling the rod horizontally with a half-hearted tug, I stagger at the sight of a three- to four-foot muskellunge arcing from the water. The back treble hook of the Eddie in the corner of its mouth, the lure whips back and forth, opposite raging head thrashes. The lure flings free at the height of the leap. The fish was no longer hooked—but I was.

Ron smiles and shakes his head. I nod back. Over as quickly as it began, a slow-motion replay brands my memory. So *this* is musky fishing: Hours, days, (perhaps weeks?) of extreme effort without an equitable payoff, settling for whatever gratification trickles from a tease, acknowledging the splash of unrequited love.

I'm good with that.

The morning's muskellunge encounter would be the only one of this trip. Won over by the method, my immersion into the world of musky hunting, however, will have to wait. Buzz-kill whispers that the significant costs to acquire specialized rods, line, leaders, and an array of expensive lures will put a strain on an already fragile home budget. Further, with no musky lakes located within a reasonable distance of my home, the inability to fish for them on a regular basis makes it an investment not worthwhile. The exhilaration of the Bone Lake experience, as Lake of the Woods years before, lays further foundation for future pursuit of the freshwater king, though just how soon still remains unknown.

∼ ∼ ∼ ∼ ∼

There will be days when the fishing is better than one's most optimistic forecast, others when it is far worse. Either is a gain over just staying home.
—Roderick Haig-Brown

On the Home Front
1975 – 1980

In 1975, one year into our marriage, Jo Ann and I purchased a two-year-old house in suburban Bloomingdale, 22 miles west of our apartment on Chicago's far northwest side. On a corner lot on Prairie Avenue (in a quirk of suburban town planning, the front of the house faced Spring Valley Drive), the second floor of the raised ranch contained the main living space with modest-size rooms: a kitchen, living room, dining room, three bedrooms, and one bath. The unfinished ground level first floor awaited completion as a family room. A picture of the builder's grade sliding windows used in every room can be found in the dictionary beside the word "sieve."

The unappealing mansard-style roof, its brown shingles cascading over the front one-third of the house, did not deter us from acquiring the property. It should have. The realty concept of curb appeal, foreign to us as young, naïve buyers, would have negative financial consequences decades later when attempting to sell our appearance-challenged residence. On a positive note, a village park with a fishing pond was located one-half block to the east, and a forest preserve, also with a pond, the same short distance to the west.

In addition to the non-intuitive street address, further confusion for the mailman, deliverymen, and others persisted by virtue of another Piotrowski family, Nancy, Steve, and their daughters Julie and Jennifer living in the house next door. On the flip side, this arrangement proved convenient for Mom and Dad when they traveled west for a visit from their home in Niles and when Jo Ann babysat our nieces during summer vacations. Also, Steve had a short commute when coming over to help me finish the family room. Okay, more accurate, I assisted handyman Steve with the installation of dark paneling, brown and beige linoleum tiles, a wet bar backed by faux-brick panels, a half bath, and a drop ceiling housing two sets of tube fluorescent lights, all prime 1970s décor. Upon completion, I affixed fishing-themed appointments to several of the walls.

Home ownership necessitated another leap up the stairway of responsible adulthood with a myriad of new duties: a lawn to mow, snow to shovel, landscaping to plant and maintain, rooms to paint, faucets to fix, and on and on. And on. The financial responsibility hit home in a subtler way, long before the due date of our inaugural mortgage payment. The many comforts of home come with a price, never considered or taken for granted when growing up or even when renting the Harlem Avenue apartment with "utilities included." The first time our air conditioner kicked on, I envisioned dollar bills flying out of *my* pocket. So too, a similar thought engaged with every activation of the furnace, flip of a light switch, or turn of a faucet handle. But of greater concern—among marriage, work, and owning a home—when will I have time to fish?

~ ~ ~ ~ ~

The solution to any problem—work, love, money, whatever—is to go fishing, and the worse the problem, the longer the trip should be.
—John Gierach

(Almost) Grown-up Fishing
Paradise Island

By 1976, more than a half decade had passed since our last Canadian fishing trip. With life events unfolding on fast-forward, the memory of that trip faded deep into the rearview mirror. Now two years after my college graduation, Larry and I broached the subject of another excursion north of the border to our dads, who agreed the time was right to recreate the magic of special days in a special place. With the camp on Kipling Island sold and privatized in the early 1970s, I spent the winter months searching for an alternative. Collected over many years, lake maps, travel pamphlets, and lodging information from Wisconsin, Minnesota, and Canada stuffed a 1940s vintage "tweed striped" suitcase that was now too old, small, and tattered to serve its original purpose. From within this fisherman's treasure chest, I unearthed and unfolded a map of Lake of the Woods. The advertisements of various resorts lined its edge with squares the size of large postage stamps, creating a colorful border. A number in each matched with ones in red circles, identifying their location on the massive lake. I wrote to several and anxiously awaited the arrival of their brochures. We sealed the deal with the first one returned, the choice mostly based on the promise of its name: Paradise Island.

On prior trips to Kipling Island, we drove into the bustling (or at least as "bustling" as a city of 10,000 can be) city of Kenora. There, we parked in a well-maintained municipal lot with numerous boat docks, where the owner met and ferried us to camp in his comfortable, 22-foot launch.

The logistics of getting to Paradise Island were different. A succession of narrow chip seal roads, little traveled, brought us to a barely discernable entrance cut into the trees. Adjacent to a rusted metal gate, an old-time telephone hung on a board nailed to the trunk of a pine tree. The phone, with a funnel mouthpiece jutting from the box and a similar shaped earpiece attached to the frame by a black wire, reminded me of those seen on the *Andy Griffith Show*, the 1960s television series set in a small town in rural North Carolina. I wondered if we were entering the Canadian equivalent of Mayberry.

Surprisingly, the phone worked and I made the call announcing our arrival. I was instructed to open the gate so we could drive the trail to its terminus at a narrow inlet of the lake where, in a half hour, our hosts would pick us up in their boat. The rutted, partially graveled road meandered through the woods, the car bouncing as it negotiated exposed tree roots and shallow depressions. Only a mile but seeming like ten, the road ended at a makeshift, unpaved parking area where a half dozen cars and trucks were wedged between the trunks of trees, their hoods and windshields dotted and smeared with dripping pine tree sap and splattered with the remains of bugs that took Kamikaze aim at them as they traveled Canadian roads.

The "prime" parking places taken, we drove our vehicle to high ground lest the soft, damp loam from recent rains suck the car's tires down to the hubcaps during our stay. We unloaded our gear, walking it to the rickety wooden-plank pier, the last several feet sloping precariously toward the water. It was from that pier, however, that a majestic vista of the lake, dotted with islands near and far, opened before us. Not long after we'd completed our task, a fair-sized boat, but one in need of a good cleaning, arrived to transport us to Paradise.

By the time we reached the island, another rain shower had begun. Quickly directed to our cabin, the outside looked like any other we'd stayed in over the years: painted plyboard siding, a screened porch, and a moss covered roof. The inside walls, plasterboard instead of the typical timber or paneled knotty pine, were coated with a chalky primer. Closer examination of what first appeared to be random red and black specks of a floral print turned out to be the remnants of swatted spiders, mosquitoes and flies. Some remained on active duty as they moved about; others took flight in search of their next meal—us. (Each night, in spite of the summer heat and to my perspiring discomfort, the incessant bloodsucker buzzing caused me to wear a stocking cap to bed and pull the blanket over my head with only an opening the size of a straw allowing sips of life-sustaining oxygen.) Inside the bathroom, hanging from the ceiling and ending a few feet above the toilet, a large diameter galvanized metal pipe served as a primitive (or unfinished) venting system. A spider with the leg-span of a dinner plate dangled from it by a single strand of web thread.

Our host and owner, Wolfgang Schultz, could well have been a "separated at birth" triplet of wrestling bad guys Baron Von Raschke and Mad Dog Vachon. (For those not familiar with these niche sporting entertainment legends, picture Procter and Gamble's Mr. Clean expressing a bad case of constipation.) On the day we arrived, Herr Schultz expelled a group of his guests, one of them having made a pass at a server during a meal at the lodge. (Had Elin changed employers, the fisherman's indiscretion would not be excusable but remotely understandable.) On that same day, Larry kept quiet about several tiny black bugs moving through the leaves of his lettuce salad, not wanting to incur the wrath of the already agitated island czar and jeopardize *our* stay. The rose-colored vision of Shangri-la was rapidly fading to the morass of paradise lost.

All of this must have made quite an impression on Larry's 15-year-old brother, my cousin Rich, joining us on his first Canadian adventure. Surely the fishing will make up for the less than ideal ancillaries.

No. On a scorcher of a Sunday, our first full day on the water, the fish pitched a shutout. Dad and Uncle Ben, in a bold and out-of-character "loosening of the purse strings" decision to assist in locating the elusive walleye, made arrangements with Schultz for an Indian guide to accompany us on Tuesday.

On Monday, Uncle Ben granted Rich permission to fish with Larry and me, though that did not entail a large leap of faith as our boats traveled in tandem. We led the way, but per their directive never fished locations more than a 5-minute boat ride from camp. Similar to our first trip to Kipling Island, our dads exhibited a marked discomfort with the possibility of becoming lost. The likelihood of stormy weather also loomed as a concern, weather fronts rolling in and out with revolving door regularity.

Larry, Rich, and I reverted to our familiar and favorite Chain O' Lakes technique, trolling with #2 and #3 Mepps across the large expanses of two weedy bays just west of Paradise Island. Minimally successful, we caught a few undersized northern pike, walleye, and perch. Of greater significance than guiding Rich to his inaugural Canadian catch, we presided over several rites of passage, which included the refreshing and celebratory consumption of his first beer, a bottle of Labatt Blue, and less enjoyed, a first (and last, ever) cigarette. We also let him captain the boat, right hand tightly gripping the tiller, concentration high but not intense, a hint of a smile appreciative of our trust.

Uncle Ben and Dad in sight but a considerable distance away, casted while drifting across the bay. Mid-afternoon, we heard their raised voices over the drone of our motor, followed by a commotion of "bangs" and "thumps," the sounds traveling unimpeded through the wild. We reeled in and motored toward them, rapidly closing the distance. Seated opposite each other and seemingly unaware of our arrival, both leaned forward with arms down, focused on an unseen task in the bottom of the boat. Throttling down as we moved closer, Larry called out, "What's going on? Need any help?"

My father looked up and shouted back, "Your dad just caught a big musky!" At that moment, Uncle Ben, still seated, lifted a metal stringer with one of the clips secured through the lower jaw of the fish. We all thought it—Rich spoke it: "Wow!" Almost the length of a yardstick (most of the fish caught by this clan could be measured with a 12-inch ruler and have inches to spare), this fish represented the largest ever caught by a family member. As I snapped a couple of photos with my Kodak Instamatic, Rich asked, "What did you get him on?"

After lowering the fish to the bottom of their boat with care, Uncle Ben lifted a tiny lure that dwarfed in proportion to his hand. I immediately identified it as a Bass Buster Beetle Spin, a one-inch lure in the shape of an open safety pin. A blade the size of a pinky fingernail spun from the top arm, and a jig with a white plastic trailer that partially hid the hook extended from the bottom. In unison, Larry, Rich, and I reached down and opened our tackle boxes to search for a similar lure that might induce lightning to strike twice.

Dad and Uncle Ben, wanting to share their moment of triumph with the camp, headed back after agreeing to let us continue fishing until dinner time, an hour later. We casted the area to a froth, with nothing to show for our efforts. Upon our return, we found our dads seated at the kitchen table, gnawing on thick chunks of meat cut from a salami log, a ritualistic munchie that Dad brought on every fishing trip. Highballs in hand, the amber-color contents of the Jim Beam bottle touched the bottom edge of the label, indicating a serious celebration was underway. Their facial expressions, however, seemed less joyous than one might expect under the circumstances.

"Everything okay?" I asked.

"Musky season isn't open yet," Dad replied. "We couldn't revive it, and Hitler's henchman wasn't happy about us bringing it in. Said we should have known better, that we'd be in trouble—him too—if the Ontario MNR caught us with it. He filleted it on the spot and made us motor over to one of the islands to dump the guts." Dad paused with a healthy swig, then continued, "When his eyes settled back into their sockets he said he'd have the guide cook it up for us tomorrow." Uncle Ben downed his drink with three big gulps, slammed down the glass, took a long drag of his cigar, and growled with a smoky exhale, "That guy's a jerkoff!"

Uncle Ben, though modest in height at 5 feet 6 inches, is wound tight, physically and emotionally. A boxer in his younger days, he still exudes an aura of toughness, in contrast to my happy-go-lucky dad. The delight of today's momentous catch unfortunately and prematurely doused, later that evening my uncle shared the innovative technique that led to the capture of the big fish. "I had a feeling something was behind us … something big … hitchhiking in the shadow of the boat. I didn't want to turn around and let him know I knew, so on the backswing of my cast I took my finger off the line to let lure drop into the water right behind me. I gave it a second or two to flutter down like an injured baitfish, and bam!" He looked at my dad, and with a wink and a grin, asked, "Fooled him good, right, Eddie?" "Right on, Benjie. *Right on*!" Dad replied with guttural emphasis, he and his best buddy healing in the beaming glow of Jim Beam.

Uncle Ben with the first Canadian muskellunge.

The next morning our guide arrived promptly after breakfast. His height similar to Larry's at about 5' 7" and with a similar slim build, his Ojibwa ancestry manifested in chiseled facial features, sun-leathered skin, and straight black hair pulled back and tied in a ponytail. Mak introduced himself as he extended his right hand in greeting, a spinning rod, burlap sack, and a Sucrets lozenge tin gripped in his left. Hmmm.

We walked down to the dock together, our dads deciding to send Mak out with Larry and me. Heavy cloud cover remained from overnight storms, blocking the sun and trapping air thick with humidity. More rain seemed a foregone conclusion; it was just a matter of when. With Dad, Uncle Ben, and Rich following, Mak motored us to our first fishing spot, stopping in an area best described as "the middle of nowhere."

He opened the rusted, white and blue Sucrets tin, revealing a small variety of jigs in various sizes and colors, each with a matching tuft of hair concealing the hook. He plucked a purple one, the lead head shaped like an M &M but half its size. A man of few words and those soft-spoken, he raised the lure to eye level and looking our way said, "Use something like this."

I opened my size-and-weight-of-a-marine-battery tackle box, somewhat embarrassed by the bloated collection of lures relative to those in our guide's possession. I recalled having purchased some jigs after the first Kipling Island trip, the lesson learned (or not?) when Mr. Weston schooled us at Indian Bay. Some of the jigs unused and still in their original packaging, I selected a yellow one, unwrapped it, and showed it to Mak. He approved with a subtle nod.

His jig already tied on, Mak dressed it with a lively minnow scooped from our Old Pal minnow bucket. He opened the bail of his spinning reel, the line uncoiling under the weight of the jig. Several seconds later the line went slack, an indication the bait had reached the lake bottom. A turn of the reel handle snapped the bail closed as he raised the rod in a slow, steady motion. An immediate bend in his rod tip signaled a strike. Larry and I watched in amazement as he set the hook, then steadily reeled with the rod held high, bringing the fish to the surface. Momentarily dumbfounded, I inadvertently shirked my duty as net man. But it didn't matter. Mak reached over the side of the boat with his free hand, cradling the belly of a fine "eating size" walleye in his palm. The 16-incher remained curiously calm and motionless during the unusual landing; unusual to us but obviously second nature to Mak. After unhooking it, he grabbed the burlap sack and swished it in the water. The coarse, dampened fabric returned to the bottom of the boat, he slipped the fish into it. Like the Sucrets tin "tackle box," the mystery of the burlap sack "creel" was solved.

Mak methodically maneuvered us in and around patches of thin-leafed cabbage weeds, periodically shifting the lever of the outboard motor between neutral and reverse. He bagged two more walleye before Larry got one, all the fish within an inch of the first one. The action slowed for a few minutes, and then it was my turn. With an exclamation point. My rod yanked down with a violent jerk, the tip plunging into the water as the fish bulldogged under the boat. Immediately registering that this was not the size-class of the others caught today, visions of a monster walleye, a fat 10-pounder like ones I'd seen in *Fishing Facts* magazine, flashed through my mind. Or maybe a big musky, like Uncle Ben's.

The stalemate in our tug of war made one minute seem like a dozen. I maintained steady pressure, finally gaining ground with grinding movement of the reel handle in fractions of inches. A big northern pike slowly came into view, rising like a surfacing submarine. The lack of fight made it seem as if the fish had no idea it was hooked. With one swift movement Mak scooped it into the net.

I'd caught northern pike before but none like this. One or two others may have been almost as long, but this one was thick, broad-backed, fat-bellied. With this bruiser stalking their neighborhood, it's no wonder the walleye cleared out. As Mak slid it into the sack, the skies opened, the heavy rain forcing our return to camp. I followed Mak to the fish-cleaning hut to measure the pike, pleased to see the tail touching the 33-inch mark, making the fish my largest to date.

A short time later, the sounds and pleasant aroma of frying fish, potatoes, and onions filled our cabin, an intoxicating parallel to a new bottle (bravo for our fathers' foresight!) of Jim Beam cracked into by Dad and Uncle Ben, shared with Mak, in generous proportion. Minutes later, our feast began. Easy to distinguish from the smaller walleye fillets, we graded the firm, surprisingly tasteful steak-size chunks of the musky and northern with a unanimous thumbs-up. During the meal, Mak explained that catching a musky out of season did not defy the law, as long as you weren't fishing for them with heavy gear specifically designed for that purpose. To catch one by accident, while fishing for another species was okay, provided a prompt release followed.

Wednesday and Thursday dawned sunny and hot, humidity building through the hours of each day. We did our best to locate the area fished with Mak, attempting to duplicate his technique there and elsewhere, but could not match Tuesday's success, brief as it was. Right or wrong (it couldn't be us, could it?), we chalked it up to the change in weather conditions. Back to the bays and trolling, we bagged a few small pike.

The view from the cabin window on Thursday evening filled with waves of rain swaying across the lake like a sheer curtain in a summer breeze, blotting out the remainder of the fishing day. Our dads exhausted their supply of Jim Beam II, and when sufficiently numbed, met with Schultz to settle-up the bill. Based on previous trips, Larry and I knew, and shared our knowledge with Rich, that we would be vanquished from "paradise" tomorrow. But at least we'd have a burlap sack full of memories in tow.

"Paradise Found"- My biggest fish to date.

~ ~ ~ ~ ~

Fishing is hope experienced.... Catching is hope affirmed.
—Paul Quinnett, *Pavlov's Trout*

Back to Illinois

Refusing to let the tasks associated with home ownership get in the way of the important stuff, I began reacquainting myself with the local fishing holes. My first journal filled, a green covered spiral NIU notebook leftover from the college days became my new piscatorial repository.

An early (too early, judging by the weather and water conditions) April 1975 outing to Deep Lake, with Chuck and Terry, required breaking shore ice with the anchor of a boat we commandeered before the rental office opened. Overpowered by a fog that limited visibility to the length of the 14-foot boat, we drowned the sorrows of the zero-catch saga with a steady intake of blackberry brandy.

On the morning of May 31 of that same year, Dad, Larry and I each scored northern pike from Channel Lake and adjoining Lake Catherine. Mood upbeat, the success of landing each of the 24- to 28-inch fish concluded with hearty swigs of Du Bouchett's dark berry elixir.

Dozens of entries spanning the negative to positive spectrum filled that year and those that followed. Outings to the Chain O' Lakes were most frequent, with some combination of Dad, Jo Ann, Larry, Chuck, Terry, or Art—my closest friends and family—sharing my passion.

The 1976 season tallied as follows:

    103 white bass   1 walleye
    32 yellow bass   4 channel catfish
    14 crappie   1 carp
    17 perch   1 sunfish
    3 northern pike   3 bullhead

Jo Ann ... Nice!

Me ... Not quite as nice...

In 1977, Cedar Lake accounted for my first muskellunge, the species recently stocked by the Illinois Department of Natural Resources into select Illinois lakes. I'd like to provide a rich-in-detail account of battling a behemoth, but the 14-incher that grabbed a floating Rapala would need at least a decade of growing up for me to realize the tackle-busting vision of my childhood dreams. That said, it was still a musky—and size-wise, there's nowhere to go but up.

On an early November day heavy with overcast, Art and I worked The Chain for eight hours, tallying the meager sum of three white bass. As late afternoon darkness crept over our final trolling run, my rod doubled over with the weight of a large fish. Was it the one we'd been waiting for—the one that would make the long, chilly hours spent on the water worthwhile? Momentarily absorbed in the throes of thrill and suspense, disappointment snuffed out the excitement as a foul-hooked, five-pound-plus carp came into view.

The 1978 Chain O' Lakes results presented much the same as previous years. My reputation and prowess in the world of angling northern Illinois waters, however, broadened via my comments recorded in an interview published on July 8, 1978, in *The Daily Herald* article, "Chain O' Lakes still a popular water playground," which read in part:

> *Gary Erickson, regional fish biologist for the Illinois Department of Conservation said there are 30 different fish species in the Chain, ranging from pike to bass, sunfish to bluegills—although the bottom-feeding fish, such as carp and bullheads, have become dominant.... To keep up with the growing number of fishermen, the conservation department has been stocking the lakes. This summer, 90,000 newly hatched walleyes were dumped into the Chain, Erickson noting, "Walleye is a tasty fish."*
>
> *And the lure of catching the elusive walleye is what keeps bringing Ed Piotrowski of Bloomingdale back to the Chain. Piotrowski, at 26, is part of a new generation of fishermen in the Chain. He is not old enough to remember the days when lunkers were plentiful and begging to be caught. So he is content to catch a dozen small fish while waiting for the big one—maybe this time the walleye—to find his hook.*
>
> *"I like the Chain because it's relatively close to home. And it's got nearly every type of freshwater fish," he said. "You always seem to catch something, no matter how big or small." Piotrowski is tanned and his hair sun-streaked from the many hours spent out on the water. But he says it is not just the fish that draw him there. "I don't know, I think catching fish is only half of it," he said. "It's also getting away from things and just being with friends."*

Oh, did I mention Chuck's wife (at the time) Debbe wrote this feature? Years later, she would be awarded a Pulitzer Prize for investigative reporting.

So, would it be wrong for me to say I was the subject of a piece by a Pulitzer Prize winning-journalist? Wrong? Let's just call it a tad misleading. It'll be our little secret.

Among the late-1970s sea of statistics, Larry's name appeared with less frequency. His job as a bank teller required he work on Saturdays, effectively cutting in half the possibilities of weekend fishing outings. His marriage in 1977 further reduced his availability. Prodded by his wife for career advancement and following the natural instinct to a bigger paycheck, his career and our togetherness took divergent paths. Excellent job performance and befriending the bank vice-president, who also became his mentor, expedited his movement up the corporate ladder. When the V.P. took a position at a bank in downtown Chicago, he brought Larry with him. Good for Larry. Bad for us.

Enough being too much, we arranged for a mid-week day off from work. With spring in full bloom, a brief discussion ensued regarding two options: attend the Cubs-Phillies game at Wrigley or head to the lake. Either option a win-win (though the likelihood of a Cubs loss would diminish one of those "wins"), there was little doubt what we would choose.

On Thursday, May 17, 1979, we trolled the waters of the Chain's Lake Marie beginning at 5:30 a.m. The typical mixed bag of white bass and perch was punctuated by Larry's largest fish ever, a chunky 30-inch northern pike.

Off the lake at 10:00 a.m., we considered overloading our day off by taking in the Cubs game, but with our 3:30 a.m. wake-up, a morning filled with fresh air, Du Bouchett, and a one and one-half hour commute down to Wrigley while hinting the fishy fragrance of northern pike, we opted to pass. With the day's success already in the books, why not close it out, albeit early, while riding high?

Here's why not. With afternoon winds squalling from the south, routine fly balls sailed, in a steady stream, into the bleachers or beyond. By the end of the first inning, the Phillies led 7-6. The slugfest that ensued included 11 home runs (three by Cub left fielder Dave "King Kong" Kingman), 50 hits, and 97 total bases. When the dust on the well-traveled base paths finally settled after the 4 hour 3 minute marathon, the Phillies triumphed in 10 innings by a final score of 23-22. Although we missed a highly entertaining game, Larry's lifetime-best catch, and from Illinois waters, no less, validated our choice.

Larry's "no regrets" northern pike.

~ ~ ~ ~ ~

Wisconsin

Horizons expanded in the late 1970s for me and my former D-2 Waco fishing compatriots. Fact or fiction, we all believed the farther north one traveled—Wisconsin, Minnesota, Canada—the greater the odds of encountering more and bigger game fish. To further explore this supposition, I purchased several *Fishing Hot Spots* books documenting Wisconsin lakes. With information on lake size, depth contour maps, bottom composition, structure, and fish species availability, I studied them in great detail. Ready to make the leap over the Illinois-Wisconsin border, I targeted Silver Lake. Why? Because I liked its name.

On a mid-September Sunday in 1976, Art, Chuck, Terry, and I ventured 10 miles into Kenosha County on our inaugural Wisconsin outing, hoping to mine fishing gold from Silver. We arrived under the cover of darkness at 6 a.m., one-half hour before sunrise, our headlights illuminating the roadside sign: "Silver Shiner Baits and Boat Rental." After turning onto the gravel driveway and exiting the vehicle, our plans hit a snag. The orange letters of the sign on the side door of the white frame, two-story building beaconed the solitary word:

"CLOSED." Multiple rings of the doorbell, interspersed with solid knocks on the glass of the storm door finally roused the proprietor from his second floor lodging. His sandpaper voice seeped through the screen of the open window, his words following a disgusting phlegm-laden cough: "Be right down."

We thought that meant he'd be right down. A few minutes passed, then annoyingly another and another before the office light flicked on, allowing a glimpse of a rotund fellow who had just entered the room from a back staircase. Outfitted in slippers, gray sweat pants, and a tattered Green Bay Packers T-shirt (looking like a relic from the long-ago glory years when Lombardi paced the sidelines), his left hand pushed a few strands of black hair across the top of his balding dome. His disheveled appearance made us question whether he even bothered to change out of his bedclothes, or for that matter, if his sleeping and daytime apparel were one and the same. He shuffled toward the front door, his right hand stroking gray-colored whiskers sprouting on basset hound cheeks. After unlocking the doors and flipping the sign to "OPEN," he muttered a "C'mon in." The unpleasant odor of unlaundered clothing and ripe, days-old malt and barley trailed his movement to the back counter.

The room's pegboard panels supported a colorful assortment of classic-but-no-longer-in-favor (as evidenced by their hard plastic packaging, yellowed with age) bass lures: Argobast Hula Poppers and Jitterbugs, Heddon Tiny Torpedoes, Creek Chub Minnows, Lazy Ikes, and Johnson Silver Minnows. The whispering hum of aerators and soft gurgle of oxygenating bubbles rose from minnow-holding tubs along the far wall.

The owner's raspy words interrupted the soothing drone: "One too many PBRs last night," the words followed by a yawn that exposed his Pabst Blue Ribbon-color teeth, the top two chipped, the opening forming a perfect triangle. He continued with questions, as if not expecting answers. "Early start this mornin', huh? ... Where you fellas from?" With another yawn imminent I turned my head, already having filled the day's quota of uninviting visuals.

Eager to get our fishing day started, eye contact among our group of four silently screamed, "Fish are waiting ... dammit ... sometime today!" We alternated replies to his questions with nods and one word answers, balancing our irritation against the fact that we did cut short the hung-over man's beauty sleep, although an infinity of same would not improve the sight before us. Shaking out the cobwebs, his questions finally turned to the matters at hand. "Need any bait? ... Whaddalya be fishin' for? ... Do you have your own cushions? ... How many boats do you need?"

Terry, Chuck, Art, and I (*Polak*, *Bohunk*, *Bohunk*, and *Polak*, respectively), parsimony laced through our Eastern European heritages that also laces shut our wallets, preferred not to plunk down the money for two boats. The same thought process applied in electing not to rent a gasoline motor. Motor-trolling illegal on most Wisconsin lakes, we planned to stay within the confines of the law by using my electric trolling motor to meander about while casting and retrieving. We also decided against the purchase of live bait, years of discretionary income already invested in the artificial lures filling our tackle boxes.

The dull aluminum hulls of a half dozen overturned rental boats leaned against one another in a jumble near the water's edge. Art and Terry righted the one closest to us and pushed it into the water before securing it to the ramshackle dock.

Before joining them to load our equipment, I walked to the far end of the dock, carefully maneuvering around several cracked and rotted planks. There, I paused for a moment to absorb the view. Looking straight across the lake to the north, thickets of trees filled the areas between homes and cottages that dotted the shoreline, contrasting with the east and west shores that were mostly devoid of development. A hint of a southwest breeze rippled the lake's surface, its size approximating that of the Chain's Lake Marie. With the better fishing areas from the map in my *Fishing Hot Spots* book committed to memory, I planned to concentrate our efforts on the shallower western half of the lake, which also contained several expansive weedbeds. I continued my scan noting shoreline landmarks, narrowing the focus to guesstimates of the prime fishing locations, my observations revving hope for a successful day.

Art's voice snapped me back to the moment: "Hey, Columbus, searching for the New World or just afraid of a little early morning manual labor?" During my reflective interlude, my friends worked on transferring our gear from car to boat. My failure to assist did not escape notice or comment.

Not missing a beat, Chuck chimed in, "Some respect for our captain, please. We don't need him pulling a vagina muscle before our first casts."

Their shuttling of equipment completed, I answered, "The minnows and chubs are in the bait tanks, but it looks like the big suckers are out here this morning."

Carefully stepping from dock to boat we boarded, single file: Terry at 6' 6", Art at 5' 10", and both comfortably over 200 pounds; Chuck and I, near bookends at about 6' and weighing in around 160 pounds. That's 750 pounds of human flesh joining the massive accumulation of angling accoutrements scattered across the bench seats and bottom of the boat, including eight rod and reel combos, four tackle boxes, gear bags (with rainsuits, cameras, sunglasses, flasks, etc.), a couple of Playmate coolers, a set of oars, landing net, Ray Jeff portable fish flasher, and the 60-pound 12-volt battery to power the trolling motor. Space at a premium, time would tell if our frugality was folly.

Although the sky hinted a lighter shade of gray, thick overcast fraught with the threat of rain shrouded the recently risen sun. The mid-60s temperature, for this time of the morning *and* this time of the year, was unseasonably pleasant. My Sears-Ted Williams Signature trolling motor, with 15-pound thrust (liken to the "power" of the 12-horse engine that propelled the *Wright Flyer* at Kitty Hawk in 1903), moaned and groaned under the strain of the overloaded scow. Low, slow, and the only boat on the water, we inched forward as if pushing through drying cement.

One man each on our rental's four bench seats, our standard fishing attire included well-worn Levi's, plaid flannel shirts, and baseball caps. I also donned a green plastic batting helmet for additional protection in the event of a partner's errant backswing. I imagine we provided an amusing visual for the lakeshore residents, early morning risers sipping coffee to a double-take as we fired off casts in all directions like a fireworks display gone wrong.

Our lures of choice included floating minnows by Rapala and Rebel, and the Bass Buster Beetle Spin. Minutes into our foray on new waters, I enjoyed the fortune of the first strike. My partners' quick positional shift to observe the tussle caused the boat to tip precariously. With water breaching the gunnel, vociferous reactions gushed from my boat mates:

"Holy crap!"

"Whoa!"

"What the hell?"

Instinct and agility driving corrective action, the immediate redistribution of their weight averted a potential disaster. My concentration unaffected by the perilous sway, moments later I landed an undersized, 10-inch bass. The close call of the near-visit to Davy Jones Locker overriding congratulations for my catch (unimpressive, granted), Terry muttered, "Titanic," rapidly followed by Chuck and Art's "Edmund Fitzgerald" and "Lusitania."

Not long thereafter, I connected with another bass and then a walleye. Art took a walleye and Terry a bass before I hooked up with another walleye. The merry-go-round continued, unfortunately passing Chuck by. Each member of the team, however, celebrated the landing of every fish with a swig of blackberry brandy. Filled with Du Bouchett or Bols, our flasks represented an accessory as important and integral to our fishing adventures as any other piece of tackle in our arsenal. Our astute wives postulated that our affinity for fishing might, in fact, be driven by the desire for a somewhat socially acceptable early morning venue for sipping alcoholic beverages. Difficult to deny, we preferred to think of ourselves as hearty multitasking outdoorsmen.

Over the next hour, from 9 to 10 a.m., the bite slowed. So did our senses, the prior and frequent flask content consumption beginning to take its toll. The lull prodded me to explore a change of lures that might return me to earlier success. I grabbed the handle of my tackle box, lifting it toward my lap. Not having properly secured the latch (Damn it!) after my first lure selection, a majority of the contents tumbled from the multiple trays onto my shoes and the boat floor. Several snagged on the shin portion of my jeans. Others entangled in my shoe laces.

Amid the laughter, Chuck bellowed, "I'll drink to that!"

Art offered another perspective: "Get his flask. Cut him off before he hurts himself."

Terry, the disdain in his voice juxtaposed with a smile said, "Jesus, how many lures do you have in there? No wonder the stores never have what I'm looking for, you hoardin' whore!"

The task of plucking and returning the colorful array of treble-hook lures to their compartments took several minutes. As I worked to reorganize the thorny mess, Terry nabbed another bass and Art caught a chunky perch. Team player that I am, I interrupted my meticulous restocking chore to join in the liquid celebration recognizing their successes. The final lure replaced, I took pride in not having nicked myself—not a drop of blood to be dabbed dry.

Just as I closed the lid and snapped shut the latch, Terry howled, "NO!" Startled, I looked up to see his line taut, a duck splashing water with the furious flapping of wings, its head below the surface at the center of concentric circles marking the point where Terry's long cast touched down. Immediately recognizing the potential for a unique catch, Chuck again offered, "I'll drink to that!"

Unsure but hoping the hooks of the floating minnow bait did not foul the fowl, Terry did not apply any pressure. As quickly as it began, it was over. His line went slack as the bird took flight, squawking, quacking, "squacking" into the distance.

With battery power dissipating, we caught several more fish before snailing back to the Silver Shiner. Our total catch included 9 largemouth bass to 16 inches, 5 walleye to 18 inches, and a 9-inch perch. Pleased by the quality and quantity of "game" fish relative to a typical catch in our Illinois lakes, the results equally amazed when considering our overcrowded angling accommodations. And not once did the backswing of a lure bounce off my helmet or impale human flesh, further impressive in the context of the cumulative effect of our empty flasks.

Upon docking, we found the proprietor slouched in a lawn chair, his garb unchanged. A loosely gripped red, white, and blue Pabst can dangled over the edge of the chair's arm. As we unloaded the boat he stumbled in our direction, slurring, "So, howdya doody?"

We stifled our laughter as I unclipped the metal stringer attached to one of the oar locks, raising the collection of larger bass and walleye that we'd be taking home to enjoy at a group dinner. His bloodshot eyes widening, he continued, "Holy tolody … wheredya get those? Not in this lake, didya?" His reaction, in spite of his "condition," led us to believe we'd done well.

Our "north is better" fishing postulate validated, we returned on numerous occasions in the years to follow. More often than not, Silver Lake shared its bounty of walleye, northern pike, and largemouth bass. The elusive musky, which also roamed its depths, remained elusive. We also tested the waters of neighboring Powers Lake, as well as Walworth County's Geneva Lake, with varying degrees of success, though neither matched the shine of Silver.

So, what did we learn? In addition to considering an investment in the Pabst Brewing Company, if southern Wisconsin produced such fine results, what might we expect by pushing further north? Was it time to up the ante, with the expectation of more and bigger fish? Yes, go north, young men, go north. In June 1978, we booked a three-day weekend at Pinehurst Resort, its cabins on the shores of 980-acre Little St. Germain Lake located in Vilas County, just 30 miles south of Michigan's Upper Peninsula. Navigation friendly, the lake is divided into large sections: West Bay, East Bay, and South Bay, all connecting to central No Fish Bay and each possessing distinct depth and structural characteristics.

Terry, Art, and Chuck. Photo by me, fourth in the boat.
(And "fashionable" flannel all around!)

Little St. Germain Lake

With Art behind the wheel of his Ford Bronco this early June Saturday, much of the seven-hour ride passed with sports-related banter, though I fueled our anticipation (not that we needed it) with the reading of a *Fishing Facts* magazine article: "Secrets of Catching Muskies Revealed!" (Allow me to let *you* in on a secret. To entice its purchase, the cover of nearly every fishing periodical lists a piece titled with the word "secret." Curious to have the mystery revealed, those of us who habitually purchase these magazines with childlike naiveté can be defined by another six-letter word beginning with "s": sucker. This cover also titillates with an open-mouthed musky coiled to strike this year's "can't miss, don't leave home without it or buy one when you get there" lure.)

After a stop for the all-you-can-eat lumberjack breakfast at Paul Bunyan's in Minocqua (the restaurant's profitability taking a downturn based on the quantities of eggs, pancakes and sausage links consumed by Art and Terry), we turned east onto Route 70. A few miles beyond Mama's Supper Club and Goose's Disco of the North, the burnt-wood Pinehurst sign came into view. We turned onto the gravel road cut among the pines, met our host, quickly unpacked and readied our gear.

Our accommodations package included two boats, each powered by a 10-horsepower gas motor. Boat pairings decided by a flip of coins, Chuck and Terry (heads) occupied one and Art and I (tails) the other. The space and relative comfort of two- versus four-in-a-boat felt like the difference between a penthouse suite at the Ritz-Carlton (never been in one, just surmising) and a ground level room at a flea-bag motel (been in plenty of those.)

By 2 p.m., our Mepps spinners and Rapala minnow baits were seining one of the lake's many weedy bays. Our offerings connected on a nursery of northern pike, most less than 20 inches. The "secrets" of catching muskies was easily forgotten amid the fish-catching flurry.

We continued our tradition of celebratory swigs after each catch. By late afternoon, our mood light from the dizzying success, I acknowledged one of Terry's many fish by blurting across the bay, "Nice going, Maretti!" With four of the larger pike kept for tonight's dinner (Terry led the way with a total of 10 "snakes," Art and Chuck each took 8 while I brought up the rear with 4), we returned to the cabin. After toasting the outing with a round of Boggs Cranberry Liqueur, I declared, "We *are* the Fabulous Maretti Brothers!"

And so, from the berries "black" and "cran" was born the Maretti moniker that remains to this day. Unaware (but obviously floating in my subconscious) of the name's source at the time of its on-water creation, I later recognized it from dialogue (though they were not characters) in the television series *Welcome Back, Kotter*. We also assumed first names: Bluto (Art); Gonzo, aka Dr. Gonzo (Chuck); Nimzo (Terry); Mondo (me); and later (absent from this trip), cousins Larry (Plato), and Rich (Rico).

A faulty heater made for a nippy overnight in the cabin, the Brothers surviving the 40-some degree temperature with the aid of the aforementioned consumption of berry "antifreeze." On Sunday morning, sprinkles fell from a dull gray sky, swirled by biting northeast winds and a temperature that hovered either side of 50 degrees.

Today's coin flip paired Art and Terry for the first session's 7:30 a.m. start. Early on, Chuck bagged two pike while I pitched a zero, the only tugs resulting from my Mepps spinner contacting the weeds. After an unsuccessful attempt Lindy-rigging minnows in the deeper water of West Bay, I moved us to a shoreline indentation just north of No Fish Bay.

In an effort to get me on the scoresheet, Chuck began with a question before offering some brotherly advice. "Do you have a naturalized Rebel?"

"Only one," I replied. "A floating, jointed walleye."

"That's the ticket," he confidently offered, likely a function of witnessing Terry's success with a similar lure the day before. "Put it on and you'll have a fish within a dozen casts."

With nothing to lose and buoyed by his optimism, I tied it to my line and began the silent count of casts and retrieves. One, two, three, eager. Four, five, six, hopeful. Seven, eight, nine, dimming. Ten, eleven, near surrender. Twelve, Whammo! A 15-inch pike torpedoes the lure. Small? Sure. But a prophecy fulfilled, nonetheless. I caught another before we adjourned the morning session, meeting Art and Terry back at the cabin for a 9:30 breakfast. While Art came up empty during the session, Terry again worked his magic with the naturalized pike-pattern floating Rebel lure, catching four more northerns and a beautiful 17-inch walleye.

Not long after completing the meal, sheets of rain began pounding our Northwoods retreat. Our return to the water delayed, the cabin confinement spawned a new Maretti competition—an egg shelling contest. (Egg salad sandwiches were planned for lunch.) Each given three hard boiled eggs, I handicapped it as follows: Terry, most experienced in the kitchen (causing me to sometimes refer to him as Mom Maretti) should win in a cakewalk; Art and Chuck will likely fight it out for second; and me, a food preparation ignoramus, should flounder in fourth. All bets off in any Maretti event, I "egg-celled" with an upset victory. Art and Chuck finished second in a dead heat, while Terry brought up the rear claiming he got "bad eggs"—whatever that meant.

Under gradually clearing skies, we returned to the fishing grounds at 3 p.m. With Chuck manning the motor, we returned to No Fish Bay. Drifting and casting an area we hadn't previously fished, I asked him for a depth reading from my Ray Jefferson fish flasher. Hand to eyebrows to shield the now shining sun, he looked into the brown-cased enclosure, answering assuredly, "20 feet."

In need of a lure that would approach that depth, I reached into my tackle box and grabbed a CountDown Rapala, advising my captain of the choice. With a fall rate of approximately one foot per second, I made a long cast and began "counting it down" after it contacted the water. At "20" I began the retrieve. Halfway to the boat a fish struck. Moments later a 13-inch walleye came to net. Three casts later the scene repeated, this time with a 15-incher. In an unexpected reaction, Chuck burst into laughter.

"What ..." my question began.

Unable to complete the inquiry, Chuck gathered himself to chortle, "You're an idiot!" Before the words could settle, he continued "But not as big an idiot as me—we're in 8 feet of water!"

Ah, my partner-imp was messing with me, but his "Chuckfoolery" backfired. My success leaving me unconcerned with the misinformation, I continued to cast. Minutes later my rod bent again, this time its curve loaded with verve. I alerted Chuck, but he nonchalantly concluded my catch was nothing more than a substantial clump of weeds rather than a fish. His analysis changed when my line neared the boat and pulled violently beneath it, causing him to scramble for the net. The fish surfaced briefly on the other side of the boat, allowing a partial glimpse of its mass and identifying it as a northern pike.

Flying in the face of good fishing form (perhaps inspired by flask-to-lips celebration of the walleyes?), instead of standing to fight the fish I remained seated in the bow. Then (too late…), in order to battle the fish head-on, I swung the 7-foot fiberglass rod over my head and lost my grip of the Mitchell 300 spinning reel's handle. The awkward maneuver proved to be my undoing, the slack line allowing the pike to rid itself of the hooks and diesel back to the depths. Disheartened, I mentally replayed my misstep with head bowed.

"Don't worry about it," Chuck said in a tone melding matter-of-fact with commiseration, concluding, "I don't think it would have fit in the net anyway."

I found little comfort in his words. An opportunity lost weighed on my mind through the next fishless hour. We agreed it was time to explore other areas, moving to fish the shoreline of a small island in lower East Bay. A half dozen casts into the drift, our decision was rewarded.

"Got one!" I exclaimed.

"Will this one be part of your early release program, too?" Chuck chided.

The darting, side-to-side movement felt typical of the undersized northern pike we'd been catching. Slack line no part of this bout, however, I reeled the fish boatside where Chuck scooped it into the net.

Now secured, we both did a double take. Though its elongated body said pike, it lacked the pattern of small yellow ovals speckling dark green sides. The subtle vertical gray-green striping of this one spelled m-u-s-k-y! Never at a loss to deliver a lighthearted jab, Chuck asks, "What the hell is that? Some kind of Wisconsin baby carp?" Measured at an unremarkable 25 inches, making contact with the elusive species still loomed large.

After returning to the cabin at the prescribed time for our dinner meal and completing same, we hopped into the Bronco for a short trip to Jack's Bait Shop. My partners planned to load up on CountDown Rapalas with the promise of replicating my multi-species success. That hope quickly deflated—not because the lure wasn't in stock but rather due to the "highway robbery" price, at least as seen through the eyes of the miserly Maretti clan. The lure, available in the Chicago area for $2.50, was priced at the-only-game-in-town Jack's for $3.85. Incomprehensible! Inconceivable! Implausible! Improbable! Incredible! Impossible! Incensed, it was "no sale" followed by a nonstop return to Pinehurst.

Monday, our last full day of fishing, found me paired with Terry. Admittedly sleepy-eyed from the action-packed days (and nights), my third cast of the morning startled with a real eye opener. No Fish Bay sited the largest fish I'd ever encountered in my days on the water. A muskellunge, larger than the Kipling Island catch of Tex though not the monster of Doc Watson, followed my shallow-running Rapala. Ever faster I cranked it, the fish keeping pace but not committing. Now out of room, I swung my rod to move the lure on a course parallel to the boat. So focused on the prize that the boat might as well have been invisible, the muskellunge perfectly tracked the lure's movement. Now trailing it by just inches, the brute opened its mouth and flared its gill, a microsecond away from a final burst to inhale the faux meal. At that critical instant, I ripped the lure out of the water...

I don't know why, either.

Incomprehensible ... inconceivable ... implausible ... improbable ... incredible ... impossible. Ed-iot!

Casting in the opposite direction, Terry did not see this drama unfold (just as well) but acknowledged his peripheral vision caught a significant swirl at boatside as the fish bolted away to conclude the confounding sequence of events.

Over a fine late night dinner of walleye and northern, the trip's "last supper," I babbled my embarrassing encounter. I'm not sure which of the Brothers commented, "Where others dream, Mondo hallucinates."

Our group totaled 1 musky, 3 perch, 4 walleye, and 72 northern pike for the 2½ day outing, affirming the decision to travel north with the hope of better fishing prospects. And as often occurs, a big fish seen or hooked on the last day teases, imbedding a memory that simultaneously haunts and beckons, solidifying the desire to return.

In four of the next five years, various members of the Fabulous Maretti Brothers would reconvene at Little St. Germain. Although the results were good, they became a little less "fabulous" in each successive year. And consistent with all other outings, a big musky was never landed.

~ ~ ~ ~ ~

Fishing is a discipline in the equality of men, for all men are equal before fish.
—Herbert Hoover

The Fabulous Maretti Brothers

Not to brag, but I don't think you'd get much of an argument if you asked each of the Fabulous Maretti Brothers about my importance to the group. Their descriptions of me, or more specifically my role within the Maretti world, would likely include (in addition to some well-chosen expletive adjectives) any or all of the following: organizer, hub, facilitator, focal point, middleman, coordinator, planner, catalyst, glue, solder, thread, bungee cord, adhesive, binder, stickum, grout, mortar, spirit, essence, heartbeat, the straw that stirs the drink (or the air in the emptied glass…). If not for me, I'm not sure there would ever be any communication among the others. I'm quite a guy.

After our graduation from NIU, I organized events and maintained statistics on a broad range of competitive events from 1974 to 1990. Each year we gathered, on multiple occasions, to compete in matches of golf, bowling, basketball, bumper pool, and the board games Risk and Stock Market. Oh, and lest I forget, tournament-style fishing.

Golf

With across-the-board pedestrian skills, we hacked up several courses in the west and northwest suburbs, among them Brae Loch (our unofficial "home" course) in Grayslake, Glendale in Bloomingdale, and Indian Valley in Long

Grove. I placed first in 8 of 19 tournaments, my lifetime average of 98.78 ranking second to Rico's 95.44. Three of the remaining four Brother's average scores placed in the narrow range of 101.09 to 103.31. Only one from our group of six, whose name and average will go unmentioned, failed to capture a title. We never handicapped skill inequality in any Fabulous Maretti Brothers competition. Innate talent, desire to improve via study and practice, ability to manage alcoholic intake, and visits from Lady Luck leveled (or further tilted) the playing fields.

Early on, I retired all my "worm burner" woods, finding better accuracy as well as decent distance (after the body had limbered up, a few holes into the round) using a 1-iron in lieu of a 1-wood driver. In that same time frame, my father-in-law, John, had given me a complete set of vintage, 1940s-50s Walter Hagen signature irons (loved the leather grips!) he had purchased at a garage sale.

Our second of three 1979 golf tournaments took place at Brae Loch on August 4. Familiar with early starts common to our fishing outings, our day on the links began before 6 a.m. beneath dawn's early light. Like our fishing decision to forego the cost of renting a gasoline motor, so too did our frugality carry over to the links. We always walked the courses, carrying our bags of clubs or pulling hand carts instead of renting motorized ones.

On Brae Loch's first hole, a straightaway 420-yard par 4, I always considered any score less than the dreaded "snowman 8" a moral victory. No matter how much stretching or how many practice swings I would take before stepping to the first tee, early morning muscle tightness generally translated to a poor score. Not surprisingly, today's first drive faded right, coming to rest in the tall rough. My second shot rifled a divot the size of a boat propeller high into the air, the spinning clot of sod traveling twice the distance of the ball that dribbled into the fairway behind it. Next, a not particularly well hit 3-iron brought me within chipping distance of the green. My "touch of a blacksmith" chip rolled well past the pin, the ball cutting a trail as it spun through the silvery droplets of dew blanketing the green. Two putts netted a six.

A par 4 scored on the 365-yard second hole staked me to an unexpected four stroke lead, the rest of the field struggling mightily in the early going. The third hole, a 140-yard par 3, sported an elevated green with only the flag, hanging limp atop the flagstick, visible in the morning calm. Behind us to the east, the rising sun illuminated the emerald leaves of the trees lining both sides of the fairway. Robins hopped among the branches, chirping a cheery tune. A hint of the day's heat began dissipating the cool, moist morning air.

I secured honors by virtue of my par on the second hole and prepared to tee-off. As part of my *Polak* par-3 ritual, I surveyed the area and found the remnant of a cracked wooden tee. After lifting the 9-iron from my bag, I moved between the white wooden blocks defining the men's tee. A MacGregor Nicklaus Golden Bear "3" ball clenched in my palm, I used its hard surface to plunge the remnant tee into the ground, the ball coming to rest a sliver above the level of the turf. Two casual practice swings preceded high concentration mode: eye on the ball ... backswing ... pause ... eye on the ball ... downswing ... eyes closed (dammit!) ... Whack! ... follow through. The shot lofted high and true, the white sphere flying toward the flag. Cognizant of golf as the "gentleman's game," one of the Brothers clapped, another whistled, and a third called out, "Nice shot, Maretti!" With the green above eye level, we'd have to wait to see just how nice.

Upon completion of all the tee shots, I grabbed the putter from my bag and led the uphill trek, anxious to see the ball's proximity to the pin. As the scene unfolded, one ball had come to rest some twenty feet to the right of the pin. The other two hugged the left fringe, front and back, their distance more than twice that of the ball on the right. My upbeat mood soured with the absence of the fourth ball, obviously mine, whose line of flight appeared to target the pin. I can't believe a 9-iron was too much club, I thought, surmising my ball had rolled into the underbrush at the bottom of a gentle slope ten yards behind the green.

Only a minute or two into the dispiriting task of poking through the tangles of branches and leaves, Bluto called out, "Maretti—you playing a Golden Bear 3?"

"Yeah," I muttered, shuffling further into the thicket.

His next words, "I found it," brought a sigh of relief, a penalty stroke and the financial consequence (minimal but annoying nonetheless) of a lost ball averted. Relief elevated to delight, Bluto stood on the green with one hand on the pin, the other pointing to the cup. I floated up the incline and across the putting surface with long strides. Silent but beaming a smile, the inner me screamed a simple "Yes!" Retrieving the treasure of the momentous event, I ran my fingers and thumb across its dimpled surface thoughtfully, almost lovingly, the subtle movement to ensure the object was real, the scene not a dream.

Gonzo, reverting to NIU Waco linguistics, commented, "No shit ... *A-hole in one!*" Nimzo took another slant: "The old man must've kicked it in for you," a reference to an elderly gentleman, a Brae Loch fixture, who set up shop between the third green and fourth tee, peddling three-for-a-dollar balls that had flown out of bounds along bordering Brae Loch Road and Route 45. I'd just pitched a perfect game, bowled a 300, and caught a state record walleye. It felt good. Real damn good.

The remainder of the round went well. My game, not capable of maintaining the par pace set over the first three holes, didn't collapse either. In addition to the eagle, I parred six holes, finishing with my best-ever score, an 87. Though I won the tourney, my ace, and a sub-90 round, would never be repeated.

I'm not sure if it was before or after that memorable round when my most embarrassing moment in golf occurred. While practicing with my 1-iron at a driving range, I somehow lost my grip on the club, propelling it straight-as-an-arrow forward some 25 yards. Observed from the concession, the loud speaker blared, "All golfers, please hold your next shot … all golfers, please hold your shots." The moments-ago clicking sound of clubs contacting balls ceased as patrons who had not seen the ball-imitating club arc skyward looked around with quizzical expressions on their faces. Hands on head I froze in disbelief, the loneliest man on the no-longer-rotating Earth. Make that the universe. Oh, for the power to cross my arms, nod my head, wink, and disappear as in *I Dream of Jeannie*. Or be beamed up to *Star Trek's* Starship Enterprise. Or spontaneously combust. Tail between my legs, I jogged out amid the disquieting silence to retrieve my club, feeling the pang of dozens of sets of eyes following my every step there and back.

Bowling

The venues for bowling outings were many and varied: Elk Grove Bowl in Elk Grove Village, Golf Mill Bowl in Niles, River Rand Bowl in Des Plaines, Brunswick Lanes in Arlington Heights, Schaumburg Lanes in Schaumburg, Palatine Lanes in Palatine, Striker Lanes in Buffalo Grove, and Mundelein Bowl in Mundelein.

In contrast to my generally successful golf results, I was the only Maretti Brother failing to capture a bowling event title, an accurate reflection of my anemic 135.55 lifetime average that placed last among the Brothers. (An additional financial consequence of my poor performance required funding most "beer frames.") Bluto topped our group with a 155.68 average, the others spread at various levels between us. Not surprisingly, the all-time high game of 220 did not roll from my fingertips, and strange but true, neither did the low of 88.

My Brae Loch hole in one provided a memory for a lifetime. So, too, did one roll from the June 11, 1977, tourney at Elk Grove Bowl. My performance that day mirrored many competitions past, the majority of frames ending without the mark of a spare or strike. Solidly in the throes of a funk midway through the third and final game, my mannerisms took on a robot-like quality. In the seventh frame my first roll missed the headpin, netting five pins. The remaining five stood in a physics-defying configuration that even St. Jude, the Patron Saint of lost causes, might have trouble picking up. Futility, thy name is Mondo, I thought. Emotionally anesthetized and sleepwalking through the motions I pushed on, head down and without pause: pluck ball from ball return and hold chest high ... push ball forward, step one, two ... ball swings back, step three, four ... ball swings forward, step five ... release and follow through ... "Maretti!"

"No!"

"What the hell are you doing?"

Shouts from the gallery of Brothers wakened me in time to see the ball rumbling on a collision course with the malfunctioned pin sweep stuck in the down position. Closed eyes and a grimaced cringe synced with the resounding metallic *thunk!* as the 16-pound sphere crashed into the metal barrier. The desk attendant was not happy. Needless to say, neither was I. But with the driving range incident still fresh, I'm sad to say my comfort level with dumb and dumbfounded was trending upward.

Basketball, Bumper Pool, and Board Games

Maretti Brothers basketball tournaments, intense one-on-one contests, took place in the spring or fall, our hardcourt the concrete driveway of my Bloomingdale house. The first segment of the tourney a round-robin, each player dueled every other in games to seven, a basket counting as one point. A victory required a two-point margin or being the first to reach eleven points. Six competitors necessitated a total of 15 matches. Differentials for each game, computed and totaled by individual, came into play in case of a tie for seeding in the second round. The top four finishers moved on, bracketed in games requiring eleven points, win by two. Nimzo and I each notched victories in three tournaments. Two of the Brothers never captured a roundball title in the Maretti-world's most physically demanding competition. Though bumps and bruises were a given, the permanent record includes no tales of broken bones, stitches, or calls to 911.

The family room of my Bloomingdale residence sited our bumper pool tournaments. Success at bumper pool, a pocket billiards game with clusters of fixed bumpers, demands knowledge of angles and a skillful "touch" when utilizing rails and bumpers to execute offensive and defensive shots with delicate precision.

Like basketball, 15 match-play games in round-robin format filled the first segment, determining position for the second round. Unlike basketball, all six contestants participated in the king of the hill, with wins in two of three games needed to advance. I was victorious in five tournaments, Gonzo three. Two Marettis captured singular tourney wins, and two failed to ever shoot their way to the top of the hill.

Mondo, Rico, Plato, and Nimzo intent on the action.
Bluto and Gonzo ... not so much.

Though not an official bumper pool tournament, Gonzo, Bluto, and Nimzo joined me for an impromptu gathering on December 8, 1980. A Monday evening, *ABC Monday Night Football* featured the Miami Dolphins and New England Patriots, the game playing in the background on our 19-inch Motorola Quasar "works in a drawer" television. Shortly after 10 p.m., Jo Ann came running down the stairs, delivering news that stunned like an uppercut from Muhammed Ali: "John Lennon's been shot."

Moments later the dispirited, staccato delivery of Howard Cosell announced, "Remember, this is just a football game, no matter who wins or loses. An unspeakable tragedy, confirmed to us by ABC News ... John Lennon, outside of his apartment building on the west side of New York City ... the most famous, perhaps, of all of the Beatles ... shot twice in the back, rushed to Roosevelt Hospital, dead ... on ... arrival."

His words welled up equal parts sadness, disbelief, and anger. We had grown up with The Beatles, following the enormously gifted, sometimes irreverent, never dull moptop quartet from Liverpool. Their music filled the background of our lives from early teens into our college years. Though they disbanded a decade earlier, we, as all fans, held out hope of a reunion. The dream died on that cold December night.

Sometime later, we returned to the pool table; the game, along with doses of Yukon Jack and Eagle Rare bourbon whiskey, provided a comforting distraction. Time lost in the game, drink, and dismay, we snapped back to the moment when Bluto opened the front drapes to reveal the light of day. It was 5 a.m. Work loomed in a few short hours, the "all-nighter" our first since the NIU days in DeKalb.

My hexagonal bumper pool table, when covered with its reversible, poker-style tabletop, doubled as the location for our board game encounters of Stock Market and Risk. Although wins and losses did not become part of the permanent Fabulous Maretti Brothers record, game intensity matched that of our physical competitions. As in the D-2 days, Bluto continued to amaze during Stock Market with lightning quick in-his-head calculations, computing the accurate purchase and sale prices of odd lots of stocks.

Risk's simple goal of world domination found complications in its execution. The most tossed-about phrase, "civic duty," chided a combatant to attack a continent controlled by another, a successful foray reducing the defender's claim to additional armies. Unlike real world pacts and treaties, many not worth the paper they're written on, the Fabulous Maretti Brothers applied a thumbs down to such politics. Each game was guided by the "every man for himself" tenet, yours to win or lose based on strategy and helped or hindered by the random roll of dice and draw of cards.

Sometimes a game or two followed a day on the lake.

Fishing

The annual Maretti calendar always included several highly anticipated on-water events. Tournaments included the Waco Fishing Derby, the Fabulous Maretti Brothers Pro-Am Fishing Invitational, and the Fabulous Maretti Brothers Bass Master Classic. Adding fun and formality to the informal, a traveling trophy was presented to the winner of each, the award made possible when friend and former Motorolan Tom left the company to take a position at a prominent trophy manufacturer located in Chicago. His employ there enabled purposefully gaudy trophies to be acquired at a reasonable cost.

I targeted the Chain O' Lakes as the home waters for The Fabulous Maretti Brothers Pro-Am Invitational, several reasons backing that choice. Haisman's Launch and Boat Rental on Lake Marie served as the departure point, centrally located to the better fishing of the Chain's northern lakes. (As a side note, the name of this business allowed us to refer to our tournament's traveling prize for overall winner as the Haisman Trophy, spelled differently but a takeoff on the annual award to college football's top player.) Don, a Motorola co-worker and friend, invited us to gather for the post-tourney refreshments and awards presentations at his home, located on the south shore of Lake Marie.

The Fabulous Maretti Brothers Pro-Am Invitational, garnering contestants by invitation necessitated, well, an invitation. This event (as most of the others) my brainchild, I fulfilled the annual task of creating, developing, producing, and distributing the multi-page invitation to co-workers, relatives, and friends. It followed a standard format from year to year.

The cover page often contained fishing-related photos of the Fabulous Maretti Brothers—sometimes as a group, sometimes individually—posed or captured in less-than-flattering candid snapshots. The second page detailed the particulars: the when (date); where (Haisman's); what time (usually 6 a.m. to noon); prizes (rods, reels, tackle boxes, lures) and refreshments; and entry fee ($1.00 in 1979, escalating to $6.00 by 1988, the quantity, value, and volume of prizes increasing accordingly). Additional information on page two always included these details:

> Winners are required to return to next year's event to pass on the trophies (28-inch overall and 7-inch big fish) to that year's champions.
>
> Tournament fishing is open to any body of water, muck, or sludge adjoined to the Chain O' Lakes. Although not prohibited, we trust no entrant would stoop so low as to fish the waters adjacent to any property they own, lease, rent, or otherwise loiter. (This was a reference to Don after he secured his third consecutive victory, the winning fish usually caught in his "backyard.")
>
> In the event of ties or disputes, the Fabulous Maretti Brothers will determine awards based on any criteria they so choose. Bribes are encouraged.
>
> Requests for refunds graciously refused.

The last page of the invitation contained the tally sheet. With slight tweaks in the early years, the point values settled as follows:

Muskellunge—Automatic Winner. (In the event more than one is caught, both/all liars will be disqualified.)

> 20 Walleye (Yeah, right)
> 12 Largemouth Bass
> 12 Northern Pike
> 2 Striped Bass
> 2 Crappie
> 2 Bluegill
> 2 Perch
> 2 Sunfish
> 1 Bullhead
> 1 Catfish
> -1/2 Carp or Dogfish
> (Maximum tally per species is 10 fish.)

The cover page of the 1979 inaugural invitation featured individual Maretti photos from various outings past, each taken while in a boat…

> …Gonzo - Crazed smile, standing, drenched from an unintended tumble into Cedar Lake during a Waco Derby, smiling, holding the skeletal remains of a small gar fish found on shore.
>
> …Nimzo - Seated, wearing shorts and a dago-T, outstretched arm lifting from the water a pair of six-packs clipped to a stringer.
>
> …Bluto - Standing in the bow, shirtless, back to the camera.
>
> …Plato - Sporting wire-rim sunglasses, down-to-the-jaw sideburns, shorts, and a white T-shirt with green scripted "Apple" across the front, seated and gazing into the distance as he drives the boat, one hand on the tiller and the other holding a bottle of Labatt Blue Canadian beer raised toward the camera.
>
> …Mondo – the image shouting, "Feeling lucky, punk?"

The second annual invitation featured a photo of a man, his right arm straining with the vertical hold of a 33-pound carp, his face blocked out by question marks and the subtitle, "It could be you—you're invited!" Across the bottom of the page flowed the following fictitious snippets:

> "Ounce for ounce, fish for fish, or pound for pound, there is not a fishing tournament in the world that carries more weight and prestige than the Fabulous Maretti Brothers Invitational."
> *Fishing Facts* magazine

> "By far, one of the greatest and most exclusive fishing competitions in the northern Illinois area, indeed the entire country."
> John Spehn, Outdoor writer, *Chicago Sun Times*

> "All fishermen love to talk fishing, weaving fantastic tales. But few have experienced the sport as it is commonly experienced by the talented, Fabulous Maretti Brothers."
> Tom McNally, Outdoor editor, *Chicago Tribune*

In response to his receipt of the invitation, I received the following letter from my friend Tom:

> *Dear Ed,*
>
> *Your Pro-Am Fishing Invitational letter warmed my winter blood! Just the thought of a 33-pound carp oozing around the bottom of a boat is enough to make anyone's blood boil.*
>
> *If the tournament ends up half as good as your invite, it should be some contest. I quickly called Al Lindner to see if he had received the honored invitation. He wasn't in, but his secretary said something about him slipping out the back door and going on an extended vacation. "Off the record" she told me that he felt he would be a fool to try and compete in this tournament, and is glad that he doesn't have to explain why he would refuse to compete if he were lucky enough to get invited.*
>
> *Please find enclosed my one dollar ($1) entry fee.*
>
> *Tom*
>
> *P.S. I hear they're hitting on wooden fluorescent yellow jig heads with split shot crimped on the back hook.*

The cover of the 1981 invitation contained nine photos of Rico, among them the trophies won and the fish he caught in the 1980 tournament when he aced the competition with five northern pike and a largemouth bass.

The 1984 invite featured the front page of an issue of *Jim Peterson's Outdoor News,* touting the cover story, "Six Inducted into Fishing Hall of Fame." Crudely cut and pasted (with scissors and tape) into the article are the names of the six Fabulous Maretti Brothers, as well as a group photo, a takeoff of The Beatles *Abbey Road* album cover. This also marked the inaugural appearance of the logo that I designed, a fish formed of the letters in "Maretti."

The cover of the 1987 invitation splashed the title, "If You Fish, Take Some Suckers Along," and the 1988 read "O-Fish-L Business." The latter included a group photo in which we're holding our bowling balls, the caption below reading, "What's wrong with this picture? Nothing! We're going bowling for bass at the 10th Annual Fabulous Maretti Brothers Pro-Am Fishing Invitational. (Ten years later, we're all still alive!)"

Some might say (I could argue with them, but I won't…) that my decade-long failure to capture the "Haisman" led to yet another tournament creation. Born as a "bass only" contest in 1981, the Fabulous Maretti Brothers Bass Master Classic was sited on either Silver or Powers Lake. Open only to the Brothers, another trophy traveled among the annual winners. The refined yet regal award, featuring a leaping bass atop a gold and blue velvet crown, adorned my bookshelf for the majority of the tournament years and remains in my possession to this day, the last Classic fished in 1987.

Late in the 1980s, I began experiencing organizer "burn out" with all events Maretti. Marriages, the birth and raising of children, divorces (*most certainly not* an unfortunate result of extensive Maretti events!), remarriages, job promotions, general work demands, occupational relocations (Gonzo's employment at *The Kiwanis Magazine* necessitated a move to Indianapolis), homes (their purchase, maintenance, and moves), expanded and extended family obligations and commitments—damn, life was getting in the way of the important stuff. Scheduling became bothersome at best, near impossible at worst. Unable to stem the tide of this unwelcomed though inevitable evolution, the Pro-Am Fishing Invitational in 1990 marked the final formal Fabulous Maretti Brothers event, also ending my self-assigned undertaking as record-keeper.

Unwilling to accept the move from undertaking to undertaker, I continued impromptu attempts at smaller, informal get-togethers. Those also generally unsuccessful ("Can anyone come out and play?" "No, go away!"), I spoke out on the subject in one of my Symposium Letters, quoting a 1962 *Twilight Zone* episode: "All kids play games, and the minute they stop, they begin to grow old." Just a kid-at-heart, I didn't want the child in *me* to grow old.

~ ~ ~ ~ ~

If people concentrated on the really important things in life, there'd be a shortage of fishing poles.
—Doug Larson

Life Goals

There comes a time, early for some, later for most, when we take stock of our lives. This involves an examination of where we've been, what we've accomplished, and desires of things yet to be experienced or attained before bidding adieu to our earthly existence.

At an early age, my thoughts and actions on career and life goals pointed in an altruistic direction—you remember—monk, then doctor. Throughout my childhood, Auntie Fran frequently mentioned that I would make a fine priest, or might one day be president of the United States. I knew that my "hands on" experience with Lizzy Rosinski disqualified me from both opportunities, although subsequent revelations of carnal indiscretions by both the Catholic clergy and numerous politicians, including U.S. presidents, would have kept those possibilities in play.

Others might dream of curing cancer, working with the elderly or infirmed, or serving the public good through the military or law enforcement. With a tidy chunk of life tucked under my belt at age 27, I noted the following achievements in my 1979 Symposium letter:

> Emptied my rack on the first turn in a game of Scrabble.

> Caught a walleye in Illinois (Lake Marie, Illinois Chain O' Lakes, May 16, 1976, 8 inches).

Made a hole-in-one (Brae Loch Country Club, Grayslake, Illinois, third hole, par 3, 140 yards, 9-iron, August 4, 1979).

Caught a musky (Cedar Lake, Illinois, June 18, 1977, 14 inches).

Attended a no-hitter (thrown by the Cubs Don Cardwell over the St. Louis Cardinals at Wrigley Field on May 15, 1960).

Caught a baseball at a major league game. (Made an outstretched, barehanded grab from the front row of the upper deck at Wrigley, fouled off the bat of Cubs utility infielder Mick Kelleher. A late 1970s Sunday afternoon game in September, a Chicago Bears away game took precedence over the broadcast of the Cubs game on WGN radio. Listening to the tape delay later that day, Cubs radio play-by-play broadcaster Vince Lloyd described my successful effort: "Nice catch, young man!")

Always striving for more, I laid out additional goals:

Catch a fish of a size significant enough to have it mounted.

Make a longer hole in one.

Catch a legal (34 inches, or thereabout) muskellunge.

What's that you say? Yes, yes, I still had some growing up to do. Adulthood ahead. Forward, full throttle!

~ ~ ~ ~ ~

Here Comes the Son

In preparing for the birth of our first child, Jo Ann enrolled us in Lamaze classes. Developed in the 1950s by a French (there's the first clue this could be trouble) obstetrician, this birthing technique popularized psychoprophylaxis. That's right—psychoprophylaxis. I'm not sure what it is, either, and it sounds insanely anti-pregnancy to me, too.

Over the weeks, we became familiar with a game plan that would minimize medical intervention and manage the pain of labor through specific methods of breathing, positioning, and massage. The tenets of Dr. Fernand "Sadomasochist"

Lamaze's natural approach also meant no anesthesia. I'll struggle through that ... but what about my wife?

As coach and provider of emotional support, my focus will be to keep *her* focused on the lessons learned. Completion of the classes will punch my ticket into the delivery room, though I question whether my emotional constitution isn't perhaps better suited to the good ol' days when the expectant father, cigar or cigarette dangling from mouth, paced the waiting room until the doctor's triumphant announcement.

During the final Lamaze class, our instructor shared letters from previous attendees, each documenting their birthing experiences from first contraction through delivery. Strange how a joyful, blessed event could read like a chapter from a Stephen King novel. The labor process of first births generally more prolonged than subsequent ones, most of the new parents detailed trials and tribulations spanning 12 to 36 hours. Upon hearing these chilling tales, I exchanged cringing glances with several of the other dads-to-be. Our wives, headlining this propagation of the species theatre in which an object the size of a bowling ball will pass through an opening the size of a quarter, seemed accepting of the daunting accounts presented. We departed the final class with "showtime," Jo Ann's due date, only a week away.

To this point, the pregnancy played out straightforward and uneventful, just the way one would hope. Good for Jo Ann, lucky for me. She retained her good-natured and even temperament throughout, largely unaffected or covertly dealing with topsy-turvy physiological changes that might easily have triggered mood swings. Morning sickness never paid her a visit.

She did admit to sensitivity to certain smells, on one occasion experiencing an upset stomach at a family function when a plate of steaming *golabki* (Polish cabbage rolls, in case you've chosen to forget) got the better of her. In her defense, even sans-child individuals of non-Polish heritage sometimes find themselves felled by the potent odor.

Perfumes and colognes also took a toll on my wife-with-child. Atop my chest of drawers, an assortment of drug store-quality aftershave scents remained capped during her pregnancy. The colorfully shaped and labeled bottles included Hai Karate and Brut (splashed on when I needed to feel like a tough guy or clear out a crowd), Canoe (radiating the balm of birch bark), and Stetson and English Leather (oozing the bouquet of an old saddle).

In this age of birthing, doctors preferred expectant mothers limit their weight gain. At the same time, they didn't impose many restrictions on the food intake of moms-to-be. Craving a BLT loaded with pork fat and mayo? Sure. A ham or salami sandwich with chips and a kosher dill from the barrel on the side? No problem. A cup of joe? Certainly. Cream and sugar with that? You bet. Jo Ann gained 13 pounds during the pregnancy, actually giving back a couple of those in the final week. Only admitting to being a bit tired, she worked until four days before delivering.

Between her nursing background and working with moms and their babies at a new job she had taken at a pediatrician's office in west suburban Elmhurst, she developed a level of comfort with the birthing process, seeing firsthand and answering questions about things she would soon be experiencing.

At 2:30 p.m. on this spring day, our department secretary (a job function soon to follow the path of the bottle boy), Jeanette, tracks me down in a conference room as I work, in solitude, on a project. No, I'm not napping, although my post-lunch doldrums plead for one. She advises that Jo Ann just telephoned (she had also called about an hour ago but didn't leave a message) and that I should return the call right away. My fingers fly across the touchtone buttons. Jo Ann answers on the first ring: "I think it's time—the contractions are ten minutes apart." The words stir a nervous excitement. "I'm on my way."

Home within half an hour, Jo Ann's relaxed demeanor helps put *me* at ease. She had just showered and suggests I do the same to prepare for the long road ahead—and I'm fairly certain she's not referring to the challenging, 15-mile ride on the cusp of afternoon rush hour traffic from Bloomingdale to Melrose Park.

Refreshed and ready we take to the road, making good time as our '75 Chevy Nova wheels down Lake Street and I-290. Two-thirds of the way there our "good time roll" slows, bumper-to-"bummer" traffic grinding to a crawl as we exit at North Avenue. Little reason for concern, I think to myself, as double-digit hours of labor await us. The worrywart within, however, sees through this feeble attempt to reassure. As we inch along, I sense the time between Jo Ann's contractions, um, contracting.

Still several miles from the hospital and with the steering wheel gripped in a stranglehold, I initiate stimulating conversation.

"Are you okay?"

"Fine."

"Are you okay?"

"Fine."

"Are you okay?"

"Fine...." Some of her responses, timed with painful contractions, eke out through gritted teeth.

I breathe a guarded sigh of relief as the pace of traffic picks up. No longer just riding the brakes, an occasional tap of the accelerator moves us along, though the speedometer never tops 25 miles per hour. Not every traffic light changes to red as we approach it. I'm feeling better ... until Jo Ann's emphatically vocalizes three little words one never wants to hear from a pregnant woman being driven to the hospital: "This is it!"

Frozen on the outside but churning, melting on the inside, I dribble, "What…" unsure of the exact words that will follow. Gratefully deprived of the opportunity to utter something foolish, Jo Ann speaks decisively: "This is it! … Your turn! Halfway into the intersection I hit the brakes and swing the car hard right, just missing the stopped vehicles in the oncoming lane.

I repeat the familiar question, "Are you okay?"

"I'm fine. Are *you*?"

"No, er, yeah, uh, fine. Sorry." After a moment to compose myself, I attempt to cover the mental lapse with a little humor, continuing, "I was lost in thought—you understand—trying to remember if the Mepps spring catalog arrived yet." The onset of another contraction swallows Jo Ann's smile. The final mile passes without further incident. We enter the hospital at 4:30 p.m.

Promptly admitted, they whisk Jo Ann away for a quick exam as I don the never-stylish trio of ill-fitting gown, surgical "shower" cap, and matching shoe covers. The assessment of her condition reveals dilation of 9 centimeters. On a scale of 10. So, that in-the-car "This is it!" almost was "it."

I overhear some of the nurses' questions and comments: "Why did you wait so long to come to the hospital?"; "We're not sure your doctor can get here in time."; and "Is that your husband looking a little green around the gills?" To this day I maintain my skin tone was a function of the fluorescent lights playing off the teal-colored scrubs.

Relieved to be in the care of the hospital's professionals, I'm further encouraged for Jo Ann—okay, and for me too—that the ordeal of labor may be shorter than longer. The nurses assure us they will check in frequently to monitor change and progress. The wall clock reads 5 p.m. We are alone, the two and one-half of us. The time has come for me to lead:

> Deep cleansing breath … inhale through nose … shoulders at ease …
> exhale all body tension through mouth … focus! …
> pant … in-breath … out-breath … 2 … 3 … 4 …
> repeat … 2 … 3 … 4 …
> inhale through nose 2 … 3 … 4 …
> exhale through mouth 2 … 3 … 4 …
> deep cleansing breath … facial muscles relaxed …
> shallow upper chest breaths … relaxed exhale with a sigh.

Okay, that felt good. Now it's time to coach Jo Ann. With the next contraction, I take hold of her hand, her grasp firm and tightening with the passing of seconds, the feeling similar to a second grade experience when childhood friend Jimmy Muscala turned my hand purple after talking me into putting it in a machinist's vise attached to his dad's workbench in their garage.

The first word of my Lamaze coaching career, the gently delivered command "focus," evokes a three-little-words response from my loving wife: "Leave me alone!" Her tone forceful and definitive, like 12-year-old Regan in *The Exorcist*, her grip threatens to turn my hand to sawdust. Before the last syllable of her command trails off, I timidly reply, "Okay, okay…" I wonder if it's too late for a Lamaze class refund. As the pain subsides, Jo Ann apologizes for her comment, explaining it's nothing personal, just that she prefers to work through the pain in her own way. I wonder if it's too late to get two refunds.

In less than an hour, we're in the delivery room: a simple, sterile, well-lit space. Dr. Hugh, having successfully negotiated rush hour traffic, tends to Jo Ann with the assistance of two nurses. I'm comfortable in my role as bystander, observing the medical crew performing like a well-oiled machine. With an "I've done this hundreds of times before" presence, Doc Hugh directs the nurses while guiding Jo Ann with confidence and empathy: "You're doing fine … push … push … push … won't be long … push … push … push …" The scene, an oxymoron of a time-stand-still whirlwind, culminates with the piercing cry of a healthy child leaving the warm, watery comfort and security of the womb to experience life's first light at 6:14 p.m. "It's a boy!"

My heart jumps to my throat as Jo Ann and I share tears combining joy, thanks, pride, and a million other good and beautiful things that words cannot adequately describe. Jo Ann cradles our son, her kiss to his forehead simultaneous with my touch to strands of his dark hair. And so, we became three.

Several days later, our baby boy now at home and peacefully asleep, Jo Ann and I stood beside his white slatted crib. The sights and sounds of his days-old world so limited, I asked, "What's going on in that little head? What could he be thinking, dreaming?"

Jo Ann smiled as she replied, "He's playing with the angels."

~ ~ ~ ~ ~

Pets – Now and Then
(It's a Short List)

Our lives are full and happy, in spite of the choice to hang with the dozen or so households in America that don't experience the joys and responsibilities of owning a dog, a cat, or some multiple of one or both. Not that we don't like them, it's just that Jo Ann is allergic to pet dander, and as for me, well, I have enough trouble taking care of myself.

Pets of the traditional four-legged mammalian variety also absent from my childhood—no dog, cat, hamster, gerbil, or other "cute" rat—I did own a couple of silver dollar-size turtles. Purchased at the local "dimestore" or "5 & 10," the now extinct F.W. Woolworth variety stores sold low-priced, low-quality items, much of its imported inventory stamped with the words "Made in Japan." Although my pet reptiles did not display those words (current imports would likely read "Made in China" and be unable to swim due to heavy lead content), their shells displayed hand-painted designs in colorful, intricate patterns, like those found on a geisha's kimono.

It should come as no surprise that I also owned an aquarium. At any given point in time, its inhabitants numbered one to ten. With a pronounced stomach and twice the size of your average, run-of-the-mill goldfish, "Goldie Gut," my first purchase, ruled the tank for many years. My next acquisition, "Spot," sported splotches of gold, silver, and white, all peppered with black speckles. Third to join, with formal ichthyologic phyla and genus nomenclature,

Oneofthoseallblackjobswithdroopyfeatheryfinsandbulgingeyes,

"Big-eyed Blackie" integrated a touch of class to the aqua-neighborhood. As I approached the tank to sprinkle the tiny fish food flakes on the water's surface, Goldie Gut alerted the others, mouthing the words, "Here comes 'Predictably Non-creative.'"

In an effort to reduce the number of times (one being too many) the tank required cleaning (a smellier, messier, more disgusting chore does not exist), I researched the subject and came up with some possible clothes-pin-off-the nose, slime-off-the-hands, fish-flying-out-of-the-net-onto-the-floor alternatives. I handed the mop and squeegee to a couple of scavengers, hoping the indiscriminating palates of a snail and mini-catfish would do the trick. Unfortunately, "Whiskers" and his escargot buddy didn't get the job done. Perhaps Whiskers might have fared better with the name "Hoover" or "Eureka."

When the summer carnival arrived, Ping-pong ball fishing brought additional residents to the tank. With overcrowding an issue, I initiated a major relocation. A large, blue plastic child's wading pool, set up in the basement, became their new home. Its size, location, and immobility made cleaning it impossible. With an unpleasant odor slowly building over the months, my parents advised me that slumlording would not be tolerated, and failure to promptly rehabilitate my fish ghetto would result in a fish "ghettaway." In spite of the clear message, I failed to act. The aquatic skid row, like boxes of my baseball cards, mysteriously disappeared during the annual spring cleaning ritual.

~ ~ ~ ~ ~

Motorola - The 1980s

In 1980, I receive my third promotion, this one to the position of contract administrator for federal government customers in the central United States. Credit worthiness not an issue, detailed review of purchase "delivery orders" is necessary to ensure they comply with the pre-negotiated General Services Administration contract. With that verified, collecting the money presents the greater challenge. Oh, it's there. It's always there. Somewhere. Therein lies the rub: the delicate, tedious, and frustrating process of unwinding government "red tape" to pry it free. Lucky for me, I'm quite good at it.

As the recipient of another stellar performance review, the $500 merit increase that boosts my annual salary to $14,500 disappoints. My voiced displeasure falls on deaf ears. Perhaps it's time to let the Motorola logo "batwings" fly off into the sunset. Resumé prepared, I begin perusing want ads in pursuit of more gainful employment.

A maker of traffic counters and heavy-duty commercial weighing devices, Streeter Amet posts a position for a credit manager in the Sunday *Chicago Tribune*. I apply, and after several interviews, receive an offer with a starting salary of $16,000. Nearly as important as the higher wage, Streeter Amet is located in Grayslake. Thirty-five miles from our Bloomingdale home, I envision and welcome the possibility of a move north, to the town that Larry still calls home. And just as good, this puts me closer to the many fishing lakes of our childhood, ones that we continue to angle.

First thing on a Monday morning, I enter the office of the Motorola controller to whom I report, handing him my letter of resignation that includes the provision of two week's notice. Dick, a former Marine officer who served in the Vietnam conflict and wears a hearing aid as a result, appears momentarily dumbfounded. A second later, as if flipping a switch, he calmly asks, "Are you sure this is what you want to do?"

"I'd prefer not to. But under the circumstances, I feel as if I have no choice. You know I wasn't happy about my raise, and I've searched out an opportunity that pays more money."

"Things are tight at the moment, but let me see if there's anything I can do."

On Wednesday he calls me into his office. "I took this up my chain of command and also talked to Vince in Fed finance, and Jim, the sales manager you support. We're all interested in having you stay. We can offer another thousand dollars to put you at $15,500. I don't know what your outside offer is, but hopefully this will be enough to allow you to stay with us."

"It's not as much, but it gives me something to consider. I'm not ungrateful for your effort, but are you sure that's the best you can do?"

"We turned over every stone. I'm certain that's it."

"Okay, thanks. I'll get back to you by the end of the week."

Two days (and nights) of hell follow—gut-wrenching, anxiety-laden, have-to-make-a-career-altering-decision days of hell. Playing in my head, I hear the crowing voice of a boxing announcer, "In this corna', your six years invested in an employee-friendly company, in business since 1928, known for cutting-edge technology, ranking numba' 125 on the Fortune 500 list, Mo…to…rrrola! And in this corna', for 500 bucks a year more, a maker of scales for whales, but closa' to your closest buddy *and* your beloved lakes, Strrr…eee…ter A…met!

In a decision surprising even myself, I opt for Motorola, choosing against money, closer proximity to my cousin-brother, and our hallowed fishing grounds. The choice displays wisdom and maturity beyond my 28 years, along with a sizeable chunk of luck. Streeter Amet shutters its facility soon thereafter.

In 1981, I earn another promotion, this one to the position of financial analyst for the Area B service business for the Midwestern territory. With that position currently not filled in the Southeast and only days on the new job, my boss volunteers me to assist with the preparation of 1982 budgets for the company-owned service centers in Area E.

The Business Trip, Late Summer 1981

United 876	27Jul81	Mon	Fr: Chicago 8:55A	To: Tampa 12:18P

As I arrive at O'Hare for my weeklong trip southeast, it's October in July: 60 degrees under heavy overcast. What a great day to be jigging a drop-off for walleye. Instead, I have to settle for a fish sandwich at 30,000 feet.

The odyssey begins in Tampa. Temperature 95. Humidity 95%. Motorola manager Wes picks me up and recommends I shed the three-piece suit if I plan to survive. Okay. And I'll loosen the tie, too. Limber up those fingers. I'm going to have an affair with my calculator this week.

    Surface   Fr: Tampa   To: Orlando

At the midpoint of the one and one-half hour drive we stop at a Southern-quaint standalone eatery on a rural stretch of road. A pair of crudely drawn strawberries anchor both ends of red letters scripted on a white background, the sign above the full-glass door identifying "Jerry's Diner." A row of tables lines the windows, opposite a counter that runs the length of the interior. Wooden barstools, mostly empty at the time of our mid-afternoon visit, snug up to it. Standing fans in the two front corners circulate the warm, grease-filled air that escapes from the cooking area behind the counter. I take a pass on the chicken fried steak, hominy grits, and biscuits and gravy, opting for giant triangle of the highly recommended strawberry pie. "Florida's the strawberry capitol of the world, you know." Can't say that I did. On to Orlando, another Service Center and the home of Disney World. I won't see it though. Only more numbers to make me "Goofy."

    Republic Air 470   28Jul81   Tue   Fr: Orlando   To: Ft. Lauderdale
                                                            4:00P   4:42P

Fort Lauderdale—the "Venice of America." Canals. Loaded with bass as big as your arm: 8-, 9-, 10-, 12-pounders. Biggest one local manager Tommy ever caught? 7 pounds. Lots of 4- and 5-pounders, too. Too bad I won't have a shot at 'em. The only numbers I see are headcount, payroll, revenues, expenses and margins, attempting to put them together in a manner that will make management smile.

"There's a Motorola production facility for portable and paging products here." (I know.) "Some call the plant the Magic Kingdom. Others call it the Tragic Kingdom."

    Eastern 796   29Jul81   Wed   Fr: Ft. Lauderdale   To: Atlanta
                                                 4:10P   5:49P

This flight does its best to put the "hospital" in southern "hospitality." The slow-moving weather front that passed through Chicago on Monday must have reached Atlanta at 5:45 p.m. today. Flashing veins of light streak through pulsing gray-black cloud pillows that smother the aircraft. Stomach-upside-down turbulence. I can hear it now: "We interrupt our regular programming for this news bulletin. Eastern Airlines flight 796, en route from Fort Lauderdale to Atlanta, crashed three miles from the Atlanta airport. Against virtually impossible odds the plane was struck by lightning, disintegrating in midair." The wild ride concludes. The metal bird prevails.

Midweek, half way home. I miss my wife and baby. He's hardly a baby, more a little boy now, walkin' and talkin' to beat the band.

    Republic Air 392   30Jul81   Thurs Fr: Atlanta To: Mobile
                                                 12:05P   1:10P

    More crass than class, recently created Republic Airlines merges the worst parts of Southern and North Central. No assigned seats. Back three rows off limits because the john overflowed, soaking the carpeting. Wings vibrate like they need to flap to fly. Upon arrival, my suitcase sports a 3-inch gash as a souvenir of the flight.

    Dilapidated Mobile screams for urban renewal: buildings in various states of disrepair with crumbling facades, missing bricks, and cracked or boarded windows; shopping cart-pushing homeless; cardboard, newspaper pages, and Styrofoam food and drink containers poked and prodded by the gulf breeze, rolling from here to nowhere like tumbleweed through a ghost town. Keep cranking out those numbers. I'd rather be cranking in crankbaits. Thursday evening score two-for-one "happy hour" at the Ramada Inn lounge with Motorolans Bob and Bill. Nothing personal, (good ol') boys, but "unhappy hour" better describes. Oh, to have Larry, Chuck, and Terry here for another south of the Mason-Dixon Line Symposium. Back to the Howard Johnson, the iconic motor lodge with orange roofs, weathervanes atop cupolas, and gaggingly bad restaurant food. Room décor is standard with thick, insulated, gold fabric drapes, a double bed draped with a same-color comforter, and a dresser topped by a 19-inch color TV. Cable TV. With WGN. I never thought I'd be so happy to see Chicago weatherman Tom Skilling spouting his customary "better suited to a student preparing a doctoral thesis in meteorology" in-depth analysis of weather minutia.

    Republic Air 402   31Jul81   Fri   Fr: Mobile To: Chicago
                                               2:10P   5:20P

    What? A stop in where? Gulfport-Biloxi? Don't they know I want to get home, *need* to get home? Okay, back in the air. I've lived a month this week. It's almost over. Catnap. Wakened by the voice of the pilot, there it is—I see it! Ant-cars move in steady streams, in all directions, on the grid of streets radiating south, west, and north. Closer. Buildings—steel, masonry, and glass—stretch to the sky, their height increasing as they approach the southwest curve of the big, blue water that disappears into the eastern horizon. Descending. Home at last. Touch down. Sweet home, Chicago.

~ ~ ~ ~ ~

The early 1980s bring about the relocation of the Mighty "B" Barracudas from Elk Grove Village to a white, two-story structure in Schaumburg, "1309." All buildings on the corporate campus, having Algonquin Road addresses, are simply referred to by their number. The move puts an end to lunches at Frankie's Two, but 1309 shares a cafeteria with the attached 1313 parts distribution facility. Rich, one of only a few "barracudas" that relocates to a different facility, necessitates a change in my dining companions. Depending on the day, my brown bag and I make our way to the caf to break bread with a variety of co-workers from multiple disciplines. I miss the sports chatter, conversations now increasingly business-related.

Late in the afternoon, on a Friday in September of 1982, I receive a telephone call from my boss, Mike, an assistant controller. "Ed, can you swing by my office before you head home today."

Most communication with him easily transacted over the phone, this request, and its timing, raise concern. "Sure. What's going on?"

"I'll tell you when you get here. I just need to see you today."

He *needs* to see me? *Today? At quittin' time on a Friday?* This can't be good. The brief conversation weighing on my mind, I hastily close up shop, scooping up and locking away the papers and folders I'd been working on. His hard-wall office in the 1301 building resides across a lengthy parking lot from my cubicle in 1309. The five-minute walk, followed by the ride up the elevator to Mike's fourth floor office, drags with the feel of five hours. His greeting does nothing to allay my fears. "Come on in ... and close the door." Seated behind his beige sheet metal desk topped with faux mahogany, I squirm into the uncomfortable plastic seat of his guest chair. Eye contact established, I nearly drain the room of oxygen with a deep breath before he speaks.

"I hate to be the bearer of bad news, but the service finance job, across all the area offices, is being eliminated." Even though I had anticipated the worst, the words still stun me. Mike continues, "We've got a month to try and get you slotted somewhere else, and some of the area service managers may try to make room for you and your counterparts under their budgets. I haven't talked to Virgil yet, but he knows how valuable you are to his organization, so hopefully that will pan out."

Instead of heading for home I decide to return to 1309 on the chance that Virgil hasn't yet left the office. Short and slight of build with a southern accent true to his Kentucky roots, Virgil boasts a lifetime in the service industry, thirty of his years with Motorola, most of those in service management. I've provided financial support to his business for several years, and we've developed a good working relationship.

Now past 5 p.m., I reenter the eerily quiet 1309, most of the workers on the way to beginning their weekend plans. Walking up to the second floor, I see his closed door from the top of the stairs, indicating he has also departed. This disappointment adds to the momentum of events rolling uncontrollably downhill and the prospect of an uncomfortable, stomach-churning weekend. Next to his office, however, an open door and light visible in the office of his right-hand man, John, provides a glimmer of hope. As I approach the doorway, I find him talking on the phone, in a subdued tone. He signals me to come in and sit down. Numb with the late afternoon's goings-on, I gaze out the window behind him, my spirit a void matching the almost empty parking lot. His conversation concludes.

Like Virgil, John is also a long-tenured Motorolan, though his experience encompasses both service and sales. His powerful build and always well-groomed, wavy light brown hair and moustache exude a commanding and professional presence. After hanging up the phone, he stares across his neat-as-a-pin desk with steely eyes behind gold, wire-rimmed glasses. Expressionless, he offers no further greeting, his leathery voice jumping directly to the matter at hand. "I spoke with Mike earlier and just finished a discussion with Virgil." My heart skips multiple beats during an extended, pregnant pause. The corners of his mouth turn up slightly as he continues, "You're an important part of our team and we'd like you to stay on and continue to work for us under the title of program manager. You'll report to Virgil with no change to your salary, duties, or responsibilities."

Yes! I'll have a good weekend, and you and Virgil do the same!

This change encompasses the best of two worlds: enjoying the day-to-day tasks without the formal finance reporting structure and, on a higher level, continued employment. In 1984, I celebrate 10 years of tenure and gain membership in the Service Club. The remainder of the decade proceeds swimmingly. Although Virgil never provides feedback regarding my work, no news is good news. I likely set a corporate record with no performance reviews for seven consecutive years, but that's okay. With annual salary increases continuing to appear in my paycheck and never a negative comment coming my way, I'm perfectly fine with foregoing the formalities.

The Business Meeting
Super 8 Motel, Fort Mitchell, Kentucky

It is the morning of the second (and final) day of an informal, off-campus meeting hosted by the Area Service Operations Management team, the group to which I provide administrative and financial support. "Over-served" yesterday evening begets oversleeping. Readying myself at a frantic pace, my mind races as I shower, "grasping at straws" to concoct a reasonable excuse for such out of character (and first-ever) tardiness.

Almost an hour late, good-natured jeers greet my arrival. As the comments subside, the comfort of my relationship with managers and other team members allows me to present, with apologies to David Letterman, "15 Reasons Why I am Late":

15. No wake-up call received
14. Didn't arrange for wake-up call
13. Alarm did not go off
12. Didn't set alarm
11. Couldn't find the meeting room
10. Long delay at front desk checking out
9. Was on the phone with broker rearranging finances to cover yesterday evening's billiard losses
8. Wanted to be "fashionably late," following in footsteps of chronic offender and former boss Sal
7. Thought we were on "Pacific Time"
6. Spent too much time hugging "My Old Kentucky (Porcelain) Home"
5. Had a customer visit
4. Couldn't locate eyeballs and stomach
3. "Evil Twin" locked me in my room
2. Floor was moving in the wrong direction
1. Spent too much time devising reasons why I was late

Horse Crap

Virgil and John make plans for the annual business review and budget "scrubs" at a rural resort in the northwest corner of Illinois. Unlike most of the corn and soybean flatlands that dominate the upper two-thirds of the state, this area escaped the glacial steamroller that grounded to a halt at its doorstep 10,000 years ago, leaving rocky, hilly, and forested terrain with elevations that allow views 10 to 15 miles north to Wisconsin and west to Iowa.

Meetings such as these typically include a recreational activity. Depending on location it could be golf, a major league baseball game, or fishing. The agenda for this gathering lists a late-afternoon-into-the-evening time slot for the event, but fails to detail it. Cleverly guised hints lead us to believe we'll be savoring a fine meal during a leisurely, paddlewheel cruise on the nearby

Mississippi River. I plan to enjoy it to the fullest and promise myself I won't even ask about trolling a line.

As our second day of meetings concludes, we pile into vehicles and follow the leader to our destination. After passing a stretch of post-and-rail paddock fencing, my heart sinks as we turn beneath a rough-hewn, woodcut sign that reads, "Ponderosa Riding Center." In the name of Mr. Ed, say it ain't so! The only horses I've ever ridden were those that pumped and whirled on the merry-go-round at the St. Hedwig school carnival and Riverview (less than two miles from our Dickens Avenue home), a 74-acre amusement park that entertained and thrilled Chicagoans from 1904 to 1967. My vehicle partners, like me city born and bred, share my concern and make light of our plight.

"Maybe the folks from the Elmer's factory will be making a pickup soon."

"Or McDonald's…"

No way out, we're lassoed. And, they tell us it's an overnighter. Horse crap!

The trail bosses parade the horses, one by one, from the stable into the corral. As each saunters into daylight, one from our group of 15 Roy Rogers rookies (we're all now wearing plastic cowboy hats) mounts his chosen steed. Each sinewy beast seemingly larger than the last, I have serious concerns about effectively relinquishing control of my physical and psychological well-being to a half-ton animal with a brain the size of a walnut. I hang back, waiting for a more manageable version to emerge—maybe a subcompact, like the Ford Pinto.

Waiting … is this the one? Massive like the Trojan horse, I can almost hear the walnut rattling around as he whips his noggin from side to side. Pass. How about the next? Looking good … beautiful chestnut coat with white go-go boots. Ready to make my move, he rolls back his lips and exposes a set of choppers, sneering my way with a crazed grin. No. Waiting…. Next, a buckskin dressage wannabe swishes its tail like a cheerleader's pom-pom, cantering forward at a disturbing angle like a car driving down the road with a bent frame. Uh-uh. *Still* waiting…. The number of rides dwindles. The next, a salt and pepper gray looks promising. Until I spot a thin stream of drool. Probably rabid. Nay. Unable to pull the trigger with the simple movement of steps forward during the introductory procession, I'm the only buckaroo left with my feet still on the ground. The next ride is mine. Ready or not, here he comes.

The gamble doesn't pay off. It's a bad roll of the Dice—my steed's name. This burly boy's got muscles on top of muscles. Why is he leering at me, giving me the "hairy eyeball?" Why is he shaking his head? Why is he snorting? Even his paint job, white splotched with cowpie brown, shouts "Renegade!" Frozen,

I hear a catcall from someone in our group: "Hey, Annie Oakley, sometime today."

Spurred on by my companions, I recall the words of the "Duke," John Wayne, when he drawled, "Courage is being scared to death—and saddling up anyway." One of the three cowhands that will accompany us gets me settled "behind the wheel," hands me the leather "keys" attached to the bit, and delivers a brief driver's ed primer: left turn, pull on the left rein; right turn, pull on the right rein; stop, pull on both reins, and, if necessary, supplement with a "Whoa!" Simple enough. Though I'd rather mount a fish than a horse, I'm on board. Hopefully Dice won't roll craps. Or me.

The line of equines and their burden of urban cowboy neophytes begins to lumber forward. Puffs of dust rise as the clip-clopping hoofs smack the dirt trail in a rhythmic cadence. Unlikely partners, Dice and I form the tail of the snake that winds through the undulating hills.

Ten minutes into the journey, our caravan of ambling equids stops along a slight incline in the pastoral terrain. Rush hour in the middle of nowhere? A red light at the O.K. Corral? A wagon train funeral procession with the right of way? A thicket of trees borders our left, and a verdant prairie extends to our right for as far as the eye can see. Moments into our standstill, Dice's muscular caboose begins swaying like a shark's tail—like a great white picking up the scent of chum. "Eeeeasy boy," I whisper, hoping to keep him in neutral gear, the dual purpose words uttered more for my peace of mind than to comfort the thousand-pound beast beneath me. "Eeeeasy, b..." Dice bolts from the line like Secretariat at Churchill Downs.

"Whoa!" My call pierces every molecule of air hovering in the moments-earlier serene meadow. "Whoa!"

What the hell!?, I think.

"Whoa!" I shout.

I pull on the reins. To no avail. Where's the goddamn brake pedal?

"Whoa!" I plead.

Where the hell's the emergency brake?

"Whoa!" Holding on for dear life, I'm bouncing on and off the saddle like a pogo stick on fast-forward. My polystyrene Stetson goes flying.

"Whoa!" With every ounce of adrenalized strength and energy I can muster I strain on the leather reins, stretching them like pulled taffy. Rumbling Dice does not respond.

Now more than a hundred yards since breaking rank, the mane of this equine-gone-crazy undulates beneath his gyrating bobblehead like Fabio's hair whipping in the breeze on the cover of a romance novel. My mind races with thoughts matching our runaway speed:

> I've got the horse's ass trophy locked up—the outing's organizers felt certain a mishap worthy of special recognition would unfold with a hayseed group of this size.
>
> The only time, ever again, I want to hear the word "horsepower" is in the discussion of outboard motors.
>
> Time to bail before we reach Wisconsin.

"Whoa, you son of a …" No dice. The final word of my impassioned howl dissipates as I launch myself from this locomotive, this living, breathing runaway iron horse. Arms outstretched, my flight more "Pooperman" than Superman, I momentarily suspend in mid-air at the peak of my voluntary dismount that angles up and out at a 45-degree angle, away from the raging hoofs. In slow-motion descent, I tuck my right shoulder and barrel roll into the down comforter of tallgrass prairie that pillows my body and soothes my embarrassment. With apologies to the Rolling Stones—roll me, tumblin' from Dice.

The gymnastic maneuver executed in one continuous motion, I pop to my feet, sticking the landing like 14-year-old Nadia Comaneci concluding her perfect "10" routine on the uneven bars at the '76 Olympics. My head and shoulders visible above the golden stalks, a quick inventory reveals all body parts intact. Even my jeans retain their original, unsoiled condition. With only a bruised ego, I look skyward, arms raised above my head to signal a safe landing. Across the hushed prairie, whistles and applauds begin drifting my way from still-in-line companions recognizing an unwitting novice stuntman's job well done.

Two of the trail bosses gallop a beeline, one in pursuit of rider-less Dice, the other hoping to find me whole, toward the goal of avoiding a seven-figure lawsuit. Successful on both counts, I'm asked if I'd like to call it a day and return to the stable. Offering as an alternative his jet black mare, Bea, one of the bosses speaks with confidence about her gentle demeanor and assures me the remainder of the journey will be incident free.

Hopeful this won't be another night-"mare," and cognizant of the aphorism, "Get back on the horse that threw you (or in this case, from which you bailed)," okay, it'll be Bea and me. Guided by our ranching attendant, we mosey back to the end of the queue and the remainder of our journey resumes.

It's steady as she goes. Until Bea makes several unscheduled pauses to relieve herself, or pluck a snack from bushes, or stop for no apparent reason, I guess, just because she can. I become uneasy as the rest of the line separates from us, and then increasingly tense as our pace quickens as we catch up. Why me?

Then, a more serious concern mushrooms when she begins butting her nose onto the backside of the horse ahead of us. With *this* malfunction also not covered in the lesson plan and no clue about how to fix it, my heart stops when the annoyed bronco rears up and delivers a twin-hoofed kick to Bea's jaw. NO! Unfazed like a heavyweight boxer taking an opponent's best punch (and to my great relief), the big girl just keeps plodding along.

From time to time, the riders in front of me glance back to check on my well-being, acknowledging my fortuitousness with some combination of a nod, a smile, or a tip of their hat. Chugging along, chugging along, chugging along, two more agonizing hours pass before we reach the terminus, a plateau offering long, 360-degree country views. A gingerly negotiated dismount and the open-air aesthetics bring welcome relief to this now-owner of a saddle sore the size of Wyoming. Steak n taters grilled up by the hired hands and a sunset enjoyed from the heights inject a bit more distance from the memory of the afternoon's events as day fades to dusk. Tummy full, eyes closed and with cool night air descending upon us, visions of a hot shower and soft mattress trot through my head. A sleeping bag tossed at my feet spurs a rude awakening.

Low-level discomfort now coursing through my body with every movement, I rise to survey the area, noting some members of our group have already turned in, strewn across the area like battlefield corpses at Gettysburg. I don't know where they've hitched our fleet of horses; they're outside my line of sight and that's just fine with me. My weary arms grab the bed-in-a-bag. I stumble about in the low light before finding a plot of grass near some exposed, smooth-slate bedrock. Fumbling with the unwieldy zippered blanket, I manage to tuck myself in, a human burrito of sorts.

Lying on my back, I stare into the starry night. Eyes closed, the unnerving events of the day come alive again. Eyes open. Let's try counting the stars. Yes. Yes, like sheep jumping over a fence. One … two … three…. Stupid! How are you going to fall asleep with your eyes open? But if your eyes are closed, you can't see the stars to count them. Damn it. Eyes closed. Brrrr, it's getting nippy out here. What if a timber rattler is looking for a warm place to hole-up for the night?" Eyes *wide* open. Crap. Horse crap! Star light, star bright, please keep this sleeping bag tight tonight. Eyes closed.

Seconds later, a neigh-like laughter begins lancing the still night air. Eyes open. Are those words I'm hearing, intertwined with the sounds of the equine? Can it be? Sure it can. It's that S.O.B. Dice, and Bea, likely yucking it up at my expense.

"That poor greenhorn's about as green as they come," Bea whinnies.

Dice, obviously happy with the wild ride, snorts, "When my turbo kicked in, could you actually see his face turn green?"

"White, actually. As white as the Lone Ranger's hat. How far were you going to take him?"

"Ever heard of Nevada's Mustang Ranch? I spent some time in that area as a young stud. It's a world-class place for horsing around."

"I'm surprised your tenderfoot bailed before you could turn him into Hobble-along Cassidy."

"He was as good as anybody to pay the price. I'm still ticked off about Trigger getting stuffed." Final squeals, then silence.

Bastards. I wish this had been a fishing outing. A fish never laughed at me. Well, maybe they did, but not as far as I know. An afternoon at the casino would've been okay too—blackjack ... roulette ... shooting dice. Yeah, shooting Dice... Sometime closer to dawn than dusk, I fall asleep. An hour or two of shuteye begins with the whispered words, "John Wayne can kiss my ass…"

A forced smile before an unlucky roll of(f) Dice.

~ ~ ~ ~ ~

During the decade of the 1980s, major corporations address the growing concern (and reality) of global terrorism by increasing security measures. As a high profile manufacturer of sophisticated electronics equipment, Motorola acts accordingly by adding gated guard stations to the corporate campus entrances. Guards also man the lobbies of every building, though the security they provide ranks with what one might expect from Barney Fife, the milquetoast deputy from Mayberry.

As time and technology march on, so do the tools of the office trade. Deep, wide, and the weight of a boat anchor, a hulking CRT (cathode ray tube) monitor reduces everyone's four-foot desk space by one-third. A CPU (central processing unit) computer "tower," the size of three stacked tackle boxes, does the same for foot space below. Keyboards either pull out from trays mounted beneath the desks, or rest on top of them. And with my telephone, Casio L.E.D. readout roll-tape calculator, and Swingline stapler, actual working space shrinks to "minimal." On the positive side, the computerized information sends the tree-killing green-bar report the way of the abacus. One thing that doesn't change is the modular furniture, though it does sport a lighter, more upbeat shade of gray.

On the board that borders the back of my desk, lit by fluorescent tubes beneath the upper shelf, multi-colored push-pins fasten a telephone list with frequently called business numbers, a Motorola financial calendar with report due dates and month-end closing dates highlighted, and a pair of single panel cartoons:

> *Belvedere*: At the lake, with the caption, "So you didn't catch any fish—so what? At least nobody can accuse you of disrupting the ecological balance."

And,

> *The Far Side*: Two fishermen in a boat with nuclear clouds mushrooming in the background, with the caption, "I'll tell you what this means, Norm, no size restrictions and screw the limit."

The shelf above my desk holds a few binders with budgets and other monthly reports, an NIU Huskies logo golf ball, and three coffee mugs that read: "Work is just something I do between fishing trips"; "I fish, therefore I am"; and "A bad day fishing beats a good day working." (Of course it's common knowledge that there is no such thing as a bad day fishing. The catching might be bad, but the fishing? No, fishing is always fine.)

In the mid-1980s, Motorola develops a business management strategy called Six Sigma, a multi-faceted problem solving technique to improve quality by reducing defects and the cost of production. Through continuous improvement, the process drives toward the statistical goal of six sigma, that number representing a minimal 3.4 defects per million. (I often feel like six sigma also represents my odds of someday catching a trophy musky.) To generate employee involvement and buy-in, the company encourages the assemblage of teams to develop projects for a Total Customer Satisfaction competition. Several rounds of presentations send the top performers to the finals, held in Hawaii. I participate on a successful team, our project developing a process to automate add-on equipment to existing customer service agreements. While some of the statistical and technically detailed concepts of the Six Sigma process escape me, I continuously remind the team that indeed, six sigma is certainly better than five, or four, or three.... In our Aloha State presentation, my teammates astutely assign me the task of manually flipping the overhead projector transparencies. My execution flawless, our project still only garners a silver medal in the administrative category of the competition. As a second, more significant disappointment, the tightly packed meeting agenda does not allow time for deep sea fishing.

~~~~~

WARNING!

To those of you who are not fifth-grade boys and may be offended by "potty" humor, please skip over the "When Nature Calls" section that follows and proceed to page 202.

When Nature Calls

In response to increasing competition from the Pacific rim, the corporation begins watching its pennies and before too long, squeezing the beard hairs out of poor Mr. Lincoln. One of the first casualties, the corporate recreation department sheds employees and miscellaneous costs associated with on-campus programs and sports leagues. Thus, mothballed is the opportunity to best my .558 batting average as a member of the Area B Cheap Thrills 16-inch softball team that recorded an 18-4 record in its final year. As a result of the rec department dissolution, informal employee networks pick up the slack for lost contacts resulting from the corporate cost-cutting hatchet.

Those of us bent to the outdoors revel in the calls of nature, among them the screech of the hawk, the howl of the coyote, and the cry of the loon (that piercing pitch eerily similar to the corporate manager who just missed a performance goal). And, similar to the employee need to follow the directives of a superior, so too we find ourselves subservient to nature, that demanding Mother.

It's May 1986, and at least a year since I last spoke to Carl, an accountant by schooling and trade. With his depth of knowledge and 6-foot 4-inch frame, he projects a commanding presence, someone to look up to, on several levels. Although we both labor for Motorola, our careers veer in divergent paths. We worked together in Area B finance a number of years ago, concurrently beginning pursuit of our MBAs through the extension program of my alma mater, Northern Illinois University. By the time Carl receives his degree, I need to complete eight courses in one semester or lose eligibility. In a bold preemptive move, I exit the program before they boot me out.

A business question necessitates my call to Carl. Seconds later, the issue handled, the conversation turns to the important matter of a fishing outing. A relative late-comer to the pleasures of the sport, Carl recently purchased a boat and seeks to satisfy his enthusiasm with any opportunity to float it on a body of water. With the Memorial Day weekend in the offing, Saturday looks good for both of us. With past success and knowledge of its waters, I suggest and we agree on southern Wisconsin's Silver Lake. We plan to target bass but know that walleye, northern pike, and, stocked some five years earlier, the mighty muskellunge also roam its depths.

Typical of the night before a fishing outing, the anticipation of the day and fear of oversleeping makes falling asleep a formidable chore. After finally drifting asleep, the piercing buzz of my alarm clock scares me awake at 3 a.m.

A cranium filled with cobwebs convinces me only minutes have passed since dropping off into dreamland. The early start fouls my body clock. Out of sync, I shower and shave, but cannot complete the third leg of man's "Three S" morning ritual.

We meet in the Motorola parking lot at 4 a.m., where I transfer my fishing gear into Carl's 16-foot Tracker. Before hopping onto Route 53, we swing into the White Hen Pantry on Algonquin Road, just east of the campus. I would normally fill a Styrofoam tumbler to the brim with hot java and grab a "nutritious" breakfast foodstuff like a Hostess Twinkie, Suzy Q, or Fruit Pie, but because of the early hour and the gurgles roiling my digestive tract I take a pass.

Back into the car, up "53," and exiting on Route 12, the tummy rumbles continue. Miles pass slowly. Every stoplight turns red as we approach, slowing our progress and giving me additional time to dwell on my disconcerting circumstances. The blender that is my stomach revs at higher speed. Carl makes small talk as I force one-word responses through clenched teeth.

Pressure builds, brewing a colonic storm of Biblical proportion. To relax my puckering muscles will unleash a tawny sea unseen since the mighty Fox River overflowed her banks during the spring floods. Misery undulates in labor-like waves of birthing. Hoping to finally cash in on the money spent, I recall the Lamaze techniques not utilized during Eddie's birth years earlier. I inhale short, controlled drinks of air under my breath in an attempt to hide my discomfort. An easing of the sphincter will springboard an immediate dilation to ten centimeters.

Unexpectedly, as if released from the grip of a boa constrictor, the spasms mercifully subside. Aside from a bit of subdued squirming, I believe I have successfully hidden my plight from Carl. Ah, sweet serenity. Responses to questions begin to flow in complete sentences. In an ironic twist, we approach a Gas for Less station. I consider requesting a stop but believing the danger has passed, elect to press on.

Big mistake. Less than a mile down the road, distress returns—with a vengeance. The brown demon's plot to escape reinvigorated, my intestines twist and squeeze with the intensity of wringing the last drop of moisture from a dishrag. The mushy monster plunges his way to the edge of my nether region, where he stands ready to ignite a fuse that will unleash energy with a force last seen during a-bomb testing. Why, oh why didn't I request we stop? Too proud? Too stupid? Too interested in wanting to arrive at the lake a few minutes sooner, to cram a few extra casts into the day? Foolish, misguided, or both, I pay the price: "excretiating," feet-through-the-floorboards pain.

We near Route 120. Can it be? Do those colorful backlit letters and numbers, bright against the still-dark early morning sky, signal another gas station up ahead? My words eek out in muffled gasps. "Carl ... I think ... I need ... to make ... a ... pit stop." As our rig turns into the parking area, I bolt out the door before we roll to a stop. Lock-kneed, I race around the building in search of a restroom. A wall-mounted air pump, its hose coiled and kinked like my intestines, stands next to a single, unmarked door. Hopeful it represents the gateway to salvation, I grab the knob and turn. Attempt to turn. Unmoving, it is locked. I am going to die.

With a high speed Charlie Chaplin gait, I waddle back to the front of the building and burst through the front door. Vision clouding, I babble at the nameless, faceless, genderless clerk in a single breath, " 'scuse . me . do . you . have . a . restroom?"

"Uhhhh . . . . yeah . . . . it's . . . . (I am one second away from diving across the counter and grabbing him-her-it by the collar to shake the words loose) . . . . outside, around the back."

Fragile consciousness in jeopardy, I mutter, "It's locked...."

After fumbling beneath the counter for what seems like an eternity, the clerk tosses a key across the counter. I grab it and exit with haste. Fearful of creating a gingerpoop trail, I retrace my steps to the side door with the speed of a 200-horse outboard pushing a 14-foot johnboat. After inserting the key I shoulder the door, slam it shut, and push in the locking button. In a swift, seamless, singular motion I unsnap, unzip, sit, and release an eruption with a force and volume not experienced since Mount Vesuvius buried Pompeii. The horrendous buildup, leading to a climax lasting only seconds, transforms to a bizarre bliss. It's over. If I hadn't given up smoking, it'd be time to light one up.

Now, only the clean-up remains, my bottom splashed with the repugnant reminder of an event I'd prefer to forget. My head, momentarily bowed in reverent thanks, slowly rises in search of Charmin, or its low-cost, sandpaper equivalent. A glance to the left draws a blank. I look right—nothing. Head now on a swivel and eyes darting in every direction, a thorough examination of the room—on and around the tank, sink, and walls—comes up empty. Reserved panic. Am I the star in some kind of tasteless *Candid Camera* episode? Is that filthy mirror a two-way, with the androgynous clerk and a gathering of customers enjoying an early morning guffaw at my expense? What now?

With pants still around ankles, I shuffle over to the waste can. Evidence suggests I am not the first to experience this dilemma, though perhaps the first today. The E. Coli clan breeds, building an impressive empire in the dreary, disgusting depths. Against better judgment but with no viable alternative (my long-nose pliers tucked away in my tackle box), I am forced to go in. Barehanded.

With the delicate precision of a neurosurgeon navigating nerves near a spinal column, I lightly grip, with the tip of thumb and index finger, scraps of paper and "whatever," each carefully removed and examined. Several small shreds appear salvageable, but lack the volume needed to accomplish the task at hand. Digging deeper, through layers "nasty," and "gross," I hold my breath to keep the wretched microbes from setting up shop in my lungs. As my oxygen supply depletes, I turn my head away from the vile container, exhaling, then quickly inhaling a new burst of air, though my earlier "contribution" in the confined space has left a no-rose-garden funk of its own. Hope dwindles as the bottom of the can nears. On the brink of defeat and dripping with equal parts diarrhea and despair, I unearth the holy grail.

The archaeological find sends my spirit soaring, an emotional high likely last matched with the discovery of King Tut's tomb. Pulling upward, slowly, to minimize the disturbance of the contagion about it, a white plastic bag with the red K-Mart logo clears the rim of the can. Though flimsy and non-absorbent, I turn it inside out, revealing a clean surface at least one square foot in size. (In my euphoria, I envision a television commercial with a young, smiling employee, in full "blue light" garb, extolling the benefits of shopping at K-Mart, closing with "...and our handy, reusable bags can double as toilet paper too!") Messy clean up completed, with handkerchief-turned-washcloth sacrificed for final touch-up, it's back to the car and we're on our way.

My luck exhausted (thankfully and without regret) on exhuming the unlikely object of a retail shopping bag, I come up empty in my pursuit of largemouth bass, and for that matter, every other species that swims in Silver Lake. Carl, however, finds himself a fine fishing hole. While pursuing bass, he scores 18-, 22-, 25-, and 35-inch muskies. He lets them all go—but I believe my "release" was the most gratifying of the day.

~ ~ ~ ~ ~

Motorola - The 1990s
Back to Business

The corporate tide continues its slide in the 1990s. On a personal level, unable to leave well enough alone, management shuffles the deck and promotes me (kicking and screaming inside) back to a position with the finance pukes. Let the ugliness begin. Past the 15-year mark in the company's employ, I pocket a fourth week of vacation. Too bad the ongoing, oppressive demands of the job will not allow me to put them all in play. With global competition ramping up, cost-cutting and consolidations begin as territories merge and offices (including Houston!) close. The work performed at those shuttered locations doesn't go away; it all backs up in an ugly pile—on my desk. My telephone rings eternal. Workdays and the workweek expand. After a second straight year of reorganizations, matrix management becomes the rave: more people to report to, more people demanding information, longer, harder hours spent with efforts unrecognized and unappreciated (by more people), jumping from fire to fire while juggling containers of accelerant, inevitably dropping one now and again, the flare from the heat scorching my backside. Asphyxiating under the stress of an exponentially multiplied workload, management offers, "You're a Chicago kid. You've got big shoulders. Just be thankful you aren't in Houston." The formerly warmhearted Motorola culture takes on the feel of ice fishing in the Arctic. The last two words of the "work hard, play hard" mantra tumble into the abyss.

I'm forced into a last minute cancellation of our family vacation and miss the week of fishing in Canada. Picture my "joy" when Terry calls that Saturday evening in August to ask my opinion on whether he should mount the 44-inch musky he just caught. My brother-in-law Joe asks if I can accompany him to Canada in September. Nope. He comes home with a 30-pounder. How about joining him for a walleye trip to Michigan's Tittabawassee River in November? "Negatory." His photo of a limit of 4- to 8-pounders still looks mighty good. Okay, cry me a river; I've still got a job.

To keep perspective in the midst of the overbearing work grind, I frequently glance at two items I've added to my shelf. The first, a photo, fills a yellow-metal 5 x 7 photo frame. A blue lifejacket tucked under his chin and stretching past his waist, three-year-old Eddie sits on my lap in a boat on Lake Marie. Father and son smiles light up a cloudy day, celebrating his first fish, a five-inch white bass held proudly toward the camera. The second, in an 8 x 10 soft-sided frame, holds the artwork of five-year-old Eddie. Hand-drawn with Magic Markers, it features three blue clouds above a red boat with registration numerals IL2318 (?) and "9.9" (designating its horsepower) on the motor. Smiling father and son "stick-men" hold fishing rods, hooks at the end of their lines baited with gobs of night crawlers. Beneath wavy line waves, a pair of curious fish approach the younger angler's offering from opposite directions. The simple visuals serve as constant reminders of simple pleasures, helping to keep the stress of the work day at bay.

Also on the positive side of the ledger, the company relaxes its dress code. No longer mandatory, suits and ties give way to "business casual": slacks, and collared, button shirts. The open collar portion of this worker-friendly change assists with reducing the constriction of the neck's jugular veins and carotid arteries, as well as the red-face condition resulting from daily job pressures. Casual Fridays take it down another notch with golf shirts, jeans, and gym shoes acceptable apparel.

The 1990s also heralds the end of smoking in office buildings. At Motorola, this plays out in a two-step process. No longer allowed to partake of the health-hazardous habit in general work areas, smokers are confined to specially ventilated "smoking rooms," with large picture windows facing the inside hallways. Passersby view the occupants, like fish in an aquarium. Puffer fish, one might say. The final ban eliminates the rooms, forcing the smokers outdoors, "no closer than 15 feet to any entrance." Not a quick study, it took me two decades, post-college graduation, to wean myself of the cigarette addiction, though the enjoyment of an evening cigar after a day on the lake would continue for some years thereafter.

Tobacco products no longer providing the smoke, other issues continue to churn and burn in the '90s. It begins with a move to the fourth floor of the sector headquarters building, a six-story "addition in black" tacked onto 1301 several years earlier. Opaque ceiling panels shower diffused light on trees and plants that fill a central atrium, bringing a tropical feel to the start of each workday. That pleasantness quickly dissipates. It's too quiet in this jungle. The morgue-like lack of *any* noise—the ring of a telephone, the sound of a voice, the click of a keyboard—causes my skin to crawl and signals the potential presence of a corporate boogeyman. Maybe that unsettling sensation simply results from the close proximity to upper management, who occupy the top floors.

"Bottom line versus employee fine," and "surviving instead of thriving," suggests the corporate metamorphosis as the decade progresses. Motorola joins the nationwide trend of slicing and dicing jobs more frequently and in greater numbers. One of my reviews includes the statement "Ed has reached his full advancement and earnings potential within this position. To continue to grow and advance he must be open to considering new challenges and opportunities." Uh oh.

The concept of employment preservation not lost on me, I take on a new challenge, a new opportunity, out of finance into a recently created bid and quote role for services. Back to a back corner of 1309, I work solo in a room the size of the three-urinal, three-stall men's room. Personal effects lining a single shelf provide my only company. But there's lots of desk space for my cascaded files and folders, slid aside at lunchtime for my new dining companion, the sports pages of the *Chicago Sun-Times*.

Short-lived, within six months management eliminates the position. I assimilate into a support team that renews service contracts. Edging closer to where my career began, I report to an individual I hired 20 years ago. Soon thereafter, our group folds into the newly created Customer Response Center, a recently built two-story building in Wood Dale, five miles southeast of Schaumburg. Back to corporate civilization with workers all around, I finally land a cubicle adjacent to the windows. Daylight, instead of fluorescent light, now brightens the gray of my work area. I add a Canada-snapped photo of the northern lights, the swirling and colorful image one of nature's most dazzling displays, to my push-pin board.

The "CRC" touts the patron-friendly slogan, "One Face, One Place." A Lucite award in the form of a star, engraved with my name as a "Quarterly Overachiever," joins the other personal items on my shelf. A subsequent review by new management that details my above-average performance includes the message of a job grade reduction. Well, sit on *my* face, to use a well-worn phrase from the old D-2 days. At 44 years of age, I've toiled for the company 22 years, half my life. I remain upright in my teetering employment kayak and survive the '90s, as does the corporation. Equally successful in job performance and keeping a low profile, a plaque recognizes my 25th employment anniversary and the new corporate mantra, "If you can't pay 'em, plaque 'em."

"Cubicled" at the office. (Yeah, I'd rather be fishin'...)

Part Four
Fishing? Seriously? – Fishing Seriously

Brothers-in-Laws
Steve

My brother-in-law Steve seldom fished, his take on the sport lining up with humorist Dave Barry's comment: "Fishing is boring, unless you catch an actual fish, and then it is disgusting." When he did fish, his preferred method involved reading a book and soaking up the sun's rays while soaking a worm beneath a bobber. On a good number of days, I'll admit there's something to be said for this approach, although we part ways where I sense he prefers to remain undisturbed by a fish that might thoughtlessly inhale his bait.

On rare occasion, Steve took fishing more seriously. Our most productive trip filled the Memorial Day weekend of 1978 when Dad, Steve, and I accompanied Steve's friend Rick and his father, Rick Sr., to Cutfoot Sioux-Lake Winnibigoshish in north central Minnesota. Familiar with the waters by virtue of fishing them annually, the father-son team shared with us techniques and locations learned over the years.

We fished out of Steve's recent purchase, a 17-foot, tan fiberglass tri-hull with white block decal letters on its stern: FOOLISH PLEASURE. Not designed as a fishing boat, its inboard-outboard motor, canopy for inclement weather, and interior configuration with cushy leather seating for seven made it better suited for tooling about open water, its occupants able to enjoy a cool beverage while taking in the scenery or perhaps reading a book. Those unconducive-to-fishing creature comforts notwithstanding, we encountered daily success drifting up catches of northern pike, perch, crappie, and walleye.

During one of our on-water sessions, Dad clipped a recently landed walleye to our metal stringer, already heavy with a near limit of walleye and northern. The joy of the catch vanished moments later, as he forgot to reattach the stringer before tossing it overboard, sending it to a watery grave. Frantic efforts to retrieve it by jigging and dragging treble-hook lures proved unsuccessful. I know he felt bad about it—who wouldn't? I've been responsible for an extensive array of fishing faux pas, more than I care to admit (though they are eking out as I continue to tell my story). By day's end, we eased his emotional pain by filling another stringer, that one including my largest crappie ever, a 15-incher.

Rick and his dad cooked our dinners, always the catch of the day. Northern pike, with firm and tasty white flesh, normally require time-consuming care during the fillet process. Extra rows of "Y-bones" stand pointedly ready to ruin the meal. Surprisingly unconcerned about bone removal, they used a preparation technique unfamiliar to me: running the fillets through a hand-cranked meat grinder. Formed into patties, seasoned, and fried with potatoes and onions, the end result satisfied as a culinary Mmmm Mmmm good. The food, as well as the fishing experience of "Big Winnie," ranked solidly in the category of unforgettable.

Years later, while on a business trip to Florida, Steve joined a group of associates on a Gulf charter and landed a 46-inch barracuda. The deep-sea predator, with elongated body and head, a mouth laden with jagged teeth, and a nasty demeanor, often draws comparisons to the freshwater muskellunge.

His catch brought back an early 1960s memory from the WGN-TV children's show *Ray Rayner and His Friends*. Live-action, seven-minute shorts of *Diver Dan*, its rudimentary underwater effects achieved by filming through an aquarium, featured an underwater explorer in an old-fashioned diving suit interacting with a cast of puppet (strings visible!) fish, among them Doc Sturgeon, Gill Espy, Sam the Sawfish, and Sea Biscuit the Seahorse. The monocled Baron Barracuda, a villain whose thickly accented voice sounded like Boris Badenov from *The Rocky and Bullwinkle Show*, appeared in numerous episodes with his simpleton sidekick-henchman, Trigger, who swam the scenes with a cigarette dangling from his jaw.

Steve's big barracuda and the clear-cut success of the Minnesota trip weren't enough to hook him on fishing. My hope to someday catch Baron Barracuda's ornery cousin, Mean Mr. Musky, in a size similar to Steve's almost-four-footer, began edging its way from the periphery to the center of my fish-catching radar.

~ ~ ~ ~ ~

Calling fishing a hobby is like calling brain surgery a job.
—Paul Schullery

Joe

With the responsibilities of adulthood loosening the ties that bound the Fabulous Maretti Brothers, the resulting void began filling in 1982 when Jo Ann's younger sister, Jackie, married Joe. I acquired a brother-in-law whose passion for fishing matched, and dare I say in some ways, exceeded my own.

Like me, he grew up in Chicago. Unlike me, he didn't attend college, instead parlaying his mechanical acumen and entrepreneurial ambition into a partnership in a transmission repair business. Similar in height to Larry, he stood a half-head shorter than me. Like Larry and me he wore glasses. Unlike Larry and me, he possessed a solid build and the strong hands of a mechanic, fingernails darkened by stains of grease.

I always felt comfortable traveling, fishing, and conversing (most of those conversations, of course, revolving around fishing) with Joe. If we encountered a problem with the car or the boat, I knew Joe could troubleshoot and fix it. (I addressed potentially troublesome car noises by increasing the radio volume.) A Chicago oddity in his love of the Green Bay Packers, I enjoyed family gatherings where Joe would engage in spirited but lighthearted verbal jousts with Steve, an overly passionate Bears fan, about each team's chances for success.

Many partners with whom I have shared a boat, based on their personalities and competitive makeup, exhibit different reactions when someone in the boat lands a fish. The reactions can range from jealousy to silence to cheers, a nod of acknowledgement to back-slapping and high-fives. I trend toward the more animated and vocal. Joe ramps it up a few notches from there. His genuine elation measures equally high whether he or his boat mate lands one. And if I'm that partner, the excitement flows contagious. His exuberance doubles *my* pleasure.

Joe's fishing knowledge and skills far outdistanced mine. To my benefit, his mentoring proved a boon to my proficiency. Fishing with Joe I learned of viable options outside a 50-mile radius of Chicago. Lakes fished on multiple occasions included Mason, Oconomowoc, Castle Rock, Powers, and Redstone in Wisconsin, Turtle Creek in Indiana, Clinton, Crab Orchard, and Newton in central and southern Illinois, Erie in Ohio, the backwaters of the Mississippi River, and the Tittabawassee River in Michigan.

Fishing with Joe, I learned the nuances of line types and terminal tackle: snaps, swivels, leaders, sinkers, split rings, and various plastic worm rigs and live bait presentations.

Fishing with Joe, I learned the concept of patterns, attempting to replicate positive results in similar locations with like presentations.

Fishing with Joe, I learned that his high quality, hand-crafted "Brushmaster" spinnerbaits consistently catch bass.

Fishing with Joe, I learned that on a late November day, with no other facilities available, walleye *can* be filleted in a motel room.

Fishing with Joe, I learned to apply the F + L + P = S (Fish + Location + Presentation = Success) formula, the "when, where, and how," taught by expert anglers, innovators, educators, and Chicago natives Al and Ron Lindner. Their humble startup of the *In-Fisherman* magazine blossomed into a communication empire that included television shows, radio programs, and videos. Their blueprint to maximize angling results targets specific species, on specific bodies of water, with specific techniques, during specific calendar periods. With an extensive array of information, the determined angler studies and analyzes these details in hopes of interlocking the puzzle pieces to form the big picture that will increase the odds of success.

Questions must be answered for the species sought: river, reservoir, lake?; if lake, oligotrophic, mesotrophic, or eutrophic?; water clarity: murky, clear, or stained?; bottom composition: muck, gravel, sand, or boulders?; structure fished: reefs, saddles, timber, or weeds?; if weeds, cabbage, coon tail, or sand grass?; species response to seasonal water conditions, the "calendar periods": pre-spawn, spawn, post-spawn, pre-summer, summer peak, summer, post-summer, fall turnover, cold water, or frozen water?; mechanics: troll, cast, or drift?; lures or live bait?; follow the food source, "match the hatch"; if lures: crankbait, top-water, or spinner?; size, color, shape, and retrieve speed?; if live bait, night crawlers, red worms, leeches, or minnows?; if minnows, fathead, shiner, chub, or sucker?

Damn, my head hurts. Maybe ignorance *is* bliss. The more you know the more complicated things become. It's a wonder I ever caught a fish before meeting Joe.

~ ~ ~ ~ ~

A stringer of walleye from Castle Rock Lake ~ fishing with Joe, of course!

It is impossible to grow weary of a sport that is never the same on any two days of the year.
—Theodore Gordon

The Club

As an additional bonus to knowing Joe, he introduced me to his fishing buddies, John, Charlie, Glenn, Randy, Billy, Bob, Chuck, and Tom. Longtime friends, some back to grammar school, their occupations casted in all directions. Blue to white collar, they included a printer, Chicago policeman, tool and die maker, salesman, owner of a small manufacturing business, quality control engineer, and upper manager of a hi-tech firm. Varied in skill level though versed and talented well above the average angler, each also possessed a passion for the sport. Any and all would make accommodations to find an empty seat in one of their boats if you'd like to join them for a day on the water. I've always marveled at the brotherhood among fishermen—how the undercurrent of common experience turns strangers into immediate friends.

Joe and John are masters. No, grandmasters. Don't ask me to select who ranks above the other. To use a religious analogy, God the Father and God the Son are both God. Would you prefer your art class taught by Michelangelo or da Vinci? A forum on philosophical thought guided by Aristotle or Plato? Talking football X's and O's with Halas or Lombardi? The fortune and pleasure of fishing with either likens to attending a writer's workshop hosted by Shakespeare, a chess lesson from Bobby Fischer, or sharing a spin around the track with Dale Earnhardt.

And the rest of the group doesn't lag far behind—fishing equivalents rivaling Rembrandt, Picasso, Monet, Dali, Renoir, and Van Gogh—while I'm working on a paint-by-number goldfish. In spite of fishing IQs worthy of membership in Mensa International, this collection of friends is unpretentious and friendly-competitive. Gosh, they're the Fabulous Maretti Brothers, only wholly devoted to fishing.

In response to highfalutin associations and bass tournaments whose members and participants (dressed in color-coordinated, neatly pressed sponsor-splashed attire) fly around the lakes in sleek, metal-flake bass boats powered by hundreds-some horsepower motors, the group formed its own tongue-in-cheek fishing club. Standard garb for this down-home collection of anglers typically includes "seen a better day" T-shirts, crooked-brimmed and misshapen "lucky" baseball-style caps, and one-step-away-from-the-trash blue jeans. Members own modest but well-outfitted and impeccably maintained boats propelled by 40- to 60-horsepower motors. With no formal meetings, no dues, no officers, and no rules, this anti-club became known as The Club.

The group gathers annually in late January or early February during Chicagoland's dead of winter and sometimes includes peripheral "members," among them Big Mike, Tony, Felix, and Frank. Hosted annually by John in his finished basement, the knotty pine walls (there's that lakeside cabin feel!) and bar, fish mounts, antique lures, award plaques, photos, bookshelves (with binders containing details of decades of his fishing excursions, a continuous source of reference), and a six-sided rack holding 36 poles (a proper "tool" for every fishing application) provide the perfect ambiance for reliving time-on-the-water tales of triumph, humor, and failure (not many of those), as well as discussing possible outings in the coming year.

Near the conclusion of this annual assemblage, a traveling, John-purchased "Angler of the Year" trophy is voted to a deserving member. Although John and Joe regularly corralled the trophy in the early going, recent years found them recusing themselves by nominating other members for a significant catch relative to that individual's history, whether one fish or a season's body of success. Although my years of association with Joe and The Club have resulted in improvements in my fishing techniques and successes, the trophy has never been seat-belted next to me on the ride home from a Club meeting. In that regard I'm like the Chicago Cubs—waiting 'til next year. And the next, and the next, and the next....

My prominence on the fishing scene burgeoned international (not!) and with members of The Club (not! not!) when my photo appeared in the May 1985 issue of *The Kiwanis Magazine* accompanying an article entitled, "U.S.-Canadian Cooperation: Preserving Wildlife." In the photo, snapped on one of the trips to Little St. Germain, I'm seated in the bow of a boat as I hint a smile. Outfitted in a camouflage rain suit (though it appears to be sunny), Motorola batwings-logo baseball cap, and aviator-style sunglasses, I'm gripping a musky behind its gills. Long-armed in extension toward the camera, I'm attempting (but failing miserably) to make a 22-inch musky appear more like a 22-pounder. (The Club frowned on that photo-practice, so I promptly removed it from my repertoire.) Oh, did I previously mention my friend Chuck served as the magazine's executive editor?

Like superstar athletes, Joe and John raise the performance of mates who share time in their boats. So it should come as no surprise that I boated my largest fish in several different species, to that point in time, while fishing with them.

Big Largemouth Bass

On March 27, 1987, the White Sox traded John Cangelosi to the Pittsburgh Pirates for Jim Winn. On a more personal level, it's also the day I caught a big bass.

With winter losing its grip, Joe and I ventured to central Illinois' Newton Lake in search of early springtime largemouth, the pre-spawn bass carrying their heaviest weight at this time of year.

Through the course of the morning, Joe hooked up with several nice ones, while I had yet to connect. He directed us to the back of one of the many creek arms, announcing he was taking a break. He stopped within casting distance of a small point from which a deadfall extended into the water, the combination flashing like a neon sign: "Bass lives here!" I had no doubt that Joe was giving me the spot, a clear opportunity to end my day's drought. How did I know? Simple. Joe never takes a break.

I casted my Shad Rap to the edge of the shore where the tree trunk entered the water. Turns of the reel handle drove the lure down the submerged incline and out of sight. A moment later, a solid pull signaled a strike. The horseshoe bend in my rod and the tussle that followed suggested a fish of considerable size, at least in relation to my lifetime catch inventory. The battle ended with Joe commenting, as he netted it, "Whoa, nice one!" The 20 ½-incher weighed 5¼ pounds.

While not a giant by Southern standards, where 5- to 10-pound largemouth are not uncommon, it measured up nicely for a lake north of the Mason-Dixon Line. And in my world, it taped several inches longer and almost two pounds heavier than any largemouth I had ever landed. In conversations past, Joe mentioned that scoring a big fish for the wall would increase my confidence as a fisherman, molding me into a force to be reckoned with in our friendly competitions. Not yet having a mount showcased in the family room, this one merited consideration.

"You keeping it for the wall?" Joe asked.

Still uncertain, additional thoughts crossed my mind. With regard to the positives, mounting a fish would garner recognition from The Club. Most members already displaying multiple species of trophy fish captured, a mount would define a rite of passage, alter how I viewed myself in relation to the others by moving the needle from protégé to colleague, farce to force. On the dollars and cents side, however, this sporting swagger would require a significant investment of well over $100. Further, will this one be as good as it gets? With the mindset of one trophy mount per species, what happens if I catch a larger one? And if I decide against the mount, what if I never catch one bigger? What if, what if, what if...?

Joe, sensing my indecision by lack of an immediate response, said, "If you want to think about it for a while, we can put it in the livewell. It *is* a beauty." I nodded in agreement on both counts, appreciative of the suggestion. Through the remainder of the afternoon Joe boated a few more, though none measuring up to the "hog" in the livewell. I can't say for sure if being shutout in those same hours played into my decision, but when Joe repeated the question before departing for the launch at the end of our fishing day, I'd made up my mind. Time to wall-hang an ego-boosting "diploma" to proclaim my graduation from pretender to contender.

"Diploma" in hand and cigar in mouth ~
Does it get any better than this?

~ ~ ~ ~ ~

Lake Erie

In little more than a decade, Lake Erie made a marvelous comeback. Its water, near-toxic "swill" in the 1970s, reclaimed to a level allowing it to support world-class walleye and smallmouth bass fisheries. What's world-class, you ask? Over three million walleye harvested each year through the mid-1980s.

For three consecutive years, my dad and I joined Joe and his dad, Joe Sr., on two-day charters. Unlike typical Great Lakes salmon and trout charters that hook fish by trolling and then have their customers take turns reeling them in, *we* did the fishing on Lake Erie, casting and retrieving Erie Dearies. From the family of "weight-forward" spinners, the lure consists of a keel weight in front of a small spinner blade, trailed by a long-shank hook that we'd dress with a night-crawler. The lure can run deep by counting it down; suspended schools and catching multiple fish from them occur when this information is shared and replicated by fishing partners.

On each day of these father-son outings, we caught our limit. Size varied, though I'd guesstimate the combined outings averaged 18 to 19 inches. I know what you're thinking—what's the big deal about plucking a couple dozen walleye out of population numbering in the millions? The Western Lake Erie Basin that these fish call home covers an area approximating 2,000 square miles.

Joe, me, Dad, and Joe Sr.
Walleye - catching and eating ... soooooo good!

~ ~ ~ ~ ~

The vast waters of Lake Erie also accounted for my largest smallmouth. Caught on a Motorola outing with co-workers Mark, Glen, and Dave, the 19½-inch "bronzeback" weighed in excess of 4 pounds.

~ ~ ~ ~ ~

Big Walleye

May 1, 1993, marked the 100th anniversary of the opening of the World's Columbian Exposition in Chicago. It's also the day I caught a big walleye.

Club members John, Glenn, and I rocked in Erie's rollers on a breezy, sunny spring day. We had taken some walleye on Erie Dearies, but John surmised a bottom-bumping presentation with jigs and minnows might increase our odds of contacting bigger fish. John stared intently at the screen of his fish locator, like a surgeon reviewing x-rays before a delicate operation. I knew from previous outings on Erie that in spite of its size, which would lend itself to vast areas of fishless waters, this "fish factory" of the Western Basin generally showed some sort of activity on the sonar. How a captain decided on one particular spot over another was a mystery to me.

Moments later, John said, "This is the spot—we start here."

"Seeing lots of 'hooks?'" I asked, hooks referring to symbols on the locator that resemble an upside-down Nike "Swoosh," each representing a fish.

"No, all the activity just cleared from the screen—it's blank at the moment," he responded.

Though the logic of the choice seemed counterintuitive, his matter-of-fact response did not warrant further questioning. I chalked it up to his sixth sense, just another tool in the tackle box of an experienced and successful angler.

Only minutes thereafter, he and Glenn connected with several hefty ones, bruisers between five and eight pounds. Anxious to join the party I considered a change in jig color. I tapped the grandmaster's vault, asking for his recommendation.

With humor cloaked in his James Bond martini-dry delivery, he answered the question with a question: "Oh, did I forget to tell you…?"

Over the years, this tongue-in-cheek question took on a life of its own among The Club members. It implied that the individual posing it possessed a fish-catching secret not shared: a tip, a twist on a presentation, a lure type or color, any or all only in his possession for this particular trip. Its origin unknown but likely another slap at the highly competitive and cutthroat world of professional bass tournament fishing, members of The Club readily shared information, cheered, and encouraged one another.

John peered into my open tackle box, eyeing an assortment of jigs with the color spectrum well represented. With no answer right or wrong, he simply provided direction, leaving the choice to me: "Chartreuse or lime work well. And they say pink is a big fish color."

With a long drive and equally long hours invested on this big water, the "good" of the green family just wouldn't cut it. I tied on the pink jig, hooked on a minnow, and within 15 minutes John's words resonated prophetic. I landed a 30-inch, 9-pound 1-ounce walleye, adding another species to join the largemouth bass on my family room wall.

*John and me with a bunch of big ones ~
Including the 30-incher in my left hand.*

~ ~ ~ ~ ~

I like fishing for musky. Why have baloney all your life when you can have steak?
—Sarah Terry, (fourteen-years-old), after catching a Kentucky state record 47-pound muskellunge.

Musky Fever

As the 1990s dawned, members of The Club added muskellunge, a top-of-the-line predator, to its list of species pursued. As most fishermen would likely agree, the only thing better than catching a fish is catching one that's bigger. As previewed on Bone Lake over a decade ago, to hunt this fresh-water colossus required another level of cash outlay: stout rods, heavy-duty reels and line, and large lures costing three to five times the amount of those purchased in the pursuit of bass and walleye. The astute fishing consumer acquires the inventory in stages to avoid second mortgages or other loans requiring installment payments for all eternity.

Big Muskellunge

September 2, 1991, hailed significant for several reasons. Nagorno Karabakh declared its independence from Azerbaijan, forming the Nagorno-Karabakh Republic. The mountainous and forested landlocked region in the South Caucasus lies between Lower Karabakh and Zangezur, encompassing the southeastern range of the Lesser Caucasus Mountains. It's also the day I caught a big musky.

Joe and I joined John and Charlie for a late summer week to ply the waters of northwest Ontario's Canyon Lake. Unlike all my other Canadian excursions to this point in time, where catching a muskellunge would fall into the category of "unexpected pleasant surprise," this one exclusively targeted them.

One of Joe's trip preparations included poring over hundreds of catch statistics submitted by Muskies, Inc. members over the years past, noting lure type and color for Ontario muskellunge caught in early September. His research paid off as he caught a number of muskies on a black Suick. John worked his own magic with a more diverse selection of lures. Both he and Joe scored muskies at a pace exceeding one each per day, averaging 36 inches. Charlie and I got a lot of practice honing our netting skills on "the fish of (way less than) 10,000 casts (if you're John or Joe)."

After several late nights spent refreshing the palate from our generous supply of Canadian Labatt Blue, we slept in on Labor Day Monday, not hitting the water until after 9 a.m. Bluebird skies and a 20 mile per hour west wind greeted us. We motored to our first stop, a mid-lake reef topping out 8 feet below the surface. Tired from the cumulative effect of "Blue" and a couple of long, workmanlike, fishless days pitching large lures, I started this one on autopilot—just going through the motions—waiting for a minimum level of attentiveness to kick in.

I casted a gray-silver Cisco Kid, a 7-inch minnow-body diving crankbait, in the direction of the underwater island. The lure's metal lip contacted the submerged rock, bouncing and scraping as I worked it back to the boat. Moments later the lure stopped—I feared a crevice snagged it. Slowly lifting the rod the tension held, and then a heavy pulsation signaled the head shakes of a fish unhappy with its first bite of a morning meal. Instantly rotating my body to the right and with the rod tightly gripped on the horizontal, I set the hook. My heart thumped with excitement as the fish stayed down and out of sight, its size unknown but feeling substantial. The butt of the five-foot "pool cue" rod tight to my side, grinding cranks of the reel handle worked the fish steadily toward the boat. Less than a minute after hookset and not knowing what craziness might yet erupt in this battle, to my surprise the musky simply came to the surface among the jostling waves, allowing my partner to easily scoop it into the net. Joe let out a whoop as he extended his hand, a vigorous handshake following. Our smiles mirrored as I worked in a couple of deep breaths to steady my shaking knees.

After removing the hooks with the netted fish still in the water, Joe explained the proper method for holding it: slide fingers inside the gill plate (avoid the razor sharp edges of the gill rakers!), clench the lower jawbone between thumb and fingers, and support the bottom of the fish between its belly and tail using the other hand. Now in my grasp, the largest fish of my life measured 40 inches. With a healthy girth, Joe estimated its weight near 20 pounds. A Polaroid photo captured the muted bars on its scaled sides that shimmered like 24-karat gold in the bright sunlight. A prompt and successful release followed. It would be my only musky of the trip but held up as the group's largest for the week.

Striking musky gold!

~ ~ ~ ~ ~

Some men would rather be photographed with their fish than their wives.
—Gwen Cooper and Evelyn Haas

CPR

Although I still had wall space reserved for a trophy musky, environmental "green" initiatives, including resource protection and conservation, rapidly gained acceptance in fishing circles. Other than fish kept for food, "Catch, Photo, Release"—"CPR"—became the mantra of conservation-minded anglers, including members of The Club.

In the pre-digital camera era, Skrudland Photo served the Chicagoland area as the preferred film developer. A roll of film with the image of a large fish often necessitated the wasteful snapping off of the remaining photos on rolls that totaled 12, 24, or 36 shots. When completed, the rewound roll was mailed to Hebron, Illinois, for processing.

The day of its return couldn't come too soon. The back of the red, white, and blue return envelope pictured the balding and bespectacled owner next to the following words: "I want to thank you for the business you have given me since 1929. I hope that you will continue to mail your orders to me. Thank you again. G. Skrudland." And beneath his name, "Mini-Bibles 10-cents each." The excitement of the envelope's arrival often fizzled, in short order, upon opening it. The photos frequently disappointed, their poor quality a function of photographer incompetence (partner unfamiliarity with the camera or the basics of framing a photo) or the roll of film not being the optimum speed (100, 200, 400, always a crapshoot) for the lighting conditions encountered.

Polaroid Instamatics partially solved these issues, becoming an onboard must-have. The ability to view the image of the fish, before releasing it, offset the marginal photographic quality the camera provided. Further plusses included immediate gratification and the opportunity to share the pride and delight of the catch without having to wait for weeks on end.

Another change in the fishing world from the 1970s to the 1990s centered on the measurement of fish. Early on, when sharing stories with family and friends, their question of "How much did it weigh?" required (at the time of the catch) use of the Zebco Fish De-liar, a small, primitive (and thus not very accurate) spring-style scale. Rarely was the length of the fish asked or offered, even though the De-liar also contained a pull-out tape measure.

Portable, battery-powered scales with digital readouts subsequently provided more precision. A final evolution eliminated weighing a fish intended to be released, as most experienced fisherman could accurately estimate the weight of various species depending on their length and girth. Now, questions about fish size are answered by length in inches, accomplished by a quick tape measurement.

Yet another leap forward in the stewardship of the sport occurred with the inception of replica mounts—trophy-size fish could be released. Cutting edge taxidermists, with only a photograph and length and girth measurements, began producing high-quality reproductions both artistic and realistic. All the better, my yet-to-be-caught musky released to swim again. Now all I have to do is catch it.

~ ~ ~ ~ ~

The muskellunge (Esox masquinongy), also known as muskelunge, muscallonge, milliganong, or maskinonge (and often abbreviated "muskie" or "musky"), is a species of large, relatively uncommon freshwater fish of North America. The muskellunge is the largest member of the pike family, Esocidae. The common name comes from the Ojibwa word "maashkinoozhe," meaning "ugly pike," by way of French "masque allongé" (modified from the Ojibwa word by folk etymology), "elongated face."
—Wikipedia

Little Vermilion Lake

November 1984. With our tenth wedding anniversary approaching, the search for a gift befitting the occasion rose to the top of my leisure-time agenda. Aluminum and tin the traditional material for tenth anniversaries, my gut told me that a six-pack of Schlitz or a cowbell would not be my best options. With similar instinct, I also ruled out fishing rods, reels, and lures for my decade-long bride. How about jewelry? Yes. Jewelry. Jewelry from water. What? Yes, jewelry from water—a string of pearls. I'll make the purchase with cash saved from my allowance, specifically for that purpose, over the course of several years. Time to hit the mall.

After work on a Friday evening, I drive to Stratford Square, an indoor shopping center near our Bloomingdale home. My pilgrimage through the mall wings includes crisscrossing the upper and lower levels via staircases and escalators to visit various purveyors of jewelry: J.B. Robinson, Zales, Rogers and Holland, and several other lesser-knowns. At each, I anxiously peruse display cases filled with gold, silver, and gemstone treasures sparkling beneath bright lights. One by one the stores disappoint; oddly (or at least I think it odd), none carries the object of my search.

On the verge of needing to rethink my gift of choice, I enter the last store, my last hope, Page Jewelers. The store manager, Alan (I know this because his nametag reads "Alan, Store Manager"), greets me.

"Hello, welcome to Page Jewelers. Where do you do your fishing?"

Hmmm ... strange. I hadn't been fishing since the previous weekend when Joe and I bagged a bunch of walleye below the Petenwell Dam, and I'd showered every day since, so how did he know? The quizzical expression on my face brought his explanation before I could answer.

"Your shirt," he said, pointing to it.

I look down to see my "Good Things Come to Those Who Bait" sweatshirt. The mystery answered, I reply, "Pretty much anywhere there's water, except for sinks, sewers, and toilet bowls, that is." He smiles, and I continue, "Mostly Illinois and Wisconsin; a little in Michigan, Minnesota, Indiana, and Ohio. I haven't been to Canada in quite a few years, but I'm looking to get back there."

"There's nothing like the beauty of Canadian waters," Alan says. "My wife Audrey and I love it up there. We go to Lake of the Woods for a week every summer. It's peaceful—a piece of paradise."

"Ah, paradise. You just triggered memories from one of *my* Lake of the Woods trips. We stayed at Paradise Island—which was anything but."

"Really. What happened?" Alan asks.

I looked at my watch and say, "You close in less than an hour ... long story ... maybe next time."

"Can't wait," Alan replies, then continues, "My wife and I have kicked around the idea of chucking this rat race and buying a place up there. When we mentioned it to a couple of people on our last trip, we were told that the owners of Fireside Lodge, on Little Vermilion Lake, may be putting it on the market soon. It's the only resort on the lake, and the fishing is supposed to be terrific: musky, northern pike, and smallmouth—all in nice sizes. And there's a half-dozen other lakes in the system connected by creeks or short portages. If the camp becomes available, we might go for it."

"Good luck following your dream," I say, knowing more often than not such thoughts are nothing more than pipe dreams. Many die-hard fishermen experience the whimsy of becoming a fishing guide, owning a tackle shop, or creating and manufacturing the next surefire-can't-miss-must-have lure. Then, we come to our senses. To turn a passion into one's life's work takes fortitude, a little luck, and a lot of guts.

Alan takes hold of my extended hand as I say, "My name is Ed. It's been nice talking to you. I'll be sure and check in with you any time I'm at the mall so we can share some fish stories." As I begin turning toward the door he tightens his grip and says, "I'm afraid I may have sidetracked us. Is there something you were looking for?"

Minutes before closing time I exited the store with a beautiful string of pearls and matching earrings, both nicely priced with a fisherman's discount. Over the next several years, at periodic visits to the mall, I would stop in at Page Jewelers. If he wasn't occupied with a customer, Alan and I would engage in pleasant conversation about recent fishing outings. Though he had the "gift of gab" common to most salesmen, he also possessed a down-to-earth demeanor. That, along with his obvious love of fishing, allowed us to click on a personal level.

On an early winter visit to Page, I planned to ask if he cared to join our upcoming annual gathering of The Club. Not seeing him in the store, I inquired if he had the day off. The sales clerk advised me that he was no longer in their employ, that he and his wife had purchased a fishing lodge in Canada.

Before his departure, Alan must have taken my address from the purchase receipt for the pearls. Each winter I'd receive a colorful Fireside Lodge brochure with information about the lakes, notable catches of the past year, and accommodations. The bottom of the back page included an image of the smiling owners. The first opportunity to reserve one of their cabins for a family vacation occurred in mid-June of 1993.

~ ~ ~ ~ ~

Greeted by our host upon arriving, Alan looked like a new man. His facial features and physique had taken on a more robust appearance. The change in career, lifestyle as it were—leaping off the retail corporate treadmill and bidding *adieu* to the stress associated with it—obviously agreed with him.

Built in 1904, the main lodge is situated on several cleared acres that adjoin a small bay at the east end of the lake. The structure, crafted from hand-hewn logs, exudes a vintage charm true to the era of its construction. The sizeable two-story space within boasts an enormous fieldstone fireplace, three guest rooms, and a dining area. The timbered walls sport an array of taxidermied (some yellowed, speaking to their age) fish native to the lake: muskellunge, northern pike, smallmouth bass, and lake trout. Fur pelts, a set of antlers, mounts of a fox, small game birds, and the heads of a moose and deer also line the walls.

Augmenting the main lodge, cabins were built at various intervals in the years that followed construction of the lodge building. While clean and well maintained, all clearly reflected their age. Alan and Audrey undertook the job of modernizing and rebuilding, their pride of ownership evident in the TLC-changes and ongoing upgrades.

Little Vermilion Lake, configured in long and narrow upper and lower sections that run east-west, finds many bays along its 60 miles of shoreline. Alan provided a lake map that included not only depth contours but additional information: shallow water hazards highlighted in red, and black arrowed lines detailing safe navigation routes around and between islands and shorelines. The lake touts abundant structure with reefs, reeds, and weedbeds. In the northeast, a rushing rapids named Twin Falls exits to Big Vermilion Lake to the north.

Our week played out at a leisurely pace. With Jo Ann and Eddie as my partners, our fishing agenda did not include any marathon sessions. We could not target muskellunge, as the season opener for that species remained two weeks away. Our efforts did, however, regularly end with positive results, all catch and release. Smallmouth bass took a liking to small crankbaits and top-water lures, a three-hour stint in a bay near Twin Falls netted 110 perch, and using small Mepps spinners we each caught a number of northern pike that ranged in size from 27- to 34-inches. With the same Mepps lure I boated "accidental" muskies of 35- and 36-inches.

Our visit to Little Vermilion Lake did not disappoint. I planned to return, to ply its waters in a more serious and thorough manner. And the next time, after the opening of the muskellunge season.

~ ~ ~ ~ ~

You can observe a lot just by watching.
—Yogi Berra

When I can't be out on the water, watching fishing programs on television ranks as the next best thing. I've enjoyed that indoor pastime since the 1960s. Instructional and entertaining, shows that have lured my attention over the years include *Jim Thomas Outdoors, Virgil Ward Championship Fishing, Outdoor Sportsman* with Joe Wyer, *The Fishin' Hole* with Jerry McKinnis, *Fishing North America, Outdoor Encounters* with Debra Johannesson, *Hank Parker's*

Outdoor Magazine, The Bassmasters hosted by Ray Scott, *Jimmy Houston Outdoors, Billy Westmoreland Fishing Diary, Fishing with Roland Martin, In-Fisherman* with Al and Ron Lindner, *Bill Dance Outdoors, Babe Winkelman's Good Fishing, Wisconsin Waters and Woods* with John Gillespie, *Discover Wisconsin* with Dick Rose, *Midwest Outdoors* featuring segments with Dan Gapen and Bobber Annie, *Fishing with Joe Bucher, Time on the Water* with Frank Hyla, and *Musky Hunter TV* with Jim Saric. Yes, indeed. And these are just the ones that immediately come to mind.

Oh, and one more—*Simply Fishing,* hosted by Bob Mehsikomer. Bob prides himself as a big fish guy, with northern pike or muskellunge on the weekly agenda. Many of the shows, filmed in northern Minnesota and Canada, include segments on Lake of the Woods. Well-timed, these 1990s episodes nicely coordinate with my life's fishing spectrum that has advanced to the pursuit of freshwater's largest species.

Not coincidentally, the Giant Jackpot that Bob frequently casts is manufactured by the program's primary sponsor, Poe. The 7-inch cigar-shaped lure, crafted from cedar, zigzags the surface as Bob imparts the action with up and down movements of his rod. Big fish attack the lure with explosive predictability (assisted, of course, by the marvel of film editing). It is a lure I need. A lure I want. A lure I *must* have. I purchase three at the annual winter Chicago Outdoor Sports Show held in suburban Rosemont, the multiple purchase justified not only to have them in different colors but to share the magic with my fishing partners on the next venture into Canada.

Further accelerating the urge to return to Little Vermilion, in 1993 the Ontario Ministry of Natural Resources opened three lakes connected to it by a creek. Under special management, the OMNR nurtured the "musky sanctuary" lakes of Maskinonge, Hooch, and Cloudlet since their closure in the 1930s. Although restrictions for the "catch and release" lakes include using lures with barbless hooks and only one hook per lure, the thought of Canadian lakes ripe with big fish that never encountered a lure still screamed "Muskellunge Fisherman's Nirvana!" To capitalize on this rare angling opportunity, time was of the essence.

Jo Ann, Eddie, and I missed the opening window in the inaugural year but with our modest success, the promise of Poe's Giant Jackpot, and the recent accessibility to a potential musky fishing Shangri-La, Larry and Art agreed to join me for a mid-July 1994 trip. Not that they needed any further convincing, but I boldly predicted we would each catch our largest musky. Relying on Joe and The Club members to lead the way on fishing excursions over the past decade, I captained this one, its success or failure squarely upon my shoulders.

On the Road (again)

We drive our normal route through Wisconsin and Minnesota, cross the border at International Falls, and proceed north and east to Dryden. Its welcome sign lists a population of 6,500, small by most standards yet the third largest city in the 200,000 square miles encompassing northwest Ontario. We stop at a grocery store to pick up some food items to supplement those brought from home.

"I'll get the bacon," I state authoritatively, as we approached the store's refrigerated cases. Although we're in Canada, I'm not talking about that goofy circle-ham-slice the Canadians call bacon. Larry and Art nod a "whatever" and continue their trek through the aisles, filling a cart with other shopping list entries, unaware that only Jo Ann harbors knowledge of my curious idiosyncrasy for bacon shopping. (No, I don't know why. Doesn't everyone harbor a dark, sometimes slimy little secret? Perhaps mine dates back to bass fishing success with jigs dressed with an Uncle Josh pork rind...)

The average shopper may be fooled by seemingly lean-layered strips staring at them through the cellophane package front, but I'm not deceived by fool's gold. Those two flaps on the back of the package are there for a reason, and I'm going to lift every one of them, package after package after package, panning for pork belly gold. Mining deep into the stack, I finally strike the mother lode. It's the Hope Diamond of bacon. Precious cargo in hand, I track down my partners, beaming as if I've just landed a 60-inch musky.

"What's with you?" Larry asks.

Arm outstretched, I present my prize.

"Look, Art," Larry says, "Ed found a package of bacon."

My domestic shortcomings well known among family and friends, Art rolls with the flow. "I'll alert the media. Can he boil water yet?"

"Laugh, clowns," I reply as I further extend my arms, tilting the package to the back and lifting the flaps: "95% lean!"

"Crazy as a loon, my cousin," Larry mutters as he slowly shakes his head.

"Yeah, Canada's already honored him with their currency," Art adds, the Canadian one-dollar coin, which bears the image of a loon, commonly referred to as the loonie.

"Nowhere to go but down from here," Larry says. "Should we just head for home?"

Their brief salvo absorbed, I retort, "The stars are aligning, my friends. And if the fish don't cooperate, at least we'll forever have this memory of pig processing perfection."

Our shopping chore complete, we check out and drive the remaining hour to Fireside. Greeted by Alan and Audrey, they escort us to a two-bedroom cabin, the same one Jo Ann, Eddie, and I stayed in last year. After unpacking our luggage and supplies, we assemble our fishing gear and carry it down to the dock. Alan meets us there, showing us the rental boat we'll be using for the week. We're pleasantly surprised that it includes swivel high-back cushion seats, a luxury we've never experienced in previous rentals always outfitted with simplistic backless benches.

Upon returning to the lodge, we belly up to the counter of a small office area, its walls filled with an array of fishing lures in various sizes and colors. Alan hands us each a lake map. A quick scan refreshes my memory of last year's success at many of the spots named on the map: Chicago Bay, Mike's Island, Ament Bay, Twin Falls, and the Muskie Pasture.

"How's the fishing been?" I ask Alan.

"Not too bad," he replies,

In "lodge owner speak," that translates to "not too good." On a positive note, however, it also means all the fish in the lake weren't caught in a "you should have been here last week" feeding frenzy.

Alan continues, "I'm looking for a big improvement with your arrival. Some of the folks that were here last week didn't have the experience you guys do."

"Oh great, more pressure," I respond with a forced faux furrow of my brow. "I'm already weighed down by the anchor of guaranteeing these guys the biggest muskies of their lives."

Larry leans forward, speaking directly to Alan in a lawyerlike and subdued tone, though purposely loud enough for Art and me to hear. "Art and I have privately discussed the merit of Ed's 'guarantee' and absolve him of any obligation, express or implied. We have no expectations and will be satisfied to catch anything or nothing." Further lowering his voice to a near whisper, he concludes, "We'll fill you in later on his fragile mental state and his recent encounter with a package of bacon."

Catching glimpses of grins, Alan gives a subtle nod, smiles, and says, "A lot of stories have been told in front of the lodge fireplace these past ninety years. Can't wait to hear this one."

After a pause, Alan shifts the conversation. "Fireside is participating in a special program just started in the Sioux Lookout District. We've joined the local Ministry of Natural Resources, Department of Tourism, and other area businesses to start a Master Angler Release Awards Program. If you catch and release a minimum 44-inch musky, 40-inch northern, or 18-inch smallmouth, you'll receive a certificate and Master Angler Release Award patch. Should be no problem for you guys to score some of those, so I'll start preparing the submission forms so all you'll have to do later is fill in the size."

"*More* pressure," I whisper, though it really wasn't—just a nice bonus to add to the family room wall that already displays a "Fish Ohio Outstanding Catch Certificate" for the big Lake Erie walleye, a Musky Hunter Magazine "Musky Hunter Par Excellence" certificate for my Canyon Lake musky, and several In-Fisherman Master Angler awards for largemouth bass.

"You guys need any lures, or are you set?" Alan asks.

"We're good," I answer with confidence.

"My cousin has watched one too many fishing shows," Larry says. "On the drive up here, he told us he loaded up with a magic lure that muskies can't resist. What's it called, Art?"

"It's his namesake lure—the Giant Crackpot."

"Jackpot, Alan, *Giant Jackpot*," I say, correcting quick-witted Art's intentional play on words.

"Hmmm, I'm familiar with a lot of lures but never heard of that one," Alan replies.

"That'll change this week," I say, before hedging my bet and concluding in a subdued tone, "I hope." Map in hand, I turn to Larry and Art and say, "Time to hit the water. Let's see if we can hit the jackpot ... or at least cast one."

The 20-horsepower outboard starts with the first pull. The long-anticipated on-water portion of our adventure underway, we slowly propel from the dock. The balmy breeze, the panorama of sky, woods, and water, the sensation of gliding, floating—all swaddled in the soothing hum of the motor—creates an intoxicating confection that exhilarates. Touched by all, touching all, the spirit soars in these moments. The pristine ambiance embodies the best Canada has to offer.

Okay, time to fish. With only a few hours until sundown, we circle Little Vermilion's lower arm, casting main lake points and island shorelines. Sticking with proven fish-catching tackle, I elect to delay the maiden cast of my specially touted but personally untested lure until tomorrow, allowing one more night to dream the dream of the Jackpot at the end of the rainbow, that special place where a giant muskellunge lays in wait to devour it. If it fails to produce, the delay at least leaves one less day to sulk over a dream dashed, one less day to rue tackle money not well spent, one less day to deflect the good-natured barbs of my fishing partners. Saturday draws to a close with the only tally a smallmouth bass that took a liking to Larry's Mepps spinner.

On Sunday, we experience an uptick in activity upon venturing into the lake's more expansive upper section. We fish Ament Bay, where my Johnson Silver Minnow fools a 33-inch northern pike. Several muskies, similar in size, follow our lures but do not strike. I repeatedly remind myself to complete a figure-8 at the end of each cast and encourage my partners to do the same, as I've read that it accounts for more than 40% of muskellunge strikes.

For each of us, bending at boatside to swirl the rod and lure in a wide-sweeping "8" is a pain—literally. Although we're "young" men in our early 40s, we all suffer some degree of debilitation from back problems. I'm less than two years removed from lower lumbar disc surgery and need to calculate every movement to avoid aggravating the always-present discomfort. Art wrenched his back only days before this trip. Larry injured his shoulder during a high school baseball game over twenty years ago and continues to deal with periodic flare-ups aggravated by certain activities, casting among them.

Our scour of Ament Bay complete, we travel a short distance to another bay, a small one adjoining Mike's Island. As I open my tackle box for a change of lures, my eyes immediately lock on the three Giant Jackpots: one with a black back and silver-glitter sides, a second with a red back and white sides, and the third with a blue back and silver-glitter sides. The time is now.

My choice simple, I pluck the blue and silver model—the one that Mehsikomer throws religiously—and snap it onto my wire leader. No words spoken as the lure dangles from my rod tip, I'm uncertain if the sound from one of my boat mates is a cough or a snicker, though I believe it to be the latter.

In response to the wordless comment, I retort, "I *will* have the last laugh," before muttering, "or cry." I stand and launch a cast that carries the 2½-ounce lure seemingly half the length a football field. After splashdown, I envision the rod and reel movements of Mehsikomer's retrieval methods, hoping to replicate them. At first awkward, halfway back to the boat I achieve a rhythm that causes the lure to sway from side to side as it pushes water, the movement causing a "bloop" akin to a vintage coffee pot just beginning to percolate. Larry and Art hold their casts, amused rather than mesmerized by the commotion disturbing the water's surface.

Art comments, "Maretti ... you've *got* to be kidding."

"If I'm a fish, that thing is scaring the hell out of me," Larry adds.

If I hadn't seen fish attack it on the television show, I'd have to agree with them. Bobbing and weaving and splashing across the surface it does look, well, quite ridiculous. Many lures have a laughable appearance or action, among them the one-by-seven inch "block of wood" Suick, bucktails dressed with fur-ball puffs of marabou feathers better suited to Las Vegas showgirls, and the Creeper, an alien with metal arms hinged to a froglike body. Yes, the Giant Jackpot stands with the best of them. After a dozen or so casts I unclip it, without fanfare, and hearing no other comments, slip it back into my tackle box.

Like the bacon, the catching remains lean through the remainder of Sunday. During several musky fishing interludes that provide needed rest for our weary backs, we target smallmouth bass with downsized gear. I catch one while Larry and Art take three each. Maybe the "so-so" fishing report was right on. Maybe Alan was giving us too much credit. Maybe I should have pleaded with a member of The Club to lead this expedition. Tomorrow we'll test one of the recently opened sanctuaries, the one tagged with the name of the object of our pursuit: Maskinonge Lake.

My culinarily challenged status no secret, Larry and Art handle the week's cooking chores. With today's plan to travel the added distance to Maskinonge and spend the better part of the day there, preparations for an extra-hearty breakfast are underway. Burner flames heat a coffee pot and frying pan atop the stove. A loaf of Wonder Bread with yellow, red, and blue balloons dotting the white packaging rests next to the toaster. Scattered across the countertop are the remainder (or so I thought) of the fixin's: a mesh bag filled with potatoes, a stick of butter, individually wrapped Kraft American cheese singles, and a carton of eggs. Just back from the refrigerator, Larry tosses another package on the counter and grabs a knife, preparing to slice it open.

"Whoa, what are you doing?" I ask, peppered with a dash of urgency.

Before Larry can answer, Art pipes in, "It's called cooking, Maretti. There's more to breakfast than Pop Tarts. Prepared food doesn't just materialize out of thin air. If you didn't marry Jo Ann right after we left NIU, I wonder which of us would've found your withered, undernourished carcass in some roadside ditch."

The subject of bacon and Art's mention of NIU reminds me of a poster in the room of one of our fellow Wacos, L.F's, I think. It pictured a pair of fornicating pigs with the caption, "Makin' Bacon." Twenty years hence the image remains unforgettably fresh.

Snapped back to the now, Larry asks, "What do you want to do—take your pig prize home and have it mounted on your family room wall?"

"Maybe he plans to use the strips as trailers on his Giant Crackpot," Art says. "That is, if he can open the package without leaving a fingertip on the cutting board."

I interrupt my friends' good natured roll. "I was thinking we could wait until we catch a musky and celebrate the next morning with the oink of a lifetime."

Shaking his head as he returns the package to the refrigerator, Larry asks, "You think you can make toast?"

"Sure," I reply, "but how do I know when it's done?"

~ ~ ~ ~ ~

The cares and anxieties and perplexities of everyday life are forgotten as the angler wades the merry stream and casts his flies on the flashing water. He is wholly obsessed with his pursuit and has unbounded faith in his methods. And while the eager expectancy of a response to his lures absorbs his every faculty, he enjoys, at the same time, in a subconscious way, the bounties of Nature surrounding and investing him. The voices of the stream are ever in his ears—the lapping and purling of the water as it sparkles on the riffle or whirls in the eddies. He is alive to the song of the birds, the hum of insects, and the whispering of the leaves as the sunlight filters through them.
—Dr. James A. Henshall

Bellies full, we depart under sunny skies and pleasantly cool low 60-degree temperatures forecasted to hold through the day. We motor west through the lake's lower section, then cut north through the narrows adjacent to Cedarbough Bay before turning left, setting course for the far western shore. There, we locate the inlet of the creek that leads to the sanctuary lakes.

Lack of recent rainfall left the narrow, winding waterway precariously shallow, making its navigation a challenging proposition requiring a high level of concentration. The outboard, now locked in a raised position, continuously churns chocolate milk silt. Our vision focused forward as cattails and reeds block views to either side, the canal runs no deeper than Grayslake's Crystal Creek that Larry and I fished as kids. Although Little Vermilion and the lakes connected to it experience little fishing pressure, the possibility of encountering another boat in the confining "passageway for one" adds a pinch of edginess. Turn after turn, the 45-minute meander through the untamed Canadian backcountry, amplified by our collective anxiousness to begin fishing, makes the trek seem as if it will never end.

This expedition brings to mind the *Journey to the Beginning of Time* serial from the *Garfield Goose and Friends* television show that aired during after-school hours on WGN in the 1960s. Four boys embark on a surreal rowboat odyssey that takes them back in time. Encounters with dinosaurs and other extinct creatures mark their travels through the eras of prehistory, concluding at Earth's dawn:

> "All we knew was that we had to push on, we had to see what lay ahead. Then, there on the horizon before us stretched the greatest spectacle of all.... We were witnessing the beginning. We had arrived at the sea, the sea in which life began. This, we knew, was the end of our journey. We could go no farther. We could only pause and stare with awe at the great drama."

As we negotiate one last bend, a simple yet spectacular scene similar to the one encountered by the young explorers unveils. We exit the creek, gliding into the impressive expanse of Maskinonge Lake. Timbered shorelines frame silky waters that reflect cotton ball clouds sunlit white, bright, against a regal blue sky. We stop, silent and humble, to appreciate the aura of virginal wilderness, experiencing a rare place with no hint of man's fingerprint, so simple yet stunning, this somewhere in the middle of nowhere.

I struggle to suppress feeling the role of interloper, justifying our presence with the thought we've invested a great deal of time and money to enjoy our sport, our hobby in this, another beloved Canadian adventure. We *will* respect this place, this paradise, as Alan referred to it years ago.

Our surroundings duly appreciated, Larry, ever the pragmatist, breaks the silence with a question: "What do we do if the motor craps out?"

"We're dead," Art matter-of-factly replies.

Indeed, having arrived "somewhere and nowhere," my friends' question and answer affirm a sad truth. Our collective mechanical expertise ends not far beyond the changing of a lightbulb.

"No better place to kick the minnow bucket," I say, my voice upbeat, my pun pathetic.

"With all due respect to my fishing partners," Art answers, "I'd prefer to cash my chips in Vegas."

In final answer to Larry's question, I conclude, "Alan will find us ... eventually."

We begin casting the shallow bay at our point of entry, bracing for a flurry of activity, fast and furious action promised, wished, hoped. I make periodic hand adjustments to the trolling motor to alter the speed and direction of our drift. Expectations unfulfilled, not a strike nor follow rewards our efforts. Moving on, we fish multiple locations—bays, shorelines, points—all with the same sterile result. The optimism of "sanctuary unlocked" begins to fade.

Minutes turn to hours. The muskellunge that live here must have invoked sanctuary of their own.

Upon locating a large mid-lake weedbed in midafternoon, the game changes. Circumstances take a positive turn.

"Follow!" Larry shouts, a muskellunge trailing effortlessly behind his bucktail.

"Me too!" Art echoes, as he retrieves his bucktail from the opposite side of the boat.

My eyes darting from side to side I hold my next cast, immersed in the double dose of long-awaited excitement. "Make sure you figure-8," I dictate, though their concentration likely has my words falling on deaf ears. I'm prepared to reach for the net should either fish strike. As if a choreographed synchronized swim event, both fish dart away (perhaps a result of seeing the strange sight of a boat for the first time?) before either of my partners has the chance to entice them with a figure-8.

"Damn," Larry mutters.

"Damn," Art echoes.

I offer a different perspective: "Damn encouraging."

The scene, at this weedbed and another, repeated through the remainder of the afternoon and into the early evening. The count of muskellunge that followed our lures swelled to 40, the remarkable number of sightings more than we, collectively, had encountered in a lifetime of fishing.

Perhaps the results would have differed had I removed the Giant Jackpot from drydock. I hadn't prepared one (not that there was anything holding me back from doing so in the boat) by removing one of the two treble hooks and crimping the barbs of the remaining one, as required by the sanctuary lake regulations. Maybe I lost a bit of confidence in yesterday's unsuccessful, albeit brief trial, finding it easier to stay in a comfort zone and stick with known fish-catching commodities.

Although no muskies came to net, Larry caught northern pike of 32 and 33½ inches. With an hour ride back to the lodge and no interest in attempting to negotiate the bulk of it through the creek in waning daylight, we launched our final casts at 7:30 p.m. Between Larry's catch and the multitude of muskellunge sighted, we agreed Maskinonge Lake merited a return visit.

The fish and I were both stunned and disbelieving to find ourselves connected by a line.
—William Humphrey

Tuesday's forecast calling for possible storms, we elect to fish Little Vermilion instead of making the long run to Maskinonge. Early sunshine gives way to increasing clouds as the morning progresses. We hit several spots in the lower arm without contacting fish before heading into the lake's upper section, arriving at a large island near Twin Falls a few minutes before 10 a.m.

In need of giving his aching shoulders a recess, Larry put down his musky outfit in favor of lighter-weight spinning gear. Several casts later his brown and orange bucktail, casted a good distance from the point and toward deeper water, stops dead. His rod arched like a bell curve, he shouts, "Got one!"

I see his line slicing through the water, parallel to the boat. Moments later it reverses direction, the whirr of the reel's drag doing its job to tire the fish and reduce the strain on the monofilament line. Slowly coaxing the fish closer, it surfaces; it's a musky—larger than any we've seen this week.

I grab the net, squeezing the handle with an intensity befitting the tension-filled scene. I thought my all-purpose medium-size net had the capacity to handle anything that might come our way, but as this fish nears I'm not so sure.

Closer … stay hooked … closer … don't bolt … closer … please…. No last minute antics in the musky's bag of tricks, Larry guides it into the waiting net, filling it with nary an inch to spare.

"What a beauty!" I shout.

I remove one hand from the net and give Larry an exuberant congratulatory smack across the back. Seems I'm more excited than my cousin, who may be in the temporary stupor of adrenaline overload. His first musky, the fish boasts the eye-catching markings of a hybrid, referred to as a "tiger." One of Mother Nature's finest compositions, it results from the natural interbreeding of a muskellunge with a northern pike. Green-gold squiggled vertical bars paint its sides from gill plate to tail, the stripes fading as they melt into the white underbelly.

Larry kneels, takes control of the net, and with long-nose pliers in hand reaches over the gunnel to pop the hooks free. I ready the camera and tape measure while passing along the gripping instructions learned from Joe. It measures 40 inches, the same length as my first musky, the natural from Canyon Lake. A couple of quick photos, one or two each with my Polaroid Instant and Kodak Instamatic, precede the release successfully accomplished seconds later. We reorganize the boat and spend a few minutes relaxing in the savory afterglow.

Ready for more, I start the outboard and shout, "Bacon for breakfast tomorrow!"

Upon arriving at the next spot, the edge of an expansive reef adjoining deep water, Art asks me, "So, have you mothballed that magic lure for good? I think Larry and I are ready for some comic relief."

His not-so-gentle toss of the gauntlet prods me to again wing the Giant Jackpot. Without his comment, it may have forever been remanded to the darkness of the tackle box, never again to see the light of day, never again to fly through the summer breeze, never again to splash down and swim across the cool, refreshing lake water. I'll give it a fair chance this time, an extended workout, similar to the one it will give me by virtue of the intensive manual retrieve it requires.

New trial underway, retrieves assume a steady cadence following long casts. The up and down movements of my rod snake the Jackpot's hypnotic dance. The rhythm has spawned a dreaded earworm that syncs to the tune of "The Lion Sleeps Tonight." Cast after cast after cast. After cast. Maybe Art is right. Maybe this lure, like hundreds of others, is more adept at catching fishermen than fish.

Disappointment intensifying, I put a little extra behind the next cast, launching a "mile-long" bomb. Aware that the distance will reduce the odds of executing a good hookset should a fish strike, I dismiss that possibility, chuckling under my breath, "Like that's going to happen…"

The lulling monotony interrupts in staggering fashion as the water explodes with the violence of a TNT charge. The Jackpot momentarily disappears … then pops back to the surface, bobbing in the wake of the watery aftershock.

"What the hell," Art says, turning in the direction of the fireworks.

Stunned, my heart racing, I groan, "Damn."

Larry, echoing my comment from yesterday when close calls were the order of the day, says, "Damn encouraging."

Partially vindicated, I decide the Jackpot will be my exclusive lure of choice for the rest of the day and will see extensive action through the remainder of the week. We work the area awhile longer, but the eruption stands as a one-hit wonder.

Heavy overcast, a positive in musky hunting, now blankets the sky as we move to Twin Falls Bay. During that brief ride, a bald eagle, white head and tail feathers alight against the gray sky, wings overhead. With a lifelong affinity for eagles, I silently hope that the sight of the majestic raptor is a sign of good things to come.

Moments later, we begin our routine, flinging casts in various directions. I rocket the Jackpot toward the outlet where the falls cascade into Big Vermilion. The annoying earworm returns during an uneventful retrieve. With the lure some fifteen feet from the boat, I pause, reaching down to make an adjustment to the trolling motor while also taking a peek at the depth contours for this area on the lake map resting atop the small platform next to my seat.

Upon looking up, a sizeable shadow suspends several feet behind and below the lure that lies, motionless, on the surface. I alert Larry and Art, who hold their casts. With little room to work the lure in its normal manner, I contemplate the next move. Intensively focused on my musky fishing "first," I slowly reel in the small amount of slack line that curves from my rod tip to the lure, hoping to leave the Jackpot undisturbed until I decide if a subtle or exaggerated movement might up the odds of enticing this lion of the lake to strike. The last turn of the reel handle causes a barely perceptible twitch of the Jackpot's nose. The fish rises to within inches of the lure: curious, perhaps hungry, menacing. It's big—bigger than the one Larry landed a few short hours ago.

Indecision be gone, I think, it's time to do *something*. A short, quick jerk of the rod propels the lure several inches forward. As if shot out of a canon, the musky breaches the surface and with alligator, tooth-lined jaw agape, engulfs the lure.

"Holy crap!" Art yells, as all hell breaks loose.

The drag on my reel completely tightened down, there's nowhere for the fish to go; it's a wild steer at the end of a lasso. Both hands gripping the rod, I'm hanging on for dear life. The frenzied fish, seesawing the surface at boatside, showers us with lake water. In spite of the chaos, Larry manages to grab the net. As the musky powers from stern to bow, he corrals it. Sort of. One of the treble hooks snags the inside netting mesh, causing the back half of the musky to hang precariously outside the hoop as its jackhammering tail flings water in all directions. With a lightning move, Art jumps to the rescue, grabbing the body just in front of the tail. Swift and instantaneous, he and Larry swing the brute into the boat.

Rattled in a good way, approaching euphoria yet grounded by the need to get the musky back in the water with as little delay as possible, somewhere in the sequence of unhooking, measuring, and holding for a couple of quick photos, I slice several fingers of my right hand on its teeth or gill rakers. Nothing a Band-Aid or three can't handle, I gladly accept the badge-of-honor wounds, like the scrapes and punctures that now scar the Giant Jackpot. At this instant, find me in the dictionary next to the word "satisfaction."

The fat-bellied muskellunge tapes at 45 inches. I support it with two hands as I return it to the water, keeping it horizontal during a brief period of recuperation. Strength regained, it swims away near the surface before a final powerful sway of its tail thrusts it to the depths.

Around 6 p.m., my Jackpot repeats the magic, enticing a 35-inch musky to strike near a main point in the lake's upper arm. Then, at our last stop of the day, Art lands his first musky, a 21-incher from Chicago Bay. Gratified by the results of a day unparalleled in the annals of Maretti fishing, we return to the lodge to share the details of our conquests.

In response to my victorious toss of the Polaroids on the office counter, Alan's wide-eyed expression accompanies sincere congratulations. "Outstanding! I *knew* you guys could do it. How big?" One by one we flip through the photos, detailing the length of the fish and where we caught them.

In the photo of the 45-incher, Alan notices a narrow stream of blood along the musky's side, originating near the gill. Showing his concern for the resource, he asks, "Was the fish injured? Did she release okay?"

I hold up my bandaged fingers as Art says, "Just another day on the water with the Bloomingdale Bleeder."

"The fish was fine," I say. "Swam away strong to fight another day."

Alan reaches beneath the counter and then hands me a Master Angler Release application. "What'd you catch her on?" he asks.

Art, quick to respond, answers, "The Crackpot ... what else?"

"If I hadn't seen it with my own eyes, I'd have never believed it," Larry adds.

"Got to get some of those for the tackle shop here," Alan says, his head turning toward his inventory of lures for sale on the walls behind him. "And a few for *my* tackle box, too."

On Wednesday, under a mix of sun, clouds, and light rain, we ventured back to Maskinonge for a 12-hour marathon, hoping to turn Monday's followers into biters. Although the Giant Jackpot did elicit a couple of "blow ups," I came away empty. My partners, however, triumphed with various bucktails, each landing two muskies: Larry 26- and 29-inchers; Art 28- and 30-inchers.

With our experience of bigger fish coming from Little Vermilion, we elected to stay in the non-sanctuary lake on Thursday. The weather mirrored yesterday's mix. During a brief downpour, a 37 ½-incher took a liking to

Larry's experiment with the red and white Giant Jackpot tossed in the bay near Mike's Island. Although failing to tally, I experienced my first follows of the Jackpot. To this point, all the explosive action had been without warning. Today, the sight of a musky pushing water, "S"-ing on the surface behind the lure, brought a whole new level of titillation to the musky fishing dynamic.

On our last day, we again fished Little Vermilion. Unlike most of the other days this week, the day's unvaried weather offered sunny skies and calm seas, providing what I would use as our excuse for a fishless Friday.

For the week, we caught nine muskies and five northern pike, and in our brief respites from the big fish hunt, seventeen smallmouth bass. Upon returning home, I wrote a letter to our hosts at Fireside Lodge:

July 24, 1994

Dear Alan and Audrey,

Based on our daily updates, I believe you're aware that Larry, Art, and I had a great time last week. I don't think there are too many fishing groups that can say each member caught the largest fish of their lives on a single trip. We can, and had we been able to convert even a small percentage of the follows into strikes, the results would have been unbelievable—almost as unbelievable as the bacon.

Our last day, though fishless, was incredible as well with three eagles sighted. And returning from our final fishing session, we saw a cow moose and her calf crossing the lake at its deepest point. (If a 1,200-pound hoofed animal and her young-of-the-year can swim, why, oh why, can't I?)

Hope the remainder of the year goes well for you. See you at the show this winter, if I don't talk to you sooner.

Best regards,
Ed

Larry's 40-inch tiger musky.

The 45-incher (most of it, anyway).

My Boat

She's a 16-foot aluminum Crestliner FishHawk, birthed in 1980. Yellow in color, I affectionately refer to her as the "Banana Boat." Based on her age you might say she's fully ripened or if we're talking about the soft, mushy feel of floorboards beneath the well-worn beige carpeting, almost rotted. Of course, if she could talk, she might say the same about me and my body parts and be just as accurate. We've been through a lot together, some of it good, most of it better. She's a reliable friend and companion, an integral participant to bunches of memorable catches, most of which are fish. (More on that later.) We've weathered every type of weather, relished numerous wildlife sightings, and shared hundreds of hours of blissful serenity when the biggest concern centers on where to throw the next cast. Each time we leave the dock and glide onto the lake, worldly stressors of work and bills and traffic jams float away in the undulating wake. I am free and at peace. I love my boat.

Pre-owned, I purchased her in 1991 from Adlai E. Stevenson III. Name doesn't mean anything to you? Then you're probably under 50 years of age and-or not from Illinois. The Stevensons are a celebrated political family here in the Prairie State, noted for their intellect, reserved demeanor, and eloquent oratory skills.

Adlai III served in the U.S. Senate from 1970 to 1981 and ran for governor of Illinois in 1982 and 1986. Unsuccessful in those later ventures, he and his family members are "burdened" by the political "flaw" of too much integrity, not fitting the profile of numerous, infamous Illinois politicians:

> Joel Matteson, governor 1853-1857: Attempted to cash in $200,000 of government scrip he "found" in a shoebox.

> Lennington Small, governor 1921-1929: Charged with embezzling and laundering $600,000 while state treasurer. Acquitted of the charges, four jurors later enjoyed the good fortune of obtaining state jobs.

> Otto Kerner, governor 1961-1968: Convicted in 1973 on 17 counts of bribery and conspiracy, sentenced to three years in prison.

> Paul Powell, secretary of state 1965-1970: Upon his death, some shoeboxes (still the preferred storage for Illinois graft a century later!) and other containers holding $750,000 were found in his hotel suite. Later, discovered in his rental storage

facility were 14 transistor radios, 49 cases of whiskey, and 2 cases of creamed corn.

Dan Walker, governor 1973-1977: Pleaded guilty in 1987 to fraud and perjury charges resulting, in part, from improper loans arranged for him from his own savings and loan institution before it went bankrupt. Sentenced to 7 years in prison.

George Ryan (aka 16627-424, Federal prisoner ID), secretary of state 1991-1999, governor 1999-2003: Convicted on federal racketeering and fraud charges, sentenced to 6½ years in prison.

Rod Blagojevich (aka 40892-424, Federal prisoner ID), "Governor Hair" 2003-2009: Impeached from office by a 59-0 vote January 2009, found guilty of 11 criminal charges related to allegations he attempted to "sell" President Barack Obama's vacated Senate seat, and 6 counts involving fundraising shakedowns of a hospital executive and racetrack owner, sentenced to 14 years in prison.

Ah, Illinois. The state where elected officials make our license plates.

Adlai III's dad, Adlai II, held the position of Ambassador to the United Nations and Governor of Illinois, running unsuccessfully for the Presidency of the United States against Dwight D. Eisenhower in 1952 and 1956. (Tough sleddin', running against a five-star general and WWII hero.) Adlai III's grandfather served Illinois as its Secretary of State, and his great-grandfather, an Illinois Congressman, ran successfully as vice president of the United States on the democratic ticket with Grover Cleveland, elected in 1893 to a four-year term.

If none of that impresses you, how about this? Adlai III and actor McLean Stevenson are third cousins. You'll likely remember McLean as Colonel Henry Blake from the hit television series *M*A*S*H*. The easygoing commander hailed from Illinois, frequently wearing his navy blue college sweater with the large orange "I," having attended the University of Illinois. He also wore a floppy hat adorned with fishing lures. Gosh, maybe some of those lures hit the water while fishing out of the yellow Crestliner FishHawk with his cousin Adlai III. Talk about a boat with provenance.

So what does it all mean? I'll tell you what it means. It means the honorable Adlai Stevenson III and I likely farted in the same boat seat.

~ ~ ~ ~ ~

High Level Health Highlights (Lowlights)
My Body - A Lemon with Lyme (Disease), But Hold the Mayo (Clinic)

(H)ELP!

Leonard is my middle (baptismal) name, given in honor of my godfather, one of my dad's younger brothers. Placing an "H" in front of my "ELP" initials creates a moniker describing much of my physical history. I understand that aches and pains befall everyone at one time or another. I further understand that 80% of people don't care about mine, and the other 20% are glad I have them (and they don't). Larry designates me as the person he most associates with the word "pain." I spend so much time in doctor's waiting rooms that if I were so inclined, I could complete a detailed replica of the Eiffel Tower from the jar of tongue depressors on each visit.

Then, and now, my mother holds fast to her belief that I was "sickly as a child." She must have struggled with the decision of whether or not to allow me to don the robes of an altar boy, gaining holy indulgences that would vault me up the stairway to heaven's eternal happiness. She ultimately decided in favor of my health; the need to cut short my sleep to serve at daily 6 a.m. masses might weaken my resistance and further compromise the already fragile (in her view) state of my physical well-being.

Other than an appendectomy at age eight (the "I can't move I'm in so much pain" affliction striking at Uncle Ben and Aunt Irene's Grayslake home, and additionally, this could very well have been the same weekend that Dad inadvertently slammed the trunk of the '52 Ford on my thumb as we packed for the trip, the damaging scar from that event more psychological than physical, the v-shaped indentation below the nail returning to normal with the quick application of an ice cube), and a tonsillectomy at ten (an innocent bystander to an appointment for my sister, Nancy, and I'm not making this up, the quack-specialist attributing the source of her ongoing hip pain to fluid draining from her tonsils, those bad boys requiring removal, and "Oh, by the way young man, as long as you're here let's take a look at yours—my goodness, yours are worse than hers!"), I believe my illnesses pretty much tracked with the rest of the childhood population: chicken pox, measles, mumps, colds, and flu.

In the category of "everyone remembers where they were when they heard the news," a low-grade fever "ravaged" my body on Friday, November 22, 1963, as I slurped spoonfuls of slender, inch-long noodles soaking in the warm broth of Mrs. Grass Chicken Noodle Soup. Slouched on the couch, the somber Walter Cronkite bulletin reporting the assassination of President Kennedy interrupted my viewing of a television show. The delirium of a 98.7-or-thereabout degree temperature taking its toll on the clarity of my recall, I'm a bit fuzzy as to which of Mom's soap operas the historic announcement interrupted. No matter, having called me in sick that day, maybe Mom *was* onto something regarding my less-than-robust health hardiness.

As if flipping a switch, good health flourished during my high school and college years, with one recurring exception. During my junior year at Notre Dame, driven by the need to be freed from the inconvenience of wearing glasses and the desire to improve my personal appearance (with the omnipresent goal of gaining female companionship), I chose to see the world through a pair of contact lenses instead of my geeky thick-plastic-frame spectacles. The corrective lenses converted my unremarkable blue-gray eyes to a deep, rich, and remarkably hokey ocean blue. While at NIU, I wore the "hard" lenses 16 to 18 hours per day, aware but choosing to ignore the fact that saliva was not a good sanitizing agent when inserting them. The nasty "Mr. Iritis" visited me on several occasions. The last bout, a year after graduating, was so severe it required an anti-inflammatory injection directly into the eyeball. Yum. Already betrothed, I returned to the bespectacled world of "four eyes" with little regret.

From my high school days with the Ted Williams dumbbell (this is not a reference to Ted's son, John, who had Ted's head cryogenically frozen upon his death in 1992) through early adulthood, Dad counseled me on using my legs to avoid injury to my back when lifting heavy objects. I always appreciated the advice, but by the time I celebrated my 33rd birthday, with twenty years of "knowing it all" tucked under my belt, his words went in one ear and with little in between to stop them, out the other.

The fateful event launching this young stallion on the one-way path leading to the glue factory occurred on a summer day in the early 1980s. Upon returning home from a successful day of catching white bass on the Chain O' Lakes, I began unpacking my fishing gear from the '75 Chevy Nova. Forgetting (er, ignoring) years of Dad's admonitions, the 60-ish-pound trolling motor battery got the best of me. My legs shirking their responsibility as I lifted the Sears DieHard from the trunk, the L4 and L5 discs showed their displeasure by bulging like frightened puffer fish.

Thus dawned my personal epoch of "oldfartitis," the periodic lower back "lock-ups" limiting me to turtle-like mobility. The trigger for these painful episodes included any number of strenuous life activities, including but not limited to: sitting the wrong way, sleeping the wrong way, sneezing, reaching for a television remote, toweling dry after a shower, coughing, blinking, tying a shoe lace, eating, wiping my butt, entering or exiting a car or boat, casting a lure, retrieving a lure, setting the hook, and breathing.

Combinations of heat, cold, physical therapy, muscle relaxants, and pain medication aided in the gradual improvement of each episode, those spanning three days to two weeks. My Cro-Magnon movements during these periods of recovery often brought comments and questions from co-workers, friends, and family, with the most frequently asked, "Why are you walking around like you've got a fishing rod shoved up your rear end?"

Something had to give. In the spring of 1992, at age 40, it did. Startled and twisting to answer a ringing telephone (wrong number, thank you very much) in the middle of the night, one of my original equipment lower lumbar shock absorbers exploded, the "fragmented disc" pressing on a nerve causing leg pain so intense that my severely hampered gait looked as if Jacque Cousteau had driven his dive boat *Calypso* up my posterior canal.

A neurosurgeon (bless his heart) returned my ability to walk, though permanent but varying levels of chronic discomfort in the lower back remained, as well as nerve damage in the legs. Calf, ankle, and toe cramps often interrupt a night's rest, requiring me to rise and "walk it off." The silver lining in an otherwise dark cloud, these involuntary leg and foot movements rarely occur during the day. Fortunately, they have not interfered when out on the lake operating the foot-petal that controls the trolling motor.

The bad back (and legs) put an end to my participation in a number of previously enjoyed sports including golf, racquetball, and the less enjoyed bowling. So much for some of the Fabulous Maretti Brothers challenges. My limited physical activity, along with heredity and diet, paved the road to blood test numbers continually tracking in the wrong direction: high triglycerides, high total cholesterol, high bad cholesterol, and low good cholesterol. Our family physician, Dr. Mark (an avid fisherman, by the way), prescribed the statin Baycol and recommended I take note of the fat content on food labels while cutting back on sweets and fast food. I'm not sure if substituting a Filet-O-Fish for a Big Mac is what he had in mind.

The hits kept on coming: allergies (the mystery of the annual April symptoms I believed to be a spring cold), bifocals, a chronic sore neck, tennis and golf elbow (although I no longer played either, perhaps "fishing-casting" elbow), and pain in the hips and finger joints. Too young for arthritis (not really), a 2001 test for Lyme disease (what a "lemon," my body) came up positive (so *that's* what that target-like rash was...) and was promptly treated with heavy duty antibiotics. Baycol got pulled from the market because of serious side effects, among them stiff neck and stiff joints. Hmmm, maybe the tick got an undeserved bad rap.

Mental Capacity (Incapacity)

Many years ago, my fishing friends believed I could remember the specific circumstances of every fish I ever caught: species, size, body of water, location, time of day, lure, weather conditions, etc. Their belief, of course, was folly. At my cognitive peak, I believe my recall capability did not exceed 99.9%. As years passed, my mental capacity for such recollection diminished to perhaps 99.8%, the freed space needed for tasks such as finding my way home from work each day, remembering to wipe foodstuffs from my face that may have missed my mouth or covertly escaped during the dining ritual, and zipping up after a visit to the men's room. I sometimes wonder if the deterioration relates to innocent activities past:

> As a preschooler, I recall visits to the claustrophobic four-room flat that Busia rented on the second floor of a rickety old building on Noble Street. The landlord didn't do a particularly good job maintaining the property, and while I can't say for certain that I sampled some of the flaking lead-based paint that peeled from the walls like Jays potato chips, I can't say that I didn't, either.
>
> My previously mentioned plastic-bag-over-the-head divers helmet when playing *Sea Hunt*.
>
> Early in my grammar school years, I played with a bead of mercury that had oozed out of a broken glass thermometer. The quicksilver provided hours of entertainment as I rolled the droplet across floors and tables, separated it into multiple beads, and then rejoined them. Such a fun little item, that toxic chemical element.
>
> Remember my previously mentioned silver-dollar size pet turtles? In 1975, (some 15 years too late for my protection)

the U.S. Food and Drug Administration made it illegal for anyone to sell turtles under four inches in length due to the ease of contracting salmonella through casual contact with the mini-reptile.

Since early childhood, I've engaged in an unquenchable love affair with the sweet treats of the Hostess brand: Cupcakes, Sno Balls, Ho Ho's, Ding Dongs, Fruit Pies, and Twinkies. The Interstate Brands Corporation announced a recall for many of those foods manufactured in Schiller Park, Illinois, on January 27, 1998. The confections produced that fateful day may have been contaminated by the illegal removal of asbestos from the plant's boiler room, the process not following prescribed emission control and disposal procedures. Removed asbestos was carted through the production facility to outside dumpsters. Asbestos fibers may have been mixed into the products or contaminated packaging. Checking our freezer, a box of ten individually wrapped Twinkies had one of the "winning" numbers: 57A006. (I should be so lucky with Lottery tickets.) Only one of the ten golden sponge cakes with creamy filling remained in the box.

Perhaps the lead residue left in my mouth from crimping split-shot weights onto fishing line with my teeth, a practice spanning some 50 years, hasn't been such a good idea, either.

In discussions with my baby-boomer contemporaries, I know I am not alone. Though the causes may differ, many of us seem to be suffering from what has been termed "Halfzheimers" or "Sometimesheimers" disease. Ever walked into a room for something and when you get there, already forgotten the reason why? Of course you have. Left a light on in the basement, garage, or closet, and not discovered it until hours later, or the next day? Of course you have. Can't come up with that ... that ... that ... "word" you're looking for, the name of that acquaintance, the title of that movie you saw just a week or two ago? Of course you have. Most of these are child's play, tales from the lightweight division. Step into the ring with this Muhammed Ali; I've taken it to a whole new level. Here's a sampling of a few of my more memorable whiffs at some of life's simpler tasks:

> Back in the contact lens-wearing days, I put them in but found my vision significantly blurred. Removing one, I found the

second lens on top of the other—I had put them both in the same eye.

Flipped the switch to open the sunroof on the car after leaving work, but didn't realize until arriving home that I failed to slide back the inside panel.

Though the same style, I wore two different color shoes to work.

At work, numbers, letters, words, and dates often don't make it from brain to paper. I'm dialing wrong telephone numbers while looking right at them. I'm dialing fax numbers instead of telephone numbers. E-mails need to be triple checked before sending, each pass typically finding a correction (or two, or more). I received a call from an out of state co-worker: "Was there supposed to be something in that Fed-Ex envelope you sent me?"

Following the eraser, my next best friend is the Post It Note. If I don't write it down, whatever "it" is, it doesn't get done: forgotten. My pain is your gain—buy stock in 3M!

Did an "Uncle Billy" from the movie, *It's a Wonderful Life*. Worked on my semi-monthly bill paying and prepared the forms for depositing checks, making transfers among accounts, etc. I also had $50 cash in the envelope I took to the Credit Union. The teller completed the transactions and handed me my receipts and the additional cash back requested. I folded and put them in my pocket, pitching the envelope into the trashcan. When the money count that evening came up $50 short, I realized what I had done. Placing a call the next morning, they informed me the trash is picked up nightly. "Silly ol' stupid ol' fool!"

I prepared two rebates for a couple of recently purchased light bulbs, sealing both envelopes. Each contained a sales receipt, rebate request form, and UPC code. When doing the "clean up," I came across one of the UPC codes. Cutting open both envelopes, I found I had put a blank piece of cardboard in one of them instead of the UPC code.

One of the two snaps securing the cover of my portable depth finder broke, so I began using a bungee cord to keep the cover in place while transporting it. Over the course of time a bit of stretch worked its way into the cord. Sure, the cover was bouncing off the base each time I carried it. I was aware, but hey, where's it gonna go? I'll tell you where. The base unit is going to twist itself out of the cover and go crashing to the sidewalk, breaking off one of the control knobs.

The circular part of the station wagon's key fob to which the key ring attaches cracked. I rigged some Velcro and it worked just fine—for a while. On occasion, the two would get separated, typically when putting the keys into a pocket or taking them out. A permanent fix was required, but hell, where are they gonna go? I'll tell you where—into the fourth dimension, like the little girl who fell out of bed and disappeared into the wall in that classic *Twilight Zone* episode. Unlike the success retrieving the girl, the fob is yet to be found.

The next week, I lost the keys.

Invited to attend a family gathering on a Sunday afternoon, I set the VCR to record the Bears game. Upon returning home I rewound the tape and settled in to watch it. Set to the wrong channel, I ended up with three hours of Bridezilla.

"60 POUNDS OF TOMATOES FROM ONE SINGLE PLANT—TREE TOMATO—ZOOMS TO AN AMAZING 8-FEET TALL IN JUST 3 MONTHS!" I knew better. I really did. But that didn't stop me. Writing the check, the voice of reason inside my head kept whispering, "This is stupid … this is a mistake." The five-inch shriveled stalk I received needed immediate life support. Stubbornly refusing to acknowledge my blunder, I gained some comfort with the 30-day money back guarantee, so, what the hell, let's put it in the ground and see what happens. Advertised to grow a foot taller than Wilt Chamberlain, the plant's DNA *had* to possess superior genetics. Over the next three weeks I staked, fertilized, and watered "Little Wilt." My nurturing went for naught: The prolific promises of the Master Tomato Race flat-lined. Swallowing my pride and acknowledging the "I told you so" of the voice that tried to warn me, I pulled out the ad to request a refund. Damn hucksters! All of their information was on the ordering coupon sent with the check, not a shred remaining about how to get my money back.

In (another) moment of flawed thinking, as I write the annual premium check for my life insurance policy I consider the advantage of dying before the policy expiration, so all the payments over the years will not have been in vain.

Confident we didn't need the motel to provide a wake-up call to get an early start for our day on Lake Erie, I assured my fishing companions that my body clock would adequately serve that purpose at 5 a.m. They weren't happy with me (nor was I and couldn't blame them) when the sun, peeking through the window shades at 6:30, ensured a place at the end of a long line at the launch ramp and a few less hours to bag our walleye limit.

A nasty snarl of twisted monofilament required I cut the line and retie my snap-swivel with the Mepps spinner attached to it. With the task completed, I tossed the lure over the side of the boat to pull the line taught before reeling it in, preparing for the next cast. As it fluttered out of sight, I realized I had tied it to an unattached piece of the clipped line instead of the one coming from the reel.

So, when I return from a fishing trip and Jo Ann asks, "What did you catch?" you understand she's not surprised if I answer, "Was I fishing?"

~ ~ ~ ~ ~

It has always been my private conviction that any man who pits his intelligence against a fish and loses has it coming.
—John Steinbeck

The Thrill of Victory, The Agony of the Hook (I)

I'm not exactly a klutz, but with regard to grace, I'd say I'm further from Grace Kelly and Gene Kelly, and more in the neighborhood of Emmett Kelly. I believe my companions, on various fishing trips, run a pool picking the date and time that I yell, "I'm cut!" The person selecting a time early on the first day is typically the winner. The first aid kit and I are best of friends.

I always make sure my tetanus booster shot is up to date, a Darwinian survival instinct not unlike a person keeping tabs on the battery strength of their pacemaker. Some of my more financially savvy friends inquire as to the timing of my fishing vacations so they can reallocate their stock portfolios toward heavier weightings in the health care industry.

Small comfort reigns if the appearance of first blood results from unhooking a toothy walleye or northern pike, slicing a finger on the gill raker of a musky, or even getting stuck by the dorsal fin of a perch or bluegill. Quite often, unfortunately, the call goes up when I reach into the tackle box to select a lure and end up receiving a prick for my pluck. With regard to the latter, inquiring minds might want to know, "Gee, how could such a seemingly simple task turn into a blood-letting? How difficult could it be?" A couple of factors play into this scenario:

> On the advice of the fishing mavens, I meticulously hone the hooks on every lure to the sharpness of a neurosurgeon's scalpel.

> My tackle boxes (some number more than eight but less than infinity), "packed to the gills" like cans of sardines, evidence the ongoing objective to accumulate at least one of every lure that has ever been manufactured, in every size and color.

My first body piercing of a fishy-kind occurred in October of 1994, at Mason Lake in south-central Wisconsin. On this outing, Joe introduced me to the joys of bass fishing with Rat-L-Traps. The one-half ounce Rat-L-Trap, a slender hard-plastic bait just under three-inches in length, profiles like a football. A chamber containing small BBs that rattle as the lure tightly quivers during high-speed retrieves sets it apart from most others. Fish instinctively respond to its vibration and motion, savagely attacking it.

After two hours on the water, Joe had landed 15 bass. My count stood at 6. Around 10:45 a.m., I hooked a 'hammer-handle" 20-inch pike. Hand-land in process, I gripped it behind the gills and lifted it into the boat. Big mistake. With a feisty flip, the slimy pike slipped from my grasp, one of the hooks from the back treble impaling my index finger, driven in past the barb. Still attached to the other treble, the fish commenced a wild break-dance. Silenced in shock and stupidity, the surreal scene lasted an eternity of some ten seconds before the flapping fish freed itself. Minutes later, we were off to Divine Savior Hospital in Portage for the divine relief of professional hook extraction.

With my finger bandaged (and ego bruised), we returned to the lake. From 1 p.m. to 4 p.m., Joe caught 21 bass. I bagged 35. Oddly, it was the first time I out-fished him. In view of my improved results, I considered taping my finger on future outings, as perhaps the bulky wrap somehow contributed to the extraordinary afternoon success by changing the speed or cadence of the retrieve as I turned the reel handle. Or not. Recognizing the folly, by golly, I took a pass on that one.

The dictionaries give twenty-three ways of spelling the word "muskallonge," but there's only one way to fight him and only one particular, peculiar kind of heart-palpitation that he gives the fisherman who catches him napping. For what the leaping tuna is to the Pacific Coast and the tarpon to Florida, is the muskallonge to the lakes of the great Northwest.

To begin with, call him by the familiar term with which sportsmen have come to know and revere him—the "musky." The very word tells of his standing as the greatest game fish in American waters, for he is the only one of them that has had his name so affectionately abbreviated. You can hear a devotee of the sport talk about the pugnacious bass, the trout, or the pike in matter-of-fact manner; but, if he knows the game and loves it, his voice takes on a different tone when he speaks of the musky.

Fishing trips are very much like love-affairs in one way: they say a man can have only one grand affair of the heart....
—John R. Rathom, *A Fight with a Muskallonge*, 1902

Musky Fishing on the Alexandra Chain of Lakes, Ontario, Canada

It's a midsummer evening in the early 1990's. At home and in front of the television, I'm viewing another installment of the unending ritual of self-inflicted punishment: The Cubs are losing another ballgame. The telephone rings. I answer, greeted by Terry's voice. I am surprised. I am surprised because Terry never calls me. Because Terry never calls me, I reply, "Who is this?"

"It's Terry."

"No, really, who is this?"

"Damn you!"

With the hint of urgency in his voice and curiosity getting the better of me, I ask, "What's going on?"

"I'm up at our place in Canada and just caught a 44-inch musky. It's the biggest fish I've ever caught and for sure the biggest anyone in the family has taken out of our lakes. Do you think I should let it go ... or have it mounted?"

"Who is this...?"

In the years following my musky-targeted Canadian trips to Canyon and Little Vermilion Lakes, I turned my attention to northwest Ontario's Alexandra Chain of eight interconnected lakes: Forest, Whitney, Edward, Indian, Bladder, Cobble, Big Boulder, and Little Boulder. With the Canadian province encompassing a-quarter-million lakes, what defined the allure of these eight? A blindfolded toss of a dart at an Ontario map? A cosmic call to my namesake, Edward Lake? Rumors of tackle-busting behemoths dwarfing the existing

249

world record? How about a simple matter of dollars and cents, framed by a 35-year friendship? Bingo!

Terry, by virtue of marrying into a family that owns a couple of cabins on the shore of Forest Lake, began hosting an annual Canadian trip that would become my primary musky-fishing destination for decades to come. The property, purchased by a consortium of his father-in-law and uncles-in-law in the mid-1960s, Terry contends this dowry of fisherman's delight did not play a role in his decision to proffer a marriage proposal. While likely true, it certainly didn't make the proposition any less attractive, either. Over the years, he and his wife, Dianna, acquired majority interest in the property, completing numerous "sweat equity" updates and upgrades while preserving its reclusive charm. In the "It's a small world" category, the northernmost bay of Forest Lake connects to Canyon Lake (though a non-navigable spillway separates them), the location of my first Canadian muskellunge excursion several years earlier.

Dianna and Terry's retreat, not road accessible, requires a five to ten-minute trip by boat. Near the spillway on the Forest Lake side, an inconspicuous turnoff from Ontario Highway 647's terminus tapers to a boat launch at the water's edge, where a 20-foot pier extends into the lake. Launching the boat on the irregular surface of rocks, depressions, and tall grass can be any combination of adventurous, troublesome, or borderline dangerous: Rain makes the ground wheel-spinning, mud-rutting slick; ticks jump for joy at the prospect of burrowing into our fresh flesh; and the hum of euphoric mosquitoes fills the air with a vampire-melodic symphony.

Once successfully launched and tied to the dock, we pack the boats to flotation-challenge level with rods, reels, tackle containers, luggage, food, and beverages—before finally cramming ourselves into any remaining crevices. It's quite a sight. I've considered contacting the product development team of the Lund Boat Company should they have interest in producing and marketing a "garbage scow" line of watercraft.

The westernmost lake of the Alexandra Chain, Forest Lake is shaped like a checkmark, its two relatively narrow arms orientated to the northwest and northeast. Dianna and Terry's property, located at the southernmost point where these sections of the lake adjoin, consists of several acres. The original structure, a quaint 20-foot by 20-foot log cabin built in the early 1950s, calls its summertime visitors from atop a rock outcropping rising from the water's edge. Down a gradual slope behind it, a small bay harbors a pier and two-slot boathouse. Decades of harsh Canadian winters have faded the once-yellow wooden-sided boathouse that stands awkwardly pitched like a precarious house of cards, one breezy day away from becoming a memory.

Built several years later and crafted from logs of native trees like the original lakeside cabin, the main lodge is centrally sited on the acreage. Stilted in front, the structure tucks into terrain that gradually elevates to the rear. Trees of the Canadian forest, pines, junipers, aspens, and birches among them, rim the land behind it and dot the grassy area from the lake to the lodge, providing privacy and a cloak of shade.

After ascending nine stairs, a screened porch stretches across the front two-thirds of the cabin, affording picturesque views of the lake and the setting sun on evenings with clear skies. The space, which catches refreshing south and westerly breezes, comfortably accommodates four to six individuals with cushioned Adirondack-style chairs, a couple of circular pine tables, and a propane grill.

Stepping into the lodge from the porch, a vintage 1950s charmingly rustic great room awaits: brown, beige, and green linoleum tiles partially hidden beneath colorfully patterned and well-worn oriental-style rugs and runners; built-in pine cabinets and bookcases; a large, pine dining room table; an open and airy ceiling, the underside of the gable roof lined with pine boards; a thick, circular pine tree-trunk support beam crossing the width of the room; couches and chairs with pine frames and arms supporting fishing-theme cushions; a square-shape pine coffee table and round, pine end tables. It's a pine place to be.

A wood-burning stove and a glass-door gun cabinet line the room's back wall, separated by a floor to ceiling fieldstone fireplace. An enlarged photo of a loon and her chick rest on the mantle, with a rack of moose antlers affixed above it. The log walls also display the head mounts of an elk and a proudly antlered caribou. These steeds of the Canadian boogeyman protrude prominently into the room. They survey all that transpires, stealth eyes following every movement of cabin occupants, ready to come alive in the dead of night and use their majestic racks to gore weary fishermen as they sleep.

An aged, thick-bellied muskellunge mount, positioned above one of the lake-view windows, sports an oxidized, hairline-cracked, golden brown varnish. A sports relic (much like myself), the mummified trophy appears poised to drop its formaldehyde encrusted scales like a cornflake rain shower the next time the cabin door accidentally slams shut.

The open feel of the cabin's interior continues to the two bedrooms, curtain panels on tension rods functioning as doors. Two beds in each room are tented with mosquito netting, the white mesh foiling the efforts of blood-sucking cabin infiltrators. A small loft, open to the great room, contains another bed.

A long day on the water, followed by imbibing locally purchased Canadian beverages containing malt, barley, and rye elevates us to a platonic state of being known as "pickled contentment." The conclusion of this daily unwinding process renders the lack of privacy with door-less sleeping accommodations a non-issue. Some find the snoring cadence a soothing rhythm to induce one's own slumber. Those who don't must repress the urge to add their names to the list of infamous mass murderers, though any court of law, with audio tape evidence, would certainly rule it justifiable homicide. More passive methods of dealing with the potentially irritating adenoid musical include ear plugs or retreating to the silence and privacy of the original lakeside cabin, now solely furnished with a pair of beds.

The main cabin scores a big "thumbs up" on its bathroom: toilet, sink, hot water shower, two small windows, and … a door! A single seat outhouse located behind the house shares a common trait with all other outhouses: enter at your own risk and only in the most critical of bowel-gnarling circumstances when the indoor facility is occupied. When tearing down a tiny shed near the lakeside cabin, Terry uncovered the remnants of the original latrine, a "two-seater." Double bum-mer.

The kitchen, not an "eat in," contains a pass-through to the dining area. Water pumped from the lake to a storage tank passes through multiple filters that supply the kitchen (for washing dishes) and bathroom (for bathing and the potty). With one ear to the W.C. Fields comment, "I never drink water because of the disgusting things that fish do in it," purified, bottled water is used for drinking and cooking,

All food, whether unwrapped fruits and vegetables, packaged bakery goods and breads, or boxed or bagged staples, are secured in cabinets, tight-fitting covered bins, coolers, or stored beneath smoke-colored plastic storage domes on the countertops. Further vigilance is required in cleaning up crumbs and bits of food AWOL from the countertops or table, caught by the sink strainer after dishwashing, or splashed from a pot or pan to the stovetop or floor. Why?

Such caution lacking, a newbie to our Canadian outback experience, just awakened and on his way to pouring a first cup of morning coffee might observe, "Hey, who sprinkled caraway seeds on the floor, countertop, sink, and stove?" unaware the tiny, black pellets represent the "calling cards" of field mice that participated in an unintended nocturnal buffet. A different kind of "rat race" exists up here. Several years ago, hearing a rumor of resident mice in need of the Jenny Craig program, a snake approximately two feet in length took up residence in the kitchen for a few days (more on that, later). Ah, the great outdoors, indoors.

Two other words come to mind when describing the "rustic ambiance" of this secluded getaway—"no electricity." If whatever modern convenience you may require isn't powered by batteries, don't bother packing it. A stove, refrigerator and hot water heater, all powered by propane (stored behind the house in five-foot, steel gray, missile shaped cylinders) complete the fully equipped kitchen. Wall sconces throughout likewise run on propane, providing all cabin lighting. A wood-burning stove radiates early and late season heat, fueled by fallen trees cut, split, and stacked between the stilts supporting the front porch. The breezes of three seasons, passing through the screens of open windows, provides the lodge's "air conditioning."

The annual "guys" outing occurs in mid-July. Depending on the year, two to six individuals participate, drawing from an expanded pool of family and friends: Cousins Rich, Ben, Larry, Phil, Richie, Alec, and friends Dan, Mike, Ken, Art, Rick, Dave, and Tom. I sharpened the ol' statistician's pencil to keep tabs on our progress (or regress) spanning almost two decades. Although the majority of our efforts target the muskellunge we also, on occasion, jig for walleye, fine table fare.

Craving to reconnect with nature while collectively enjoying the sport we love, Dianna and Terry's sanctuary provides a glorious retreat "far from the madding crowd." As our weeks unfold from this venue of simplicity and solitude, each annual excursion imprints images—frequently adventuresome, occasionally heroic, and sometimes bumbling—that forever imbed in the memory of its participants.

I have wondered if it is the wildness in fish that somehow renews the wildness in us. After the hook is set and the shiver of something wild comes dancing up the rod, we seem somehow to be released from the confines of our over-civilized selves. It is as if the fighting fish is the longed-for iron key that opens the golden door to our uncensored souls and what might be wild in us.

I have seen children squeal, women scream, and men bellow with delight at the first mad run of a just-hooked fish. I have heard their voices and my own ring out over a still lake. And in that instant, in that moment of abandonment too pure, uncluttered joy, there is, suddenly and momentarily, a brief glimpse into the untamed, unfettered, wild nature of what man once was, and what he still needs to be from time to time.

And afterward, after the fish is brought to hand, the catcher seems somehow recharged, revitalized, renewed. Having shed the burden of self-consciousness, if only for a few moments, he seems somehow relaxed and more at one with his nature.

—Paul Quinnett, *Pavlov's Trout*

Freespool Flashbacks from the Alexandra Chain of Lakes
1995 - 1999

Carpe diem! Unfettered by the burdens of civilization, our days in the splendor of the Canadian wilderness unfold long and full. Rigorous daylight hours on the water, casting and retrieving in a labor of love, yield to relaxing evenings on the screened porch. The sun long gone, citronella candles now flicker a golden glow. Blackberry brandy no longer a part of our in-boat ritual, we now share libations of consolation or celebration upon conclusion of our day on the water. Later, the call of the loon punctuates conversations and fishing tales of yore that linger well into the late hours. Then, solid shuteye and on to tomorrow.

The cabin's creaky floorboards announce my status as "first to wake" each morning. The ritual begins in the kitchen, where I fill the aluminum coffee pot with water and ground coffee, then igniting the stove burner that will percolate it into an addictively aromatic and piping hot liquid heart-starter for all to enjoy as they awake, one by one, in no particular order. That task underway, I navigate to the screened porch, deeply inhaling a dose of the new day. Its greeting may be cold or cool, temperate, or tropical, sometimes surprising, never upsetting. Morning sun can cast a glow on distant shorelines, or rain or mist may obscure them. Swaying tree branches and waves suggest wind direction and velocity. I delight in the absorption of these solitary morning moments in this small plot of rough-hewn paradise on the edge of northern wilderness.

July 1995. On the lakes, my adrenaline pumped with vigor through numerous muskellunge encounters. Although bucktail offerings drew a fair amount of follows, the Giant Jackpot worked its magic for me, with 31-, 35-, and 37-inchers coming to net. Turns of the reel handle to retrieve a top-water lure likens to the childhood experience of rotating the crank of a Jack-in-the-Box toy, though without the catchy "Pop Goes the Weasel" tune that provides a "heads up" before clown-face weasel "Jack" (a creepy, albeit inanimate boogeyman of sorts) comes bolting out of the box. Sometimes the wake behind a top-water lure tips-off the angler to an impending strike, though often the surface explosion occurs without warning. When fishing for muskies, the only thing better than catching one is catching one on a top-water lure, the heart-racing thrill unparalleled in my fishing world.

Thank you, Dianna and Terry, for a truly enjoyable week. Contributing to the carefree spirit of holiday, not necessarily in order (for their order is of no consequence): fine fishing, food, scenery, and camaraderie. It's all good.

Equally satisfying ... on the lake, or on the porch.

The Thrill of Victory, the Agony of the Hook (II)

July 1996. Cousin Ben, thirteen years my junior, captained us on that "I wish I could fuggidaboudit" day. I'd recently acquired the bad habit of not returning used lures to their proper place in my tackle box, instead hanging them from a strip of wood that trimmed the red Lund's aluminum bench that served as my seat and casting platform.

All proceeds according to plan with the netting and unhooking of a small musky that chomped down on my black bucktail. Ready to release the 30-inch fish, I lower myself to a kneeling position and place it in the water, left hand beneath its jaw. Concentrating on the task at hand, I give little thought to a pinch on the outside of my left knee. With my right hand gripped in front of its tail, I make small adjustments to keep the fish upright as it regains its bearings. Pulsing movement a signal of reclaimed strength I ease my grip, give it a gentle push forward, and watch it sway out of sight.

I swish my hands in the 70-degree water and then grab the gunnel preparing to return upright. My progress impeded, I look down to find a hook from one of the trebles of my Cisco Kid crankbait imbedded in my jeans at the knee. So … that was the pinch experienced during the release—just a surface scratch, I surmise.

That scenario fades in seconds. Each tug of the hook stabs and burns—a big clue that it's not just buried in the material. Uh oh. While I hold the lure and hook, Ben uses a pocket knife to cut through the denim, revealing the hook point of one of the trebles straight into my flesh, buried past the barb. The disturbing sight churns my innards like a school of frenzied minnows racing from stomach to throat. Here we are in the middle of nowhere, hours away by boat, then car, from a medical facility.

Ben comments on the oh-shit moment. "Oh, shit."

"That's not what I want to hear," I say, the words eking out past the lump in my throat. "Any ideas?" I ask, after a bewildered pause.

"When I was in the Boundary Waters a couple of years ago, one of my buddies took a small hook to the forehead, past the barb, just like yours. We had him gulp down a whiskey anesthetic, held him down, pushed the barb back out through the skin with a pair of pliers, severed the shank with bolt cutters, and slipped out the two pieces."

Momentarily at a loss for words I ponder the potential treatment, then listlessly repeat his original observation: "Oh shit."

Though dumbfounded, my mind begins to race in search of an alternative. My knowledge of anatomy and physiology limited to my childhood gynecology practice with Lizzy Rosinski, I nevertheless intuit that an attempt to twist and push through the perpendicularly inserted heavy-duty hook might encounter bone, tendon, or ligaments, each of which would be better served remaining in their current undisturbed condition and location. Equally, nay more important, we have no flask of whiskey.

In spite of the hot, midday summer sun, anxiety spawns a cold sweat. Lightheadedness on the verge of eliminating clarity of thought, I recall a magazine article read a number of years ago that detailed a hook removal procedure. Nostradamus-like, I had committed it to memory: the "String-Yank Technique."

Unlike the well-schooled Dr. Ben Casey from the mid-1960s television series, my Dr. Ben lacks familiarity with the procedure:

1) Patient (victim) and field surgeon (unfortunate sap in the wrong place at the wrong time) insert earplugs. In the event the procedure fails, both will expel obscenity-laced screams that will reverberate to the Earth's molten core.

2) Field surgeon dons eye protection (eyeglasses or sunglasses). In the event of procedure success, the needle-like hook becomes a projectile that can "put your eye out," requiring a procedure repeat in a much more delicate body part.

3) Field surgeon threads a length of fishing line ("String") in the bend of the hook, firmly gripping both ends of the twine.

4) Patient presses down on the eye/shank of the hook and prays an Act of Contrition:

O my God, I am heartily sorry for having offended Thee, and I detest all my sins because of Thy just punishments, but most of all because they offend Thee, my God, Who art all-good and deserving of all my love. I firmly resolve, with the help of Thy grace, to sin no more and to avoid the near occasions of sin, including, but not limited to always putting all unused lures in a properly covered storage receptacle. Amen.

> 5) Patient and surgeon close eyes, grit teeth, and tense all body muscles to maximum torque as surgeon gives a firm, quick pull ("Yank") on the line.

I could sense Dr. Ben had his doubts. So did I. I'd have signed a no-fault waiver for him if we had a pencil and paper. As the lesser of two evil alternatives, it's time to rock and roll. Besides, it's my idea, my leg, and my pain.

"String"... press ..."Yank"... pop!

Pain free, blood free, how could this be (it's me...!)? In grateful thanks, and as a public service announcement, check out the entire library of fish hook removal techniques at:

>http://www.aafp.org/afp/20010601/2231.html

I have.

~ ~ ~ ~ ~

July 1997. Another excellent week, catch-wise our best yet. Our group scores 20 muskies, 10 on Friday, the last full day of fishing. The week also pitched us a roundhouse weather event. In advance of those details, allow me to provide some important background information.

When the subject of swimming comes up and I acknowledge my inability to do so, people often ask, "Ed, how is it that you spend all that time on the water doing all that fishing, and yet don't know how to swim?" It is a reasonable and logical question, to which I answer, "Gosh, I don't know." Actually, I do. I've always had a healthy respect for the water. Expressed another way, I'm pretty much afraid of it, at least in those instances where there isn't the bottom of a boat separating us.

On a sunny summer Saturday in 1959, the seven-year-old me experienced a life-altering event at a family picnic at Druce Lake, located a few miles south of the Wisconsin border.

Cousins Jim, Larry, and Peggy, early arrivals with Uncle Ben and Aunt Irene, are already taking advantage of the refreshing lake water. Before joining them, I detour to a nearby pier with fishing pole in hand. After landing and releasing a handful of bluegills and sunfish, I enter the water to join them. Unfortunately, they frolic in the deeper water near the drop-off, an area outside my physical and psychological comfort zone.

The dreaded drop-off looms at the outer edge of the swimming area, where the lake bottom takes an immediate and precipitous vertical plunge from six feet to 20,000 leagues. The water boogeyman, first cousin to the Dickens Avenue attic and basement boogeyman, prowls the waters of the drop-off. Giant squid and octopi also lurk there. Their slimy tentacles, the length of 400-year-old redwoods and covered with suction cups the size of tubas, undulate in the murky depths waiting to coil around unsuspecting swimmers who inadvertently wander into their lair.

These indisputable facts, along with my inability to swim (or even tread water, for that matter) explains my need to avoid waters that extend beyond my waist. On this day, however, responding to my cousins' continuing gleeful urgings I inch forward, with caution, my advance ending as the water begins tickling my armpits. Uneasiness fades with the preoccupation of engaging play.

Then … it happens. Lost in the moment's frivolity, I let down my guard. Feet losing contact with the bottom, I clamshell beneath the water's surface. Panic. Arms and legs flail, whipping like a Mixmaster on high speed. I'm sucking in lake water at a rate that would make a Shop-Vac proud. Struggling to avoid a watery, water-logged end, a five-second eternity passes before my feet reconnect with the lake bottom. I springboard toward the diffused sunlight, head popping through the surface in the form of a water-spewing gargoyle. Gasping to exchange the lake water for air, a coughing spell ensues. My palpitating heart eases its way back into my chest.

Not interested in "getting back on the horse," I trek toward the beach. Slowly at first, I slog through the heavy, wavy water. Into the shallows, with less resistance, my pace quickens. Lips pursed in the aftershock of distress and anger, my toes dig deep into the lake bottom for additional traction, the grains of sand and smooth pebbles kicking up watery puffs of fury. Steps later I tumble to the warm, dry sand. Exhausted, my mind replays the near-death experience. I resolve to never again enter any body of water without flotation equipment.

As my life clock added years, it dawned on me that water wings, and later, the bright orange "Mae West" life jacket screamed "Uncool!" when I took to the water—natural bodies and hotel-motel pools inclusive. And because I spent a fair amount of time on the water fishing, the time had come to confront this fear head on. I accepted offers from family members and friends to teach me to swim. The lessons always took place in the shallow end of the pool, and always within reach of the safety-net sidewall. (On an additional note, a member of the boogeyman's clan lives in the deepest, 10-foot section of the pool, in the shadow of the diving board.)

In spite of their optimism (like each new Cubs manager believing that he can bring the team to the promised land of a World Series championship), each of my well-intentioned instructors failed, ultimately convinced that my skeletal structure is indeed laced with lead weights that defeat any and all methods attempted to keep me afloat.

Thus began my relationship with Mr. Stearns, whose flotation-in-a-vest accompanies me on every fishing trip. A disquieting incident would link us as lifelong friends. Those who lived it and recall it, with equal parts respect and angst, simply refer to it as:

The Storm

By their nature or as part of nature, certain events leave indelible imprints upon the psyche. A Wednesday in July, the midpoint of our weeklong trip to the Alexandra Chain, found me paired with Cousin Ben. Both of us players in my uncomfortable though successful in-boat surgical event last year, today's experience would further strengthen our bond as fishing partners and friends, sharing the stage as unwitting prey in a relentless display of fury from a restless Mother Nature. Our 16-foot aluminum Lund, displaying the unsettling registration numerals "6666," carried us into the day's adventure, nay, misadventure. Maybe Ma Nature missed that extra "6," inadvertently serving up one devil of a day. While the recollection is vivid, only the words may fail to do justice in describing the afternoon when fate held us captive in her whimsical hand.

The fishing day begins pleasantly enough, our "milk run" taking us to familiar spots on several of the interconnected lakes. Our group's ongoing tradition enables the person catching the first musky in a new location to name it. Today's string of stops includes "The Brush Pile," "The Godfish Hole," "Blood Bay," "The Badlands," "Bill's Boulder," and "Pass-Me-By."

Early efforts produce no strikes and only a couple of lazy follows. Since our arrival on Saturday, heat and humidity escalated with each passing day. As today wears on, our enthusiasm wanes under the oppressive midsummer sun, our mood paralleling the lethargic muskies. With the sun beating a drum solo on my skull, my imagination starts playing tricks on me. As one of the larger followers slowly turns away from my bucktail halfway through the retrieve, I thought its scales flashed the words: "Too hot to eat."

Late afternoon finds us in one of our comfort zones, "Musky Bay," a particularly productive section of Edward Lake. After throwing perhaps a dozen casts, we notice an unsettling collection of dark gray clouds rapidly building on the western horizon, no doubt a function of a cold front scheduled to move through the area before day's end. The avid fishermen within us demands we stay; we are both aware that muskellunge become increasingly active in advance of severe weather. The inner voice of responsible adulthood, however, mixed with a dose of the self-preservation instinct (also known as the innate cowardice gene), urges us to depart for the 20-minute ride back to our home base, located squarely in the direction of the oncoming storm. Supporting that thought we both recall our moms' gentle words of wisdom spoken to us since childhood, prior to departing on fishing trips: "Have fun, be careful, and wear your life jacket!" Our dads always wished us well with similar words, but with the oft-repeated addendum, "And don't do anything stupid!"

Decision making not one of the strong suits of the DNA shared by my cousin and me, we engage in a "should we stay or should we go" conversation reminiscent of the elementary school days.

"What do you want to do?"

"I don't know? What do you want to do?"

"Age before beauty, you make the call."

"You're younger. Less of your brain has rotted away. You decide."

"You've got the family, your call."

"You're the captain, it's up to you."

"So, what do you want to do?

"I don't know. What do you want to do?"

Precious time wasting, we finally agree: ten more casts each. We concentrate on the final flings for glory, soon realizing the folly of our compromise decision. The ominous clouds expand toward us like blacktop being squeezed under the weight of a Lucifer Construction Company steamroller. We shut down our gear posthaste, "batten down the hatches," and head for home.

Several minutes hence, shortly before entering a stump-field channel connecting Lakes Edward and Whitney, we stop to don our rain gear. The water-logged lesson learned from the less than adequate rain-shielding qualities of inexpensive and flimsy ponchos from the first trip to Lake of the Woods, we now confront the downside of quality protective gear as we scramble to "suit up." Unlike unfolding the one-piece poncho and slipping it over the head, outfitting in a heavy-duty two-piece is fraught with delays, accentuated by the frantic game of "beat the storm/clock": remove from boat bag, unfurl, lose balance as heel continuously catches in pant leg, thread suspenders over shoulders, clip on and adjust, put on jacket, zipper catches on drawstrings....

Had we known what that hiatus would mean just a few minutes later, the time would have been better spent strapping on a pair of Depends.

We resume our journey through the stumps and around the channel point, the next leg of the trek taking us across the large expanse of Lake Whitney. The clouds, now directly above us, bespeak eerie tones of amber to onyx. Headwinds rise, as does our adrenaline, pumping in concert to bolts of lightning, darts thrown about us to the thunderous laughter of Thor.

We press on, entering Forest Lake through another set of narrows, bracing for the final five-minute straightaway run. Ben pushes the tiller handle to full throttle, propelling us with all the power 20 horses of Mercury can provide. In the distance, adjacent to the area near the cabin, a low-hanging mass of gray obliterates the far shoreline. Over the noise of the motor, wind, thunder, and flapping of our raingear, my lack of outdoorsman savvy surfaces as I shout, "Ben, what's that cloud hanging over the water?"

Without hesitation he replies, "That ain't no cloud—it's a sheet of rain—and we're gonna get blasted!" Halfway down this final run, no more than two to three minutes from "home," it hammers us.

Ben immediately reduces our speed as a fierce burst of cold wind and rain begins pelting our rain suits and stinging the exposed skin of our hands and faces like a continuous spray of buckshot. My first thought (my mind works in strange ways, when it's working at all) under these distressing circumstances? "I wonder if anyone has patented windshield wipers for eyeglasses."

Seconds later, the wind and waves begin lifting and pounding the Lund, ready to crush it like a flimsy aluminum beer can. Seated in the bow, I lean forward at a 45-degree angle, my raingear billowing on a perfect horizontal like a Rolls Royce "Spirit of Ecstasy" hood ornament. As waves jolt the boat, my hands clutch the gunnels in a death grip. A long way from ecstasy, I push downward with every ounce of force I can muster, the misguided instinct being that somehow it might help to keep the nose of the boat on the water. My immediate fear envisions a gust of wind catching us on top of a wave with the bow exposed and flipping us over like a half-cooked flapjack. Another concern, less crucial, involves having to explain to my wife the softball size bruises being created as my butt slams the metal bench seat as we ride the tsunami. Visibility now near zero and uncontrollably spun in a 360 by the spewing breath of The Beast, we're tossed about like a toy tugboat in Beelzebub's bathtub.

I take little comfort when Ben shouts, "What should we do!?"

I turn back with a "deer in the headlights" look to see him kneeling in the bottom of the boat. Swell. My captain is making peace with his Maker while I'm doing a Charles Atlas isometric exercise in the bow. No, wait: His hands are not folded in prayer to Poseidon. One grips the tiller attempting to maintain whatever control possible, while the other shields his eyes against the nearly horizontal downpour (or would that be sidepour)? His low profile, making a smaller target against the onslaught, lessens the odds he might be tossed overboard, and also provides the boat with a measure of additional stability. Consumed in the moment and obviously forgetting we share the "indecision gene" come Ben's next words, barely audible in the tumultuous roar. "Should we beach it!?"

Life-threatening circumstances require split second decisions. Genetics be damned, I need to step up to the plate. Absorbing the variables at hand, my mind analyzes them with the speed of an abacus. Knowing most of the shoreline in this section of the lake to be steep and rocky (and not visible at this time), and control of the boat minimal to nil, I do not consider this a good alternative. The possibility of slipping into the water and being pummeled against the rocks before crawling ashore holds no appeal. Apparently not familiar with the concept of insurance, a dollars and cents aspect also enters the equation, though it shouldn't have. Even if we successfully disembark, the boat, motor, trolling motor, battery, and a king's ransom of rods, reels, lures, cameras, and nautical electronics would likely be pounded to smithereens against the rocky shore, or swamped and sunk by the huge waves. That would put a real damper on the remainder of the fishing week. No, beaching the boat would not be in our best interest. Genetics again surfacing, I shout back to Ben, "Do whatever you think is best!"

He continues the valiant fight against wind and waves but the storm, still flinging bolts of lightning amid the roar of thunder, retains the upper hand. It seems that for every foot of progress forward, the roll of a wave in the unrelenting squall pushes us a yard back. Amid the mayhem, I experience a measure of comfort in the security Mr. Stearns provides, tightly wrapped 'round my heaving chest.

Ben, an accomplished swimmer but against the advice of motherly love, has not taken the time to put on his life jacket. In the event we capsize, I imagine a replay of the tragedy and glory of PT109. Bad back and inability to swim notwithstanding, Mr. Stearns and I, in the role of John F. Kennedy, with the drawstring of Ben's rain suit hood clenched in the steel grip of my jaw, would successfully bring my cousin-captain to safe harbor. More likely, envision Mr. Stearns and I, bobbing neck deep in the raging waves, appendages spasmodically flailing as anguished screams mingle with inconsolable tears lost in each rolling whitecap. A calm and collected Ben would swim to me, execute a series of rapid-fire slaps to bring me to my senses, and grab Mr. Stearns to swim the three of us to safety with a confident, Michael Phelps-like effort.

With the storm still roaring about us I scream, "I'll toss out a crankbait and you throw a top-water—we've got a heckuva drift going and the big ones gotta be moving!"

"Yeah, make sure you're using the graphite rod so if we don't hook one, at least you can shock one up!" Ben shoots back.

"Okay…" I howl. "I'm depending on you to have the fish and me mounted in a flattering pose, and make sure the taxidermist gives you a quantity discount!"

Moments after this exchange, the lightning and rain subside, along with winds now whipping at only 30-plus miles per hour. Ben regains control of the Lund. With progress slow and steady, he skillfully negotiates the last stretch of shoreline before turning into the bay and boathouse sanctuary. Words failing, we spend a minute or two in silent exhausted non-reflection: The totality of this experience would take some time to digest. The harsh winds, now reduced to a gentle breeze, push a fine mist that now fills the air under a lightened gray sky.

After exiting the boathouse we surveyed the grounds, Mr. Stearns still snug and reassuringly vested on my torso. A large branch had fallen atop the roof of our lodging, and chunks of insulation sucked out from beneath the cabin plastered the porch and window screens like wads of water-soaked toilet paper. A total of 13 pines and birches lay scattered about the property, snapped like toothpicks by what we later learned was a microburst, its winds exceeding 70 miles per hour. Thankful for having weathered "The Storm" unscathed, a hint of a smile came over my face, confident Mom would be proud I heeded her advice, "Wear your life jacket." Moments later, recalling Dad's parting words, I believe he would not likely be as pleased.

~ ~ ~ ~ ~

July 1998. Several "firsts" occur on this trip. I bag a 33-inch musky on my first cast on the Saturday of our arrival. As we pull up to the spot, I ask Terry, "Do you want me to set up the net before we start fishing?"

"Nah, don't worry about it … plenty of time." Fire drill follows.

Satisfaction peaks in the form of "money well spent" when a fish attacks a newly introduced lure. Being the first to take a chance on such a purchase can often draw good-natured scoffs (recall the Giant Jackpot at Little Vermilion) from one's fishing peers, quickly silenced by the first hook-up. I liken the use of a new lure that catches a fish on the first cast to scoring a hole-in-one with a newly purchased club. My "first cast of the trip" musky grabs such a fresh-out-of-the-box lure, a five-inch, perch-pattern crankbait Salmo lure, handcrafted in Poland. More heritage pride: Pulaski's Revolutionary War accomplishments and now this! Unfortunately, the joy of the catch on the inaugural cast slowly dissipates through the week—little did I know that would be my only fish until Friday evening, the day before our departure.

Another "first" of this trip involves the delight of guiding my younger cousin Rich to his first muskellunge, partnering with him for the first time on the sixth day. In advance of Thursday evening's last light, I suggest a move to Indian Lake's "Honey Hole." His top-water strike on a Giant Jackpot thrills. In spite of the fish measuring a modest 32 inches, the catch punches his admission ticket to the compulsive world of musky hunting, from which there is no turning back. To catch a muskellunge is to have muskellunge fishing catch you.

My last "first" of the week, not fishing related, concludes with a glowing natural wonder, the northern lights. Shortly after nightfall on Wednesday, they appear as a haze against the dark, star-sprinkled sky. Varying intensities of white undulate, fade, and reappear—the dance of an angel's gossamer robe swaying through the heavens.

I fish several days with Ben, the evening session of the final Friday particularly memorable for pleasantly non-storm reasons. Instead of motoring to other lakes of the Chain as would be typical, we choose to remain in the solitude of Forest Lake. A southwest breeze swirls perfect 77-degree air about us as a spellbinding composite fills the senses: a rich, blue sky cradles clouds that reflect white to gold from the descending sun; shoreline conifers stand resplendent in their deepest green beneath the solar spotlight; opalescent ripples dance atop the lake's surface. I cherish this gift, this artist's masterpiece, this peek into nirvana. At one with our surroundings, I feel a bit uneasy about picking up a rod, afraid to disturb the perfection I am absorbing, the perfection that absorbs me. Undistracted by my cousin's fishing efforts, my mind drifts with our boat. Then, electrified words shatter the peaceful silence. "Got one!"

Jolted from the euphoric trance, my typical reply of positive acknowledgement, "Alright!" is replaced by an acerbically lighthearted "Damn you!" We land the musky. Later that evening, he also guides me to one of my own. The week's final hours embody the ultimate Canadian experience: Great fishing in a great venue, wrapped in the bond of friendship, all boundaries blurring in the immersion of body, mind, and spirit. What a fine ending to another unforgettable week north of the border.

~ ~ ~ ~ ~

July 1999. Aaaa-ver-aaaage: 4 guys, 14 muskies, one 40-incher.

Since the psychosomatic melodrama of the border guard interaction that occurred with my first crossing in the late '60s, all have gone smoothly—till now.

Single and a guitarist and vocalist in a local band, Ben's hair flows to shoulder length. This combination of talent and looks creates the total package known as "chick magnet." On the trip north, his long locks are neatly tied in a ponytail and tucked into his hooded sweatshirt. Alert, clean shaven, and wearing contact lenses, his appearance raises no suspicion. As we enter Canada, the border guard doesn't give him a second look. Okay, maybe a second, but not a third.

On our return to the U.S., we inch forward in the row of vehicles heading southbound. We're now those sad faces sporting an acute case of fisherman malaise. We all battle the week-long accumulated effects of long days under a scorching sun, reduced hours of sleep, and significant, late evening doses of rye, barley, and Havana's best. As we pull up to the guard station, Ben rests in the back seat with hair disheveled, a seven day 5 o'clock shadow, and wire-rim eyeglasses with round, blue tint lenses masking half closed eyelids. His burnt-out appearance makes him the "separated at birth" twin of John Lennon following the former Beatle's exhausting two week "Bed-In for Peace" in Montreal in '69. Lennon, of course, worked different kinds of "weed" and "beds" during his Canadian visit versus the weedbeds that received Ben's casted musky lures. I'm thinking anything short of a strip search will be a moral victory.

I hand the U.S. Border Patrol Agent our driver's licenses, the task completed with faux aplomb, concealing a near-debilitating level of respect that can fog the mind and trigger fumbling fingers. Curiously, he ignores Ben during the standard line of questioning. Apparently satisfied with our answers, he turns his attention to the neglected passenger. Resting his "I wrestle grizzly bears for fun" forearms on the car door at the base of the open window, the agent pokes his head in toward the back seat, his bionic glare stopping within a foot of Ben's face. Following an uncomfortable pause lasting the time it takes to retrieve a long cast of a slow-moving top-water Creeper, he breaks the silence. "Tell Yoko I'm still pissed-off about her breaking up your band."

Backing out of the window with a smile on his face, he taps the roof of the car, sending us on our way with a pleasant, "Have a safe trip home, boys."

By golly, they *are* human after all.

~ ~ ~ ~ ~

Thanks, O'Hare
The Battle of Bloomingdale

To the best of my knowledge, neither Chicago's O'Hare airport nor our home physically moved during our 23-year residency in Bloomingdale. Situated approximately six miles "as the crow flies" west of a runway (though 17 miles by vehicle to the terminals), disturbance from incoming and outgoing flights was never an issue. That changed in 1997 when the *blitzkrieg* roar from wave after wave after goddamn wave of low-flying airliners began taking our life away.

Enjoyable evenings on the back porch became a thing of the past. An imperceptible mist of jet fuel exhaust built a thin, oily film coating all things outside, among them the aluminum siding, the cyclone fence encompassing the yard, and the old swing set tucked in its corner. No more basketball games in the driveway. No more open windows—not if you wanted to hear the television or the person who called on the telephone, that is. Even when we shuttered ourselves in, the muffled waxing and waning of engine noise infiltrated the roof and walls in a continuous and maddening assault.

Sensibility and sanity under siege, calls to the Chicago Department of Aviation Noise Hotline pleading, imploring, begging for answers and, more importantly, relief, brought nothing more than a report detailing a numeric summary and graphic representation of the jet-age Chinese water torture. On the 6th and 7th of November, 579 and 608 planes, respectively, flew over our home, one every two-plus minutes in the 48-hour sample period.

What caused this change, tossing our lives topsy-turvy? A shift in runway usage? Pilots incentivized to save fuel by approaching "long and low"? Were we mystically teleported as lead characters in a *Twilight Zone* recurring nightmare episode? Of no consequence, the reason or reasons remained unknown.

From annoyance to irritation to anger, nerves grated raw. When outside working in the garden or mowing the lawn, I greeted the unending line of airborne intruders with one-finger waves. I also toyed with the idea of pulling the pitching wedge out of my golf bag and launching a Titleist with the hope of planting it between the pilot's eyes. No, I wasn't proud of these out-of-character responses, but fighting for self and family elicited primal and irrational thought and reaction.

Aware that our frumpy little house on Prairie would never appear on the cover of *Home and Garden* magazine, we nevertheless dressed her up with factory-fresh beige vinyl siding and a pretty new "hat" of brown-tone architectural-style shingles in the months leading up to our unconditional surrender in the Battle of Bloomingdale. Then, as she slept with her window shades down and painful as it was, we planted a "For Sale" sign in her landscape apron next to a bed of colorful, recently planted petunias.

Priced in line with the market, people came. And ran away. Screaming. Feedback remained consistent. Strangely, none of it involved airline traffic but rather some form of "no curb appeal." One woman, so repulsed by the exterior, refused to step inside.

She wasn't that grotesque ... (was she?)

As weeks turned to months and the psychological drubbing (from the planes as well as lack of buyer interest) continued to take its toll, I offered suggestions to our realtor with thoughts on a new angle for the listing of our architectural pariah:

> Ugh!-ly. Come one, come all—take a peek at DuPage County's most hideous house. Current owners deal with disgusting exterior by living *inside* this clean and well-kept raised ranch. Grotesque but maintenance free, if the outside of this house wants to make you vomit, come inside and vomit in the newly remodeled bathroom. This housing horror is certain to repel solicitors and other undesirables. Sorry, no picture provided; FCC regulations prohibit display of grossly offensive materials.

To add divine assistance to the marketing mix, Jo Ann purchased a St. Joseph Home Sale Kit. In my mind (simple as it is), this ranks as one of the more bizarre Catholic rituals of folklore and faith. Per the kit instructions, bury the four-inch plastic statue of Jesus' earthly dad, blood-rushing-to-his-head upside-down, in the yard. No kidding. ("Get in the ground, carpenter Joe, and don't give a thought to chiseling your way up for a drink of air. We'll fetch you as soon as you bring us a qualified buyer.") As months passed with no positive results, Jo Ann suggested we double down with the purchase and burial of a second, the task completed in early November. Through the winter months, activity remained dormant with snow falling and anxiety snowballing. Early in March, Mom gifted a third statue, which I promptly entombed by hacking into the partially frozen ground.

March 13, 1998. With Jo Ann and Eddie out for the evening, I stand alone on the porch under stars sparkling the night sky. Arms outstretched, I lean forward and grasp the railing in the near-freezing air, further chilled by a brisk breeze flowing through the mane of March's lion. Cold to the touch, the wood hints the oily residue of jet fuel exhaust. An eerie silence hovers—a peculiar respite from the dreaded repetition of approach, crescendo, and fade of roaring aircraft engines.

The quiet void fills with images of days past, fondly remembered. This is the first and only home Jo Ann and I ever owned, the only one our son has ever known, this "house made a home" where we watched him grow: in the back yard playing catch ... fishing for bluegills in the park pond a half block to the east ... equal time to play and learn on the popular and affordable Commodore 64 computer in the third bedroom, the "study."

Many family parties and holidays were hosted within these walls: children opening birthday and Christmas presents ... men sparring sports conversation in the family room against the backdrop of a televised Bears (how exciting and satisfying the '85 season, led by "Da Coach" Mike Ditka, culminating in a Super Bowl XX victory), Cubs, White Sox, or Bulls game (and what a joy to watch "Air Jordan" and company dismantle opponents with a pair of "three-peat" championship runs from '91-'93 and '96-'98!) ... women in the kitchen preparing meals, the mouthwatering aroma of roasting turkey, stuffing, and mashed potatoes wafting through every room.

The Fabulous Maretti Brothers spent many a day (and some long nights) here: shooting hoops in the driveway ... discussing plans for upcoming fishing trips ... contesting games of bumper pool, Risk, and Stock Market, the activities often fueled by the golden nectar of Yukon Jack.

My next thoughts bring a grimace turned smile: crouched beneath the rafters scoping out the attic for storage space, I inched along atop and beside insulation-covered joists, progress halted as my feet punched holes through a bedroom ceiling ... the shocking incident of forgetting to turn off the electricity when changing the dining room chandelier ... swinging the fishing net to and fro, attempting to capture a frantic sparrow as it darted about the laundry room, the terminus of its journey from chimney through furnace.

Back to the moment, negative superstitious connotations of Friday the 13th notwithstanding, I muse the evening's abnormal silence (and another 10% reduction in our asking price) may foreshadow our escape from this war zone, allowing *us* to take flight.

~ ~ ~ ~ ~

In the months preceding the sale, Jo Ann worked tirelessly in anticipation of the move, her look to the future a partial remedy for dealing with desperation. Her research revealed that a 30-mile buffer from O'Hare would ensure freedom from flight-related noise. The metro area more heavily populated north and south, the logical move pointed west. To stay near arterials that would keep the commute time to our jobs (currently five- and twenty-minutes) under one hour, while satisfying the distance-from-the-airport criteria, a scan of Rand McNally targeted the towns of Huntley and Hampshire. Early on, we enlisted the services of a Huntley-based realtor to assist with the search that occupied most weekends.

Of numerous properties viewed, we found a new-construction ranch floor plan townhouse in Hampshire most appealing from the standpoint of size (downsizing) and price (limited to anticipated Bloomingdale proceeds). With two bedrooms, two baths, and approximately 1,400 square feet of living space, its vaulted ceilings in the kitchen, living room, and master bedroom gave it a feel much larger than its actual size. The basement, half finished with a family room, also contained a good amount of unfinished storage space. With a two-car garage, it suited our needs perfectly.

I'll admit I had reservations about townhouse living: common walls, an Association, and limited outdoor common areas instead of owning a yard. On the flipside, however, for a reasonable fee, no more lawn mowing, snow removal, or outside home maintenance. Freedom from those chores would offset some of the "windshield" time resulting from the longer commute. And the idea of living in Hampshire, a significantly smaller agricultural community anchored by a quaint downtown area of less than three blocks (reminiscent of Larry's hometown of Grayslake during our childhood), also held strong appeal. And a location a half hour closer to my beloved Emerald Lake (details to follow) put another check in the plus column.

Prepared to make an offer, our realtor set up a meeting at the townhouse with the builder. True to the rural locale, his appearance was farmer-like: overalls, a flannel shirt, work boots, and a John Deere baseball cap. His weathered face, forehead lined with wrinkles, and cheeks and chin dotted with salt and pepper whiskers, bespoke an age on the far side of sixty. After exchanging pleasantries, I confidently proceeded: "My wife and I like this property very much. If we can agree on a price…"

Cut off in mid-sentence, the moments-ago affable Mr. Green Jeans morphed to a frowning Ebenezer Scrooge, sternly and matter-of-factly stating, "The price is the price."

Alrighty then. So much for the artful craft of negotiation.

In the days preceding the meeting, Jo Ann and I agreed on our desire to make the townhouse our new home and were prepared to pay the list price. I had no trouble putting aside my heritage-based financial fret, which paled in comparison to the mental anguish gnawing at us daily in Bloomingdale. We signed the contract. At the price that *was* the price.

The "contingent on the sale of our Bloomingdale blight" clause prevailed as a blessing and a curse. On the positive side, no duel ownership and associated dual debt; on the negative, if the builder received another offer (the price is the price unless the price is better), we'd have three days to come up with the cash or lose the opportunity to own it.

~ ~ ~ ~ ~

March 14, 1998. Jo Ann, Eddie, and I run some errands. Upon returning home, the chill of a cold Saturday is warmed by messages waiting on the answering machine. Three realtors want to show the house tomorrow. Return calls set the appointments.

On Sunday, we receive two offers, accepting the one with the most advantageous combination of price and closing date. Never underestimate the power of St. Joe cubed—and a significant price reduction.

Hampshire

Settled in 1835, Hampshire's fertile farmland supported more than 1,000 residents by the 1870s. Slow growing in the decades that followed, only 2,900 people resided within its boundaries at the time of our move in April 1998. Though airport noise served as the driving force for our displacement, we took comfort in relocating west and looked forward to our days in "the country" as needed relief from the relentless growth and inconvenience of suburban congestion.

In the early going, we adjusted well to townhouse living, our end unit sharing a common wall with a retired couple. Jo Ann enjoyed the size, natural light, and configuration of the eat-in kitchen. The basement family room had wall space for my decorative, fishing-related paraphernalia. And, most important, what blessed comfort, the sounds of silence as we drifted off to dreamland that first night and all those that followed.

One of the previously acknowledged downsides necessitated by our move involved extra time and gasoline expense associated with 25-mile, 45-minute commutes to our work places. I was still employed by Motorola at the Schaumburg campus. Jo Ann worked as a first grade teacher's aide in Roselle, the town adjoining Bloomingdale to the north.

Dad and Mom, now in their late 70s, still lived in Niles. Our move to Hampshire significantly increased the distance between us. Dad's ability and desire to maintain their 40-year-old home justifiably waned with each passing year. Health issues popped up with increasing frequency. Based on this combination of factors, I suggested they move to a townhouse in our development. Six months after we arrived, they purchased an end unit similar to ours, less than a block away.

As luck would have it, not long thereafter a number of negatives began eroding our contentment with townhouse living:

> On several occasions, our neighbor's smoke detector malfunctioned. When they were away, the muffled screech pierced the wall for hours on end. Also, on the subject of not-well-noise-insulated common walls, the elderly couple's elevated television volume periodically seeped into our living quarters.

> Enforcement of association regulations deteriorated mightily from "rigid" under the control of Ebenezer Green Jeans to "nonexistent" when transferred to the homeowners upon completion of the development build-out. Violations of the

covenants and restrictions, many and frequent, related to renters, parking, and pets. The lack of action on one in particular was disgusting and egregious: a minefield of dog excrement, expanding by the day, accumulated atop the grass between the back of our unit and the dog-owning ignoramus who kept his huskie chained to his deck each day.

A serious financial concern arose with the discovery that the Association did not carry liability insurance covering the common areas. Additionally, there was no oversight confirming individual homeowners carried proper insurance in the event of vandalism or weather-related damage to the buildings' exteriors.

Thanks, O'Hare.

Jo Ann and I talked about making another move, returning to a single family home with the understanding that we'd stay within several miles of our present location to retain precious flight-free silence and proximity to my parents. After broaching the subject to them, their response included the words "feeling abandoned." They also expressed a level of dissatisfaction with townhouse living. The arrows of their annoyance pointed to three children living in the adjacent unit. I surmised the thumps heard filtering through their common walls resulted from the three active youngsters bounding up and down a staircase, slamming drawers, or playtime activities. Also bothersome to Mom and Dad, the children frequently played in the yard spaces outside their front and back windows. And, last but not least, Mom felt the townhouse rooms were too large (though they weren't, just a function of the vaulted ceilings!), too much to clean.
Well, didn't this work out well? Thanks, O'Hare.
May 1999. Back to the proverbial drawing board. We both wanted out. With the circumstances complicated two-fold, what's the answer? Is there an answer? How about a duplex? (No! Don't repeat the mistake of common walls, even if it's family on the other side.) How about a single family home with in-law quarters? Good thought, but a review of real estate listings revealed none available in our target area. How about pooling resources to *build* a house to accommodate both families?
We consulted with a local builder. Back to the drawing board, literally this time. I sketched a floor plan (the task not foreign to me, somewhere around the tender age of ten I penciled plans for my "when I grow up" dream home) that included living space for Dad and Mom, with back-to-back walls only in the

laundry rooms. The builder roughed out a price based on square footage and our selection of a lot in a newly developed subdivision. The cul-de-sac location with abundant oaks and hickories, a relative rarity in the flat farmlands of Hampshire, promised privacy. To our collective relief, the number came in as doable. We allocated the cost pro rata based on square footage, with upgrades tacked on to the family requesting them.

Excited at the prospect, we relished brief moments of calm in the eye of a building storm. Soon to swirl about, we'd face the uninviting reality of selling two townhomes before giving the go-ahead to start construction, coordinating sale and purchase closing dates, relying on the builder to meet a completion date, and finally synchronizing the physical moves if and when all of the above fell into place. Here we go again—same story, different town—with stress rivaling the siege of Bloomingdale, multiplied by two. Thanks, O'Hare.

Jo Ann, honoring the Association covenants and restrictions by not digging in the common ground outside our unit, instead buried one of the three St. Joseph statues in our inventory in a small decorative planter adjacent to the front door. Mom chose to follow the Home Sale Kit guidelines with a below-grade enshrinement in the yard, Association rules be damned.

"It's a vibrant real estate market," we were told in May. *But* ... June ... *not* ... July ... *for* ... August ... *us* ... September ... *no* ... October ... *not* ... November ... *for* ... December ... *us* ... January.

Then, in a pleasant February surprise (the extended competition of dueling St. Joes, each refusing to be outdone by the other?), we both received and accepted offers on our respective townhomes. Giving the builder the go-ahead, he assured completion of the 3,600 square foot house within 4½ months. We agreed to close on June 30 to avoid a double move for Dad and Mom, the closing of their townhouse also set for that date. Wheels now in motion, we breathed a sigh of relief, short lived, as family and friends express doubts about completion of such a large home in such a tight timeframe. More intestinal squeeze. Thanks, O'Hare.

Jo Ann and I didn't fare as well with our closing date. Set for the end of March, it necessitated a three-month layover at an apartment in Roselle. I likened our stay in the second floor one-bedroom apartment to dorm living gone bad. The building's main entry and lobby adjoined our bedroom wall. Neighbors on the other side frequently hosted evening parties during the NBA playoffs, their rooting interest readily discernable from cheers reverberating through the living room wall. The odors of unidentified foreign cuisines wafted in the hall, seeping under our door. The brothers living in the apartment below chain-smoked, the fumes of their habit creeping into our living space. A perpetual motion three-year-old scampered the hall nightly between 9:30 and 10:00 p.m., occasionally knocking on our door before ducking into the stairwell. Thanks, O'Hare.

Aside from the "joys" of apartment living, the March through June period delivered new levels of stress and inconvenience. The distance from our temporary living quarters to Hampshire made weekday visits impossible, leaving only weekends to keep tabs on construction details and progress.

With the project clock racing, time was of the essence regarding color selection and option choices for items inside and out: bricks, garage doors, roof shingles, siding, carpeting, hardwood, vinyl, countertops, cabinets, lighting fixtures, and on and on and on. And double that "fun," needing to prod my mother to timely decisions.

Frequently interrupted while at work, I dreaded the telephone conversations with the builder: "You can't do what? You told us this … now it's that? Why is that extra?" And tasked with watching our nickels and dimes as well as Dad and Mom's, I also assumed the role of conduit, filter, and messenger between them and the builder. "Are we getting what we're supposed to? Aren't we paying for this and not that? That's not what I thought it would be. When is he going to get back to us with an answer? Is it all going to be done in time?" Thanks, O'Hare.

June 29, 2000. Ready or not, moving day arrived, one day before closing with the builder's okay. Heavy rains turned the crushed stone base for the not-yet-blacktopped driveway into an opaque gray ooze. A moving crew of six tracked the sloppy muck into the house as they carted furniture and boxes across virgin flooring, not all of which was properly covered with cardboard or sheets of plastic. The movers, and a half dozen subcontractors working feverishly to complete their tasks on this day before the deadline, scurried *Frogger*-like inside the home, all in each other's way. All were annoyed. All casted disparaging glances our way.

Although agonizingly slow and emotionally draining, that day, too, passed. A tumultuous life chapter ended that first night as we slipped into peaceful slumber, blanketed in the sublime silence of our new home. We closed the next day, as scheduled, with items on the page-long punch list clearing in a timely manner over the weeks that followed.

From every room in the house, groves of trees fill the view through each window. Mom loves the cozy feel of the rooms in her new home within a home. Flooded with natural light from a bank of windows, Dad prizes the lookout basement and the workshop area he set up, always busy with small projects: constructing family requested made-to-order benches, shelves, and nativity stables, trimming out the basement windows, painting this or that. Jo Ann enjoys her large eat-in kitchen much as she did the one in the townhouse, though this new one has even more cabinets and counter space allowing an expanded area in which to enjoy her cooking craft. We both savor time spent on the screened porch and the solitude provided by the curtain of mature trees that begin at the edge of the backyard downslope. This indoor-outdoor room truly pleases through three seasons, a place to enjoy reading or writing while sipping a cup of tea or coffee, the only sounds the rustling of leaves or the whirring wings of hummingbirds dining at the nearby feeder.

Our master bedroom and laundry room, both conveniently located on the first level, allows us to avoid daily trips up and down stairways. The living room, though not grand in scale, has the bright and airy feel of a "great room." Four large windows, topped by smaller square transoms, fill the southwest wall. A staircase at the back of the room parallels the slope of the vaulted ceiling that leads to a modest loft area and two more bedrooms, one of those Eddie's room. I commandeered the other, filling it with an array of items themed from my treasured sport-hobby.

A quilt wall-hanging with freshwater fish species, handmade by Cousin Rich's wife, Sue, adorns the door of the "fish room." Inside, a row of fish circle the room in a wallpaper border. Calming sea green-colored walls hold many objects, the most prominent the mounts of my 30-inch walleye and 20½-inch largemouth bass, and five bulletin boards, each tacked with thirty to fifty fishing photographs from 1962 to the present.

A canoe shaped-shelving unit displaying fishing-related tchotchkes stands in one corner. A two-shelf bookcase holds 24 books, sandwiched by fishing lure bookends. Prized among the titles is a classic, first edition of *Spoonplugging, Your Guide to Lunker Catches* by E. L. "Buck" Perry.

A five-shelf bookcase presents another "fishing stuff smorgasbord": In-Fisherman Master Angler patches; the Waco Fishing Derby and The Fabulous Maretti BassMaster Classic trophies (the traveling nature of these trophies ended when I stopped organizing the events—these two in my possession at that time); and liquor decanters sculpted in the forms of a bluegill, crappie, bass, and muskellunge.

This bookshelf also holds a few more piscatorial titles: the 1962 Golden Book *Fishes* (the one Dad purchased for me as a ten-year-old on a visit to the Shedd Aquarium), *Muskie!* a 1964 work by James A. Lind, and a 1988 reprint of *THE COMPLEAT ANGLER, Or, The Contemplative Man's Recreation*, Izaak Walton's 1653 title.

Back to the loft area, a couch and end table, the latter overflowing with all things Blackhawks hockey (with emphasis on Stan Mikita and Bobby Hull, including autographed books, photos, and pucks) line the back wall. Available at my fingertips with the spin of my desk chair, another five-shelf bookcase holds a printer, compact stereo, a modest collection of classic rock and Native American flute music CD's and a dozen books on Native American history.

One side of my L-shaped desk overlooks the living room, the other borders two large windows that bring the outdoors in. In addition to the computer monitor and cubbies holding traditional office miscellany, other personally important odds and ends fill most of the available desk space: some wartime photos of Dad and a 1913 half dollar given to him by Busia upon his induction into the Army during World War II, the good luck piece carried in his pocket through his three-plus years of service; a pair of Chicago Transit Authority tokens from Uncle Stanley's days as a bus driver; a vintage 1953 Motorola AM radio; a chessboard to track the daily moves sent and received via e-mail games contested through cyberspace with Chuck in Indianapolis; a dozen miniature decorative carved eagles; and an ever-expanding assemblage of rocks and minerals in various shapes, colors, and compositions collected during vacations near and far.

How comfortable and content I feel when seated at my desk. Perhaps someday I'll pen a book. Maybe when I retire.

Thanks, O'Hare!

~ ~ ~ ~ ~

When the winde is south, it blows your bait into a fishes mouth. Next to that, the West winde is believed to be the best: and having told you that the East winde is the worst, I need not tell you which winde is best in the third degree.
—Izaak Walton
THE COMPLEAT ANGLER
Or, The Contemplative Man's Recreation - 1653

Freespool Flashbacks from the Alexandra Chain of Lakes
2000 - 2005

July 2000. We celebrate the millennium year with our best trip ever, 25 muskies. A "camp record" falls: Terry's friend Dan catches 9 for the week. Cousin Ben bags a 44-incher, tying Terry's largest from the early 1990s. Like 1997, we score another 10-fish day.

~ ~ ~ ~ ~

July 2001. I've heard it on multiple occasions, and if you've ever taken a fishing vacation, chances are you have, too. Full of anticipation for the long-awaited week of fantastic fishing action, the resort owner greets us upon arrival. Milliseconds after the introductions we pose the question, "How's the fishing?"

The reply often includes, "Fish have been jumping into boats like never before. Hope it keeps going." Sometimes there's a hint of truth to this version of "You should have been here last week." More often, however, the owner is simply setting reduced expectations to protect the reputation of his lake and livelihood. More forthcoming (though not good for business) responses never heard? "There's an unverified rumor that one of our camp guests caught a fish last week," or "The local grocery store has a sale on fresh fish. You may want to stop by and pick up some fillets if you're planning on eating any fish dinners this week."

The better indicator of fishing prospects occurs if you arrive in time to speak with camp guests lingering before their departure. With no vested interest, the information they provide is generally more accurate, detailed, and truthful. If their report includes the statement "You should have been here last week," well, by golly, you *should* have been here last week.

I'm pleased to report that the week of July 14th to July 20th, 2001, *was* "last week," and we were the guys who were there. To what can we attribute our outstanding catch? Besides my new fishing hat (Indiana Jones style, wide brim to keep those nasty UV rays off my face, ears, and neck—something I should have thought about 30 years ago), Jo Ann boils it down to the simplest level—being in the right place at the right time.

Of course, our group of seasoned anglers recognizes that so much more goes into creating such success: selecting a week with a full moon or new moon phase, those celestial occurrences triggering increased fish activity; optimum weather conditions; properly executed boatside figure-8s to entice following fish to strike; continuous additions to the musky fishing knowledge base including the correct selection of lures and lure colors based on location, weather, mood of the fish (negative, neutral, or aggressive) and time of day; upgraded boats getting to fishing spots quicker and in comfort, allowing more time to fish with less strain on the body, and improved boat control to thoroughly fish the locations selected.

Or ... we were in the right place at the right time.

Upon arriving early Saturday afternoon, we begin our vacation week by getting the major yardwork task out of the way: mowing the ankle-deep grass left unattended for over a month. Next, we unpack clothing and food, prepare our fishing gear, grab a bite to eat, and hit the water before 5 p.m. This first fishing session of the day works out the kinks, "clears out the cobwebs," and fine-tunes the body and equipment for the upcoming week. In my world of reserved expectation, any fish caught on the first day are a bonus.

Today, as every other midsummer fishing day in this Canadian wilderness, concludes at precisely 9:37 p.m. At that exact moment, mosquitoes the sizes of B-52 bombers magically materialize out of thin air and attack in a bloodthirsty blitzkrieg. Proximity to land means nothing; even if miles from shore and quietly adrift in the center of the largest lake, the evil insects will find and kill you. The shriveled carcasses of fishermen not mindful of the time can be found, blood-drained and lifeless, in the bottom of their boats at 9:38 p.m. You never want to hook a fish after 9:35 p.m. At 9:36 your partner will exchange the landing net for a knife to sever your line in the interest of preserving precious platelets and corpuscles.

Terry and I in one boat and Rich and Ben in the other, we return to the sanctuary of the cabin before Dracula's winged army can inflict their damage. Eight Polaroid instant photos scatter the dining room table, four from each boat. Everyone scores at least one musky. Several other fish had been hooked, though not landed. Elated with the unprecedented start to a fishing week, the bite is on—right place, right time.

The hits keep coming. Sunday's first on-water session matches yesterday's 8-count, all fishermen again finding the score sheet. Then, glory fleeting, the evening outing pitches a shutout. Still, 16 fish in a day and a half already tops weeklong trips of years past. Can it get any better?

Sure it can. On Monday, the camp record of 10 fish in one day falls as 11 muskies come to net, including a 43-incher by Rich. In three glorious days, we boys from Illinois land 27 muskies (30 inches or longer), surpassing the previous best total of 25 caught in a *week*.

A downward trend begins on Tuesday, the group catching "only" 8 more. Wednesday it drops to 4. On Thursday, one straggler fails to get the message from his buddies about the food imitations concealing sharp metal hooks. Nine on the final Friday one-ups the total from last Saturday's opener, the team finishing with 49 for the week.

Terry leads the way, averaging 2½ muskies per day, his total of 17 almost doubling the best week ever by Dan. Fishing out of Rich's new boat, Rich and Ben each tally a dozen. I bring up the rear with a "measly" 8. One of those, an early Sunday morning catch from the dock, takes place as the rest of the crew sleeps in.

A Polaroid of 49 musky Polaroids!

~ ~ ~ ~ ~

Nothing makes a fish bigger than almost being caught.
—Jerry Smith

As I cast and retrieve a 4-inch Rapala Husky Jerk minnow-bait in a firetiger pattern (chartreuse and fluorescent orange body sporting black vertical stripes) with my bass rod, 10-pound test line, and no leader, a musky follows then grabs the lure as I execute a figure-8.

Aware of the delicate nature of playing the toothy critter on light tackle, I make my way to the far side of the dock with slow, backward baby steps while holding the rod, one handed, high in the air. My body contorting in a move that would do Baryshnikov proud, I reach into Terry's boat to grab the large, unwieldy net, slowly retracing steps across the dock to scoop the fish. The commotion of my one-man act awakens Rich, bringing him down to take a photo and assist with the measurement and release of the 37-incher.

Early Monday morning, a similar scenario ensues. On my second cast, the lure is grabbed in mid-retrieve. Because of the distance and depth, the size of the fish remains unknown. The line slices across the surface, rapidly moving toward deeper water. Seconds later, the rod springs back. All resistance gone (fish and lure), the line must have run across the brute's razor sharp teeth. No, that's not the end of the story.

Two days later, during our Wednesday pre-dinner break, I'm at the dining table thumbing through a stack of *AARP* magazines (how fitting, in the land of innumerable lakes, that the equivalent Canadian organization goes by the acronym CARP ... seriously, if you doubt me, look up Canadian Association of Retired Persons) when Ben enters the cabin. Having heard the story of the big one that got away, he tosses my distinctively colored Rapala across the table in my direction.

"Is this yours?"

Surprised, several scenarios quickly flash through my mind. Has the fish washed up on shore, mouth unfortunately clamped shut by the lure's pair of small treble hooks? Did the predator with an insatiable appetite, undeterred by the dining mistake that still hangs from its lower jaw, latch onto one of Ben's offerings cast from the dock?

"It is!" I gleefully acknowledge, anxious to hear the tale of its retrieval. "Is the sow that grabbed it a 50-incher?"

"The only thing that's 50 inches is your hat size," Ben dryly replies.

"A 40-, then?"

"Be happy you got the lure back."

Remarkable but brief, the story begins with Ben entering the boathouse to check some of his gear. He notices the brightly colored lure just beneath the water's surface, hanging from the corner of a musky's mouth. Stealthily grasping a net from one of the boats and with the lightning quickness of a fishing ninja, he scoops the fish in one deft, fluid motion. After removing the lure, he sends the fish on its way.

My "brute" taped at 22 inches, and Ben said he thought he heard the adolescent fish gurgle that his old man would be coming back to even the score with me. Yeah, right.

So, that's the highlights for 2001. Oh, did I mention the *one* cast where *two* muskies follow my bucktail, or the bear swimming across the timber-filled channel connecting Lakes Whitney and Edward? (If a 500-pound bear in a water-logged fur coat can swim, why, oh why, can't I?)

As I report the tally of our week's catch to family, friends, and co-workers, I am keenly aware of how ridiculous it sounds: 4 fishermen catching 60 muskies, 49 of them 30 inches or more. Though not a mind reader, I have a good idea what most of them are thinking, and I can't say I blame them. If I didn't know me better, I'd say I was full of crap, too.

As it's been said, "Even a blind squirrel finds an acorn (or 49) once in a while." Finally—right time, right place—"last week!"

~ ~ ~ ~ ~

"2001 - A Musky Odyssey"
The Happy Hunters—Terry, Ben, Rich, and me—there "last week."

September 2002. No Canada trip this year due to a timing conflict with the "vacation of a lifetime," a land-cruise excursion to Alaska. My absence from the standard mid-July outing opens the door for a September journey to the beloved waters of Alexandra. Ben and Rich clear their calendars for the week of Labor Day, so we book a cabin at one of the four resorts on the 8-lake Chain. Although Dianna and Terry leave a standing invitation for use of their cabin, we decline their generous offer based on our handyman incompetence and fear of any number of things going awry, including but not limited to the failure of the water pump, water line, water tank (or any of the hoses or connectors linking them together), failure of the propane stove, propane fridge, propane lighting, propane water heater, or propane tank supplying all of them, failure of the indoor plumbing or septic system, or the failure to properly extinguish a stogie, reducing a 50-year family legacy, a cherished heirloom, to a pile of ashes.

Even during summer primetime, the Chain's limited number of resorts and private residences results in an abundance of water to fish, sans competition from other fishermen. With vacations having wound down by Labor Day, the lakes approach aquatic ghost towns.

This being our first excursion to the Alexandra lakes without Terry, we hope he will not take offense as we fish his home waters without him. During the course of the week we chuckle at minor mishaps, viewing them as the "Wrath of the Terry-god." The first few days go well. We catch six muskies amid pleasant, seasonal temperatures in the low 70s. We surmise that Terry, busy with his Labor Day holiday weekend activities, has forgotten about us. On Monday night, however, he remembers our intrusion and expresses his displeasure via international telepathy. As I stand near the stove, conversing with Rich and Ben as they prepare dinner, spaghetti sauce jumps out of the pot, poltergeist-fashion, splattering my shirt.

On Tuesday, the vengeful Terry-god brings out the big artillery: The daytime high stays in the 50s with high winds and the threat of storms. We lightheartedly ruminate that he has purchased three fishing action-figures to use as voodoo dolls in his bathtub. The darkened sky and approaching flashes of lightning result from him flicking his bathroom lights on and off. An oscillating fan on the edge of his tub whips the gale-force winds and heavy waves that toss us about. A violent twist of his shower faucet handle opens the skies, pelting us with cold rain. His devious sorcery continues on Wednesday giving us beautiful, clear weather but not a single fish.

By Wednesday night, all appears to be forgiven. Starting as a white haze just after dark, the northern lights appear, gradually building to fill more than half the sky, swirling white, dim, then bright. The show captivates us for hours, periodically enhanced by a shooting star. Sometime after 2 a.m., an exhilarating, multi-color grand finale ensues. White rays pulse in varying lengths and intensity before blending to form a snaking "S," followed by an explosion of shimmering shades of rose and green.

Well, maybe not all was forgiven. Strange but true, in spite of multiple attempts during the course of the week, we did not catch one fish in Forest Lake, site of the Terry-god's cabin.

~ ~ ~ ~ ~

July 2003. Deuces wild.

Over the years, our group averages one 40-inch fish per week. For one individual to catch two over the course of seven days is significant; to catch two in one day, remarkable; to catch two on consecutive passes on the same piece of structure, an unheard of triumph! Ben did it with 43- and 40-inch fish on a rainy Monday afternoon in Edward Lake, both fish biting at boatside on well executed figure-8s.

At 8:45 p.m. on Wednesday, Ben and I team up for a fishing deuce of another kind—a "double." In the fishing world, a "double" occurs when two people hook a fish at the same time. It's not an uncommon occurrence when fishing for bluegill, crappie, perch, or other species known to school. The odds decrease if the targeted species is higher on the food chain, this due to their larger size, reduced numbers, and non-schooling habit. "Doubles" are rare when fishing for muskellunge.

With day's light dimming, we cast bucktails toward "Big Ass Rock" and the group of boulder outcroppings in a large channel connecting Lakes Edward and Whitney. As my copper-blade spinner approaches the boat, I see a shadowy image following behind and below it.

As I sweep my rod into the first turn of a figure-8, the fish rises and grabs it.

"Got one!"

I catch Ben out of the corner of my eye swirling his rod at boatside. A split second later, his rod bent, tip in the water with the weight of a fish, he howls back, "So do I!"

Tumult instantaneous, we burst into spontaneous laughter. Ben blurts out, "What do we do now?"

Amid the water-splashing commotion, I answer his question with a question: "Whose is bigger?"

Not missing a beat, Ben replies, "For chrissakes—we've got two fish hooked and you're wondering how your manhood measures up?"

Our continuing banter determines neither fish is significant in size, both likely in the low 30-inch range. With the long, cork handle of the rod tucked in my armpit as I cradle the rod in one hand, I reach for the net with the other. "Ben, steer your fish over here. Women and children first."

The musky secured, he puts down his rod and takes the net. I suggest he unhook his fish, but the caring captain, wanting to ensure mine does not escape, replies, "My fish is looking for her baby brother to join her, so bring him over." Mission accomplished. Over 60 inches of musky bulge the bottom of our net. Now, if only it was one fish that size. We'll have to keep working on that.

~ ~ ~ ~ ~

July 2004. "O(uch) Canada!" A personal spin on the Canadian national anthem nicely sums up the week. The reasons will become painfully clear as the tale unfolds.

It begins with limited participation—all of our fishing buddies pitch a variety of excuses to beg off this year's trip. That leaves Terry and me, a couple of borderline menopausal men, to test our 30-year friendship with a week of vacation confinement.

On the car ride up, Terry asks if I have any goals for the trip. (What the hell, am I on a job interview? It's a damn fishing vacation!) I'm guessing his question relates to the size and quantity of muskies I hope to catch, and perhaps he expects a response something like "One more than you." Instead I reply, "Not to die." I would meet that goal, though not without distress.

Dan and his wife, Barb, joined us at the cabin from Saturday through Tuesday. They fished Lake of the Woods the previous week, enjoying great success catching 27 muskies, a number of those taping between 40- and 49-inches. We have no way of knowing if a similar bite occurred on the Alexandra Chain and can only hope it's not the dreaded "We should have been here last week" scenario. Time will tell.

Dan and Barb bring their golden retriever, Riley. His predecessor, Woody, was the poster child for retrievers: a bundle of energy, always ready to run, fetch, and swim. A polar opposite, Riley displays the laidback personality of a basset hound. About the only time he drags himself off the chair or floor is when attempting to sneak a sip from my glass of whisky and water or thrust his lengthy tongue toward the bottom of Terry's almost-empty beer bottle. Well named, he's well-suited to the life of Riley.

It's noon on Saturday. As I prepare my gear and baits for our first on-water session, a hook nicks one of my fingers, causing my oft heard call, "I'm cut!" Typically, drawing first blood doesn't occur until I'm in the boat, but my earlier-than-normal declaration does not surprise Terry. Though fishless on Saturday, a dancing-ribbon display of the northern lights provides a delightful consolation prize that evening.

Beautiful Canadian summer weather graces us for the first three days with temps in the low to mid-70s, sunny, and breezy. Good weather for fishin', but as it turns out, not for catchin'. Barb and Terry take one fish each; Dan and I are shut out. I'm not happy about my lack of success but take solace in the fact that I'm in good company.

The most notable event of those first days occurs inside the cabin—a 24-inch snake takes up residence in the kitchen. Caught and released on several occasions, the mouse buffet continues to entice the slithering reptile. "Crocodile Dan" makes the final capture and Terry dispatches it with the whack of a shovel. Foot-long spinnerbait trailers, anyone?

On Tuesday morning, Dan, Barb, and Riley prepare to depart in their sleek, new, Ranger boat. I stand on the dock and implore them to stay, joking that they can't leave me alone with my imposing 6' 6" friend, his Lizzy Borden imitation still fresh. I offer Riley unlimited access to my Alberta Springs Canadian Rye Whisky. Schedule not permitting they say their goodbyes and pull away. The roar of the 225-horsepower engine drowns my good-humored plea, "Don't leave me, DON'T LEAVE ME!"

Moments later, our friends' visit now a memory, I reach into Terry's boat for one of my fishing rods. I select the one with a bucktail spinner and throw a cast that lands parallel to the reed-studded shoreline. My spirits perk up as a musky follows, but it turns away as I perform a figure-8. I continue to cast. The fish follows two more times before becoming a no-show. Encouraged then discouraged, I step into Terry's boat and put down the rod. I slump onto the passenger seat, arms folded across my chest while waiting for Terry to come down to start our day on the water. Upon his arrival, I mention my experience with the "following" fish.

Without saying a word, he picks up one of his rods and flings a long cast toward the middle of the bay. He begins to retrieve the Giant Jackpot with an air of confidence and determination. Facetiously delivering some fishing wisdom, he comments, "After you've had a follow and it doesn't come back, you should throw toward the deep water. I've told you that before. Did you do it?" Before I can answer, the water explodes. He's got her. Time to revert to my familiar roles: net-man, measure-man, and photographer. "My" fish is a nice one, a 38-inch. Teacher takes me to school, and I'm still fishless going into day four.

Wednesday brings a change in the weather. We're hopeful it will bring improved fishing results. Cloud cover rolls in, temperature cools to the 60s, and periods of light rain sprinkle the fishing day.

Terry motors to our first stop, "Doughboy," a small, bay-like indentation along the north shoreline of Forest Lake. I clip on the blue and silver-glitter Giant Jackpot, the same one that caught the 45-incher at Little Vermilion. I wing a cast deep into the far left corner, several yards to the right of a beaver hut. It splashes down near a large exposed boulder fronted by the trunk of a downed tree lying parallel to the shore. After passing a small patch of submerged vegetation, a large shadow rises behind the zigzagging lure.

Consistent in my retrieve, the fish keeps pace with slow, steady movement. In an effort to entice a strike, I begin altering the speed … faster … slower … faster …. The fish remains noncommittal, maintaining its distance several feet behind and below the lure. With time and space waning as the Jackpot approaches the boat, I recall the unconventional method "discovered by accident" on Little Vermilion. I ease the lure to a complete stop. The fish holds behind it, motionless. Seconds pass. Tension rises in the aquatic standoff. I wonder … when should I pull the trigger? Just like at Little Vermilion, a subtle, almost imperceptible movement of the lure causes the musky to inch its gator-like snout closer.

NOW!

Just like at Little Vermilion, I twitch the Jackpot forward. Just like at Little Vermilion the musky lunges forward—and engulfs it. Just like at Little Vermilion, all hell breaks loose and, fortunately, just like at Little Vermilion, the fish doesn't. Amid anxious moments including strong runs, it powers a last-gasp dive beneath the boat. Holding tight before finally winching it to the surface, Terry slides the net beneath it. Relief replaces futility—my week has just taken a dramatic, positive turn. Just like my Little Vermilion musky, this one tapes at 45 inches, setting the camp record for our group's decade of outings on the Alexandra Chain.

This fish also heralded a fine fishing day. I caught one more, a 31-incher. Terry, however, set a one-day camp record by landing five, those measuring 31 to 39 inches.

Pleased with our success, we wondered if our efforts would bring equal reward on Thursday.

There is a fine line between fishing and just standing on the shore looking like an idiot.
—Stephen Wright

The Thrill of Victory, The Agony of the Hook (III)

If you grew up in the Chicago area in the early 1960s, you may recall a Saturday evening program on WGN-TV, *Jim Thomas Outdoors*. Viewers would send in letters and questions (or Jim would make them up), then answer with a vintage (and cheesy) film clip that had been collecting dust in the video library for years on end. Jim always narrated the clips, and without fail, as the fisherman retrieved a cast Jim would comment with nasally, Chicago-tone, hesitating anticipation, "Then ... suddenly ... without warning ... WHAM!" as a fish strikes. Hold that thought.

As years fly off the calendar, the "vacation" part of "fishing vacation" gains increasing importance. The need to be on the water every waking moment is a younger man's game. The days of casting caution to the blustering wind, blistering heat, driving rain, sleet, or snow, are distant reflections in the rearview mirror. Late night "dates" finding me dressed in a mosquito net tuxedo and lathered with Deet cologne flicker as a fading memory. The torch that illuminates the pre-dawn and post-dusk path to the cabin has been passed to a younger generation of musky masochists.

A gradual process, these changes have been mandated by unrelated events: my aging body and Terry's schedule. Terry is a lot of things, some of them (alright, most of them) good. One thing he is not, however, is a "morning person." By the time he wakens from a Molson-induced slumber and the caffeine from his cup of java has kicked in, the hands on the clock approach 10 a.m. In years gone by, this pained me like a hook into a finger or leg.

No longer annoyed by his relaxed, late start to the fishing day, I'm usually on the screened porch with a book, jotting notes about this or that, or simply allowing my senses to be overwhelmed by the blissful stupor of the Canadian wilderness as I recover from the blissful stupor brought on by generous portions of Alberta Springs consumed the evening prior. On this glorious mid-July Thursday morning, a gentle breeze caresses me as the subtle cadence of waves lap ashore, which along with the rustling leaves, creates a soothing concerto. Okay, enough flowery baloney. Time to do some fishing.

With Terry in the cabin tending to his morning ritual, I head down to the dock. My first cast, parallel to the shore, draws a follow. Unfortunately, the fish turns away before it has a chance to be fooled by my figure-8. Tuesday's lesson still fresh in my mind, I launch the next cast toward the deep water and begin a slow, steady retrieve. Plop, ploop, plop, ploop … the tantalizing topwater bait churns merrily … plop, ploop … its rotating tail sending a gentle spray skyward … plop, ploop … watery diamonds glistening in the sunlight … plop, ploop, plop, ploop … the subtle "V" of its wake gently displacing water as it returns … plop, ploop … now halfway back …

SKERRRRPLUSHHHHHHH!

The surface detonation initiates an instantaneous string of events: breakfast bagel returning from stomach to throat, knees buckling, pulse racing, adrenaline pumping, rod throbbing, heart throbbing more, rod throbbing *more*. Thoughts blur: the net is in the boat … the boat is in the boathouse … THRASHHH! … SPLASHHH! What to do? My fishing partner is preoccupied and unaware of my predicament … What to do!?

Seconds later, I hear the creaking spring of the cabin screen door as it opens, immediately followed by the reverberating crack of wood on wood as it slams shut. Terry, having heard the commotion, races down to see what is going on. The battle in view, he diverts to the boathouse for the net and returns post-haste. The timing impeccable, he scoops the played-out fish as I guide it to the edge of the dock.

With everything now under control, Terry heads back to the boathouse for the measuring tape and camera. When he returns, we'll complete the routine we've been through dozens of times before, performed with speed and precision: measure, photo, and release.

What a great start to the fishing day! As I bask in the rosy glow, the excitement of the morning success winds down with another sequence of events: blood pressure and pulse retreating, breakfast bagel returning to stomach, brown spot drying.

In three-feet of water near the sandy lake bottom, encircled by the oversize rubberized bag of the landing net, the fish lies, docile. It appears to be of average girth and slightly longer than a yardstick, putting its weight at approximately 15 pounds. I kneel on the net handle, the yolk secured on the edge of the dock. During the netting process the lure had popped free from the fish's mouth, both sets of treble hooks becoming entangled in the netting near the hoop.

Awaiting Terry's return, I begin a high stakes game of Cat's Cradle, working to free the lure. Then … suddenly … without warning … WHAM! The fish, patiently biding his time, chooses the precise moment to rush forward, pulling the net taut. In a painfully disbelieving instant I peer down, eyes widening to the size of silver dollars, to find one hook of the large treble penetrating my right index finger, the point and barb of the hook exiting on the other side. Pulse races, adrenaline pumps, heart throbs, breakfast bagel returns to throat, brown spot expands. I've been had!

Turnabout fair play, the fish contorts wildly ... Slash! Thrash! Gash! ... pleased with his accomplishment of vengeful glory. As my head bobs in a momentary swoon, do I hear the words "Got him!" emanating from the water?

A shock-induced silence strangles my vocal cords, but my brain screams, "WHOAAAA @#$%&*@#$%& (NELLIE!!!)"

Instinctively, I grab the lure with my other hand attempting to stabilize it so flesh will not be ripped from the bone. As the fish continues his romp, I feel the point of the second treble beginning to pierce my other hand. I am a second away from becoming captive in a unique set of Chinese handcuffs. Another thought flashes through my mind:

"OH, MAMA, THERE WILL BE NO WAY TO EXPLAIN AND LIVE THIS ONE DOWN, @#$%&*@#$%&!!!"

A nanosecond from further disaster I yank my hand away, grabbing the netting at a safe distance from the tangled hooks. My knee slips off the handle and the hoop slides vertically into the water. The fish, sensing victory, turns with a cat-that-just-swallowed-the-canary grin, casually gliding out of the net as if on a Sunday stroll. Rising to the surface, he splashes water on me with a slap of his tail and in a final act of defiance and poor sportsmanship, "flips me the fin" as he swims away. Further into the surreal I think I hear the words, "Payback for junior's encounter with your Husky Jerk, jerk."

So, here I am, kneeling on the dock, net half in the water, lure attached to the net, and my finger attached to the lure. Woozy in the aftermath, I sense the fish has returned with a group of his buddies to view his catch. "He's a trophy, man, a 72-incher! Average girth. Probably goes 180. Got him on a top-water." I'm momentarily blinded. Is it the sun reflecting off a wave or the flash of a Polaroid from the murky depths, making *me* the latest addition to the musky's "Angler Wall of Fame?"

Unaware of the calamity, Terry exits the boathouse and approaches with the camera and measuring stick in hand. This is not going to be good. I am kneeling and bleeding, attached to the fishless net, looking stupid, feeling stupid.

"What the hell happened to you ... and where's the fish!?"

The physical pain matches that to my ego. Still under extreme duress and a witty reply not forthcoming, I humbly understate the obvious: "I'm hooked ... and the fish is gone."

My reputation for fishing related self-inflicted bloodlettings well documented, Terry addresses me as if he's reprimanding one of his undisciplined students, his tone authoritative but the message tongue-in-cheek. "I can't leave you alone for a second, can I?" After a thoughtful pause to ensure the words sink in, he follows with, "Wait here. I'll get the hook cutters."

Wait here? Wait here? Like, where am I going to go? Okay, I know what he meant. This is no time to be smart-alecky. I'm the one with the treble clown-ring through my finger; can't alienate my backwoods surgeon. During his absence my mind replays the lurid event, searching for a face-saving explanation. Terry returns with his cutters, the metal-on-metal "pop" snapping the hook beneath the barb, the five-second operation complete as both ends of the severed shank are extracted.

Detached from the lure and net, with pulse level retreating from three digits to two, I give it my best shot. "I did what you told me to do. I had a follow, then casted to the deep water … and look what happened."

"Is that the best you can do?"

"Yeah."

"Go back to the cabin and I'll bring the first aid kit."

"Okay…"

Our week ends with a respectable total of 14 muskies, the math teacher taking 9. Arithmetic properly served, that leaves me with 5. Ever the statistician and while on the subject of mathematics, the importance I place on number of fish versus their size varies from year to year, not unlike the spin a corporation's CEO puts on the year-end numbers at an annual shareholder meeting. For instance, in 2001, length reigned. My 8 fish, averaging 33.625 inches, took precedence over Terry's 17 (hmmph, big deal!) that averaged "only" 33.264. In 2000, quantity was key. Although Terry's 2 fish averaged 37 inches, I doubled his total with 4, their 31.75-inch average length of no consequence. In the year just completed, I advised Terry that he had come up short again, size trumping quantity. My muskies averaged 35.9 inches, his a paltry 35.44. And in those years when tugs on my line have been few and far between, I find that crunching the numbers isn't, well, just isn't very important at all.

~ ~ ~ ~ ~

Summer 2005. I don't remember why I didn't make the trip this year. Maybe I wasn't invited. Maybe they left without me. Maybe the traumas of 2004 wrought permanent psychological scars manifesting amnesia. Maybe I went and don't remember. It's hell gettin' old.

~ ~ ~ ~ ~

The Forest Lake 45-incher.

~ ~ ~ ~ ~

One thing becomes clearer as one gets older and one's fishing experiences increases, and that is the paramount importance of one's fishing companions.
—John Ashley-Cooper

Fall 2005. As each of my musky fishing friends and relatives reach a landmark 40th or 50th birthday, I present them with a Giant Jackpot fishing lure that I customize with their name, age, and other decorative elements symbolic of their likes and lives. For instance, if I made one for myself, it would display the medical Caduceus symbol, a bottle of Bactine, and a Band-Aid.

I encourage my fishing partners to use their lure, hoping it will result in a catch that will bring lasting memories. Some are reluctant to do so. Though their words indicate they do not want to take a chance on losing the thoughtfully created "work of art," I believe some think the gaudily decorated gift has no chance of ever enticing a fish to strike.

My absence during the summer of 2005 enabled a September trip with Ben, Rich, and Larry. Unlike other members of the group, Ben occasionally clips on the 40th birthday Giant Jackpot I "tricked-out" for him. Imagine my delight when a fish struck it near "The Throne" on Tuesday evening. He fought it to a distance just beyond the reach of the landing net when the fish broke free.

Upon examining the birthday lure, Ben found a compromised rear eyelet—opened just enough to allow the hook to slip free. He offered a good-natured suggestion that perhaps the gift-giver had sabotaged the lure. Replying in kind, I "admitted" the entire eyelet should have pulled out, releasing a pop-up flag reading "SUCKER!" (During porch talk that evening Ben disclosed that earlier in the day the lure had snagged on a stump, and his vigorous pulls to free it likely loosened the eyelet.)

Larry didn't fish much this trip, generously relinquishing his place in the boat so as not to overcrowd it. He did, however, play the parental role to perfection. As his brothers and I would leave the dock each morning, he would comment with a stern voice but a smile on his face, "Wear your life jackets … and don't do anything stupid!"

~ ~ ~ ~ ~

Motorola - The 2000s

Into the new millennium, the corporation pays the price for serious blunders (and I mean beyond the monetary and psychological expenses of trail ride bonding) committed over the course of recent years. First, betting on the continuation of analog technology, it falls woefully behind the competition as the cellular industry switches to digital. Second, its Iridium business rockets $5,000,000,000 into the black hole of space with 66 satellites that will allow communication anywhere in the world, including its remotest locations. Technologically brilliant but a commercial bust, the limited population of potential customers find fault with a $3,000 phone the size and weight of a brick, $3 to $8 per minute usage charges, the inability to communicate inside buildings, and spotty communication if not remaining stationary when outdoors. Picky, picky.

Despair and desperation bleed from the workplace in levels never before seen in my 25-plus years. Weekly messages from CEO Chris Galvin are edgy, almost threatening. His lineage as the founder's grandson provides no protection from the sniping of Wall Street analysts and shareholders justifiably short on patience. Business news too often includes the headline "Motorola today announces another X,000 layoffs." Rightsizing—the word rolls off the tongue, unthreatening, like the attempt to match and balance a rod and reel combination. For workers, the news disturbs like a thick-barbed hook impaling a body part. Everyone knows someone felled by the corporate Grim Reaper. The Motorola Service Club, its employment assurance and intrinsic badge of two-way loyalty deep-sixed, lives only as a memory of better days past.

The payroll cuts and collateral damage from demands of maintaining the company's "bottom line" becomes a frequent lunchtime topic among the long-tenured service reps, Dave, Judy, Jim, Cindi, and Patty, with whom I now frequently dine. Comments on any given day (after Jim's reading of our horoscopes) could include:

"The company is stopping their contribution to profit sharing."

"Our health insurance premiums are going up."

"The cafeteria is serving soup made from the blood the company is squeezing out of turnips."

"Every department has to cut another 10%."

"This place sucks."

"Pay freeze just announced."

"The work doesn't go away when the people do."

"The cost-cutting death spiral continues."

"I hate my job. I sure hope I don't lose it."

The bulk of the conversations, or at least my involvement, occurs before I complete my lunch, which culminates with a Hostess Suzy Q—two rectangular chunks of devil's food cake sandwiching a thick, white cream filling that oozes out with every bite. This brownbag grand finale, on top of my sandwich, chips, and fruit, always induces a glucose-carbohydrate coma. Remnants of the last bite savored, I slump in my chair, arms crossed, eyes glazed-over. My dining companions accept this "sugared away from the depressing negativism of the workplace" as part of our daily ritual, some attempting to pinpoint the exact time it will occur.

Employee terminations result in a significant excess of facility space. Relocations, to consolidate the survivors and shed the cost of the "brick and mortar," accelerate at a ridiculous pace. My travel log includes stops at Commerce Drive and Basswood Avenue facilities in Schaumburg, interspersed with stays at 1309, 1301, and 1313, as well as several moves within each move, pinballing to the point that I often don't even bother unpacking, referring to my cubby du jour as my "office in a box." The issuance of portable laptop computers eases the burden of the moves. No more clunky CPUs and CRTs. But no matter the stop, the narcoleptic gray modular furniture remains a constant.

The Business Trip, February 2003

Unlike my work counterparts who might be headed to San Diego, Orlando, Phoenix, or upstate New York, my territory dictates occasional business trips to less glamorous locations. This month my itinerary takes me to one of these "garden spots," Cleveland, Ohio. Located on the south shore of Lake Erie, I'm reminded of the 1970s *Saturday Night Live* "commercial" for "Swill," a thick-pouring, debris-filled, domestic mineral water bottled directly from the (not so) Great Lake.

It is Monday, February 10, 2003. My ill-timed departure from the Chicago area finds me solidly squeezed in morning rush hour traffic. Before I can say "Son of a b...," I am an hour behind schedule. The logjam loosens on the eastern fringe of the metro area, allowing me to nudge the accelerator closer to the floorboard, taking flight on Indiana's 80/94 toll road, which runs parallel to the Michigan state line.

The six cylinders of my garnet red, 1992 Chevy Lumina whine as never before, the speedometer needle fluttering several miles per hour short of "85," which maxes out the dial. The banter of sports talk radio, courtesy of Chicago's 670 AM *The Score*, plays clearly in my CD-less, cassette-less vehicle. Mileposts come and go with increasing rapidity: hurry LaPorte, South Bend, Elkhart. Cars and semis left in my wake fuel a giddy euphoria. I pass a Lincoln Town Car: "Hey grandpa, suck on my Michelin molecules!"

An eerie mist rises from the snow-covered farmland on both sides of the road, veiling signs until nearly upon them. I catch one that reads, "Entering LaGrange County." After rocketing through an underpass, my mood takes an immediate and decided downturn. Out of the corner of my eye, I catch a white vehicle tucked behind one of the bridge's support pylons. With no time to react, radar beams have certainly spun their trapping web. My eyes lock on the rearview mirror. The vehicle begins pursuit, lights flashing. Thoughts likewise flash: further delay, financial consequence, and the likely end of a 30-plus year run of ticketless driving. I roll my Chevy to a stop on the road's shoulder, a shoulder to cry on.

The trooper pulls up behind me, exits his cruiser, and approaches on the passenger side, safely away from the vehicles I had passed over the last number of miles, now passing us. (I envision those drivers nodding in smug and gleeful affirmation, happy that the God of Road Justice is alive and well.) Seconds later, the Mountie-capped (Dudley Do-Right look) trooper peers into my vehicle. In my role of unlikely scofflaw, I wonder what aspect of his field of vision he may find most intriguing:

The Spiderman pillow, used as a lumbar support, that squirted free as I reached across the passenger seat to manually crank down the window of one of the last vehicle in America without power locks and power windows?

The Rand McNally Atlas, folded open to Indiana, scattered with Post It notes?

My Mototola identification badge, with mug shot circa 1992, attached to a SpongeBob SquarePants lanyard?

"May I see your license and vehicle registration, please?"

Of course. Good morning. No need to explain, we both know why you stopped me. How kind, you wanting to tell me that my right rear wheel is without a hubcap. Oh, that's not it? Alerting me to the overpowering smell of rotten eggs emanating from my failing catalytic converter? No? Interested in a closer look at the classic, decorative, non-functional luggage rack adorning the trunk?

"Yes sir."

After a minimal amount of nerve-induced wallet fumbling, my license surfaces. I hand it to the officer, glad I did not act on high school classmate Tony Dee's long-ago advice of clipping a twenty-dollar bill to the back of it for situations such as this. While such a not-so-subtle payola may have success in Chicago (the "City that Works"), its use elsewhere may draw ire in the best case, or prison time in the worst.

Hopefully, sir, there are no hard feelings from that blustery, winter day in January of '72 when your fifth-ranked Indiana Hoosier hoopsters traveled to the cornfields of DeKalb to do battle on the hardcourt with my alma mater, the unranked Northern Illinois University Huskies. So sorry (not really) to have sent Coach Knight and your team, led by All-American George McGinnis, back to Bloomington smarting from an 85-71 loss.

Next, I open the glove box, releasing an avalanche of eclectic items original to the vehicle or accumulated over the past decade: tire warranty information and pressure gauge; owner's manual; film canister holding miscellaneous coinage; a ChapStick; a clear plastic box of green Tic Tacs; a couple of toothpicks; a packet of Handi Wipes; Dunkin' Donuts napkins; and beneath them all, the car registration.

> *How's that two-way radio working for you, sir? I'm sure you're aware that my employer, Motorola, supplies your mission-critical communications equipment and service. I'm on my way to a meeting to discuss how we can best provide for the service needs of first responders such as yourself, ensuring dependable and affordable coverage as you serve and protect the citizenry of the great State of Indiana.*

Documents in hand, the trooper returns to his vehicle. His background check will reveal the following: if I were bald, on steroids, wearing white pants and a white t-shirt three sizes too small, I could easily be mistaken for Mr. Clean. A few minutes later, he returns.

Time to face the music. I've been bad. Not real bad, but bad enough. The trooper hands me a green carbon form. Glancing at the bottom, the "Speed" box is "X'ed," and the "Details Box" notes: "Excessive." My eyes gravitate to the top of the form: "Indiana State Police Warning." He departs with the words, "Just slow it down a bit."

> *I will. I will indeed. Good day, sir! My sincerest apology, and a thousand, heartfelt "thank yous!"*

~ ~ ~ ~ ~

Corporate Colonoscopy

The world "shrinks" as a result of rapid and unending advances in communication: spiffy black desk telephones with call waiting, caller ID, voice mail, speed dial, conferencing capabilities, and later with wired, then wireless headsets (under critical circumstances, along with the "mute" feature, allowing a trip to the men's room while on a call, "always connected"); laptop computers, enabling the ability to work while on the road, at home, evenings, weekends, vacation days, 24 x7 if that's what it takes! (and often it does…); "net-meetings"—follow along on your computer as the meeting host runs through a real-time slide presentation, viewable, long distance, on your very own monitor; an in-person meeting or visit to your desk from a boss or co-worker, validating human beings do, in fact, still exist; e-mails, hundreds by the week; an instant message popping up on your screen to interrupt a net-meeting, e-mail, visit from a human, or maybe just the job you're supposed to be doing, assuming you remember what that is; and an occasional snail-mail thrown in for good measure. Ah, the fast-pace world that demands multi-tasking, defined as simultaneously working to resolve a continuous string of interruptions that unrelentingly bombards every fiber of your being.

In January 2004, the Motorola Board of Directors names Ed Zander as Chairman of the Board and CEO. Wall Street lauds the move, reaching outside the company for new leadership with a fresh perspective. I also view the change as positive, though for different reasons. It's as simple as this: Ed and I have the same first name. And his last name, Zander, is a sport and food fish native to Europe, the species similar to the North American walleye.

In seemingly less time than I can say "Fish On!" my whimsical hopes tank. Even the wildly popular and iconic RAZR cell phone doesn't spare the company from continued rounds of nasty cost-cutting. Cold-blooded, like a walleye and every other fish, Eddie Z. leads the company as it continues to sever employees with the ease of filleting a bluegill with a rapier.

On December 2, 2004, I receive several letters from upper management in recognition and celebration of my 30th anniversary with the company. Although the envelopes with these congratulatory messages don't contain a bull's-eye or rifle sight hovering over my name, it wouldn't have surprised me if they did. Exactly one month later I receive the following communiqué:

> *Your employment status is being changed from exempt to hourly. There has been no change to your job responsibilities, tasks, and goals. As an exempt employee, your annual salary was within the highest tercile for that grade. As a result of your classification, your annual salary now falls outside the upper limit for your new grade. Your base pay will not be reduced as a result of this review process; however, you will be ineligible for base pay increases. You may be eligible for lump sum increases depending on individual performance. Motorola Incentive Pay targets are linked to grade level. Your MIP will be reduced as a result of your reclassification. Hourly positions such as yours have been reclassified and are not eligible to participate in the annual stock option grant program. As always, Motorola reserves the right to review employee pay against market data and adjust up or down as appropriate.*

I refer to this information as BoE—Beginning of the End. A not-so "welcome" to the new Motorola.

Not long thereafter, management selects me to assist in training a third-party vendor who will be taking over some of the job functions handled by our current Customer Support Manager crew of six. Heavily laced with the career-ending handwriting on the wall known as outsourcing, this momentum-gathering concept of payroll cost reduction has already jettisoned thousands of Motorola employees in manufacturing, repair, purchasing, IT, cafeteria, special projects, and security. Now, chum has been tossed into our midst. The sharks are circling.

Generally good throughout my career at leaving work-related issues at the office, this one throws me for a loop—that "loop" configured in the shape of a noose. Jo Ann senses a cloudy tone during our dinner conversation on the day I learn of this ominous turn of events. She jumps in with a direct question. "What's wrong?"

"Nothing," I reply, fairly certain the conversation won't end there.

Recognized as a feeble attempt falling between masquerade and charade, she queries a second time, in a firmer tone. "What's *wrong?*"

Perhaps the diversionary tactic to humor will work. "I stapled my finger to a stack of papers this morning. It was quite embarrassing walking around all day like that. And quite a problem when I went to the bathroom. They would have sent me to the company nurse, but we don't have one anymore. Her job was outsourced to Beijing."

Not happy with that response either, Jo Ann gives me the "you've got three seconds to tell me the real story" look. With our 30-plus years of marriage, I have a full understanding and appreciation of this look, one that combines equal parts concern and (justified) impatience.

I acquiesce, "On the subject of outsourcing, I'm being sent to Denver to train an outside company to do my job."

"That can't be good," Jo Ann replies in masterful understatement.

"Great minds think alike. Being crusted with Motorola barnacles that have been accumulating over three decades, I put the question to my boss, point-blank. He assured me we'll still have jobs, handling more important stuff, confident about us 'moving up the food chain,' I think he said."

"In this corporate environment, it seems like carnivores and cannibals are just one step higher on the food chain," she added.

"Thanks for that pleasant visual. But you're right. In sports, the general manager or owner gives a vote of confidence to the coach, and then fires him the next day."

"So, what are you going to do?"

"I'm planning my retirement refrain."

Fishing for Fairness
The 2006 Performance Review with the New Mnemonic: DUMB (Demeaning, Unattainable, Moronic, Bastardly)

Throughout the course of my employment, I've sensed that certain managers expected to hear some version of the following during the career planning portion of the annual review process as a positive indicator of employee potential: "Next year I'd like to have your job, and the year after that your boss's job, and in five years I'd like to be God, and the year after that be God's boss." That observation aside, generally straightforward performance evaluations through most of my career used the SMART mnemonic—Specific, Measurable, Attainable, Relevant, and Timely—for setting objectives and managing performance. In the latter years, allowing you to keep your job prevailed as management's only and not-so-subtle motivation technique.

It's time for my annual performance review. I'm feeling good. Damn good. As in most other years, I've done well. This year, exceptionally well. I hit high-water marks on each of my performance goals, not only achieving the "plan" numbers but also significantly exceeding the prescribed above plan "reach-out" numbers that always justify an overall above average rating. Additionally, the positive results were achieved under burdensome conditions: reporting to three different managers, dealing with new system platforms that frequently malfunctioned, and picking up the workload for several department members that moved on, voluntarily and involuntarily. And I did it all without having to forego any vacations, becoming a veritable poster child for efficiency and productivity.

Performance Results:

Business Goal 1:	Excellent
Business Goal 2:	Excellent
Business Goal 3:	Excellent
Business Goal 4.	Excellent
Behavior Goal 1:	Very Effective
Behavior Goal 2:	Very Effective
Development Action 1:	On Plan
Development Action 2:	On Plan

Manager Checkpoint 1 Comments: Great job overall. Employee appears to be on track for another good year of increased overall business and customer satisfaction results.

Manager Checkpoint 2 Comments: Employee is a key member of his team, always showing consistent performance with high results. Employee conducts himself professionally, and is well respected by his peers and customers.

Manager Summary Comments: Employee ended the year ahead of plan on all of his goals. He demonstrated the behaviors necessary to be successful, especially when it came to customer satisfaction. Employee received a letter from one of his customers praising his efforts over the last several years. Quality Manager also sent in some nice comments about the job Employee is doing.

(Ratings are as follows, with the number next to each noting the percentage of employees that management must allocate to each category [apparently regardless of performance]: Outstanding [10%], Excellent [25%], Effective [55%], or Needs Improvement [10%]).

Final Performance Rating: Effective

The dialog:
Me: How could you arrive at my final rating of "Effective" versus "Excellent" based on the documented performance and the summary comments?
Boss: Maybe your goals were too easy.
Me: Huh?
Boss: We're all expected to do more.
Me: Huh?
Boss: The bar was raised; we just didn't get around to telling you. We can do that, you know.
Me: Huh?
Boss: The Corporation is changing. We used to be valued employees, almost family. Now we're just commodities.
Me: Huh?
Boss: In the grand scheme of things, your job just isn't that important. The higher ratings are saved for people whose jobs have more value to the corporation."
Me: Huh?

Boss: The formal "relative performance" calibration, you know, the one where you were compared and rated against other employees in completely different jobs and disciplines officially went away this year, but you are still being compared to other employees, but we don't have to tell you who or why, and we pretty much have to shove you all into certain slots to hit the management assigned level of distribution, regardless of performance.

Me: Huh?

Boss: I really shouldn't share this with you, but I've only been rated as "Effective" too.

Me: Huh?

Boss: "Effective" is a good rating. But based on your experience and grade level, I expected you to exceed all your goals, so, you see, you met my expectations and thus were just "Effective." If it'll make you feel better you're welcome to speak to HR or use the Open Door policy to speak to the next level of management. They'll just tell you the same things, though.

Me: "Huh? ... Let me see if I understand with this simple analogy. As a seasoned fishing veteran, I'm participating in a three-day bass tournament. At the end of the first two days, I receive compliments from the tournament directors for my outstanding catch as well as sharing information about locations and lures I'm using. I experience success in spite of the fact that my tournament-provided boat springs a leak and suffers a motor breakdown on consecutive days, reducing angling time and maneuverability. At the tourney's conclusion, my total catch exceeds all others. I am not awarded top honor, however, because, well because I was expected to win with a superb catch. And if I don't agree with this logic, I'm invited to take it up with the sponsoring Bass Anglers Sportsman Society (B.A.S.S.), though their prearranged agreement with the tournament directors has already made the decision final.

Boss: That pretty much explains it. I knew you'd understand. You're a sharp guy. And, by the way, you're rating isn't going to change."

Me: I won't be getting a merit increase this year, will I?

Boss: I don't know. I'll have to check with your previous bosses.

Me: But...

Boss: But the point is, the Corporation is looking for more, bigger, better, faster—there are high expectations that we must deliver on! What makes i'Moto? Customers! Innovation! Performance!"

Me: You left out "Principles."

Boss: We can pretty much do whatever we want and don't have to explain anything to anybody.

Me: Have we somehow been teleported into a *Dilbert* cartoon?

Boss: Huh?

Me: Do you find it difficult to shave in the morning when you look in the mirror and don't see your reflection?

Boss: Huh?

Me: How does it feel to be the "ass" in associate?

Boss: Huh?

Me: If only the good die young, you're going to live forever.

Boss: Huh?

Me: Talking to you makes me want to take a RAZR to my wrists.

Boss: Huh?

~ ~ ~ ~ ~

Most of the world is covered by water. A fisherman's job is simple. Pick out the best parts.
—Charles Waterman

Emerald Lake

Most people who fish have cast their lines in many bodies of water during the course of a lifetime. Like finding a soul mate with which to spend one's life, some of us have the good fortune to develop a special connection with a particular body of water. These magical, mystical places are our "home waters." They do not have to be in close proximity to where we live or work, nor are they necessarily the place we have experienced our best catches, although that is an obvious plus. Rather, by my definition, "home waters" soothe one's soul with a transcendental comfort and solitude.

We speak to them and about them with love and reverence. As a best friend, they understand and accept us unconditionally. Wisconsin waters embrace the hearts of my friend Mike, Cousin Ben and his best friend John, and Cousin Rich with their connections to Green Lake, Lac du Flambeau, and Dam Lake, respectively. For me, it is Emerald Lake, a shining jewel in my home state of Illinois.

Relatively small, an undeveloped shore thick with trees and dotted with rock outcroppings cradles its modest and under-fished acreage. Sections of the shoreline gently slope to weed-dotted bays. Others rise tall and steep with exposed sandstone bluffs. Whitetail deer quench their thirst from it, muskrats scamper its shores, and the long-legged blue heron stalks its shallow water for meals. Hawks, turkey vultures, and eagles soar above it. Bluegills, crappies, perch, largemouth and smallmouth bass, channel catfish, walleye, and tiger muskies roam its depths, all willing to inhale a worm, minnow, or artificial bait. I've enjoyed, savored, reveled in the experiences that have unfolded in untold hours fished there, sometimes solo but more often with my father, son, wife, and a long list of friends and acquaintances.

Through no fault of its own, however, perfection eludes Emerald Lake. To wit:

The Emerald Lake Tournaments

What better way to bastardize the peace and serenity of a body of water than by introducing the invasive species known as tournament fishermen? Much to my dismay, tournaments on Emerald Lake began in the 1980s. Although small and localized, I viewed these disturbing competitions as having no upside. To get an inside look and confirm my disgust, I entered the 1990 tourney with Joe, and taking first place as we each landed a bass in excess of 4 pounds (in the midst of a violent thunderstorm, no less), I had a change of heart; by gosh, tournaments could be fun! The enjoyment and success continued in subsequent years, winning with Joe as my partner in 1991 and 1992.

What characteristics do good fishing partners possess, especially in a tournament environment? How do personalities mesh to create a winning combination? Is "being on the same page" regarding fishing location and techniques a better route to success, or does "begging to differ" prove more beneficial to reaching the winner's circle?

When fishing with Joe, I defer to his knowledge and "sixth sense" regarding the sequence and timing of locations to fish, as well as suggested baits. Our partnership works well. I am a parasitic lamprey, content with a comfortable ride on the side of an angler possessing the prowess of a great white shark. Unfortunately, after the success of the early '90s, work, scheduling conflicts, and other life events kept us from continuing our joint participation in the tournaments.

With the passing of years, my partners encompassed a wide range of age, gender, and skill level, the rigid compatibility criteria for joining me defined as follows: anyone who likes to fish, has a free Saturday, and doesn't mind seeing a small entrance fee flush like water propelled from the bottom of a boat by a bilge pump.

Jo Ann accompanied me in 1993, her 3-pound 6-ouce bass earning us first place. She subsequently retired from the circuit, preferring to "go out on top." Lifelong fishing partners, my younger cousins Rich and Ben, as well as my son, Ed, joined me on occasion for the one-day contests. Mike, the husband of one of my wife's co-workers, a passionate and proficient fisherman, joined me for a number of other Emerald Lake tournaments. Although I normally contribute a fish or two to our total catch regardless of who joins me, the importance of the "E" in "Ed" and "tEam" often manifested itself as nEt-man and photographEr for my partners' catch.

An impenetrable force-field surrounded the tournament winner's circle over the next, oh, plus or minus 15 years. This lack of success contributed to sketchy record-keeping and a temporary abandonment of my avocation as a detail-oriented pseudo-statistician. A few undated tournament scorecards list one to four fish caught, and do not indicate where we placed. Several of the better finishes did contain that information:

$1997 - 4^{th}/24$

$1998 - 6^{th}/35$

$1999 - 11^{th}/28$

$2002 - 6^{th}/22$

A number of factors played into our inability to sustain success: a continuous increase in the number of skilled tournament contestants (They had to be cheating!); refusal to learn new techniques ("We've always done it this way!"); failure to adapt to changes in the lake affecting fish location (They've got to be somewhere, so why not where they've always been?). Oh, and supernatural circumstances, too.

The 2004 Tournament

Cousin Rich joins me for this one. Traveling the last leg of highway to the cabin on Friday evening, a black cat scurries across the road in front of us. Stopped on the shoulder, it swivels its head in our direction, the car's headlights reflecting its piercingly eerie, green eyes. We chuckle guardedly, wondering aloud how the classic, superstitious feline foreshadowing might play out in the tournament.

It does not take long for the first incoming salvo. Before turning in for the evening, I inadvertently set the alarm for 5 p.m. instead of 5 a.m. Fortunately, my body clock, set for the 5 a.m. workday start, wakes me in time. Is that the best you've got, cat?

That bullet dodged, Rich and I take care of morning business, arriving at the marina with plenty of time to spare. We pony up the entry fee and are handed Flag #7. Rich nods in approval. "It's the Mick's number," he says, referring to Mr. Mantle of New York Yankee fame.

Soon after readying our equipment, the horn blares the 7 a.m. start and the din of idling motors grows to a roar as the boats depart. Go, ladies and gentlemen, go to the far side of the lake where all the fish can be had. As in most other tournaments, I linger behind to begin our quest in the fertile and under-fished waters of the marina bay. Hello? What's this? Four of the boats stop abruptly in the bay and begin fishing the favored locations I have always called my own. Okay, cat, we'll deal with it.

We proceed up the north shoreline toward another spot that has served me well over the years. Upon cruising around the point, we find two boats camped there. I put the motor in neutral to contemplate this unanticipated sequence of events. Decision made, it's back to the marina bay. Though my prime sites are occupied, we'll work some adjacent areas. Within ten casts and but 15 minutes into the tournament, I hook and land a bass—a good one at 4 pounds, 10 ounces. With that beauty, and 6 hours and 45 minutes to get the rest of our limit, I'm optimistic about finishing in the money. Take that, black cat!

Anglers near us bag an occasional fish but nothing the size of the one in our makeshift livewell, a 22-quart aerated cooler that sits on the platform in the boat's bow. After an hour lull in the action I catch another, more the standard fare at 15 inches and 2 pounds. Both fish are released after being tallied by a tournament weigh boat

At 9 a.m., Rich lands a nice 16-incher exceeding 2 pounds. Into the Coleman he goes. Things are looking good, and then get better. "I've got another one, Rich!" Up yours, black cat! While fighting the fish, I hear "thump, thump" and a minor commotion behind me. I'm thinking Rich may have stumbled while moving to ready the net. A moment later he mutters, "You're not going to believe this ... the fish in the cooler just knocked off the lid and launched himself back into the lake." A jail break. A damn jail break! And cleverly plotted in wait of a diversion before bolting. Touché, black cat!

Amid the commotion we manage to land my fish, a nice one at almost 18 inches and 3 pounds. It's into the cooler that now sports a new hood ornament—the anchor. 10 a.m. We have three fish and four hours remain to get three more. Little did we know that the escapee must have sounded an alarm, apparently alerting every fish in the lake to his experience of alien abduction Cast and retrieve. 10:30. Cast and retrieve. 11:00. Cast and retrieve. Is there a black cat antidote?" Cast and retrieve. 11:30. Cast and retrieve. 11:45. Fish On! 13¾ inches, one quarter-inch short of the minimum: Doesn't count. Nice touch, cat. High noon. With two hours to go, we're casting and retrieving the Dead Sea.

At 12:30 the fish lunch bell must have sounded as Rich, Mr. Clutch (just like "the Mick") breaks the dry spell with a 14½-incher. We're back in the game—only two more to fill our limit. Around 1 p.m., a jolt to my rod signals a solid strike. Battling deep, I feel the weight of a good fish. Now directly beneath the boat, I apply subtle pressure to raise it when my rod suddenly goes limp. As I reel in the lifeless monofilament, both the fish and the lure are gone. Was the line frayed by feline incisors? Damn you, cat!

In a final kick of kitty litter to our faces, Rich and I each hook a couple of undersized 13-inchers. When the horn sounds at 2 p.m., our four fish total 11 pounds. We finish 7th out of 20 boats, 2 pounds out of the money paid through 5th place. Two pounds. Either of two fish—one hooked but lost and the other named Houdini.

~ ~ ~ ~ ~

The date of an upcoming tournament seems to ring a bell. Ah yes! Our only child, son Ed, will be married that day. Although the ceremony commences at 2 p.m., tournament hours span 7 a.m. to 12:30 p.m. And it's only a two-hour drive from the lake to the church…

Weeks before the special day (what could be more special than a wedding and a fishing tournament on the same day?), I joke that I'll be at the ceremony on time, though likely wearing my lucky "I Fish Therefore I Am" T-shirt, a gray checked flannel shirt, and gray cargo pants. I generally don't concern myself with color coordination of my fishing clothing, but I reason that such attire, complementing the blue and silver theme of the wedding, will be an appropriate and thoughtful touch. Some of my "friends" suggest I save time, while raising the eyebrows of tournament participants, by fishing the tournament in my father-of-the-groom tuxedo.

Of course I didn't fish the tournament. "Tying the knot" this day did not include an "improved clinch," "Palomar," "snell," or any of the others a fisherman might tie during a day on the water. Sunny and in the 70s, Ed and his beautiful bride, Brandy, scored a perfect day to say "I do," and I fully enjoyed a delightful reception with family and friends that followed a lovely ceremony.

~ ~ ~ ~ ~

I know the human being and the fish can coexist peacefully.
—George W. Bush, Saginaw, Michigan, September 29, 2000

(Hmmm ... can we?)

The Thrill of Victory, the Agony of the Hook (IV)

"Outstanding"—an understated description of Emerald Lake's bass fishing in 2007. Jo Ann and I caught over 300, with a good number of those measuring between 17 and 22 inches.

When we fish together, I handle the landing and hook removal for Jo Ann's catch, as well as my own. Lip-landing the bass—reaching over the side of the boat and making a quick move to grab the moving-target fish by the lower lip with thumb and forefinger—the possibility of sharpened metal piercing my epidermis looms large. The danger magnifies with smaller fish, as there's less room to insert the thumb and closer proximity to the hook(s).

(On another, lesser note regarding the hand-land, a good day's catch of largemouth or smallmouth bass results in the malady known as "bass thumb." The handling of multiple fish by the rough edge of their lower lips causes the inside surface of the thumb to become raw and bloody, like having run it across a cheese grater.)

On a sunny midsummer outing, a 10-incher caught by Jo Ann flipped wildly while in my grasp, the tail end of the plastic worm whiplashing one of its three hooks, past the barb, into my left *digitus minimus manus*. Oh, my poor pinky. Woe, is me. Poor me. Why me?

A pinky payback?

The small hook size and its location in the finger make it impossible, even with Jo Ann's nursing background, to implement any of the field extraction techniques. I pull, push, and twist the hook shank hoping to work it free, but the effort only serves to work my half-digested bowl of Cheerios up my gullet. The tiny piece of sharp metal won't budge. Calling it quits, we're off to the hospital where the Doogie Howser ER physician successfully employs the "Advance and Cut" technique. (Refer to previously listed website for details.)

I'd later refer to that little fish as the "$250.10 Bass—total patient responsibility, $85.74."

That, my friends, would have bought a lot of plastic worms.

The Thrill of Victory, The Agony of the Hook (V)
The "Dumb Ass" Alarm

Maybe stamp collecting, instead of fishing, would be a safer hobby for me. Nah ... paper cuts to the fingers and tongue are no fun, either.

With an April birth date, many of my good intentioned but not well thought out actions have led some to jokingly refer to me as an "April fool." I did have an epiphany, oddly enough, which occurred on April Fool's Day. I've termed this wake-up call the "Dumb Ass Alarm." Experience has its price, and by gosh, having paid dearly and often with cash, flesh, blood, pain, inconvenience, and embarrassment, it was time to cash in one of the wisdom chips.

My low profile, low-end Ambassadeur reel "bit the dust" last fall. When purchasing it several years ago, I looked past the third-world country imported maroon plastic parts, instead keying on the Ambassadeur name and quality long associated with the brand. Wrong. Seeing it with a $29 price tag on the shelf at K-Mart should have been a clue.

Of winter sporting activities in the Midwest that include ice fishing, snowmobiling, cross-country skiing, and trying to find a parking space on the unplowed side streets of Chicago, the most beloved for the outdoorsman overcome with cabin fever is this: poring over outfitter catalogs to identify new, technologically advanced equipment to replace worn or broken down gear, or, adding to one's inventory, well, "just because." The joy parallels that experienced in childhood, thumbing through the Sears Christmas Catalog to prepare the wish list for Santa's upcoming visit.

With fishing reels, the research includes spool composition and capacity, gear ratio, line retrieval amount in inches-per-turn of the reel handle, type of drag system, number of ball bearings, anti-backlash braking system, anti-reverse feature, frame material, handle design, spool release mechanism, reel weight, and price. After many winter weeks spent in this pedantic endeavor, the trip to a sporting goods retailer may still find me racing into the store, perusing the display case, and telling the clerk, "Give me the shiny blue one!"

For the past several years, I have made a conscious effort to keep purchases of fishing hardware and lures to a minimum. Though largely successful, this creates a condition I refer to as PUD—Pent Up Demand. When PUD builds to a point of severe pressure, its release can lead to PP—Premature Purchase.

With spring in the air, it's off to Bass Pro Shop for their "March Madness" sale. I've done my homework, but overloaded with PUD I hope to avoid PP. In addition to a baitcaster, a new spinning reel is also on my list. I christened my daughter-in-law, Brandy, a "bassin' gal" when she caught three bass, the largest 18 inches, on her first fishing trip ever. Believing she might become "hooked" on the sport based on the Emerald Lake success made it easy to justify the purchase of another reel in honor of the newest member of the family.

Upon entering the store, each step toward the fishing department takes me deeper into a thickening school of fishermen. Attracted by this "reel" good sale, most shoppers hold baskets overflowing with angling items, reflecting the rampant nature of infectious PUD. Worming my way through the piranha-like feeding-shopping frenzy, I arrive at the displays of reels adorning the walls and showcases. What I *thought* I wanted to buy based on my extensive winter catalog homework becomes convoluted in a sea of choices that overwhelms:

> Gear ratios: 4.7:1, 5.3:1. 6.2:1, 7.1:1 ...
> Shimano ...
> Line capacities: 110/14, 120/20, 150/12, 210/14 ...
> Quantum ...
> Ball bearings, roller bearings: 4+1, 6+1, 9+1, 10+1 ...
> Abu Garcia ...
> "Thumb" vs. "button" spool release ...
> Pfleuger ...
> Front drag, rear drag, star drag ...
> Penn ...
> $49.99, $89.99, $129.99, $159.99 ...

My head is going to explode. Analysis paralysis. And no matter which ones I choose, the bane of buyer's remorse awaits upon my arrival back home.

"Can I help you, sir?"

"Uh, yeah. Give me that neat looking gold job, and the shiny blue one."

That task unsatisfyingly completed, I stroll down the aisle displaying the pricey musky lures. To my credit, or a function of the transaction at the reel counter, I successfully manage to keep PUD in check. At least for a minute or two. Indeed, short-lived, it ends in the next aisle as I'm brought to my knees by the

> New! Rapala! DT-10!
> Dives faster and stays in the ten-foot strike zone longer!
> Made from high quality balsa wood!
> Perfectly designed, weighted, and tuned!
> Tough polycarbonate lip!
> Rattles!
> Suspending!
> Bluegill pattern!

Yeah, baby!—into the basket you go! Lost amid the euphoria, "Two VMC treble hooks with six finely honed, needle-sharp points!"

I opened my 2008 fishing season at Emerald Lake on Saturday, April 1st. Typical of this year's cold spring, the temperature hovered in the mid-40s with moderate northeast winds, gray skies, and leafless trees giving no thought to budding. The weather and landscape resembled a November day. Last night's rain turned the water turbid. Weed growth, an all-season fish attractant, had yet to bloom. All factors pointed to low expectations for a successful fishing day. Weather be damned, this first day on the water signaled the end of a long winter hibernation.

The time of year and weather conditions favored a slow-moving plastic bait presentation, but new equipment begged to be used. I motored to the north bay, turned off the outboard, and released the trolling motor from its bracket, sliding the shaft and prop into the water. Ready to roll. Leading off will be the Ricky Clunn 6.3:1 baitcaster sporting the New! Rapala! DT10!

I eyed the lure, in its just-out-of-the-box newness, with reserved delight. The reel received a more thoughtful and thorough examination. Cold aluminum cradled in the palm of my hand, the gunmetal gray embossed accents bespeak a classic look, sophisticated against the cobalt blue frame. A subtle nod validated a purchase well made. All was right with the world.

As with any new casting outfit, I began a fine-tuning process of multiple casts from the center of the bay. Each resulted in adjustments to the spool, magnetic anti-backlash, and drag, all tweaked until reaching the desired level of precision. That pre-work completed, I used the trolling motor to ease the boat within casting distance of a steep-dropping shoreline that will provide the perfect start for the Quick diving! Rattling! Perfectly designed, weighted, and tuned! Suspending! DT10 bluegill that will stay in the strike zone until pre-spawn Mama bucket-mouth engulfs it!

Ready for the maiden voyage I eased down the thumb bar, releasing the spool. Adrenaline energized, the backswing and follow through launched the DT10. Frozen, I watched in slow-motion disbelief as the lure rocketed skyward like the Space Shuttle Discovery jettisoned by a million pounds of propellant. Higher. (Jimmy) Houston, we have a problem! Faster. What the...? Farther. NOOOOO! Reaching the shoreline trees the lure began looping an upper branch, slow on the rise, speeding on the descent, like an Olympic gymnast preparing to dismount the uneven parallel bars. Round n round n round she goes, strangling a branch some 15 feet above the water's surface. Minutes into the new season, the bloom was off the rose.

With the trolling motor on slow, I approached the shore. The DT10 indeed well out of reach, I grabbed the line and applied a few gentle tugs that confirmed its entanglement. I eased further in and when directly beneath it pulled on the line with increasing vigor. Seconds into that exercise, the "Dumb Ass Alarm" sounded. Loud and clear, the alarm voice comprised an intriguing combination—pitiful, helpful, and condescending: "Hey, Dumb Ass, how do you think you'll look when you pull into the Marina with a balsa bluegill nose-ring, your lips hooked together, or a couple of treble hooks hanging from your eyeballs?"

Immediately releasing the line, the leafless branch bobbed momentarily before coming to rest. With no retrieval alternative, I reluctantly cut the slackened line. Saddened to be leaving a lure that held much promise, saddest of all was the loss of $6.99 (plus tax). The gray clouds of April, however, contained a silver lining. I returned to the dock with my face intact.

While whole of body, my day on the lake ended fishless. Later in the month, the Marina posted pictures of an angler proudly displaying his catches of April bass that weighed in at 7 pounds 4 ounces, 7 pounds 8 ounces, 7 pounds 12 ounces, and 8 pounds 1 ounce. April fool? I'm just not sure.

Jigging the Tube

Tube jigging is another method, another weapon in the vast array of one's fishing arsenal. A tube jig combines a lead-head jig tucked into a soft plastic "tube" that sports tentacles or twister-tails that vibrate in a subtle yet tantalizing manner. Tube jigs can be casted and hopped or crawled back to the boat, or vertically jigged. Small versions work well on smallmouth bass and, to a lesser extent, largemouth. Larger tube baits are sometimes used in the pursuit of muskellunge, especially as a throwback to change up the look for a fish that just followed but did not strike a different bait offering.

Proctologists employ their own technique of tube jigging. (On a side note, what motivates a doctor to specialize in proctology? A score to settle from an unpleasant childhood experience with a tootsie-roll?) Many of us in the 50-plus age category have experienced the distinct displeasure of a colonoscopy. (I know better, but...) I define it as follows:

COLONOSCOPY – *From the Greek for "Up Your Bucket," the colonoscopy is a degrading, invasive, and medically questionable practical joke proliferated by medical professionals of the modern era. Primarily targeting a segment of the population known as "Baby Boomers," members of this generally well-educated and reasonably affluent and savvy demographic group are* *encouraged to drink a gallon of laxative, crap their brains out for 12 hours, and then have an "aqua-view" camera on the end of a roto-rooter shoved up their rear end. The "doctor" plays a macabre 21st century version of Polyp Pac-Man in the unwitting patient's poop chute, the procedure likened in spirit to the use of leeches and other bloodletting techniques practiced in the Middle Ages. In addition to the sadomasochistic humor provided to the medical staff, the colonoscopy also affords significant monetary gain to the hospital-clinic conglomerates.*

Upon completion of the procedure, a gurney transported me from the "video-game studio" to an adjacent recovery area that contained eight beds, compartmentalized by curtains that moved on tracks mounted to the ceiling. In that minimally private venue, Jo Ann later advised that I provided her with a number of entertaining moments—"You had me laughing my ass off," I believe was her true-to-topic phrase. She further commented that she had not witnessed such a combination of pathos and humor since Woody Allen stepped out of the orgasmatron in the movie, *Sleeper.*

Eyes struggling to open, I weakly utter my first post-procedure words: "Has … the … doctor …been … here … yet?"

"Yes, dear, the doctor has been here."

Back to momentary slumber, then struggling to lift the tons of imaginary weight pressing against my eyelids, I dig deep to find the strength for my next words, "Has … the … doctor … been … here … yet?"

"Yes, dear, the doctor has been here. You have to try and stay awake so we can get you dressed and go home."

"Okay … has the doctor … been here yet?"

"Yes, the doctor has been here. He took out one polyp. Everything is fine. He said you were nervous, and because you're young and healthy…"

"Who's young and healthy!?"

"Okay. Because they *thought* you're young and *relatively* healthy, they really 'bombed' you with the anesthetic."

"Okay. Has the doctor been here yet?"

"Yes, dear, the doctor has been here."

"Okay. Do you know which albacore tuna has a better price … the Chicken of the Sea or the StarKist?"

"No, dear. I'll check. Do you think you can sit up?"

Voice beginning to tremble, I utter, "Oh, Charlie. Poor Charlie Tuna. He wanted so badly to please the StarKist folks. And they just broke his heart … every time." Upper lip quivering, "The bastards!"

"Shhhhh! Settle down!"

"Has the doctor been here yet?"

"Yes, dear."

"I had one polyp. Snip-snip. My mouth is dry. Can I have some water?"

"Here's a cup of ice chips." Raising the cup, I miss my mouth, spilling the chips about.

"Uh oh…. The doctor said I had one polyp. Snip-snip."

"Let's try and get you dressed."

"Where are my glasses?"

"You're wearing them, dear."

Attempting to relieve an itchy eye, I bring my index finger toward my face in a slow, steady motion. Having forgotten the question and answer from moments earlier, my eyeglasses deflect the effort. Second and third tries from different angles prove equally unsuccessful. "Why do I have fingerprints all over my glasses?"

"Come on, let's try and get you dressed."

A blue plastic bag provided by the hospital contains my street clothes. Helped from the bed to a chair, my loving and highly entertained wife assists in dressing me. As I bend forward to put on my shoes, she catches me before completing a slow motion header, reminiscent of Artie Johnson keeling over while riding his mini-tricycle on *Laugh In*.

I have no recollection of the wheelchair ride from the recovery area to the hospital's front door. I have no recollection of calling Mom from the car as my wife drove us home. I have only one memory from that trip. Looking in the backseat and seeing the empty blue clothes bag, I ask with increasing urgency, "Did we forget my clothes? Did they steal my clothes? Where are my clothes!?"

"You're wearing them, dear. We'll be home in a few minutes. I've got a nice tuna salad sandwich waiting for you for lunch. And there's a message from Joe on the answering machine. He wants to know if you can go to Lake Erie this weekend. He said something about big smallmouth bass being taken on something called a tube jig."

~~~~~

The Eyes (Don't) Have It

In 2005, my already-corrected-with-glasses distance vision began to lose its sharpness. The optometrist's prescription for stronger lenses failed to correct it. In need of another opinion, an examination by an ophthalmologist revealed cataracts. Swell: more body parts breaking down years before their time. On the upside, who among my fishing partners would lambast the poor-sighted me for incorrectly estimating the size of a fish caught? (All of them, that's who).

In the summer of 2006, my clouded "original equipment" lenses were replaced by permanent, prescription-correcting ones. The silver lining in these clouds? No more glasses. But don't start the celebration just yet.

In the days surrounding All Hallow's Eve, the lightning-imitating *Department 56 Grimsley Manor* Halloween village decoration in our living room could not claim responsibility as the sole source of flashing light that streaked with each blink of my eyes. The next morning, the vision in my right eye contained a partial blind spot. This sequence of scary symptoms prompted a call to my ophthalmologist, who spoke those six little words one never wants to hear: "You better come in *right now*." In a whirlwind day, he confirmed a detaching retina and then arranged for an emergency appointment with a retina specialist who presented the immediate-action options:

"Surgery…"

The word, spurring thoughts of knives and needles poking around *inside* my eyeball, caused a temporary audio shut-down. Good thing Jo Ann was there to take in the information. I regained my composure (and hearing) in time for the next possibility.

"Injecting gas bubbles…"

Stunned again, my psyche whisks me to a happy place where children run across a sundrenched flower-filled meadow, the doctor's words encrypted into musical tones—fa la, la, tra, la, la. Then, an awkward silence filled the room as we waited for option three. What was option three? Certainly some sort of miracle capsule I can swallow to make everything right. There *must* be an option three, yes? For the love of God, tell us about option three!

No. Nada. None. Without a clear choice among two equal evils, we relied on the specialist's recommendation: gas bubbles it is. I'll spare you the nasty particulars other than to say the procedure involved a hypodermic needle thrust into the eyeball … hold … inject … don't move … inject … hold … inject … don't move … inject … almost done … inject…. Oops, I guess that was the nasty particulars. The post-poke required ten days of lying-face-down immobility to allow the bubbles to push the retina back in place. As a minor consolation and my only viewing pleasure for a week and a half, the bubbles were neat—purple iridescent—small at first, slowly moving, then joining and gradually expanding. Far out. Ah, simple pleasures.

Post-procedure maintenance included use of a laser that "glued" tiny rips in the retina. I didn't mind the initial moments when multi-colored "shooting stars" distracted me from the subtle, pricking pain. With each zap of the "gun," however, the discomfort intensified to the level of a Black and Decker, loaded with a masonry bit, drilling a hole through the back of my skull.

Other follow-up visits carried similar levels of "delight." A recurring ritual involved the use of a gizmo I privately referred to as "Mean Mr. Metal Stick." This round-edge medical utensil the size of a ballpoint pen pushed the eyelid back to places it had never been—and was never meant to go—the fully exposed eyeball defenseless to the assault of a bazillion watts of light beaming from the doctor's miner-helmet headset. I'd have preferred almost anything to that stick in the eye. Unfortunately, it didn't end there.

Oh Say, Can You (Still) See?

A few years later, the nasty flashes returned, signaling another detachment episode. With my wealth of experience regarding issues of the eyes, I bypassed the ophthalmologist-middleman, contacting the retina specialist directly. He confirmed my self-diagnosis. The bubbles not an option on a second-go-'round, this time it'll be scleral buckle surgery.

Summarized from WebMD:

> A scleral buckle is a piece of semi-hard plastic wrapped around the white (sclera) of the eye and sewn into it, to keep it in place permanently.
> The element pushes in, or "buckles," the sclera toward the middle of the eye, relieving the pull on the retina, allowing the retinal tear to settle against the wall of the eye.

Not sure how they do it and not really wanting to know, I did confirm that a melon baller was not among the instruments used in the procedure. My eyesight saved through these multiple delicate procedures (thanks, Doc!), retinal debris roils my field of vision in both eyes. Not limited to the microbial-looking dots known as "floaters," my viewing of the world must permeate permanent smoky swirls. That was much more fun when, by design, it occurred courtesy of a Macanudo. These ocular issues taught me many things, foremost among them how to spell "ophthalmologist."

Over the next couple of years, my body cut me some slack, at least as far as major health problems go. Instead, a number of outward signs trumpeting the onset of old(er) age began manifesting themselves:

> The hair that has vacated my head, now exposing an area whose edge defines a "receding hairline," makes an unwelcome appearance in a number of unlikely and undesirable locations. Unsightly wild hairs sprout from the ears, nose, knuckles, and eyebrows like a fertile landscape planted by Johnny Appleseed's bastard step-brother, Johnny Hairseed.

> An inch-long crevice in my forehead rises vertically from between my eyebrows (also sprouting a wayward stalk on occasion) creating a facial "ass crack."

> As if a bowl of *czarnina* splashed on me, "liver spots," the burly cousin of sun-spawned freckles, appear with increasing regularity, the look akin to some sort of bizarre connect-the-dots game.

~ ~ ~ ~ ~

My biggest worry is that my wife (when I'm dead) will sell my fishing gear for what I said I paid for it.
—Koos Brandt

A Fishy Encounter in the Retail Garden of Eden

I estimate my decades-long accumulation of musky lures follows the "80-20" rule. Taking some liberties with the concept, following are several fishing related examples of this maxim: 80% of the fish swim in 20% of the water; 80% of fish are caught by 20% of fishermen; and as it applies to my musky lure purchases, 80% haven't caught one—only 20% have had the pleasure of bringing a musky to net. In formal fishing vernacular, that 80% fall into either of two categories: "costly mistakes," or "very costly mistakes."

The weight of my musky tackle box exceeds most of the muskies I catch. With so many lures crammed into it, I've tired of the Barrel of Monkeys game that occurs when I reach in to pluck one of them and end up with a three-foot-long chain of lures which, by the way, is longer than most of the muskies I catch.

Musky lures are pricey, most in the $15 to $30 range. With my humongo-box in overflow status, my annual goal is zero new purchases. This self-imposed restriction can turn a visit to a sporting goods retailer into a brow beading, brow beating, and sometimes otherworldly experience.

It starts innocently enough. Upon entering a store, I am a dog on the point, making a beeline to the aisle with the musky lures. My happy endorphins pump wildly, like a five-year-old in Toys "R" Us the week before Christmas. Jo Ann understands the dynamics of this scenario, having witnessed it on numerous occasions in wonderment and pathetic disgust. She recognizes the male fisherman's genetic code is encrypted to open a wallet and have cash fly out in the face of reason. She is not with me today, but I can hear her words, repeated on numerous occasions, simple, eloquent, and indisputable: "If you are in the right place at the right time and the fish is ready to bite, the type of lure and its color are of little, if any consequence. Lures catch more fishermen than fish." Translation: YOU DON'T NEED ANY MORE LURES!

I reach the promised land, greeted by a kaleidoscope of colors, sizes, styles, and shapes that mesmerize: spinner bait styles: in-line, overhead, singles, doubles; spinner blades shapes: willow-leaf, teardrop "Indiana," round "Colorado"; blade finishes: nickel, gold, copper, smooth, hammered, fluted; hook-hiding skirts: marabou, horsehair, squirrel-tail, rubber, silicone; top-water styles: walk-the-dog, propeller, tail-rotators, buzzers, creepers; minnow imitators: lipped, lipless; crankbaits: shallow diving, deep diving; gliders; jerkbaits: weighted, not weighted; lure composition: wood, hard plastic, soft plastic, rattling; patterns and finishes: spots, stripes, glitter, prisms, colors in every shade of the spectrum. Sensory overload whisks me to the junction where dream challenges reality.

"Pssst!"

Euphoria interrupted by the subtle sound of someone seeking my attention, I swivel my head in both directions. Not a soul to be found, it must be my imagination.

"Pssssst! Over here!"

Is it my imagination? It *must* be my imagination. "Who is it? Who's there?"

"It's me ... Eve. I've been waiting for you."

Befuddled, I move in the direction of the voice. After but a few steps, a vision of singular beauty comes into view. Stunning beyond compare, I fixate on a voluptuous pair of rounded blades, golden delicious. The sweetest apples in this Garden of Eden are ripe for the picking. Blonde highlights swirl the length of her silky, cinnamon-colored hair. The refined charm and innocence bespeak a classic aura last captured in the *Mona Lisa*.

"I knew you'd come looking for me," her words now toned in an enticing, throaty whisper.

Ensnared in a Salvador Dali painting-come-to-life, my arm moves toward her but my conscience stops me in mid-reach. I don't need another lure! I could fish through the continuum of eternity and not catch a fish on every musky lure I've ever purchased!

"I'm glad you're here," the "al-lure" of her voice becoming increasingly sultry.

My ability to reason lost in her words, I lift her off the rack with great care and tenderness. My fingers gently stroke her kitten-soft hair, sliding to the trebled tips of Cupid's arrows before finally tracing the perfectly shaped twister curve of her soft, alabaster-color tail.

I snap back to reality. No! This is wrong! This is so wrong! I don't need any more lures! Not a one! Back you go!

As I turn to leave, her voice again beckons, this time a thick pouting plea, as if wounded by my intent to depart. "Oooooh, please, please don't disappoint me. I know how difficult this must be for you. I just don't want *you* to be disappointed. This will be our secret. No one else has to know—certainly not your wife."

Time machine transporting me to next week in the Canadian wilderness, I see myself lifting her out of my tackle box for the first time, newlyweds crossing the threshold as a Canadian breeze seductively lifts the irregular edge of her delicate skirt, wafting hair surrendering to the zephyr, like a model in a swimsuit photoshoot on a tropical beach.

She continues, "You work hard. You deserve the pleasures in life that I can help bring. You can't afford to take me ... but can you afford *not* to? Those big, mean muskies have never seen anything that looks like me. Can't you picture us working in harmony next week on Forest Lake? With each smooth turn of the reel handle our moves will be synchronized as you work me with delicate and masterful precision over the reefs, around and through the stands of reeds. My pulsing vibration will be irresistible. Let's do something wild—let's go leaderless! Envision a fish of massive proportion rising from the depths, following me in hot pursuit. Nearing the boat with rhythmic bursts of speed, our hearts will race as one. As daylight gives way to evening and the full moon rises you can bulge me over the milfoil bed, the beautiful Canadian sunset the stage, the call of the loon the music for our dance on the lake's mirrored surface, each choreographed cast culminating in a long, fluid, perfectly executed figure-8, the symbol of infinity connecting us. Take me, take me now!"

"Yes, YES, I want you, but I can't have you! If I take you, both of us will be cast into the River Styx! Coming here was a major mistake! I have to go home now!"

At that moment, a couple of heads peer around the corner, wondering what all the commotion is about. I glance down the length of the aisle, as if looking for the responsible party. My bluff fails: I am the lone occupant, caught deep, to the elbow, in the proverbial cookie jar. Re-engaging the gaze of the wide-eyed and mildly frightened observers, I flash them a Gomer Pyle smile wrapped in a rosy-complexion blush. My sheepish acknowledgement sends them scurrying, their heads negatively nodding in disbelief before turning my way for one final look, as if to make sure I am not following them.

Emotionally spent by the series of strange events I move toward the exit, the tear-filled voice fading with my every step. "If you don't take me ... someone else will. I don't want you to miss the fish of a lifetime. Just know that I really, *really* want to go with *you!*"

I freeze in my tracks, the furiously pounding beat of my heart filling every ounce of my being with uncertainty. The classic and complex struggle of heart versus mind, love versus logic, demands a decision.

The next voice I hear is the store clerk behind the register. "That'll be $24.95, sir—cash, check, or charge?"

During the ride home, I am not pleased with my lack of resolve. After entering the garage, hints of shame and disgust surface as I tuck the bag behind the tackle boxes stored on a shelving unit. As I walk through the kitchen, my inability to put on a poker-face betrays my attempt to conceal the illicit purchase from Jo Ann, who queries "So, what did you buy?"

I reply to the simple question in a defensive tone. "... Whaddaya mean?"

"It's okay dear, I understand. There are worse vices. You could be gambling or out carousing with other women. So, what is it? A rod? A reel? Did Rapunzel spin her golden hair into a new and improved super-braid line that wrapped around your brain then plucked 30 dollars from your wallet?"

Removing the receipt from my pocket and placing it on the table, I slither out the door, mumbling, "Something like that, hon, something like that."

Eve

Fishing is not an escape from life but often a deeper immersion into it."
—Harry Middleton

Freespool Flashbacks from the Alexandra Chain of Lakes
2006 - 2009

July 2006. You've heard it on multiple occasions, often from the mouth of an "old fart." That means I utter it often: "The older you get, the faster time flies." This year's trip, with Terry, Rich, and his teenage son Richie, however, defied the "speeding time" axiom. Time stood still. Okay, it didn't stand still, but it did move at a pleasingly s-l-o-w pace, exactly the feel one hopes for on every vacation.

Fourteen-year-old Richie, on his first fishing trip to the big water north of the border, caught his first musky on Sunday morning, our first full day. As most mornings here, I was milling about the dock (perhaps checking my wallet for my "tetanus booster valid-until" card) waiting for Terry to come down to start our fishing day. From the boathouse, I heard Richie shout for help. I scrambled to the ramshackle structure and saw him in the midst of a battle, his walleye rod doubled over with the weight of a musky that grabbed his jig. With light six-pound test line spooled on his spinning reel, he played the fish with the finesse of a veteran. His call timely, I assisted by netting the 31-incher. Although it would be the only musky of the week for Rich and Richie, they allocated a significant portion of their time pursuing walleye, catching a good number of the fine eating fish.

With the exception of one dinnertime storm, (a doozy that took down a 20-foot pine), clear skies and high 80-degree temperatures prevailed. This enabled us to play the "too sunny" and "too hot" cards to explain our mediocre fishing results. Maybe we should have been here last week. Maybe we should be here next week. Maybe we're spoiled. Maybe we've become complacent, victims of routine: same spots, same lures. Maybe it doesn't matter.

Terry and I weren't seeing many fish either, all of our on-water time spent musky hunting. The learning curve unending in the sporting contest of man versus fish, when the "milk run" sours, it's time to refresh and rethink. On Tuesday, in a dairy-theme coincidence, we tried an area where several floating plastic milk containers marked the location of propeller-eating rocks lurking just below the water's surface at the entrance to a narrow passage connecting the main body of Forest Lake with its fairly sizeable northernmost bay. I casted a top-water Giant Jackpot past the makeshift markers. As the retrieve neared them, the water exploded. A good fight followed with much surface thrashing, not surprising due to the shallow water. A 37-incher, the first musky netted from this new location, granted me the right to name the site, which I labeled "The Jugs."

Thursday brought another sunny, calm, hot day. With the afternoon high touching 90, we're prepared to catch a sunburn and not much else. A short distance east of "The Jugs," we casted another area never previously fished, this one a shoreline. Pleasantly surprised during these "dog days of summer," my Salmo golden roach minnow-pattern crankbait drew a follow. The musky remained curious as I swirled as many figure-8s as Kristi Yamaguchi practicing for an Olympic gold. With my body about one crazy 8 away from succumbing to heat stroke, the fish lined up the lure and bolted forward, grabbing it on one of the straightaways. Wary before striking and now elusive to net, the fish's valiant fight stretched the small lure's split ring (a circular piece of metal doubled over itself, attaching hooks to the eyelets of lures) to within a fraction of an inch of completely opening and breaking free. Not a moment too soon, Terry netted the musky that taped, like yesterday's, at 37 inches. Again, my spot to name, I took into account the close proximity to "The Jugs" and christened the small shoreline protrusion where the musky struck, "The Nip."

With over a decade of musky fishing on the Alexandra Chain, certain spots fall out of favor from time to time as a result of multi-year dry spells, with no fish caught nor even sighted as follows. With this year's successes at a couple of new locations, I suggested to Terry that we revisit some of the haunts from our old "milk run," ones that haven't received a casted lure in several years.

My specific suggestions paid dividends—not for me, but for "us." Captain Terry scored thrice:

> A 33-incher on his first cast in "Musky Bay." (In years gone by, a lush weedbed filled this bay, which shared its bounty of dozens of muskies. For unknown reasons the weeds disappeared, and the fish along with them.)
>
> A 40-incher striking in two feet of water in "Walleye Bay." (A short distance from the cabin, this shallow bay, with interspersed weeds, would give up an occasional musky feeding on a resident population of small walleye. Like "Musky Bay," the weeds and walleye disappeared from this location as well.)
>
> A 34-incher a short distance from "The Throne." (A submerged circular rock, symmetrically surrounded on three sides by a stand of reeds. This feature, and the stretch of

shoreline on either side of it, was never on Terry's list of locations to fish.)

After Terry's success there earlier in the week, we returned to "Walleye Bay" where a small musky in need of an optical exam entertained me. The fish twice launched airborne, missing my Giant Jackpot. Its aim improved on the third try, the 30-incher solving the mystery of the top-water lure snaking across the water's surface.

For the week, Terry took 4. I bested him with 5. The consummate host, I thanked him for shaking off a leaping 40-inch fish that he hooked at "Clark's Weedbed" on the final Friday, allowing me to finish the week with a higher total. It was another one of those years where average size just wasn't important.

Wildlife seemed more visible and active this year, beyond the normal fare that includes ducks, gulls, bats, turkey vultures, loons, beavers, and eagles. Although sighting an eagle is not uncommon, we had the good fortune of witnessing the majestic bird swoop down with talons engaged, grabbing an evening snack in a successful display of top-water fishing. Two eagles, side by side, sat on a high branch of a dead tree on the peninsula between "Bay 1" and "Bay 2." The following day in the same location, one remained perched as the other arrowed in low level flight near our boat before disappearing into the trees.

Loons proliferated: in addition to multiple sightings of the black and white pattern mature birds, we witnessed a mom carrying a chick on her back, and at another location, a protective adult overseeing a diving lesson of a fuzzy, brown-down adolescent.

A doe and two fawns sipped from the lake near the "Fifth Avenue" beaver lodge. And speaking of beavers, an industrious nocturnal vandal targeted the tree closest to the cabin's front door, even though thousands of others closer to the lake shore seemed to provide more logical choices. Chiseled chunks of fresh shavings surrounded the tree's base beneath the perfectly carved, cartoon-like hourglass form. (Only the application of a chicken-wire deterrent stopped the crime that would have been completed the following night.)

Three clumsily statuesque pelicans, stark white with long yellow-orange bills, stood on a symmetric row of exposed boulders on Indian Lake. A buck with an enormous rack patrolled the shoreline of "Doughboy," the area that gave up my 45-inch musky in 2004. A fox, a fawn, and a bear scurried along Highway 647 in separate sightings, a moose on Highway 502. The "pet" groundhog near the cabin made numerous appearances.

The fetching likeness of an Indian appeared on a boulder on the shore of the small island in the middle of Indian Lake. The profile, eerily sculpted in its namesake lake, required our boat be specifically positioned during a brief, late afternoon window when the sun brought it to life in warm hues of sandstone, copper, and burnt orange. The noble portrait was further enhanced by the backdrop of the island's solitary, stately spruce, and the white spear-like remnants of a multi-trunk birch that succumbed, years earlier, to the onslaught of time and weather.

No northern lights this year, but no snake in the cabin, either: coincidence or cosmic balance? Enjoyment and satisfaction reigned again in this year's installment of the annual saga. Though many aspects of our trips follow a certain routine, each year writes its own memorable signature.

~ ~ ~ ~ ~

September 2006. It's that time of year when deciduous trees, including the prominent birches and aspens, transform their leaves of summer green into shades of yellow, orange, and gold. Sunlight sets the citrine jewels aglow, flickering in the gentle breeze atop towering, chalk-white trunks, resplendent against a curtain of verdant Northwoods pines. It's that time of year, the autumn air crisp, when I especially love to ply the nuances of my favorite sport. Arrangements made, I'll join Rich, Ben, and Larry in another excursion north.

Unfortunately, Larry had to cancel, so the kinship of this adventure was shared with my two younger cousins. Our first stay at a resort on Indian Lake, the lake-view cabin compared favorably with our lodging on Edward Lake from previous fall visits. A screened porch provided a key feature of this rental accommodation, not necessary for mosquito protection at this time of year but rather a security blanket in the event of inclement weather, ensuring the enjoyment of traditional evening rituals of conversation, beverage, and for some, tobacco. Additional plusses of this lodge included a harbored dock and camp-provided helpers for gasoline and other miscellaneous services.

The weather, at least the first five days, threw us a curve: too nice—too summerlike. A high-pressure system locked in with sunny daytime highs hovering around 80 degrees. Winds, minimal to nonexistent, combined with a very dry summer and low water levels to produce a never-before-seen-on-these-waters algae bloom, coating the lakes with a disgusting "pea soup." During Wednesday evening's porch time, I commented that I had never experienced so many consecutive days and evenings without hearing the lapping of waves on shore, and how a change to this weather pattern would be appreciated.

Indeed, be careful what you wish for. Thursday obliged with a cold front and high winds, keeping us in dry-dock most of the day. Friday's high didn't make it out of the 50s (now there's some of that early autumn weather I'm talkin' about) and the overnight low dipped below freezing (that's *not* what I had in mind).

At least we scored well with nature. The northern lights appeared one evening, its 10 p.m. start the earliest ever witnessed. Walking out to a deck built on a small point near the boat pier, we anticipated a show that would captivate into the wee hours of the morning. Unfortunately, it ended minutes later. An eagle appeared at our first fishing destination each day, a fine "good morning" at the diverse locations selected. One evening, from the screened porch, we viewed the silhouette of a fox trotting along the lakeshore, its long marabou-like tail swaying with each step. The ride through northern Minnesota provided my first-ever sighting of a gray wolf, distinctly regal versus scraggly coyotes seen with some frequency.

Hey, was this a fishing trip or a Marlin Perkins episode of *Mutual of Omaha's Wild Kingdom*? Never having experienced "great" September fishing (here or anywhere else, for that matter) this week landed squarely on that norm. The lack of exceptional results fed into our pleasantly relaxed vacation pace. We put in an unremarkable 27 hours on the water over the better part of seven days, approximately two-thirds of that fishing for walleye and the remainder for musky. We caught walleye in a number of different and new locations in spite of the sunny, calm conditions. This success flies in the face of conventional wisdom that heralds overcast, rainy, and breezy weather as preferred when fishing for this species. The catch, with overall size better than in years past, provided fine dining and a limit for home.

While jigging for walleye, Rich and I each caught a musky, both just under 30 inches. I also bagged a 33-incher along a little fished stretch of a large island separating the main body of Edward Lake from the channel leading to Indian Lake. I christened the location "Split Pea Point." Minutes before that catch, I set a personal record—from the wrong end of the spectrum. I unintentionally foul hooked a 9-inch musky (yes, 9 inches, you read it right) that had the misfortune of being in the wrong place at the wrong time. My 10-inch TopRaider landed on his back as he sunned himself beside a patch of lily pads.

As with any trip, a few glitches arose: breaking a walleye rod; twice forgetting to snap the clip to close a tackle box, dumping its contents in the bottom of the boat; being locked out of our motel room (on the balcony) on the overnight in Fort Frances; taking a wrong exit on the drive home; and the occasional snag resulting in a lost jig while walleye fishing. In the big picture, however, tally this week as most pleasant and "snag free." In fact, not once did I shout the words "I'm Cut!" Hmmmm ... a one-time aberration, or turning a new, "autumn" leaf? Perhaps I should quit while I'm ahead. Not bloody likely.

~ ~ ~ ~ ~

July 2007. Rich, Ben, and Richie arrive early at La Place Rendez-Vous in Fort Frances. Terry and I check in an hour later, joining them outside our lake-view rooms, relaxing with a pre-dinner "cold one." After eleven hours in the car, it's time to unwind and soak up our first dose of Canadian serenity, supplemented by a barley booster. After dinner we reconvene outdoors to enjoy another beverage or two, some also stoking a stogie. What a great start to the annual musky pilgrimage!

We "call it an evening" in anticipation of a busy tomorrow that will include four more hours on the road, purchasing final provisions, packing, unpacking, and repacking (cars to boats, boats to cabin), and setting up for the week's activities. I turn on the television to check the weather report before retiring. As I flip through the channels, I happen upon one of the raciest and most bizarre shows I've ever seen on the non-pay airwaves: *Ed and Red's Night Party*. Though a variety show, the old *Ed Sullivan Show* it ain't.

Ed is a crass, insult-hurling, foul-mouth, cigar-chomping sock puppet. A Playmate-quality redhead, voluptuous Red overflows a satin scarlet nightgown. Unlike Regis and Kelly, Ed and Red's bawdy verbal intercourse and carnal conversations revolve around other activities occurring on stage, in this episode: three scantily clad young ladies on a futon simulating untold stories of an all-girl slumber party; a heavily tattooed Bowflex commercial stud sharing a hot tub with a blonde harem; caged pole dancers; and an interview with a porn star. Terry and I are repulsed, "yet we cannot look away…."

We only hurt ourselves with less sleep as a result of our viewing indiscretion, paying a groggy-skull, beady-eye price the next day. Upon arriving at the launch in the early afternoon, the docked aluminum Lund used as a transport to the cabin is swamped, an indicator that significant storms have recently moved through the area.

I begin bailing with a five-gallon bucket and then a one-gallon milk jug. The cardiovascular exercise under the midday sun brings on a healthy though unwelcomed sweat. The recent rains have also spawned an ill-timed explosion in the daytime mosquito population, gleeful with the arrival of their tasty human buffet—me. In a continuation of the "we're not off to a good start today" theme, Rich's truck gets stuck in a muddy rut after launching his boat. My task as human bilge pump complete, I assist in the effort to free the truck by pushing from the rear, the spinning wheels splattering my clothes with a shower of mud.

On a positive note, the recent rains have raised the lakes' water to a level not seen in many years. At least in theory, this should result in better fishing. The forecast for a week of beautiful weather favors us. Temperatures are expected to range from the low 70s to low 80s with low humidity and light and variable winds.

The week's fishing ended up a mixed bag. Terry caught a 25-inch walleye while casting a musky plug. We hooked a number of small (18- to 25-inch) northern pike. Believed to have negotiated a dam from an adjoining lake during high water, the "snakes" and "hammer-handles" compete with the muskellunge for spawning areas and food supply. Some believe their unwanted introduction (like me moving into a new neighborhood) will prove detrimental to the resident musky population. A positive is the beautifully stripe-pattern hybrid "tiger" musky that results from the cross-breeding of the two species.

Rich did well with four fish, setting the camp record with a 38.38-inch average. One of those fish entered our records as a remarkable accomplishment, likely as satisfying as the steak dinner he prepared for us that day. Foreshadowing the upcoming evening event his mood was upbeat, humming a tune while keeping tabs on the thick cuts of prime beef sizzling on the grill. Shifting to his right, he tapped the tongs in rhythm against the deep-fryer, periodically checking the thinly sliced potatoes turning a golden brown. The delectable meal served and then consumed with gusto, it was time to go fishing.

Terry and I left first and returned several hours later, unsuccessful in our musky catching efforts. Ben and Richie chose to fully enjoy the afterglow of the marvelous meal, deciding to take a pass on the evening fishing session. Rich proceeded without his boat mates, in a solo venture.

With the onset of dusk, worrisome paternal instinct for my younger cousin's well-being kicked in:

> What if he has a problem with the boat that strands him on any of the various lakes, his location unknown, and miles from the cabin?
>
> What if a fish hooks him?
>
> Those safety issues override earlier thoughts of less important fishing concerns:

What if he hooks a (big) fish? No one is there to help him net it.

What if he catches a (big) fish? No one is there to take a picture.

Soon thereafter, my internalized uneasiness dissipated with the drone of a motor heard in the distance. The smooth purr increasing as seconds pass, Richie headed down to the dock to greet him. He returned to the cabin ahead of his father and provided a preliminary report detailing the boat floor stained with a few dark drops of what may be blood, the hooks of a TopRaider snipped, and his dad, not appearing in need of medical attention, having a story to tell.

In anticipation of his tale, I prepared our drink of choice: Alberta Springs, ice, and splash of water. Entering the screened porch and plunking himself onto one of the cushioned armchairs, he gulped a healthy swig of the Canadian cooler. A satisfying smile on his face, he began:

"I was ready to call it an evening. It's about 8:45 and I'm pitching one of my last casts with a TopRaider near "The Throne." The water explodes. He's thrashing, running, diving. I'm holding tight, then he tires a bit and I guide him toward the boat. Then it's contortion time; I've got the rod held high in one hand keeping the tension while I reach back for the net with the other. The fish and the net are SOBs to try and control with one hand. Anyway, I get it done, sliding the hoop into the water and guiding the fish into it."

"Ah, the Baryshnikov move," I commented, "I remember it well from one of my dock-caught fish. It was the unhooking part I'm trying to forget."

Rich paused as he lifted the frosty glass to his lips, refreshing his body and spirit with another healthy swig. "Yeah, I have to thank you. I immediately recalled the nightmare when you played the role of "Captain I'm Hooked.""

"The lack of blood and Band-Aids leads me to believe you fared better?"

"Yeah. It was getting dark and I still had the long boat ride back to the cabin, so I figured I'd just cut the hooks. Safer for me and the musky, and it saved time."

"Smart move. Glad I could help. Did you have a chance to measure it?"

"I put the stick on it while it was still in the net—43 inches."

"Beauty! Too bad you couldn't get a picture."

After another hit of Alberta Springs, the gold liquid now covering only the bottom third of the ice cubes, Rich answered with a question, "Who said I didn't?" as he reached into his drybox and pulled out his camera.

"Did you grow another arm?" I asked.

"It's called a self-timer, Ed," Terry chimed in, shaking his head.

Rich continued, "It was pretty tricky, but I managed to hold the net in the water with the fish in it while I positioned the camera on the front pedestal seat."

"*You* my friend, are from the planet Krypton," I said.

"Not quite. I lifted the fish out of the net, clicked the timer button, stepped back, and a second before the shutter clicks the camera falls forward."

"No..."

"Doh yes! I've got a great full-frame shot of a gray vinyl boat seat, if anyone's interested."

"So...?"

"So, I ease forward, right the camera, click the timer button and decide if this one doesn't work, I'll be sending the fish on its way." With that, Rich drains the final ounces of Alberta Springs, then turns on the camera. As good a photo snapped by any fishing partner, a beautiful musky solidly in the grasp of the grinning angler fills the camera's LCD display.

Like the steak dinner he prepared earlier that evening, well done!

Let's see—what else? At 1 p.m. on Monday, I nicked myself with a hook, drawing blood and sounding the "I'm cut!" call.

Terry bagged five for the week with an average size of 33.1 inches. I took two, a 36 and a 31. With an average of 33.5 inches, I advised Terry that quality outweighs quantity in 2007.

Not because of its size but rather the timing, my 31-incher deserves a few words. Upon returning to the dock after Friday's final on-lake session, we began breaking down our equipment in preparation of tomorrow's early morning departure. Before dismantling my last rod and reel combo, I stepped out of the boat onto the dock, announcing my "last cast" of the trip. The fish struck my TopRaider mid-retrieve. Landed and released without incident, what a fine 31-inch exclamation point to another great week!

~ ~ ~ ~ ~

2008. It all comes together but not in a good way. Out of work, Rich can't make it this year. Ben has family issues denying him the opportunity to attend. Teaching summer school occupies Larry. Dan prefers to allocate his vacation time to bigger fish possibilities at Lake of the Woods. Art doesn't care to fish any more. The lenses that replaced my cataracts in '06 need a tune-up, and I have a work commitment in Denver to provide training to a third party vendor on how to do my job. Gasoline skyrockets over $4 per gallon. No trip this year.

July 2009. I'll describe this year as "the good, the not so good, the very good, kismet, and karma."

Good: The long drive from home to International Falls passes without incident, just the way we like it: no delays due to road construction, accidents, vehicle, or trailer problems. Rich and I plan to meet Terry and his friend Tom over the border between 5 and 7 p.m.

Not so good: Typically, a short line of vehicles rolling through Canadian Customs on Friday evenings moves quickly. This year, however, we crawl in a backup stretching several blocks. Forty-five agonizingly slow minutes pass before successfully crossing the international border.

Good: With Terry and Tom a half-hour behind, we make a trip to The Beer Store, a small building in a residential section of the city, a half mile off the major Fort Frances thoroughfare. The facility inventories a fine selection of Canadian beers not currently available in the States, two of which have become staples of our annual sojourn, Upper Canada and Sleeman. The store also stocks Labatt Maximum Ice, Terry's beverage of choice. He enjoys the "high octane" alcohol content of this brew, allowing him to attain the desired level of rapture while minimizing volume intake. At our age, this is an important consideration in the endeavor to maintain uninterrupted slumber, if you know what I mean, and I think you do. Rich and I purchase a case of "Maxi-Ice" for Terry as a precursory "thank you" for hosting the upcoming week.

Not so good: The uncertainty of who will be participating in this year's north-of-the-border adventure caused a delay in making overnight reservations. Six weeks in advance of our stay, I called to reserve two rooms at La Place Rendez-Vous. Unfortunately, but not unexpectedly, the well-kept inn on the shores of scenic Rainy Lake had no vacancy. We are forced to lodge at the Makabi. Some of my fishing partners refer to it as the "macabre-ie" and liken it to the Bates Motel in Alfred Hitchcock's *Psycho*; I don't take it that far, though it is a notch or two below the Rendez-Vous.

Good: A great restaurant with outstanding and reasonably priced food, one of La Flambe's Friday night specials is steak and lobster, priced at $19.95 in Canadian funds. With the U.S. dollar currently garnering a favorable exchange rate, there is no finer nor economical way to tantalize the taste buds and fill one's stomach at the end of a long day's travel. The joy of the Burger King Cheese Whopper Value Meal consumed for lunch in Eau Claire becomes a distant memory, though the plaque it deposited in my arteries, sadly, will remain.

Not so good: La Flambe's one-and-the-same hostess, waitress, and bus girl, who we believe to be the owner's wife, will not adjust our bill downward to account for the payment with U.S. funds.

Good: We live through the night at the Makabi, not bludgeoned to death by someone named Norman.

Not so good: While eating breakfast in Fort Frances on Saturday morning, two of the locals at a nearby table are talking about a tornado that tore through a fishing camp on Thursday evening near Ear Falls, Ontario, some fifty miles from Dianna and Terry's place. Several cabins destroyed, one was hurled nearly a mile into the lake, killing the three fishermen inside. Ironically, they were vacationing from the "Tornado Belt" state of Oklahoma, which owns the dubious distinction of the highest occurrence of supercell tornadoes in the U.S.

Good: The shelves at the retail LCBO (Liquor Control Board of Ontario) in Vermilion Bay, our final stop for supplies before the remaining 20-mile ride to our destination, are void of Maxi-Ice. We made the right decision by purchasing Terry's "gift" in Fort Frances. In stock, I purchase a super-size bottle of Alberta Springs.

Not so good: Not having been mowed in over a month, the lawn around the cabin stretches to mid-shin height. Terry issues an informal "tick alert" before taking the wheel of his recently purchased riding mower. The groceries and my clothes unpacked, I ready my fishing equipment and then go out to help, using the lawn mower to trim around trees and in tight areas Terry cannot reach with the rider. With the mower humming like the thousands of mosquitoes that will be hovering outside the porch screens later this evening, I hear Terry shout, "Don't forget to cut around the culvert." After a pass near the lakeshore and around several seedling birches, I head over to the partially exposed circular metal pipe that drains toward the lake. The grass reaches to the knee here. As the mower dips into a gully at the culvert's edge, the screech of metal on metal, the sound of the gates of hell swinging shut, pierces the air. An instant later the mower lay silent. My head bowed and mumbling a few choice profanities, Dr. Terry comes over to examine the lifeless patient, the remains revealing sheared pins and a bent shaft.

Good: Rich and I stay back while Terry and Tom hit the lake from 5 to 6 p.m., making the inaugural casts for the '09 week. Terry catches the first musky of the trip, a 32-incher, from Lake Whitney.

Not so good: Fishing from 7 to 9:30 p.m. everyone draws a blank. The overnight temperature dips into the low 40s. Noses and toes are uncomfortably chilled in spite of layered sleep clothing and additional blankets.

Good: It's a sunny Sunday, a glorious day to be on the water. Though midsummer post-cold front conditions typically do not bode well for successful fishing, I still prefer pitching musky lures with temperatures in the 60s versus working up a sweat in oppressively humid 90-degree July days experienced in years past. Though we do not catch any muskies in the morning to mid-afternoon session, Tom bags three walleye, providing a great start for some fine table fare later in the week.

After dinner, Rich and I head out to fish Forest Lake, starting at the south shore of "The Big Island." This stretch of shoreline has not yielded any fish during the past couple of years, but two-thirds of the way down the controlled drift and a few minutes before 7 p.m. Rich connects with a nice 41-incher on a copper-blade, brown-hair bucktail.

Next stop, "The Jugs." Top-water baits are the safe play when fishing this shallow, snag-filled area. Running the trolling motor from the bow as any boat owner and captain, Rich has first cast at any waters we fish. As we enter the narrows, Rich casts a TopRaider. I throw a fresh-out-of-the-package walleye-pattern Maas Marauder, a top-water lure whose side-to-side action, like a Giant Jackpot, is imparted by up and down motion of the rod in cadence with reeling up slack line. As Rich makes the turn to cast the far side of the narrows area, I point out that we are approaching three exposed boulders adjacent to deeper water that gave up a couple of nice fish several years ago. Immediately after my comment, in a most gracious gesture, Rich begins casting in the opposite direction, giving me first shot at the new water. As he inches the boat along, I make a long cast that lands perfectly in the "Forest Lake triangle" of exposed rocks. Imparting two twitches, the lure disappears as the water erupts. Feeling the weight of the fish, I set the hook. A toe-to-fin battle ensues, Rich netting a healthy 43-incher. After a successful release, I acknowledge my captain's kindness.

"Thanks, Rich. I know you gave me that spot. I appreciate it."

"It had to be done, I couldn't get in your way. You were working the "Marauder" like an artist. That spot was your blank canvas. You're very welcome, Picasso...."

Rich motors us to the next spot, the east side of a small island sporting multiple deadfalls extending from shore into the lake. The deep water adjacent to the island also holds submerged trees given up by the island from summer storms and frigid winters past. This small stretch of shoreline, referred to as

"The Brushpile," has also graced us with many good fish over the years, though like "The Big Island," it pitched a shutout against our group last year.

Rich breaks out a new lure of his own, clipping on a MagTinsel inline spinner bait that sports twin, size-10 copper-color blades, their shape and proportion similar to the bowl part of a serving spoon. Behind the big blades flow shiny strands of gold and red tinsel that overlap two sets of large treble hooks. This lure would not be out of place hanging from a Christmas tree or attached to the body part of a French Quarter Mardi Gras reveler.

A few minutes after 8 p.m., on his third cast, a musky with a hankering for "bling" engulfs the lure 10 feet from the boat, creating a water-splashing commotion at boatside. Rich prevails in the battle, rewarded with a "good karma" 42-inch fish.

As previously mentioned, our group has averaged one 40-inch class musky *per week* over the 15 years that we've fished the Alexandra Chain, known to hold good numbers of muskellunge but not trophy-size fish. To catch three of that size in one evening, at three consecutive spots, is like a baseball player blasting home runs in three consecutive at bats.

Not so good: A month before the trip, I decide it's time for my three 35- to 40-year-old Abu-Garcia Ambassadeur "red" reels and 10-year-old Shimano Calcutta to undergo a preventative "once over," a reel colonoscopy, so to speak. A leather strip, stitched to the right interior of the Ambassadeur's original brown leather case, holds a small tube of lubricating oil as well as a red-capped, clear plastic cylinder containing a small wrench and some pinhead size replacement parts. I consider undertaking the project on my own.

My first issue? I have no clue what a worn or compromised part looks like. Undeterred, I open the owner's manual to the page with the schematic, which contains several thousand interconnecting microscopic parts, all looking quite identical to my mechanically challenged eye. Although I'm reasonably certain my two left thumbs can take the reels apart, the more daunting hurdle centers on what to fix and then, how to reassemble. With doubt creeping in, I even question my ability to open the lubricating fluid, pristine as originally packaged decades ago. Further, I envision popping the cap off the spare parts tube and have them fly about the room. If I decide to proceed, unscrewing the reels' side plates would be like Homer Simpson cracking into a skull to perform brain surgery.

Aware that discretion is the better part of valor, I recall a recent newspaper feature about a reel repair service, *Reel 'em In*. Stan, the proprietor, has served the needs of the local fishing community for some 20 years since his retirement as an auto mechanic. Operating the business out of the garage behind his quaint bungalow on the northwest side of Chicago, I decide to give him a try.

Upon arriving, I meet the elderly gentleman who will perform the work. He sports a long white beard that accompanies the features, voice, and mannerisms of Kris Kringle, as portrayed in the classic Christmas movie, *Miracle on 34th Street*. His workbench contains dozens of small tools one might expect a watchmaker to use. Multi-drawer and compartmentalized utility boxes contain his inventory of thousands of amoeba-size reel parts. Aside from a small path to reach his work area, the remaining space of the one-and-one-half car garage overflows with vintage fishing equipment and paraphernalia: rods, reels, lures, bobbers, minnow buckets, photos, fish mounts, posters, and fishing-theme tchotchkes. These items line the floor, fill shelving units along the walls, and hang by the hundreds from the ceiling joists and rafters, the extensive collection a shrine to the history of 20th century fishing. Many of the unique items would not be out of place in Hayward's Freshwater Fishing Hall of Fame. I feel good, believing my reels cannot be in better, more experienced or competent hands.

Two weeks after dropping them off and one week before departing for Canada, I receive a call that they are ready and hop in the car to pick them up. When presented with the bill I nearly choke on the amount; by golly he's giving *me* a colonoscopy of sorts. "Parts for these old reels are expensive…" Okay, let it go. Sure, I could have paid for half my trip with what he's charging, but now I've got four reels set to go another thirty years. A decade or two down the road that will be good news for the winner of the eBay auction sponsored by my son, as I sit in a rocking chair trying to figure out why I tied my shoelaces together with a double uni-knot.

I get the reels home, ready to spool them with fresh line. Picking up the first and pushing the free-spool button, it doesn't stay engaged. An instant replay occurs with the second. On the phone with "Staniclaus," he tells me to bring them back in. He works on them while I wait, replacing the springs. "These parts aren't as reliable as they used to be when Abu-Garcia made them." Great. You failed to mention the parts were shitty when you rang them up as if they were made of gold. All of a sudden I'm viewing the *Reel 'em In* name in a whole new perspective. Oh, and by the way, wouldn't pushing the free-spool button and engaging it with a turn or two of the reel handle been a final part of your maintenance procedure? Okay, let it go. *Now* they should be good for another thirty.

Not a dozen casts into the first day of the trip, the free-spool button malfunctions by not popping *out*, so turns of the reel handle fail to retrieve the line and lure. The next day the identical problem occurs with a second reel. Then, onto the third, the magnetic anti-backlash adjustment fails so the spool has to be thumbed at the end of every cast or the dreaded "birds nest" tangle of line will result. Little did I know my "good for another thirty" thought related to number of casts, not years.

Caught in the purgatory bounded by anger, despondency, and disbelief, I wonder if Rich can actually see the blood pressure induced steam rising from my brow. If not, he and every other person in the province of Ontario heard the words I bellowed, still likely reverberating through the Canadian wilderness: "If it ain't broke, don't fix it!"

Good: Monday morning. With the boys in the cabin munching Cheerios and sipping coffee, I stroll down to the dock to make a couple of casts with a TopRaider. I am wearing recently purchased sunglasses with interchangeable lenses of varying tints, allowing sharper subsurface viewing under different light conditions. While not my first choice, this "outdoorsman" model was only manufactured in "camouflage" style frames.

I see a musky following my lure as it nears the dock. The fish, fooled into thinking I am a tree, hammers the bait. No one hears the commotion. Defying my historical pattern, I successfully land, measure, and release the fish without incident.

Not so good: The fish is 30 inches, bringing my average down from 43 to 36.5 inches.

Good: In pleasant temperatures and light winds, Rich and I spend the morning walleye fishing on Cobble Lake's "Grand Banks." We hit the jackpot between noon and 1 p.m. with a limit of 15- to 17-inch fish, which along with Tom's catch, ensures a tasty meal.

Not so good: To ensure a tasty meal later in the week, the walleye have to be filleted at the open-air table while fighting off flies and mosquitoes.

Good: Tuesday morning begins partly sunny with the temperature in the high 60s. Rich and Tom, boat partners for today and tomorrow, fish Cobble. Action aplenty, they bag 25 walleye.

Not so good: The walleye, all undersize, need to be released.

Good: No fish have to be filleted.

Not so good: My Calcutta reel begins to malfunction, the screws on the side plate loosening for the first time in ten years. As I tighten them in small increments taking care not to over-tighten, one is still turning when it suddenly snaps, disconnecting the screw head from the threads still imbedded in the reel. Staniclaus is gonna die.

Good: High noon. Terry and I pull up to the weedbed lining the north shore of Whitney. He positions the boat for a drift to take advantage of a breeze, building in strength through the course of the morning. After years of fishing these waters with Terry, I have a good sense of what lure he will be using at the various locations we fish, allowing me to set up with something different. I considered clipping on a Suick, but anticipating that would likely be Terry's choice, instead attach a bucktail.

After lowering the trolling motor Terry blurts out, "It's kismet!"

No longer (if ever) surprised by unconventional actions or comments from my friend, I nonetheless reply, "What the hell are you talking about?"

He explains that his fire-tiger pattern Suick, hanging with a dozen other lures from the boat carpeting that lines the bow wall above the casting deck, had dropped to the deck floor as he contemplated his lure selection for the drift. (Kismet confirms what I anticipated would be his lure choice.)

Now affixed to his hardwire leader, he throws a cast toward the shallow weeds. The instant it lands, the water explodes with the power of an M-80. A 39-inch musky, hooked and landed, defies the "finding a needle in a haystack" odds that are associated with the "fish of 10,000 casts," in this case assisted by the kismet of a lure that cried "Use *me*!"

Not so good: By early afternoon, the sun, which will not be seen for the remainder of the week, disappears behind heavy overcast. Daytime high temperatures will not exceed the mid-50s. North and northwest winds will blow vigorously and unabated for our remaining days, pushing occasional waves of mist and rain across the watery landscape. Strong winds make many of our productive spots unfishable. October weather arrives three months early.

Good: After an unsuccessful pass at "Pass Me By," Terry motors along the south shoreline to an area where it cuts back some thirty yards. I "discovered" it years ago, and although no one in our group shares my opinion of this likely looking spot, I feel it's always worthy of a few casts. I *know* there's a musky that calls this home: Each time I insist we throw a few, I can hear it laughing at me. (Or is that my boat partner…?)

Lily pads line the shore, and a narrow alley of open water separates them from a circular group of more pads dotting the surface closer to the main lake. This smaller cluster of pads is fronted by a rare (for this body of water) patch of coontail weeds. Many weeds, but particularly this variety, provides cover for small fish, which in turn attracts larger predators of the food chain that consider them a tasty meal.

As Terry turns off the motor, he gamesomely comments, "Well, here we are, 'No Fish Bay,' your favorite spot in the whole world."

I respond with a lighthearted, spirited tirade. "This is *not* 'No Fish Bay.' It's nothing, until *I* catch a fish here. Then I'm going to name it 'Ed's Bay.' I found this spot, and I'm the only one who believes in it. The time is now. Don't even bother picking up your rod. You just run the trolling motor and take me where I tell you. Get me in there, where I can lay a cast between those two sets of lily pads. Got it?"

"Yeah, I got it," Terry replies with an impish grin as he fires a cast into the bay.

The copper-blade brown-hair bucktail I'll be casting was given to me a number of years ago as a 50th birthday present from Rich. He customized it by taping the blade with a "50," along with a goofy photo of my smiling countenance topped by my wide-brim "Indiana Jones" fishing hat. The lure has served me well, having caught several muskies. I speculate those fish were able to contain their laughter just long enough to take a shot at my ugly mug.

As Terry moves the boat across the deeper center section of the bay, our casts are landing near the front edge of the central cluster of lily pads, but our distance and angle do not allow me to get my lure into the pad "alley." Knowing Terry's modus operandi for working small spots like this, I expect he will be moving us to a new location at any moment. I am pleasantly surprised as he turns the boat to make another pass, this one closer in. The boat moving a little quicker than I prefer, I know I'll have only one good shot at the lily pad passageway. Anticipating the moment, timing and accuracy are critical. With the window of opportunity about to close, I launch a long cast. Splash down—perfect! After three cranks of the reel handle the lure stops dead in its tracks. Rearing back to set the hook I feel the strong head shakes of the musky transmitted along the line and pulsing through the rod now doubled over with the weight of the fish. "Got one!"

How sweet when a plan comes together: pulling up to a spot and calling the shot like the Babe, a 35 ½-inch muskellunge christens "Ed's Bay," the fish caught on a special "Ed" lure. The total "Ed" fish catching experience appropriately concludes with a bloody finger, sliced by the musky's gill raker during the release.

I tape myself up as Terry motors us to the next location, the intersection of wide channels connecting Edward, Indian, and Whitney Lakes. "Big Ass Rock" surfaces near the east shoreline of the channel leading to Whitney. Several good-size rocks emerge from the water here, with "Big Ass" the largest at some six to eight feet in height and width. It's one big rock. It's one big, damn rock. It's one big, friggin' rock. And while it's one big ass rock, "Big Ass Rock" was named, and is pronounced with the emphasis on "ass"—"Big *Ass* Rock." Why?

The rock's geological composition gives it a pinkish hue when the sun illuminates it at a certain angle. A perfectly centered crack extends from its top to half way down the rock face, creating a pair of symmetrical "cheeks." A sprig flatulates from the crack, and dripping guano from nesting gulls splatters the rock face. So, there you have it. Too much information?

Not so good: With the wind really whipping, one of Terry's casts results in a nasty backlash.

Good: As he works to untangle it, the boat drifts out over 20 feet of water toward the center of the wide, featureless channel. Now several long casts away from our standard drift and casting route and seemingly in the middle of "nowhere," I continue to cast the "50" bucktail. Terry cannot believe his ears, when the shout goes up again: "I got one!" A bonus 31-incher comes to net.

Not so good: Wednesday, mid-50s, cloudy, misty, rainy, windy. With layered clothing of a t-shirt, long sleeve shirt, sweatshirt, hooded sweatshirt, rain suit, and life vest, my appearance combines the robotic movements of Gumby with the elephantine characteristics of the Michelin Man and the Pillsbury Doughboy. The muskies, stunned, frightened, or in a state of uncontrollable laughter, do not offer at the baits presented. No fish caught.

Still not so good: Thursday, 45 degrees overnight, 55 in the cabin, high for the day 50, cloudy, misty, rainy, windy. Did we get beamed up and deposited in early November? To close out the final two days of the week, Rich and I reunite as boat partners. "GumDoughMichieManPillBoy" reappears and gets skunked again.

Good: Lightning strikes twice: Rich bags another musky at the "Big Island." A nice 39-incher, this one follows his bucktail to the boat before grabbing it on a figure-8.

More good: Friday. Rich connects with a 41-incher from Whitney, closing out the week with three muskies over 40 inches. His total of 4 muskies, averaging 40.75 inches, sets a camp record.

The group catches 10 muskies for the week; not spectacular but not bad either, considering the tough weather conditions and the amount of time spent walleye fishing. The size of Rich's catch ups the overall group average to 37.3 inches, another camp record. If this upward trend in fish size continues, by my calculations, our catch will average 50 inches by my 120th birthday.

The 43 inch "Picasso" musky.

~ ~ ~ ~ ~

If fishing is interfering with your business, give up your business.
—Sparse Grey Hackle

Motorola - (At) Last

By 2009, I've lived as many years as Heinz has varieties—57. I'm getting older. Faster. Or so it seems. I've been an inside service representative, formally a "customer support manager," for several years now. In this role, I serve as a lightning rod, focal point, and flashpoint for all things askew in this defined business universe, the human conduit alchemizing the receipt and transmission of negatives into the miracle of profitable total customer satisfaction. It's quite challenging. Like trying to catch a musky.

Facilities management shuffles our group of six from 1309 back to 1301. The latest in confining and minimalistic furnishings awaits us, in smaller sizes of gray. Two-person pods find their "privacy" via a dry-erase board panel on wheels, pulled out to separate you from your arm's-length-away neighbor. A five-foot-tall side panel, with another neighbor on the other side, resides two arm's-lengths in the other direction. A couple of small storage cabinets cram the already cramped space. The desk surface accommodates a laptop and its docking station, a 19-inch flat screen monitor, calculator, and phone, leaving room for perhaps a folder or two, assuming neither of them are open.

Ergonomic, mesh-back chairs on wheels (be careful about not taking out a knee if you're thinking about swiveling around) replace the cushioned ones from days of yore. Completing the ensemble, a piece of thin fabric angles at 45-degrees from the top panel of each corner cubicle. Seeing through the designer's failed psychological "seclusion and noise abatement" ploy, the goofy "sail" provides the same amount of privacy as a pair of crotchless underwear.

I've been assigned one of those (no, not crotchless underwear but a corner cube), mine at what has to be the busiest intersection in the building. One aisle runs the length of the fourth floor. The other leads to vending machines and lunch tables. Directly across from me, a noisy and much used copier-scanner serves dozens of co-workers. It's difficult giving customers my undivided attention in this fishbowl adjacent to a junction constantly astir with the frenzy of a school of piranha crashing a minnow convention.

I start my work day early in an attempt to make some telephone calls uninterrupted, but that plan often fails because of the roar of vacuum cleaners pushed and pulled by the blue-uniformed cleaning service contractors through the modular maze. Instead of having the facility cleaned overnight, management moved the disturbance into the workday to save a few bucks. Eureka(s)!

Recalling my boss's comment from that DUMB 2006 performance review, "We used to be valued employees, now we're just commodities," our new office sets up sterilely devoid of shelving and wall space for personal items. My photos, trinkets, and items of recognition now stare at the inside of a cardboard box in my basement. All but one. Several years earlier a service manager, Jim, gifted me a specially crafted advertising item, a Rapala Rattlin' Rap fishing lure, imprinted with "Motorola" and the batwings logo. It now hangs from my cubicle "sail." The lure colors tell the inside joke. In fishing circles, the red head and white body form the pattern known as "clown," perfect for this circus environment.

The bulk of my work contemporaries having moved on or out, I no longer find much joy, or even mood mitigation for that matter, in the occasional sharing of a lunch table with any of a group of young whippersnappers. The only thing we share are the opposite ends of a generation gap. When the conversation turns to sports and I mention the name Johnny Morris, no one finds it interesting that one founded Bass Pro Shops in 1972, and the other, a sports announcer on WBBM-TV, was also the Bears all-time leading receiver and member of the 1963 NFL champs. Hell, I can't blame my co-diners—some of them weren't even born in '72, let alone '63. It's time for the permanent transition to lunchtime recluse.

I look forward to the days when winter loses its grip, when sunshine's warming winds wedge their way into my lunch break. The hunger bell tolls as 11:30 a.m. nears. Generally prompt in answering it, my work surface transforms from desk to dinner table for the midday repast. I ponder how many more days this ritual will continue, with over three decades having passed since my employ began. Someday, sooner than later, one of these meals will be the Last Supper.

Each day, ready as celebrant, I unfurl and drape a napkin altar cloth. One by one, I remove the edibles from my brown paper tabernacle, placing them in front of me with deliberate precision. A small bag containing host-like potato chips adjoins slices of rye bread that sandwich ham or salami or roast beef. An unconsecrated bottle of green tea, two chocolate chip cookies, and a blood-red McIntosh apple completes the configuration. As the beatitude of satisfying the pangs of hunger begins, I read the liturgy of the daily newspaper's box scores. The last morsels consumed, let the pilgrimage to waters begin.

The leg-stretching journey takes me through several parking areas (once filled with employee vehicles, now less than half so), then over a rise abutting the extinct remains of the basketball-volleyball courts that sprout chunks of grass and weeds through zigzagging cracks in the worn asphalt. I continue past the silent baseball and Frisbee fields, and the dark, smoky windows of the always-as-if-in-mourning corporate tower, and finally onto a red brick walkway that rings the multi-acre pond. My pace slows as wind-induced ripples that glitter the surface come into view, the welcome sight initiating a spiritual sabbatical, brief as it may be, that whisks me away from the mental strain of job tasks and the stifling confinement of my cubicle. Gently curving to the right, the path skirts the roots of a hulking willow, branches tumbling a thinly veiled umbrella that filters the rays of the midday sun. A few steps beyond waits my destination: a 20-foot wood-plank bridge edged by a chest-high, brown metal railing, the structure traversing a neck-down of the larger pond into a smaller pool.

My stroll, along with this bridge, links a vanilla present with colorful memories of days past and a future undefined. I recall the sight of six-year-old Eddie, only a few yards further down this path, beaming with pride as he strained to hold up a carp the length of his forearm. He'd just caught the fish in the annual fishing contest, part of the family picnics long ago discontinued when the corporation abandoned the noble concepts of employee appreciation for the shortsighted view of a few more dollars to the bottom line.

Swan Song

I stand on the bridge-pulpit, ready to rendezvous with my daily visitors. Two white-as-new-fallen-snow swans approach, gliding across the velvet water. They provide counsel on various work and personal matters. How fortunate, my ability to translate their guttural honks.

I begin today's give and take. "How's it going, my friends?"

"Swimmingly ... not a care in the world here, other than an occasional run-in with our filthy Canadian cousins who feel every inch of earth is their personal toilet bowl."

"Amen. I can't tell you how many times I've almost pulled a muscle avoiding the minefields of goose-crap graffiti. It's disgusting."

"So, what's on your mind today? Unhappy customers? Unhappy bosses? Unhappy subcontractors?"

"No, not the customer service trifecta today. I'm finding it tougher and tougher to drag my rear end out of bed before 5:00 each morning with the prospect of spending another long day in the pressure-cooker. Then, the Indy 500 tollway drive home, dinner, and vegging-out in front of the tube for a couple of hours till my head hits the pillow at 9:30. In the blink of an eye, it's time to do it all over again. Spending half my waking hours here for the better part of 35 years is getting old, just like me. I'd love to call it a career, but there's that little issue of money, not the least of which was the stock market recently turning many workers' 401Ks into 201Ks."

"Not sure how much help we can be with that—for us it's pretty simple: eating, sleeping, and paddling about. But we'll give it a shot."

"Please do."

Back and forth without pause, the swans squawk out questions: "How long are you and your wife going to live? How big is your nest egg? What's your estimated annualized percentage of investment return? What are your living expenses? How will they change if you retire? How healthy will you be—how much will you have to 'donate' to the medical community?" Thoughts swirling, my eyes dart as I follow the yellow-orange blur of their clacking beaks. "What kind of income will you have? What's your projection for annual inflation? What are you going to do with all that free time?"

Swimming in their words, only the last question registers for a response. "I like to write."

"We've heard your prose. Don't count on making any money at it. Your cousin Ben read us some of the compositions you've scripted regarding your fishing escapades. They're like that 'tough as a bulletproof vest' Kevlar line that snapped like a wishbone after a dozen casts—not all it's advertised to be. By the way, we haven't seen Ben in a while."

"He fell victim to the corporate chainsaw that recently cut another swath through the employee forest."

"You should have mentored him in the skills of corporate survival."

"Much as I would have liked to help, that would be like Roland Martin, 9-time B.A.S.S. Angler of the Year, by the way, handing him his fishing pole and saying, 'Here, fish like me.'"

"Well, he shared his thoughts on your retirement dilemma with us. Care to hear?"

"Sure."

"Painfully aware of how your body is breaking down piece by piece, he believes you'd be well-advised to do some heavy-duty traveling, fishing, drinking, and smoking. You can have a hell of a good time while cutting short your lifespan so there's no need to worry about the money running out."

"Very thoughtful, his twist on 'Live fast, die young, and be a pretty corpse.'"

"In your case, aside from dying young and being a pretty corpse, it could work."

"I'll take it all under advisement. Thanks. Until tomorrow…"

"No problem. If you'll excuse us, we're going to sneak under the bridge and work on making some cygnets."

~ ~ ~ ~ ~

In spite of the ominous possibility of outsourcing and the reality of a job grade reduction and salary freeze, management makes good, to their credit, on their promise to keep our group employed. Months of hand-wringing follow the day the swans quacked out the deluge of retirement issues. So many unknowns. My first lunch buddy, Rich, passed away a couple of years ago, and Jo Ann's sister, Jackie, is terminally ill with leukemia at age 52—both shortchanged on the joys retirement might bring. So many variables. In the realm of financial and lifestyle considerations, this ranks right up there with the decisions to marry, and later, have children. In a simplistic sense, it's like buying a musky lure that calls out to you from the shelf; sometimes you've got to close your eyes and just grab for it.

December 11, 2009. The clock twirls as I feverishly work to tie up loose ends on my final day on the job. Like all others toiled here, I keep a low profile. No mention of the day's significance made by me or to me, it passes without fanfare. By 5 p.m., most of my fellow associates have vacated the building to begin their weekend, forgetting (or so I'd like to think) that it was my last day, and not stopping to offer a final goodbye. No phone call from my remotely located boss. No local manager from whom to accept a final pat on the back or handshake. Silence instead of thanks. No one in management to be found, I gather up my laptop, badge, and cabinet keys, and walk slowly through the graveyard aisles. In the distance, the sound of pecking on a keyboard brings optimism about finding, who I believe, may be the last living soul in a dead building. My final mission accomplished, Liz, a sales administrator and friend, offers to secure the items. After chatting briefly, we exchange heartfelt goodbyes.

Unlike the stifling elevator ride up on my first day, today's final ride down wraps me in equal parts numb and surreal. Glazed eyes open, riding solo as I did on my first day, the numerals above the door light and dim slowly, as if ready to begin their weekend slumber ...... 4 ...... 3 ...... 2 ...... 1......

Hand-carried to and from work each day for the past twenty-some years, my tattered, zipper-top, navy blue cloth "Motorola—Rise to the Challenge" bag holds a few personal papers regarding retirement, insurance, and the like. Upon entering the lobby, I open the bag for the guard's nonchalant perusal, and then nod a goodbye. Wearing a hooded, baseball-style jacket with black torso and beige sleeves, its insulation cushions my right arm as I lean into one of the glass and stainless steel double doors, vacating the premises for the final time. Now outside, I reach back and flip the hood onto my head as the door closes behind me, breaking the eerie stillness with a distinctive, metallic "click." The audio cue announces a sad finality, like pushing the spool release lever of a reel before making the called "last cast" of life's final fishing outing.

My exit meets the total darkness of a late December afternoon. I stop for a moment to snap a mental photo. Lights randomly checker the windows of our building as well as the corporate tower. The permanently shuttered 1299, 1309, and 1313 lay dark, silent. Flecks of snow dance in the shining amber of light standards geometrically spaced within the parking lots. Smatterings of cars remain between yellow, fishbone lines, soon to disappear under the cover of snow, much like the anticipation-laden morning of my first day of work on December 2, 1974.

How fitting, this solitary departure. As a long-lived-but-no-longer-valued corporate dinosaur, I plod in my black galoshes, none of the four buckles latched, across the asphalt that swallows me like the La Brea tar pit of eons ago. My 35-year era ends without a word, whispered or whimpered. On Monday, the business of business will go on without me. I envision my *former* associates scurrying about, oblivious to my empty chair, as if I'd never even been there. Or so it feels, in this melancholy moment.

Thoughts again race back to Elk Grove Village—the building, the names, the faces. As I exited after that first day on the job, I recalled the words of my Psychometric Affiliates evaluation: "…youthfully anxious, fairly solemn, and somewhat original…." In line with those words, over dinner with Jo Ann that evening, I whimsically decided on a career objective—retire as soon as possible. Well, the "as soon as possible" part didn't quite work out in the timeframe I had hoped but better late than later, or not at all. My long-term symbiosis with Motorola represents a trade most undertake: a significant chunk of life's precious hours exchanged for a sustenance-providing livelihood for self and family. At least I'm going out on my own terms, unlike thousands of others "rightsized" out the door, herded from the manufacturing plant to the proverbial rendering plant over the past number of years.

Geez, snap out of it. They bought you a fishing-theme decorated cake to share with your current associates, and the key members of that old gang of yours joined you for a truly enjoyable farewell dinner, remember?

Indeed. And in addition to providing the means to a fair livelihood, the corporation also provided the venue to initiate and develop friendships, many of those lifelong. I view the key component of my long-term success as relationship-building: customers, vendors, co-workers, and management. I sent my farewell e-mail to 172 of my closest work partners, and feel gratification upon receiving replies from most of them: "I'm happy for you!" "I'm jealous!" "You'll be missed!" "Congratulations!" "Bastard!" Over the years, conversations bared not only work-related feelings but a stake in all of life's ups and downs. Comfortable inside and outside the boundaries of the workplace, we grew up, we grew old. That first day in Elk Grove Village marked the beginning with Tom and Sharon. Others relationships flourished in subsequent years, many lasting decades, to this day. With some, the camaraderie deepened with time spent in a boat and on drives to and from a lake.

Like the end of each *Romper Room* broadcast, I'm looking through the magic mirror (big inhale here); I see Dave, and Donna, and Patty, and Glen, and Mary, and Jim, and Cindi, and John, and Vern, and Chuck, and Rich, and

Liz, and Carol, and Ellen, and Paul, and the other Jim, and Bob, and Steve, and Charlene, and Christine, and Eric, and Connie, and Michelle, and Lisa, and Judy, and Darwin, and Wayne, and Dale, and Mark, and Carl, and George, and Chris, and Tony, and Harley, and the other Dave, and Laura, and the other Mark, and Rene, and Tammy, and Deanna, and Scott, and Kim, and Mike, and Lauren, and Jennifer, and Greg, and Tony, and Sam, and Jerry, and Dick, and Anita, and Roberta, and Rebecca, and Marsha, and Karen, and Tracy, and Larry, and Sue, and Ron, and Gary, and Judy, and Joan, and Leanne, and LaVonne, and Fred, and Linda, and Ann, and Anne, and Barb, and the other Carol, and the other Tom... (Sorry, I just ran out of breath. For the other hundred-some not listed, I see you, too!)

(Un)Happy Father's Day, 2010

Six months after I left Motorola, Jo Ann joined me by retiring after 21 years as a first grade teacher's aide. Her 2010 school year just completed, we're three days into an early June vacation at Emerald Lake. Storms have rolled in and out over the past couple of days, but I managed to hit the lake between raindrops for three hours yesterday evening. The good news? I caught a dozen bass. The bad? In a worst-ever hook-setting performance, I lost more than one fish for each one I landed. I'll work on rectifying that tomorrow.

While fishing provides some exercise (especially fighting a crazed musky), aerobic it's not. I want to be a good boy—get my heart rate pounding at something above couch-potato level and stretch the ol' muscles that began whispering "atrophy" through a winter of limited activity. Time to start limbering up, getting in shape for the annual Canadian musky trip next month. With the return of storms on Monday, I decided to shoot some hoops at the Emerald Lake gym.

With the court to myself, I'm getting a good workout, alternating jump shots with layups and free throws. Rust factor considered, I'm generally pleased with my game, a good number of shots tickling the twine with an endearing "Swish!" Near the end my hour workout, I race (as fast as a somewhat out of shape 58-year-old can go, that is) toward the basket for a rebound put-back of an errant 18-footer. I grab the ball, make one dribble, and leap skyward, envisioning myself in the pose of the about-to-dunk "Air Jordan" logo. (I'm three feet below the rim instead of three feet above it, but no matter.)

On my launch from the hardcourt, I hear a sound similar to monofilament line breaking under pressure when attempting to free a snagged lure: "Snap!"

The touch down of my flight concludes in a tumble to the floor. Momentarily dazed, I attempt to stand but stumble, looking as though I had just consumed a liter of Alberta Springs. I steady myself against the cinderblock wall a few feet behind the basket.

Aware the ankle hadn't twisted upon landing, I suck in a few deep breaths to regain my composure. I put weight on my right foot and then lift it—it hangs loosely, as if no longer connected to my leg. Though not painful, the sight and sensation bring on momentary lightheadedness. Unintentionally replicating the gait of Igor from *Young Frankenstein,* I shuffle through the facility and back to the car. The drive to the cabin is only a mile, and midweek traffic is light. With the right ankle sustaining the injury, accelerating and braking are dicey and uncomfortable, though manageable, thanks to the hyper-rush of adrenaline still pumping through my system. I make it back without incident, where Jo Ann's cursory exam reveals a mushy area behind the ankle. She drives us to the ER where the doctor confirms a tear of the Achilles tendon.

That brings an immediate end to what should have been an enjoyable week, celebrating Jo Ann's retirement, in one of our favorite places. I flirt with bouts of nausea on the two-hour car ride home, sitting with my casted-through-mid-thigh leg fully extended across the back seat. Every turn and every bump in the road brings pain, as the cast cuts into both sides of the area surrounding my swollen ankle bone.

A Tuesday appointment with the orthopedist blueprints next-day surgery and a recovery itinerary including no weight-bearing for the first six weeks, temporary and permanent casts, crutches or a walker, a month in that clodhopping boot (if man's limitless ingenuity can put men on the moon, surgically replace knees and hips, transplant hearts, lungs, livers, and kidneys, why am I stuck in footwear made fashionable by Boris Karloff in the 1931 cinema classic, *Frankenstein*?), a month (or more) of physical therapy, and a total recovery process to encompass 6 to 12 months. Happy summer! Maybe imitating Mr. Potato Head on the La-Z-Boy wasn't such a bad idea after all.

With day surgery scheduled for 10 a.m. on Wednesday, Jo Ann preps me to give the post-operative stint a "bright-eyed and bushy tailed" demeanor so we can promptly depart for the comfort of home. I'll give it my best shot. She alerts the nurses to my past problems with post-procedure nausea caused by anesthesia. They provide a pre-surgery preventative pill.

In my last recollection of the operating room, the anesthesiologist puts a mask over my face and mumbles some lame instructions. The next time I open my eyes I recognize my surroundings as a recovery room, the wall clock reading 12:30. A nurse asks if I want something to drink. I request a cup of ginger ale, believing the fluid will assist toward the goal of getting home as soon as possible.

Not long thereafter, our hopes for an on-time release face a potential setback as the room begins spinning—not in carousel fashion as I recall from an occasional Saturday night at NIU but vertically, every flick of my eyelids changing frames like a rapidly advancing View-Master. Over the next several hours, I doze in and out of consciousness. Each waking event includes the now out of control View-Master, refunding a few ounces of ginger ale, and consuming a nurse-provided anti-nausea pill.

The Surgi-Center closes at 5 p.m. Jo Ann believes my unstable condition will result in admission to the adjoining hospital building for an overnight stay. Although I retch again at 4:55, the nurse, unfazed by my inability to keep anything down and apparently intent on keeping her dinner plans in place, facilitates the approval of my discharge papers. Just as well—this will allow me to barf in the familiar and comfortable surroundings of my own home. Completing an hour-long, back seat, stomach-anxious ride home, the dry heaves continue into early evening. I hope the nurse enjoyed her meal.

On Thursday, the sun rises, my stomach settles, the View-Master locks in, and I'm able to down a cup of tea and a piece of toast, the first solid food since a half sandwich at 10 p.m. on Tuesday, the evening before the surgery. Over the next couple of days, my meal habits get back to normal, and as a pain-preventative surgeon-recommended measure, I'm taking codeine-based pills in the morning and evening. Well, the food and the pills are going in, but nothing is snaking its way out. Jo Ann "connects the dots"—the codeine and anti-nausea pills have constructed a dam at the exit ramp of my nether region.

Friday is "Day 3," but only the second day back on my regular meal regimen. It's no big deal: I understand it takes time for the composting pile to make its way through my abdominal sewer pipes. I figure nature will take care of things in its own timeframe, so if a day or two passes but my stuff doesn't, I'm on the okay-with-that side of the "rectum anxiety spectrum."

I'm trying to emphasize the "ass" in "assist" by eating grainy foods and fruits. Jo Ann thinks it may be time for some countermeasures. She makes a trip to the store, returning with a macabre bagful of items: Colace stool softener, Miralax laxative, and a Fleet enema. When my wife-nurse expresses concern, especially when the phrase "you've got shit for brains" could be taking on a literal meaning, I'm all ears—to a point. The Colace pills are popped, the Miralax crystals mixed into a cocktail and consumed, but there is no way the "wet and wild Big E" (as described in a Seinfeld episode) and I will become intimate friends. As the day concludes, this had not been a good Friday.

The discomfort level dials up on Saturday, "Day 4." I continue stepping into the batter's box but keep striking out. Every move around the house, including the visits to Sir Thomas Crapper's plumbing innovation, are complicated by use of the walker and the awkwardness of the casted leg and the doctor's decree that the leg be completely non-weight bearing. "Anxiety" can now be added to my ever-expanding list of physical and psychological maladies. The oral remedies prove ineffective in breaching the levee. God dam.

Sunday. Happy Father's Day. "Day 5": cry, die. I'm on the verge of the former and would welcome the latter. Condition critical, my misery level ranks with some of my greatest infirmed moments: appendicitis, fragmented lumbar disk, any of multiple occasions finding a fishing hook imbedded past the barb, or taking a hypodermic needle in the eyeball.

A second morning visit to the throne remains fruitless, toot-less. On the verge of passing out, I call for a cold compress. Like an overstuffed sausage, my 29-feet of intestinal tubing bulges with 30-feet of compacted decomposing food sediment. The kryptonite plug refuses to budge.

One-legged, walker in hand, hop-hobbling back to the bedroom, I collapse on the bed. I have run a five-day marathon of sorts but still not crossed the finish line: In fact, the starting line still remains in sight. It's the nightmare of recurring days as in the movie *Groudhog Day*, except a painful colonic twist accompanies my psychological distress. Jo Ann expresses deep concern and sympathy, with a dose of brutal realism: "You've got to try the enema—that stuff *has* to come out. If not, we'll have to take you to the hospital and they'll dig it out with their fingers. That's how they do it, you know."

OH MY GOD!

I'm stuck between a rock and a hard place with a rock *in* a hard place, a hard rock in a bad, bad place. Barely audible, I whisper, "o…….k……."

WARNING!

The reader of squeamish constitution may want to pucker up and skip to the middle of page 352 to avoid the disturbing details that follow.

The "dreaded apparatus" is four ounces of saline solution in a clear, pliable plastic bottle with a white, two-inch nozzle. I envision the Surgeon General's warning on the box:

> *Use of this product defies all laws of God and nature. Should it relieve your physical disorder, severe mental side effects are possible, nay, will haunt you forever.*

Lying on my left side, Jo Ann gingerly inserts the "ohmygod ohmygod ohmygod ohmygod ohmygod ohmygod ohmygod ohmygod!!!!!!!!"

My pillow in a death grip, a few short spurts of moisture rush upstream, against the natural flow.

"areyoudone areyoudone areyoudone!!!!!!!!!?"

"What's the matter!?"

"Nnnmmm …… gdmsh …. ohowohouwo!" (Muffled gibberish as teeth slice through lower lip, translation: "Everything!")

"What?"

"Gdmsh ….. nnnmmm …… ohowohouwo!"

"Am I hurting you?"

"It burns, too!"

"It must be the saline hitting a hemorrhoid. Okay, I'll stop, but not much went in." After a slight pause she continues, "My gosh, less than an ounce—that's not going to do anything."

"……..oh ……..my …….god……"

Hands on walker and casted leg in tow, I plod to the bathroom. The injected fluid simply trickles out. Hands and feet getting clammy and continuing consciousness in jeopardy, I again call for the ice pack. Upon stabilizing, I ooze back to the bedroom, pouring my dishrag carcass onto the bed.

"Do you want to try it again? I'll fill it with warm water in place of the saline."

"I don't know. I…….. don't………. know………"

Jo Ann implores, "We've got to do something…"

"o…………… k………………..."

The white-tipped devil engages for Round 2.

"areyoudone areyoudone areyoudone!!!!!!!!!?"

"I haven't even put it in yet! Settle down! Take slow, deep breaths or you're going to hyperventilate!"

Fleet meets seat. After a fifteen second eternity, a discouraging report follows, "Barely an ounce…."

With what I believe to be my last ounces of strength, I grip the walker and negotiate the path back to the bathroom. A hint of seeping sepia gives a first glimmer of hope. Back to the bedroom and bed, the ghastly Island of Doctor Moreau.

"Can we try it one last time, or do you want to go to the hospital?"

The dribble of progress and the graphic image of a stranger's finger imitating an auger in my sacred tabernacle makes this decision a no-brainer.

"Easy .... Good .... Hang in there .... Good! All done—almost three ounces!"

The voice of an angel speaks the words, energizing, uplifting. Upward! Onward! Outward! My arms regain strength. My stride regains purpose with each hop of the walker. This final pilgrimage to the throne concludes as I position myself upon the holey seat. The lyrics and melody to Led Zeppelin's "When the Levee Breaks" swirl, soulful, amid the scent of victory.

Sunday, 2:23 p.m. Success. Happy Father's Day. No greater gift...

~~~~~

Of course, it's not just a simple matter of having a problem, getting it fixed, and strolling merrily along. Like most of my other anatomical failures, the repaired ankle functions at about 75% of its pre-injury capacity. As the body compensated, collateral maladies arose. The inability to use my right leg for an extended period of time caused the muscles to atrophy. Medical reference books define atrophy as "withering to size of a toothpick."

My foot and ankle also began exhibiting edema (most appropriate, the "ed" in edema), the collection of fluid that causes the skin to expand and tighten like an overfilled water balloon. The physical therapist recommended a compression stocking to help with this condition. Like "the boot," the heavy duty nylon hosiery made another striking fashion statement. A paisley *babushka* and pulling a shopping cart would complete the Busia makeover.

Tendonitis developed on the inside of the ankle bone, courtesy of the exercise prescribed to help reduce the fluid, relieve the tightness, and bulk up the toothpick. Heel pain and toe cramping also materialized, though those only manifest when standing or walking, some relief realized with the purchase of pricey shoe inserts. Cost be damned, I held firm to the opinion that the ability to stand and walk without significant pain is a life "plus." Numbness at the back of the heel heralded more nerve damage. During my quarterly follow-up visits to the surgeon, he expressed pleasure with my progress that indicates a normal, on-track recovery. Recognition as his star pupil humbled me. (God help the other folks.) I've learned that when a doctor answers my questions and concerns with "Just give it some time," what he's really saying is, "It's not going to get any better—you'll learn to live with it if you *just give it some time*."

Months and months without the ability to exercise (or fish, or walk normally, for that matter) further impeded my original goal of getting in and staying in shape. The impact of this cardiovascular inactivity hit home upon answering the telephone, the voice of my sister greeting me. "Hi. Were you exercising? You sound out of breath."

"Uh, no. I just reached across the desk to answer the telephone."

(Note to the Long Term Health Care Insurance Company holding my policy: Not to worry—I am sort of, um, really okay and fine.)

~ ~ ~ ~ ~

Freespool Flashbacks from the Alexandra Chain of Lakes
2010 - 2012

2010. With my Achilles tendon on the mend, I am unable to join my friends this year. What a "delightful" way to spend the carefree days of summer: pain, immobility, and confinement, hobbling on one leg with the aid of a walker, bed to bathroom, bathroom to kitchen, kitchen to living room, living room to bedroom. On the bright side, my confinement means I won't impale myself with a fish hook and will also serve as fine preparation for my imminent incarceration in the Hayward Home for feeble-minded fishermen.

Terry, Tom, Rich, and Richie make the trip this year along with first-timers Cousin Phil and his friend Rick. On Monday, I receive an e-mail (Terry and his guests have the ability to communicate from the hinterland via computer dial-up) that includes a photo attachment. Staged on the screened porch, the picture's focal point is a bottle of Alberta Springs. One-third of its contents have been consumed. Noticeably empty in the background is "my" chair. The e-mail reads:

> *Ed (and Red?),*
> *I'm lonely and miss you! I'm smaller and only serve one now that you are gone. Your vacant chair matches the void in my heart. The absence of the smell of cheap cigars and insect-repelling citronella sunscreen is almost too much to bear. Oh, how I long for your company! I miss the touch of your hand across my label, your strong grip across my midsection. This*

place is not the same without you!
'Til next year,
Love,
Miss Alberta Springs

With the physical pain of my ankle accompanying the psychological strain of being housebound, the "missing you" communiqué provides a modicum of comfort, though I'm not pleased that Miss Springs (the little slut!) has opened her top for the intoxicating pleasure of another.

Early on, I am reluctant to inquire about their fishing success (or lack thereof). With no unsolicited information forthcoming, I fear the group may be sparing me further pain by not regaling me with stories of a banner year. By Tuesday evening, I can no longer handle the suspense and fire off a "so how's it going" e-mail. Lack of a response feeds my apprehension.

On Thursday evening, a reply arrives:

Fishing is great! Some are having a "career" week.
We don't miss you!
The TEAM

Ouch! Now there's a mountain of road salt in the wound.

In search of any positive resulting from the dark cloud that is my absence, I find a thread of silver lining, albeit thin as 4-pound test monofilament. The time affords me the opportunity to do some on-line shopping for fishing equipment, the funding supplied by the cash not spent on the trip.

As is said about diamonds, bank accounts, and certain body parts (the brain, for example, shame on you) "bigger is better." This maxim also applies to fishing and the evolution of baits and equipment used in hunting the muskellunge.

Utilized primarily when casting, in-line spinner baits (bucktails) with one (or two) size-10 blade(s) have been the recent craze, responsible for hooking many trophies exceeding the magical 50-inch mark. With no end in sight regarding "how big is too big," King Kong size-13 teardrop blades have recently hit the market. It won't be long before the "latest and greatest" bucktail will be sporting a pair of twirling pie tins. I can envision casting this next frontier of mega-lure and being lifted out of the boat by the updraft like a whirlybird taking flight. Fifteen-inch Super Magnum Bull Dawg Pounders (yes indeed, weighing a pound!) are also shot-putted by musky fishing fanatics, and some troll crankbaits upwards of 20-inches in length and weighing more than two pounds.

Casting and retrieving these mammoth baits age both fisherman and their gear much before their time. Carpal tunnel syndrome and the need for rotator cuff surgery build with each outing. And at $28.99 or more, the lures lighten the wallet while weighing heavy on the conscience.

In accordance with the convention of the time, my first musky rod mimicked the thickness and length of a pool cue. For as many muskies as I was catching, it would have provided better service in a billiard room. With the passage of time, I've gone with the flow, purchasing increasingly longer rods, stout with "heavy" action, yet limber with "fast" tips. Longer rods cast the big baits more efficiently, are better at setting the hook and playing the fish at long distances, and assist in performing more effective figure-8s. Now, even the seven and seven-and-one-half foot rods just don't cut it for pitching the new mega-lures.

I consulted with my friend John, fishing guru and one of The Club founding fathers, recently elected to the Master Division of the Chicagoland Chapter of Muskies, Inc. (I am also a member of the organization but belong to the South of the Border [S.O.B.] chapter, its home waters in the northern Illinois Chain O' Lakes area just "south of the Wisconsin border.") He advised me that an eight-and-one-half foot rod (I'm sure nine- and ten-footers are on the manufacturer drawing boards if not already in stores) gets the job done. He has one in his arsenal, casted the big-blade baits, and stamped it with his seal of approval as a result of catching numerous muskellunge of significant size. I located the budget friendly Hawg Chaser model he recommended and placed an order with a Wisconsin on-line retailer.

The house arrest brought by my Achilles recovery adjusts my outlook on the satisfaction associated with the ability to complete some of life's simpler tasks. Yes, like going to the bathroom. And in that vein, I recall the innocent and unbridled joy of Navin R. Johnson, portrayed by Steve Martin in the 1979 movie *The Jerk*, as he shouted, "The new phone book's here! The new phone book's here!"

A UPS truck pulls into our driveway *one day* after I placed the order for the rod, the driver strolling up the walkway with my purchase on his shoulder like a bazooka on steroids, resting the long cardboard tube at a 45-degree angle against the house, next to the front door. *My* new phone book's here!

The smile on my face matches the determination in my soul: that jousting lance is coming in the house right now, non-weight bearing casted leg and walker be damned. I'm ready to grapple with the front and screen doors, the only things separating me from the highlight of my summer. One hand on the walker, I use the other to pull open the steel front door. Next, I turn the handle and push open the screen door, almost tumbling onto the concrete stoop. I pull back on the handle and regain my balance before giving the tension-loaded door another push, quickly grabbing the long tube and dragging one end inside the house, the door just missing my hand as it slaps the sizeable length of tube still outside on the landing. Both hands on the walker and the tube tucked in my armpit, I manage to drag its nine-foot length into the entryway, the screen door slamming shut.

With the unwieldy cylinder still in tow, I clumsily negotiate a couple of walls (leaving a few souvenir abrasions marking the happy occasion), an end table, cocktail table, and the couch. So far so good, I plop onto an armchair and pull off the "X" of tape and the tube's end cap. Heaven's gate open, I reach in, fingers circling the smoothness of the Fuji Alconite line guide on the tip, the first of nine gracing its length. I begin the methodical removal of the rod from its shipping container, as if drawing an antique Samurai sword from its wood-carved scabbard. With the concentration of a ninja, my eyes fondle each inch of the carbon-color 33 million modulus graphite (I'm not sure what that means, but by golly, 33 million, well, that just has to be fantastic!) rod as it slowly emerges in measured lengths. As the handle nears, I spy the gold-embossed information: "8 foot 6 inch Extra Heavy Power"; "Fast Action"; "Premium Graphite"; "50-100 lb. Test Line"; "4-12 oz. Lures." I nod approvingly. The front of the extra-length handle next appears, its premium cork material as well served here as capping a bottle of Dom Perignon.

Fully enraptured with the unveiling of my new lunker-taming saber, I'm unaware that I have been passing its massive length up and beyond my shoulder, forgetting the tube and rod total over 17-feet of length in a room that is 16-feet wide. The mathematics of this situation announces itself as the rod tip, out of sight behind me, nudges a picture on the wall, sending it crashing to the floor. Startled, I swing around, the tube hitting the end table, the lamp wobbling precariously. As I dive to steady it, I knock over the walker, which tumbles to the cocktail table and sends a dish of candy shattering to the floor. There will be some explaining to do when Jo Ann returns. At least the rod escaped unscathed.

That ordeal safely in the livewell, I spent the rest of my "Canadian vacation that wasn't" ogling my prize purchase until my fishing friends returned to provide a debriefing of their trip. Their account detailed a mixed bag.

Rich caught four, including a 40-incher. His son Richie recorded his best week ever with five, as well as his largest, a 40-incher. Tom, who allocated most of his time to fishing for walleye, took his first-ever musky, a 35-incher. Unkind to Phil and Rick, the musky gods pitched a shutout in their first visit to new waters. They did, however, catch some walleye, including a 25-incher by Rick.

As Tom and Terry fished Indian Lake on Wednesday, the motor propelling Terry's 15-year-old Lund crapped out, requiring a long tow back to the cabin courtesy of a Good Samaritan. Insult added to injury, the needed part was not available locally, keeping him off the water the last two days. (Cosmic retribution, revenge of the Eddie-god for the mid-week e-mail about "career years, record catches, and we don't miss you…"?) Up to that point, he caught three muskies.

I conceded those as more and bigger than my non-catch of the "summer that wasn't" but mused that perhaps the delivery and unpacking of my rod may have, for a few brief seconds, matched his excitement battling one of those fish. Aside from that, all I could do was mirror the annual rally cry (emphasis on cry) hurled by Chicago Cubs fans over the past century-plus: "Wait 'til next year!"

~ ~ ~ ~ ~

July 2011. Next year is here! Jo Ann promises the boys she'll keep me safe by ensconcing me in bubble wrap. Habits altered, I tread with care in all daily tasks. Accident aversion activities include the suppression of sneezes for fear of popping a blood vessel or pulling a muscle, negotiating stairways one step at a time to avoid taking a tumble, and sleeping on the floor so as not to fall out of bed (okay, I didn't, but I thought about it…) An April bout with a sore back (source unknown, possibly a result of thinking about sleeping on the floor?) resolves with rest and over-the-counter medication. I'm ready to go. Anticipation runs high.

In addition to last year's acquisition of a new rod and reel, a chunk of my previous fishing-less summer included customizing some musky lures with logos from my beloved 2010 Stanley Cup Champion Chicago Blackhawks. I believe, tongue-in-cheek, that the Canadian muskellunge will attack these lures with reckless abandon, upset that the prized hockey trophy does not reside with a team from their country, where the sport is believed to have originated.

Terry plans to pick me up at 7:00 Friday morning. The phone rings at 6:45 a.m. I assume this call will advise me that he's running late, not totally unexpected and certainly not a big deal. Oh, for something that simple.

"Bad news: A mile from the house I saw smoke coming from the wheel of the boat trailer and had to go back to the house."

After a brief pause digesting the news I reply, "Did you have your wheel bearings repacked?" Before he can answer I repeat, with more urgency, "Did you have your wheel bearings repacked?! You didn't have your wheel bearings repacked, did you?!" (I really don't know what that means, but over the years I've overheard that if you don't perform this standard trailer maintenance procedure on a regular basis your wheel can lock up, catch fire, or fall off, any of which will put a damper on the fishing plans at hand.)

In as calm and contrite a tone as Terry can muster, he replies, "I use a kit with a liquid lube that's supposed to last two years. The stuff has been in there only a year. I didn't see any evidence of a problem before I left, but it must have leaked out somehow."

One of those rare instances where *I'm* not making a tail-between-my-legs announcement, I must take advantage (a reach as it may be) of this possible "due diligence" lapse. My good friend, who teaches AP calculus and can build a house from scratch, has taken for granted a simple yet important travel checklist item.

"Jeez, Terry, the wheel bearings—they've got to be packed. They've got to be packed and repacked, rammed, slammed, and goddamn jammed full of whatever it is they're packed and repacked with." Letting the good natured rant soak in for a moment I close with, "So what time are you picking me up?"

Already having phoned a local boat dealer to prep them for priority service, Terry drops off the crippled rig and returns home to await the details of the time frame for repair based on the damage and parts availability. With a minimum delay of several hours in the offing, I pass the time conversing via e-mail with Chuck (who has chosen to decline the annual Canadian adventure invitation with excuses running the gamut from rebar-strong to single-ply toilet tissue thin), hoping to close out our cyberspace chess game that nears its conclusion. Upon relating the trailer problem, one of his reply e-mails includes the following: "You and Terry are destined for a fiery death as your rig explodes in flames at the Canadian border. Nah, that won't happen, but I'm thinkin' the karma for this trip is all wrong now. You should just stay home and pull weeds. Maybe prune some bushes and trees. Take up knitting...."

Several hours later, the unfortunate news arrives. The needed parts cannot be secured until next week, so we'll be making the trip without Terry's boat.

This year's six participants, Rich, Richie, Phil, Phil's friend Dave, Terry, and I will have to fish three people out of two boats instead of two people out of three. Everyone will need to be alert and cautious when flinging the big musky lures that dangle two or three trebles, six to nine needle-sharp hooks ready to snare a skull or put out an eye during a caster's forgetful moment. Pack some extra Right Guard for the doable but less than ideal nautical close quarters, too. In the category of dark clouds with a silver lining, a new excuse to explain potentially poor fishing results is primed and ready for use.

Terry picks me up at noon, pushing our typical 6 p.m. arrival in Fort Frances back to 10:30 p.m. The delay aces us out of several annual traditions. We will forego a tasty, reasonably priced meal with an international flair from *La Flambe* (substitute a mid-afternoon BMT from the Subway in Eau Claire), as well as an enjoyable evening of post-drive decompression libations while relaxing on the La Place Rendez-Vous patio that overlooks picturesque Sand Bay of Rainy Lake. Our late arrival also renders useless the view from our premium, lakeside room. Is that darkness a blackboard centered between the panels of floral print curtains? Hungry and road weary, we simply drop off to sleep.

Heavy rain splatters the windows of the Rendez-Vous restaurant as we savor a leisurely breakfast on Saturday morning. Watery waves of gray shroud the lake view. Varying intensities of the showers continue on the two-hour drive up Highway 502, but the precipitation subsides as our three vehicles, traveling in tandem, pull up to the Safeway store in Dryden to pick up supplemental grocery items. Light showers trickle during the final hour push to Vermilion Bay, but the sky lightens as we arrive at the launch. This fortunate timing means the six fishermen, our gear, and provisions will not be subject to a distasteful soaking. The absence of Terry's boat, however, makes the transport of people and supplies more difficult and time consuming. The task defaults to Rich's boat and the small, 16-foot aluminum Lund with a 10-horsepower motor stored at the launch dock.

The loading process complete, the ferry "barges" ride low and slow, the motors straining as they push their tonnage to the cabin peninsula. I welcome the deliberate ride, the extra time allowing me to fully absorb the surroundings—the water, islands, shorelines, big sky—all sorely missed with last year's Achilles absence. Memories rush forward as beams of the sun break through the clouds, spotlighting locations of muskies caught: "The Jugs," "The Brushpile," and "Doughboy." All's right with the world.

At least until we reach our destination. Mid-shin-high grass greets us. Mowing a path between the cabin, dock, and adjacent areas becomes the first order of business. A higher than usual number of deer flies, airborne thorns that love to use human heads as trampolines, confirms my belief (from my daily watch of weather maps and temperatures for this area spanning the past month) that the season lags by several weeks, more like late spring than midsummer. Excuse number two for below average fishing results stands ready on the runway.

No-see-ums

In support of the hypothesis of seasonal delay relative to the calendar, the no-see-ums, another earlier-in-the-season flying pest, feast with vigor on members of the group (finding me particularly tasty) both in the cabin as well as on the screened porch during what should be our relaxing "downtime." Also known as a biting midge, minute biting gnat, punkie, (or as I would growl, the "u-son-uva-bitch"), they deliver irritating discomfort with stealth, virtual invisibility, the bite simulating the sensation of a pin-prick followed by a radiating itch. They upstage even the mosquitoes (whose visibility and buzz can at least give the intended bitee a sporting chance) on this year's "most annoying insect" list.

The unwelcome harassment would have been more tolerable had not the muskies also become no see-ums. Biters or follows, we just didn't see many of –um, though the Saturday evening session starts on a good note for Rich. Fishing with Richie and Dave he corrals a 36-incher with a Double Cow Girl, twirling the lure's big blades in a watery, lasso-style figure-8 at boatside. Terry, Phil, and I pitch goose eggs.

Bad juju hovers Sunday, with our trolling motor malfunctioning as we prepare to fish the first spot of the morning. We lose almost an hour of fishing time while Terry trouble-shoots the problem to the foot petal and dismantles it in the bow. The mechanically-minded Phil assists with thoughts on a fix. I chip in by asking if there are any wheel bearings that need to be repacked, then shut up and stay out of their way. Their efforts result in success, unlike the day's quest for muskies that comes up empty for both our boat and Rich's.

Things look up on Monday, as Rich and Richie land 34- and 33-inchers respectively, and Phil breaks through with his first Alexandra Chain musky, boating a 32-incher on a top-water turbo-bait, a noisy, fish-calling contraption that agitates the top of the water like an eggbeater. On Tuesday, Dave just misses our self-imposed minimum-size-to-be-recorded cutoff of 30 inches, landing a 29.

With three days of extensive usage, I am pleased with the performance of the 8 ½-foot rod and Abu Garcia Revo Toro Winch 60 reel (not to be confused with Abu Garcia's Revo Toro Winch 61, Revo Toro Winch 50, Revo Toro Winch 51, Revo Toro 50, Revo Toro 50 HS, Revo Toro 51, Revo Toro 51 HS, Revo Toro 60, Revo Toro 60 HS, Revo Toro 61, Revo Toro 61 HS, Revo Winch 50, Revo Winch 51, Revo Winch 60, Revo Winch 61, Revo MGX, Revo Premier, Revo Inshore, Revo STX, Revo SX, Revo SX HS, or Revo S, and no, I didn't buy one of each to make sure I got the right one) that I also purchased while incapacitated last summer. The only thing to please me more would be to have a musky strike a lure thrown with my new set up.

"Hawg Chaser" rod in hand to fish Cobble Lake with Rich and Richie, today is the day. I catapult a monster cast to the back of a wood-studded bay with the assistance of the lengthy musky wand and the high capacity line spool on my new reel. The rod's extensive span also allows me to steer my TopRaider around the stick-ups and through narrow passages in clusters of lily pads. As the lure churns through one of these openings the surface erupts in watery rage. The bait disappears and the weight of the fish transmits through the line to the rod. The tug-o-war begins. Touché!

With my left hand cradling the low-profile ergonomically designed reel and my right hand gripping the rod blank in front of it, the positioning allows the engagement of my entire body for additional leverage in the battle. The easily adjustable star-drag on my reel is tightened down so the fish will not run into the tangles of timber. I work the 102-inch saber to and fro. Thrust! Parry! Lunge! Riposte! I move my right hand with ease from the rod to the reel's enlarged power-handle, turning it in short bursts to winch the wench. The battle turns in my favor. Now safely away from the forest of jagged hazards, I prevail against the final deep surges. The "Hawg Chaser," elevating to "Hawg Tamer," commands the fish to the surface and toward the net. Rich and Richie simultaneously chuckle, "What the hell is that?"

In another personal musky fishing first, the front treble hook of the lure protrudes through the back of what later measures as a 26-incher. Many fishermen have had the experience: Any fish foul-hooked in the back or near the tail can make runs with the full forward force of its body that conveys the misleading impression of a fish much heavier than that of a mouth-hooked specimen. How this fellow ended up with the hook in his back serves as another illustration of the mysteries of fishing physics. Popping the hook free from the 50-that-wasn't, perhaps he had an itch and couldn't believe his good fortune when the "backscratcher from heaven" came zipping by. During the little guy's release one of his gill rakers nicks my finger, drawing first blood of the trip. I have the bizarre hope that perhaps this will change our luck for the better.

Un-uh. Like Tuesday, Wednesday pitches the group another 30-inch or better shutout. It's also a fishless Thursday until one of the last stops of the evening. Shortly after 9 p.m., Terry, Phil, and I pull up to fish the "Big *Ass* Rock" shoreline. Over the years, several fish from this location succumbed to the customized 50th birthday bucktail given to me by Rich nearly a decade ago. Hoping to repeat past triumphs, I clip it on. We launch a salvo of casts as we inch along, neither the glory of a strike nor the tease of a follow to reward our early efforts.

With the boat approaching casting distance of the buttocks-shape rock, I fire off a long cast that lands near its outside edge. Another uneventful retrieve nearing completion, the lure comes into view some 15-feet from the boat with no fish following. At that instant my lower back becomes the target of a biting insect, species unknown. Instinctively releasing my hand from the reel handle to whack the out-of-sight aerial assailant to the eternity of bug hell, my lure stops dead and flutters into the watery darkness. A thorough and relieving multi-second scratch completed, I re-grip the reel handle. On the first turn, my rod bends with the distinctive weight and powerful movement that translates to "Musky!" Unsure (and not caring) if the fish inhaled the lure as it drifted downward or grabbed it when the blade began its forward motion upon the restart of the retrieve, a 30-incher, my only countable fish of the week, comes to net after a short battle. With an assist from my flying tormentors, I father a new bucktail retrieve method: "The Stop, Slap, and Scratch."

On Friday afternoon Rich nabs the group's last (and biggest) musky of the week, a nice 38-incher that follows and attacks a Double Cowgirl at boatside. Undeterred by a weed the lure snagged during a deep turn of the figure-8, this health-conscious musky, unlike most that would find a weed-trailing lure a turn-off, grabs the "salad" with the entrée and ends up as the co-star in a brief photo session.

The philosophy of the yin and yang twirls through the events of our week:

> The sun shines brightly most days as daytime highs hover in the pleasant, low 70s; clouds rule on the day three muskies accept our offerings.

> Big breakfasts go down with gusto and fill the stomach but cut short our time on the water, the start of most fishing days

delayed until almost noon. (I hear, loud and clear, the collective disbelieving gasp of fishermen everywhere.)

Hearty portions of gourmet dinners bring a smile to the face but mellow the mood for the evening musky hunt.

Wildlife sightings include eagles and eaglets, rabbits, beavers, does, and bucks (the latter two morning visitors to the property viewed in close proximity to the screened porch), and a playful fawn romping a Lake Whitney shoreline on several occasions. The muskies choose not to match the above-water activity level, becoming "no shows" at "show time."

Wildlife *non-sightings* (the no-see-ums) tag my arms, ankles, and shins with 170 "souvenir" welts. Some of the patterns created are heavenly, among them constellations and the Big Dipper. I'd like to take an Orion's-Belt-sander to them to relieve the itching. Repellent doesn't do the trick, the "Bite Stick" provides only temporary relief, and after a day or two the problem compounds as I can't distinguish between the itchiness of the old bites and the new.

Rich and members of his boat score a nice pre-sunset walleye bite most evenings, providing a fine meal and limits for home. Terry will not fish for them, preferring not to be "bothered." (It's a difficult call for me. Those precious, waning minutes of daylight scream "prime time!" for connecting with a muskellunge. On days when the fishing is tough, I've always said I'd rather not catch big fish than small ones.)

My Blackhawk customized lures look cool but the muskies apparently disagree, rarely taking a peek let alone smacking one. I can relate, with a puckish grin, that the lures seem to repel rather than attract the desired quarry.

Okay, time for the final 2011 debriefing. We've come full circle on the musky catch, our group landing a total of six for the week, a paltry one-per-man average not seen since our inaugural (and novice) effort in 1995. The arrow that tracks our catch-per-man slopes flaccidly downward since proudly peaking at a 12 musky average in 2001. What potential reasons loom to explain this disturbing trend?

Lush weedbeds disappeared, a possible victim of the invasive and ecologically disruptive rusty crayfish. Areas without weeds lack ambush points that conceal predators. The absence of weeds also eliminates the important first link in the food chain. Healthy weeds produce oxygen for phytoplankton, the food for baitfish, which in turn draw forage fish that ultimately sustain larger game fish. Or something like that.

Northern pike infiltrated the Alexandra Chain from an adjoining lake during a period of flooding a number of years ago. Pike compete with the muskellunge for spawning grounds (and "win" because the slimy bastards "do it" earlier in the season) and food supply, the negative impact mushrooming with the passage of time.

Late spring seasonal conditions keep the muskies away from their normal summer haunts. We fail (too lazy, too stupid, or both) to adjust.

Two boats, three in a boat. The middle man, physically lower, "in the hole," (vs. partners on the casting decks fore and aft) has a limited area in which to cast, reduced lure selection, and cramped quarters (console and seats in the way) for setting the hook and performing effective figure-8s to entice following fish to strike. A third boat also enables additional areas to be fished, perhaps with different methods and the possibility of uncovering a pattern to share with the group and enhance overall results.

Perhaps my cutting edge, high performance equipment may be ahead of its time for these lakes caught in fishing's Paleolithic era. (Nah.)

Too much time eating and relaxing instead of fishing: The evolution from "fishing vacation" to a "vacation during which we fish" roars ahead full speed.

Maybe we just suck.

At least we didn't die a fiery death at the Canadian border. So, where does it go from here? Maybe I'll take up knitting…

~ ~ ~ ~ ~

Maybe

July 2012. Maybe I *should* take up knitting. That pastime would certainly produce more tangible results—scarfs instead of scars. Knitting needles don't have sharp points like fish hooks, which as we know, frequently find their way into my epidermis. That angle, however, isn't an issue during this year's outing. In fact, a number of positives stitch their way through the week.

> The well-packed wheel bearings of Terry's trailer enjoy a smoke-free journey.
>
> Spring, this year arriving in the normal time frame, leaves me no-see-um bite-free. No see 'em, no feel 'em—thumbs up!
>
> The boats and motors operate flawlessly.
>
> Late on Saturday, the northern lights streak across a moonless sky to the haunting vocals of howling wolves in the not too distant distance.
>
> The tradition of culinary delights continues. Crafted by the chef du jour, each entrée includes an out-of-this-world gourmet sauce, marinade, or rub: lamb chops as thick as your fist; venison steaks; Buffalo wings; boneless pork chops as big as *two* fists; succulent beef tenderloin; fresh caught walleye fillets. Tasty sides, salads, and wine accompany all. My fishing companions enjoy this undertaking, their presentations worthy of a fine restaurant. They derive nearly as much satisfaction in the preparation as I do in the consumption.

The chef du jour for our weeklong adventure is defined as follows: anyone but me. Unless your palate craves Pop-Tarts, SpaghettiOs, or a packet of string cheese, I'm not your guy. Not proud to admit it, even grilled burgers, brats, and hot dogs are at risk under my watch.

Cousin Ben permanently banished me from the cabin kitchen years ago. With French fries on the menu for a burger meal accompaniment, I had poured some cooking oil into a frying pan sans heat and began filling it with potatoes I had peeled and sliced (without incident, as I recall). Ben peeked in to check on my progress, and the brief encounter that followed went something like this:

Ben: "What the hell are you doing?"

Ed: "What?"

Ben: "The oil needs to be hot before you … otherwise they'll just soak up the … just get the hell out of here."

Lesson learned, I do my part in other ways that my fishing companions find acceptable:

> I set the table for each meal: plates, salad bowls, napkins, goblets, and trivets. And utensils. Including knives. Sharp, steak knives. My history with hooks having taught me respect for sharp edges and points, I exercise great care with this seemingly simple task. The group only cares to see red liquid from a thick cut of beef prepared medium-rare, not flowing from one of my sliced digits.
>
> There is no food I won't eat. Nary a morsel remains on my plate at the conclusion of every meal. I further assist with the reduction of potential leftovers by consuming overages not plated in the initial sitting.
>
> I eat at a speed half the pace of most, doubling my delectation.
>
> My post-meal thanks and compliments often include the non-verbal: a hearty belch and a contented sigh.
>
> I shuttle the dirtied tools of consumption back to the kitchen, and along with crusted pots and pans, commence washing, drying, or both, then place them in their respective cabinets or drawers for a brief period of rest before their call to serve at the next feast.

Over the course of several years that include intensive study, design, and installation, Terry fulfills his dream of bringing the convenience of electricity, solar-power-style, to this isolated summer retreat. A shed he and Dianna built for the rooftop panels also house an inverter, deep-cycle batteries, controller, capacity meter, and other electro-scientific stuff that's as Greek to me as, well, Greek. Now, if the chefs sleep in, I can burn a bagel in a toaster instead of on the metal monkey bar camp stove toaster. And the cabin rooms, previously lit by the flame of wall-mounted propane sconces, now sport lamps and ceiling fixtures with compact fluorescent bulbs, all countrified with imitation antler lightshades and controlled by switches.

So, what about the fishing? If I must…

We begin the on-water festivities with a fishless Saturday evening. No problem—just a two-hour warm-up for the long week ahead. What about the shutout on Sunday, under enticingly overcast skies and temps in the mid-70s? We can blame a lack of wind, resulting in waters too calm for the finned predators to let down their guard. Or perhaps our habitual, lazy-late start time, today 10:45. Okay, we'll chalk it up to either—or both—of those.

Downcast at the end of a long day of unproductive casts, Terry revisits thoughts of recent years regarding the downward trend, now approaching a musky-catching drought. "Maybe we need to do something different. Maybe the fish hang in 20 feet of water now, instead of the old haunts. Maybe we should do some trolling. Maybe we need to cast Bull Dawgs toward the deep water. Maybe the small northern pike are upsetting the ecological dynamic. Maybe we should fish new spots. Maybe…" Of course, each-next-morning (-afternoon, and -evening) the routine never changes. Terry captains by a method that wraps responsibility in a Teflon tackle box, the standing joke repeated by his question each time we pull away from the dock. "So, where do you want to go?" With old habits dying hard (or not at all, actually) we race off to begin the "milk run" of tried and true spots of past glories.

Heavy rains blanket the area overnight. The precipitation lingers into Monday morning, though as intermittent sprinkles. Phil, arriving early this afternoon, will be accompanied by his younger brother Alec who will be participating in his first Canadian fishing excursion. We hope the timing of the pickup will coincide with a precipitation interlude.

My retirement body clock moving my status to "no longer first to wake," today Terry prepares our caffeine jump-start with the only method known by this cabin in its 60-plus year history: a 12-cup stainless steel stovetop percolator. With the recent run of wiring and electrical outlets, however, how long can it be before Mr. Coffee ventures into our piece of the Canadian Northwoods?

At 8:30, I slither out from beneath the mosquito net that tents my twin bed. Leg, arm, back, and shoulder muscles, individually or in combination, scream, ache, or whimper from yesterday's first full but fruitless day of pitching and retrieving monster musky baits that failed to rouse monster muskies—or any muskies, for that matter. Coffee beckoning, I shuffle to the kitchen in focused pilgrimage, pouring the fresh-perked java until it sloshes the mug's brim like ocean waves crashing a breakwater. Next stop—the porch.

Relaxed and semi-reclined on the living room couch, I pass an engrossed Terry as he scrolls through the pages of his Kindle, his sandaled feet resting on the edge of the thick square of varnished light pine held by angled, sturdy timber legs. The coffee table also holds his cup of hot breakfast blend, steam curling toward the nostrils of the impressively racked caribou head on the adjoining wall. Brown eyes shiny and alert (the caribou, not Terry), it's as if the imposing mount has come alive, sniffing a share of the pleasing aroma.

After exiting the cabin, I nestle in the cushioned porch armchair closest to the vintage wooden door that separates the two spaces. Both hands cup the warmth of the ceramic mug, my index fingers outlining the pine trees, bear, and moose that silhouette atop an orange background of a rising or setting sun. Lifted to my lips with increasing frequency, sips of the precious elixir fuel my mind as it lilts through green, brown, and blue washes of trees, water, and sky, accompanied by the non-sounds of cool morning calm.

"Oh my God ... look at the size of this one." A voice from nowhere wafts through the 9 a.m. air, thoughtlessly interrupting the leisurely movement of my mind's eye view of nature's kaleidoscope. The matter-of-fact tone of the words, whose content could certainly evoke greater emotion and volume, strikes me as odd. What the hell? ... Who the hell?

SKERRRRPLUSHHHHHHH!

Just out of sight, behind a stand of tall reeds and heavily branched pines on the north edge of the property, the succession of words and violence of rapidly displaced water announces a successful hookup. Hurriedly making my way down the porch stairs into the yard, I scurry a course that will allow me to glimpse the goings-on. My arrival coincides with the victor raising his prize from the landing net. Seconds later, the flash of his partner's camera captures the scene: a smiling, gray-bearded angler, red and black flannel shirt and red baseball cap matching the color of their boat, grasps the musky in a horizontal hold. The well-proportioned fish extends comfortably beyond the width of the man's shoulders. Occupied with the tasks at hand, including the fish's prompt release, I am certain my inconspicuous presence has gone unnoticed.

I return to the porch, eyes still trained on the lake, waiting for the boat to come into view when the fishermen resume their path of shoreline casts. Cooled coffee now consumed in gulps rather than sips, I call to my host through the closed door. "Terry..."

Waiting for a simple acknowledgement before continuing, I hear the muffled words, "Get your own coffee."

Temporarily derailed, I shout back, "I'm perfectly capable of pouring my own damn coffee."

"*Are* you?" he retorts without hesitation. Expected and accepted, good-natured barbs fly with frequency any time of day or night. In an attempt to redirect our conversation to its intended path, I open the cabin door, step inside, and reply, "Are *you* interested in the 40-inch class musky that just got plucked out of your backyard?"

His interest piqued, Terry rises and moves quickly, uncharacteristic for him at this time of the morning. He steps past me onto the porch as the red boat slides into view from behind the thick greenery. Seated fishermen plunk casts, the type of lures indistinguishable but definitely smaller than the baits we throw, within inches of the shoreline. Their bow mounted trolling motor pulls the boat forward, slow and silent. Unsuccessful on the short stretch, the Alumacraft again passes out of our line of sight, behind the boathouse and original cabin standing elevated on the point. The boat's next appearance will be in the bay containing our pier, with Terry's 17-foot navy blue and beige Lund tied to one side, and the 16-foot, red aluminum Lund to the other.

My curiosity already having gotten the better of me, Terry verbalizes my unspoken thought process. "Why don't you go down and see what you can find out when they come around the corner." And not part of my plan, he additionally commands, "And while you're down there, bail last night's rain out of the small Lund so it'll be ready when we pick up Phil and Alec."

My middle finger prominently forward on the hand cradling the almost empty mug, I present it to Terry, replying, "Fill 'er up, your majesty."

I hustle down to the pier, kneel next to the small Lund filled front to back with eight inches of rainwater, grab the half-gallon milk carton bailer floating behind the driver's bench seat, and begin waterfalling rhythmic scoops over the gunnel into the lake. Moments into the task, the Alumacraft rounds the corner. The fishermen hold their casts upon spotting me but speed their boat's pace, presumably to resume their lure lobbing as soon as possible. I pause from my chore to offer a greeting and try to ascertain the details of the catch before they move out of earshot. "Mornin' guys. How's it going?"

The fish-catcher, smile peeking from beneath his beard, replies as his voice trails off, the distance between us widening. "From the looks a things, better n you, I'd say! Just got a 41-incher around the corner." I raise the milk jug in congratulatory acknowledgement while exclaiming, "Nice!" My task as human bilge pump complete, I return to the cabin.

Terry anxiously queries, "So, what's the scoop?"

"I don't know...40, 50 gallons maybe," I reply.

"The fish..."

"Maybe we should be getting earlier starts on our fishing day."

"How big was it?"

"Maybe we should try some new spots."

"Here's your coffee refill."

"41 inches."

Moderate rain returns, without the lightning and thunder that would, without question, keep us under roof. Now, only Terry's recently growing reluctance to ply our pastime in the midst of raindrops might keep us from venturing out. Delicately broaching the subject, I query, "So, are we going out, or are you afraid you'll melt?"

In a tone tossing the decision back my way, he offers, "We can if you want, Dorothy."

In an effort to link the iffy weather with fish-catching potential, I reply, "I have a note in my files, that unlike you, the muskies become active in the rain. Ben caught two, both over 40 inches, within ten minutes of each other on a rainy day in aught three."

Not missing a beat, Terry comes back with, "And do your files indicate how many *you* caught that day?"

Not to be outdone, I quickly reply, "Yeah. As many as I'm catching standing on this porch. Suit up, Scarecrow. Let's go."

Our pickup of my cousins scheduled in two hours, staying local to fish Forest Lake is the logical plan. A few minutes hence, we're pulling away from the dock. Over the din of the motor and the drops splattering our raingear, Terry shouts, "So, where do you…"

Before he can complete the question, I call back, "Head over to 'The Power Line.' But instead of just casting the 50 feet on either side, we're going to work the entire shoreline west to 'Doughboy.'" He nods, putting the boat on a course directly across from the cabin where a power line, strung on timber utility poles lining a clear-cut path through the trees, enters the water on its tubular trek along the lake bottom to provide electricity to Forest Lake Lodge and a cluster of privately owned cabins tucked into the trees along the southern shoreline.

Within a dozen casts, the large twin blades and pulsating tinsel skirt of my Double Cowgirl draws a follow, but the fish turns off during the figure-8. In the first pass along the lengthy stretch of shoreline, two more muskies in the 40-inch class come up for a look, one of them taking a swipe at the lure but missing the hooks. Pleased with the sightings, Terry returns to our starting point to make another pass. Well past the actual power line and at a point beyond where he would have stopped working the area, Terry hooks and lands a 39-incher. Likely one of the previous followers, the fish succumbs to a small, twin-bladed bucktail with a skirt streaked with yellow and black hair.

The ferry of Phil, Alec, and their provisions follows shortly thereafter and flows without a hitch under cloudy but dry skies. After unpacking, Alec nicely acclimates to the kitchen, whipping up a gourmet treat with shrimp and approaching-the-size-of-hockey-puck scallops. The leisurely meal concluded and feeling the part of fatted calves, we force ourselves to tackle the final two hours of daylight on the water. As we back away from the dock, I'm prepared for the question launched my way like clockwork. "So where…"

Index finger lined up with a cabin on a point opposite the "Power Line" shore, I cut short his stock query, barking above the rumbling motor, "The

Nichols place." A well-maintained homestead, the water around it has a lot going for it, including its close proximity to deep water, a dock, reeds, and a small cutback bay with a smattering of lily pads and large boulders. I'm not sure why we don't give it an occasional try. On second thought, I do. Terry has never caught nor even seen a musky there, thus removing it from his Forest Lake list of locations to fish. Near a deadfall entering the water where the bay meets the main lake, Terry nails a 33-incher with the same bucktail inhaled by the 39- earlier in the day. Maybe there's something to this "trying new places" game plan; at least for my boat mate.

Or maybe not. Tuesday draws another blank for our foursome.

On Wednesday morning, I pull out the lake maps in search of inspiration, anticipating Terry's decision deferral. We rarely fish the large, deep lakes of the Chain that leapfrog to the east: Cobble, Big Boulder, and Little Boulder. With a maximum depth of 105 feet in Big Boulder, these lakes lack the shallow cover of the others that capture our casts on a regular basis. The intimidating surface area and depth give the fish further advantage in the fisherman-initiated game of hide and seek. Other reasons also play into our angling neglect of these waters, including the vigilant negotiation of a shallow, stump-filled, propeller-eating channel; increased travel time and gasoline consumption; and last and most importantly, Terry's historic lack of success there.

Before he can pose the "So where do you want to…" question, I answer it. "We're going to the far end of Little Boulder and work our way back. I'll pick all the spots. If we don't catch anything, at least we'll not be catching fish in different places, looking at different scenery." I sense a "not happy with the choice" for the previously noted reasons, but also a bit of relief that today's success or failure rests squarely on my aching shoulders. The three lakes we'll be fishing today offer sights on a grander scale. Sheer cliffs, heavily forested shorelines with higher elevations, more and larger islands, and massive bald rock outcroppings all provide additionally pleasing visuals. And if we don't catch any fish today, at least the sun warms a beautiful day for a boat ride, a silky summer breeze refreshing the skin as it pushes the 75-degree air.

A half-hour after departure we arrive at Little Boulder, proceeding to the farthest shore on the east end. We begin fishing where a flow of water spills down the face of a smooth, six-foot boulder. A narrow, nonnavigable stream, sourced from adjacent Augite Lake, meanders downward through a hundred-yard stretch of rock and trees until it bubbles into Little Boulder. As we cast this area, then another shoreline and a bay connecting them, my "perfect" week remains uninterrupted by the strike of a musky. Next up—a cluster of four islands, neatly aligned as corners of a square.

Time for a break from throwing the heavy and hard-pulling Double Cowgirl, I change to a 9-inch perch-pattern Suick, a slender slice of wood but a fraction of the weight of the chunky, double-bladed spinner with a two-layer skirt. Terry circumnavigates the islands with masterful precision. The shadow of a deep follow eyes my bait, but the body language of the stealth submarine speaks curiosity rather than hunger. As we make a pass along the final side of the "square," I drop a cast into the narrowing of the two islands closest to the lake proper, landing it equidistant between them. Imparting action with the downward motion of the rod, the lure stops dead on the second pull. My arms, along with the upper half of my body, turn quickly to the right, the momentum of the move to drive home the hooks. A short tussle foreshadows a short fish, a 32-incher coming to net. But I'm on the board.

Later, in Big Boulder, I land a bonus 16-inch smallmouth on the same Suick. Casted tight to the point of an island, the startled fish strikes instantly. The splashdown of the lure, its length more than half the size of the bass, likely triggered a reaction of self-defense or anger rather than a miracle meal of manna dropping from the heavens. The musky and the bass, our total catch for the day, does not disappoint me. My lakes and location selections validated, it might be two more than I'd have caught on a lately-gone-sour milk run of the Forest, Whitney, Edward, Indian Lake quartet. Maybe.

On Thursday, we pick up a new kitchen stove in Dryden, hauling it back to the cabin via vehicle, boat, and the strain of our backs. Phil and Terry complete a successful installation, taking me up on my offer to assist by staying out of the way. "No, Ed, there are no wheel bearings to pack on a stove," Terry comments in my direction. He and I catch as many fish during our errand as we do in the hours spent on the water, though Phil breaks through that evening with a 35-incher on a boatside figure-8 of a top-water lure at the "Godfish Hole."

~ ~ ~ ~ ~

May the holes in your net be no larger than the fish in it.
—Irish Blessing

Landing Net Nuggets

Fish don't like nets—seeing them, or being in them. How inconsiderate, in view of the time and money we've invested in the research and purchase of this critical-to-the-catch tool. Landing any fish but especially a big, toothy one can be tricky business. With musky hookups few and far between, coordination between an angler fighting the fish and his or her net-person weighs critical in bringing these prized moments to a successful conclusion.

Advances in landing net composition and construction have tracked with the needs arising from the increased popularity of musky fishing. They've come a long way since the (not so) "good ol' days" when gaff hooks, billy-clubs, and revolvers were among the tools used to subdue a hooked behemoth. Other than a bump in the road with the "cradle" (a nice idea but a reality rivaling the Edsel) it's been onward, upward, and outward. Though certainly not on a par with the discovery of the Higgs boson "God particle," NASA rover Curiosity's historic soft-landing on Mars, or face replacement surgery, improvements to nets in a world of kinder, gentler musky hunters who promote catch and release are still significant.

Flimsy aluminum frames have given way to "aircraft quality" aluminum alloys molded for strength. Ergonomically configured, kiss goodbye any concerns about wrist and elbow tendonitis or carpal tunnel syndrome from landing all those big muskies. Hoops in round shapes have been joined by teardrops and pentagons, all available in sizes capable of scooping Shamu. Handles telescope with yoke locking pins. Nets of yesteryear collapsed under the weight of a big musky; today's collapse by design, for easy storage. Rubber-dipped, weighted, anti-tangle, knotless mesh bags, some with "holding pen" flat bottoms, reduce the likelihood of damage to fins and the fish's protective slime coating. They allow our catch to remain in the water during the delicate and dicey task of removing hooks, reducing stress on both fish and fishermen.

Fact: Most musky hunters have been on both ends of an "Oh crap!" netting experience. These can play out in several gut-wrenching ways. Perhaps the net-bag catches on the not-well-placed tip of a rod, handle of a reel, or hook of a lure. Or, if your boat is neatly organized, perhaps the unwieldy bag will snare the edge of a windshield, throttle, or cleat. If you've cleared those hurdles and you're poised at boatside, don't fool yourself to thinking you've got it "in the bag."

As your partner guides the fish, head first, toward the waiting net, the musky may have saved its best for last: an unanticipated, lightning change of direction can put the landing in jeopardy. Net in hand, to reach or pull back—that is the question—with only a split second to decide. (By the way, whatever your decision, it will be wrong.) To lunge and miss puts the 'llunge in the driver's seat. A prolonged open water fight may include runs, turns, and jumps, any one of which may pop the hooks free. Or worse, if a treble snares the hoop or the netting near it, the musky can leverage the mishap, twisting, contorting, and writhing its way to freedom.

We've all experienced both sides of "landing net hell." If your partner is holding the net (or should be), tolerance is encouraged. Though we may never forget an opportunity lost, we must forgive. Anglers in (fiber)glass boats shouldn't throw downrigger balls.

~ ~ ~ ~ ~

Friday. The last hurrah. Without the hurrah. Our final day plays out musky-less. Alec will go home without his first musky. Phil and I don't fare much better, each of us catching only one for the week.

I did, however, hook one along the "Power Line" shore. (Yes, we now beat it to a froth, daily.) The fish grabs my Double Cowgirl as I juice the speed just before turning the first loop of a figure-8. "Got one!"

The boatside eruption would typically stir Terry into immediate action—rapidly reeling in his lure, setting down his rod, and hopping to the center of the boat from the front casting deck to ready the landing net. Although my focus centers on controlling the fish, the lack of noise and movement from my boat partner is curious. And reason for concern. Or panic. Only a single hook of the back treble, imbedded in the corner of the fish's mouth, maintains our connection. As I ease the fish to the perfect netting position, only one thing is missing—the net. Seconds feel like minutes. I hold my breath, waiting … waiting … waiting …

My partner missing in action (though a mere 10 feet from me), the upper hand in the tug-o-war takes an ugly though not unexpected turn. The musky leaps out of the water, twists a somersault, and throws the hook before splashdown. Unencumbered, it bursts past the outboard, freedom regained.

My eyes lock on the spot where the final, rapid sway of its tail propelled it to the depths. I utter a hollow, "Terry…?"

"Sorry," his mumbled response.

"Where…?

"I couldn't move."

"What? … Why?"

"My pants were around my ankles."

Taking a few seconds to digest his words, I chuckle, "I don't think I want to know. No, I *know* I don't want to know. Maybe you should be fishing with Pee-wee Herman."

To further explain, he continues, "This wasn't the best day to be out here in cutoffs. The horseflies have been doing a number on my ankles, so I was in the process of putting on my rain pants."

The picture now complete, I reply, "Pants around the ankles ... You've broken new ground, my friend, with an excuse likely never heard in the annals of unsuccessful musky netting."

Coming to grips with the opportunity lost, I conclude the discussion. "Maybe it's time to call it a week."

And maybe next year we should try Lake of the Woods. Maybe.

~ ~ ~ ~ ~

The charm of fishing is that it is the pursuit of what is elusive but attainable, a perpetual series of occasions for hope.
—John Buchan

Lake of the Woods - 2013

Who knows how many casts remain in this body in decline: the arthritic hands, the neck knifing pain with every head turn, the chronically sore lower lumbar, the nerve-damaged legs, the never the same snapped-like-a-wishbone Achilles attached to the now-toothpick calf, the eyes with multiple retina repairs seeing through a permanent swirling haze, the hearing impaired ears in need of aids, the arrhythmic heartbeat...

With my "aging clock" shifting into hyperdrive and the details of a coveted yet-to-be-caught 50-inch musky still absent from my journal, I approached Terry about the possibility of spending the week of our Canadian musky hunt at Lake of the Woods instead of the Alexandra Chain. Big water, conducive to growing and supporting trophy specimens by virtue of its expansive area, structure, and forage, could tilt the odds of such a catch in my favor.

Over the past sixteen years, Terry and Dianna embarked on numerous trips to Lake of the Woods with their friends Dan and Barb. During those outings, Dan and Dianna scored 50-inch-plus muskies, and all four anglers landed muskies in the upper 40-inch class. With a pair of 45-inchers, I'm anxious for a shot at a new personal best. After reviewing our calendars, Terry and I agree upon a mid-July venture of 2½ days at Lake of the Woods that will precede a week at his cabin, where Rich, Phil, and Rick will join us.

Known for on-time or fashionably late arrivals, Terry surprises (scares the hell out of) me as I do a double take after catching a glimpse of his face through the kitchen window, staring Lurch-like in the early morning shadows—a half-hour early. Visible behind him, parked on the street in front of the house is his SUV with a new, sleek, black and gray Lund in tow, ready for its maiden voyage. My luggage and fishing gear neatly stacked in the garage the previous evening, the loading process quickly completes.

As in trips past, the first four hours to Eau Claire, where we gas up and have a bite to eat, fly by as we catch up on life's goings-on. Unlike trips past, a dozen or so miles short of Eau Claire, Terry says, "Uh, the 'miles left on this tank of gas' gauge is reading five miles."

"Excuse me?" I ask in reply.

"Towing this bigger boat is cutting down our gas mileage."

Here we go ... things were running too smoothly. I was hoping this trip didn't peak when you showed up ahead of schedule this morning."

"There's usually a gallon or two in reserve, so I don't think it'll be a problem."

"You don't think. You don't think ... *that's* the problem."

"Should I get off at the first exit or go to the last one, where we usually stop? It's only a few more miles up the road."

"Take however much rope you need to hang yourself. I'll be staying with the vehicle if you have to huff it with a gas can."

Terry tempts fate—and wins—pulling off at the final Eau Claire exit. We fill the tank with gas (later calculating a cushion of three gallons remained) and our stomachs with Subway sandwiches. The remainder of the drive pleasantly uneventful, we arrive at our overnight accommodations in Baudette, Minnesota, just south of the U.S.-Canadian border.

The next morning, we cross and then travel about an hour to our launch point, where we begin the 20-minute boat ride to the island that will house us for the next several days. Under sunny skies, we travel into waves roiled by a northwest headwind. As his new rig cuts through the chop, an occasional spray of water leapfrogs the hull and windshield. The droplets splatter my sunglasses and tingle the exposed skin of face and hands in a refreshing way. Terry utilizes a GPS unit that will guide him to our destination across expanses of open water and through the clustered mazes of islands. More passenger than co-pilot, I kick back to relax and enjoy these early moments, touching, touched by the airy Canadian surroundings.

My thoughts drift back to the first trip to Kipling Island and Mr. Weston's reliance on landmarks to negotiate the route sans technology. With Terry at the helm, along with his knowledge of locations where he and his fishing partners caught muskies, Lake of the Woods seems less intimidating than it did when I fished it as a novice.

A final turn brings us to the island—a modest several acres, like Kipling Island—housing New Moon Lodge. The owners and some of the camp helpers greet us as we pull up to the dock, securing the boat and toting our luggage to the cabin. With several larger groups already in camp, Terry and I have been assigned the "Honeymoon Cabin." I'm ready to return to Baudette, but a quick check of the cabin, crimson colored like all the camp buildings, reveals two double beds, neither decorated with rose petals or chocolates, and no bottle of Dom Perignon on the nightstand between them. Deal breaker averted and monster muskies waiting, it's time to go fishing.

With my years of musky fishing experience, outfitted with the proper equipment, and a seasoned partner-guide, I'm feeling good about my chances to do battle with a big one from the big lake. Confidence builds in the early going as muskies follow at several locations, but none finds our offerings or boatside figure-8s irresistible and none approach trophy size. Over the course of the afternoon and evening, Terry catches three small pike, the sum of their length totaling that one musky we seek. As Scarlett O'Hara mused at the end of *Gone with the Wind*, "… tomorrow is another day."

We wake to cloudy skies and a distinctive shift in wind direction. The low light, wind-wave action, and falling barometer of an approaching storm often triggers aggressive behavior. Oh, and it might make the musky fishing better, too. Hopeful of improving our results, we begin the day on the water traveling in a new direction. As we pass several guided camp boats, one of the guides extends his arms wide above his head signifying a member of his boat caught a muskellunge of considerable size. Yes! The muskies are moving! (One less biscuit at the breakfast table and perhaps we'd have fished that spot first…)

Anticipation high, we work several areas—alas, without success. Positive vibes fade as the sky further blackens to the point where safety becomes a concern. Bolts of lightning and the rumble of thunder urge us to hightail it back to camp. Our return well timed, sheets of rain begin blanketing the lake seconds after we scamper up the hill to the refuge of the cabin. The storm rages through lunchtime, the last drops plinking the cabin roof around 1:30 p.m. As the sun peeks through breaks in the clouds, we return to the water.

At our first stop, Terry bags the first musky fishing out of his new boat, a short but chunky 28-incher. Now to find one twice that size…. Fish at the next two locations also take a liking to Terry's bucktail. Unfortunately, they're "hammer-handle" northern pike.

Our next move requires a 15-minute cruise to a complex of tightly grouped islands that Terry and previous fishing companions dubbed "The Matrix." Adjoining large expanses of deeper open water, certain wind directions (as the one blowing today) can result in a current flow that pushes baitfish through the area. In addition to an easy meal, stands of weeds add another feature muskies find to their liking. Our first pass along an interior shoreline yields a few small follows. Terry then directs the boat toward a cut between two islands, the alley perpendicular to the shoreline just worked.

Fully aware that these two days represent the pinnacle of my life's big fish quest, Terry holds his cast and points his rod off the starboard, wanding it horizontally. "We've taken some nice fish here," he says, "cast in that direction," graciously offering me sole ownership of the prime fish-catching real estate. I appreciate the gesture. My senses sharp with heightened awareness, I nod and begin fanning long casts with a twin-bladed spinner. The large nickel blades churn the water in front of its black and rainbow tinsel tail that pulses with each turn of the reel handle. I vary the retrieve speed during each cast in hopes of finding a cadence that will entice a local brute to bite. Terry, working the trolling motor from the bow, alternates casts to the port side and directly ahead of the boat. The rhythmic "plop-ploop" of his top-water lure abruptly stops with a water-thrashing commotion at boatside. "Got one! It's big!"

Fire drill underway, I retrieve my lure with rapid cranks, toss down my rod, and grab the net, spinning the handle to uncurl the net bag. Terry holds tight as the musky bulldogs short but powerful runs, eventually coaxing it back toward the boat. He reemphasizes, "It's big!" My glimpses of the struggling fish and Terry's declarations lead me to believe the fish is big. So as not to interrupt his concentration, I refrain from wisecracking "I heard you the first time," "Don't wet your pants," or "So?" As those thoughts pass, Terry muscles the musky to boatside and I net it without incident.

It *is* a big fish. "That's a big fish," I confirm matter-of-factly, juxtaposing his excitement.

Terry unhooks it in the security of the net and then struggles to lift it into the boat. His words eek out in short breaths: "Geez … this is a big fish … I can barely…"

Measuring stick in one hand and camera in the other, I speak a few words of encouragement. "For chrissakes…"

"It's big…"

"You're bigger, damn it. Get it in here."

"It's heavy…"

"Whimpering like a little girl..." I mutter in a tone loud enough to ensure my fishing partner can hear it.

The big fish measures 47 inches. The thick muskellunge quickly photographed and released, I extend a congratulatory hand to Terry. He shakes it, saying, "That was supposed to be your fish."

"Thanks," I reply, "I know." Unable to hold a straight face, I continue, "But I'm out here looking for a *big* fish."

"Dog," Terry says, using the word we've tossed back and forth at each other since our college days.

"There's got to be a *real* fish out here with my name on it."

"I'll let you know when I see a 50-incher with 'asshole' stamped on its side," Terry retorts.

We cast adjacent areas for a few more minutes before moving on. Next stop, "Terry's Turn." Another site of success for Terry and companions on trips past, like "The Matrix" this area boasts multiple structures: deep water, a tiny island, and an irregular shaped reef extending from it. I hope it's Ed's turn at "Terry's Turn." Similar to our last stop, Terry points toward the structure. He says, "I'll move us along the edge of the reef and face of the island. Cast toward them. Let me know when you need the net."

I appreciate his optimism. With hopes of lightning striking again in the now sunlit late afternoon, I'm throwing the same type of tail-rotating top-water lure used by Terry at "The Matrix." Through each retrieve, I'm poised and ready for the surface explosion that will take *my* breath away. Cast after cast gurgles over the shallow rocks. Terry casts a Suick jerkbait in the opposite direction, toward the deeper water.

As we reach the far tip of the island, a fish strikes.

"I got one!" Terry shouts.

Rewind. Repeat. Rerun. Recur. Rejoice. He's again rewarded, this time with a plump 42-incher.

"Dog..." I drone with the next round of congratulations. "I know, I know, that was supposed to be my fish. This isn't working out the way you planned, is it? Or *is it?*"

Terry shrugs his shoulders as he smiles. "Too small for you. You should be thanking me."

It was our last fish of the day. Tomorrow is another day. Tomorrow is the last day.

Saturday dawns warm, sunny, and calm—a musky fisherman's bane. The good news is that I've got my excuse if I don't score. In addition, of course, to blaming Terry for leading my casts astray.

We revisit all the haunts of the previous two days—and a few more. One by one, they pitch zeroes. By midday, the summer sun scorches. I'm struggling to maintain concentration, fighting the urge to simply go through the motions. On top of my standard aches and pains, the two days of pitching large lures has exacted an additional toll on my arms, shoulders, and back.

Terry directs the boat along the shoreline of an island he'd never fished before. The clock winds down, hope dwindling. Then, at 3 p.m., it happens—a tug. I pull back to set the hook, bracing for a forceful reply that will answer with anger and substance. The anticipated response not forthcoming, I continue to reel against minimal resistance. Is the fish swimming directly toward the boat? Is this competitor saving its best for last, a surprise tactic in the offing? What gives in this watery game of cat and mouse?

The questions answer as a northern pike, several inches longer than my 9-inch lure, surfaces at boatside. I utilize long-nose pliers to unhook the fish as it rests in the water.

The task completed, I remark to Terry, "The size of your catches was trending downward, so I thought I'd save you the inconvenience of dealing with the little fellow. That was your fish, you know."

"Thanks," he replies, "and you didn't even have to tell me what direction to make my casts."

Although our tradition of naming the lake location is reserved for the first person to catch a 30-inch-plus musky there, I take pause and recount the events of this big fish hunt, commenting, "I think I'll name this spot 'My Musky Destiny.'"

The trip would end with the little pike my only fish of the day, the only catch of my long-awaited return to Lake of the Woods. Although I didn't connect with a monster muskellunge, the one often swimming through my dreams, the past days played out pleasantly enough: enjoying my favorite pastime, with a good friend, landscaped in the beauty and solitude of woods and water.

Oh, I'll keep trying, health and other circumstances permitting. One never knows what the next outing, what the next lake may hold. That's the fascination, the mystery, the allure one experiences as a fisherman. Hope and anticipation reign eternal. The consummate fisherman *knows* that no matter how big the catch, a bigger one, the legend of the lake, swims the shadowy depths. Should my dream not come to fruition, if that is my muskellunge fishing destiny, I'm okay with that.

Part Five
Favorite Things

I used to like fishing because I thought it had some larger significance. Now I like fishing because it's the one thing that probably doesn't.
—John Gierach

Places, Sights, Sounds, Smells, and Other Stuff

Not just things I like. Things I really, really like. Like...

...the walk, steps methodical and measured, from the front door to the end of the driveway to pick up the newspaper, delivered daily. Because of the early hour at which I rise, darkness still rules the morning. The season matters not. Mother Nature's greeting sways hot to warm to cool to frigid, dry to rain or snow. All are welcome. Perhaps rustling leaves will disturb the silence, and that in a most pleasing way. Under cloudless skies, the moon often lights my way, peeking through the maze of branches that fountain from huge oaks. Stars and planets may also be visible: The Milky Way, Mars, Venus, Saturn, Jupiter. I smile a silent hello to whatever the heavens may offer.

...the smell of freshly ground coffee.

...Jo Ann and I, settling in on most Sunday evenings to view a DVD episode of our friend, Lieutenant Columbo.

...the number 44.

...the approach of a thunderstorm.

...our at-home fondue dinners celebrating special occasions, the menu including steak, chicken, shrimp, zucchini, cauliflower, broccoli, mushrooms, tempura batter, steak sauce, sweet and sour sauce, and a bottle of Asti.

...at lakeside, the hauntingly beautiful call of the loon reverberating through the silent night.

...the Sunday morning ritual of reading the newspaper while sipping a bottomless cup of coffee. Winter in the living room, the other three seasons find me on the porch, its screened frames filled with a backyard forest.

...root beer floats.

...the northern lights.

...games of Risk, with a full complement of the The Fabulous Maretti Brothers seated around the table.

...various shades of green.

...bald eagles.

...my fishing headgear—"Indiana Jones" hat (2001) and Philadelphia Eagles cap (1994). (Note: Not because the team from the "City of Brotherly Love" is my NFL favorite but rather because of the colors (green and silver) and eagle-in-flight logo.)

...Chicago Blackhawk games, all the better now televised in high definition. And Sunday afternoons with the Bears.

...my Timex Expedition watch. Worn daily and true to the manufacturer heritage, it's had the hell beat out of it over the decades and "keeps on tickin'."

...the appetite-inducing aroma of Jo Ann's homemade spaghetti gravy.

...the hilly, treed terrain of Jo Daviess County, a treasure in the otherwise flat farmland of northern Illinois.

...the Syposiums.

...the front window view of sparkling snowflakes on a moonlit night, juxtaposed against the fireplace glow, setting the cozy scene for our Christmas Eve custom, my favorite movie, *It's A Wonderful Life*. ("Sentimental hogwash!")

...fishing. At Emerald Lake. And in Canada. Or anywhere. Any time.

~ ~ ~ ~ ~

One fish. Two fish. Red Fish. Blue fish. Black fish. Blue fish. Old fish. New fish. This one has a little star. This one has a little car. Say! What a lot of fish there are.
—Dr. Seuss

Emerald Lake Summary

To my audience: For those of you who have made it this far, thank you very much. If you're as fatigued from reading fishing stories as I am from writing them, I'll save us both a lot of time and me a lot of effort by summarizing the "game" fish caught out of my boat (self and guests) from Emerald Lake. Bass the targeted species for 99% of the hours fished, here are the 20 year totals from 1993 to 2013:

Largemouth bass	3,240	(largest 22 1/2 inches)
Smallmouth bass	7	(largest 14 inches)
Walleye	99	(largest 25 inches)
Tiger musky	43	(largest 44 inches)

And, several brief highlights:

I caught bass on five consecutive casts.

Jo Ann landed bass of 17, 20, and 21 inches on consecutive casts.

I netted 35 inches of bass on one cast: gluttonous 15- and 20-inchers simultaneously and successfully attacked a multi-hook plastic worm.

Within a two-hour period, Jo Ann caught bass measuring 16 ½, 17, 17 ½, 18, 18, 18, 20, and 21 inches. In that same session, Eddie landed largemouth of 16, 18, 20, 20½, and 22 inches. (Giddily busy assisting my "clients" with netting, photographing, and releasing the catch, I managed to land a solitary 14-incher.)

Rich and I averaged one bass every 2 ½ minutes during the first hour of an outing.

At 22 inches, my biggest bass weighed 6-pounds 1-ounce. (Yes, it was one of the rare occasions I used the digital scale.)

You're welcome.

Jo Ann and me with some samples from Emerald Lake.
(Hey, where's that life vest???)

Wheels

Some automobiles, shiny and new, were purchased directly off a dealer's lot. Others, with their better years behind them and acquired from immediate or extended family, spent time with us before their final road trip to the auto graveyard. Not necessarily in the order of their procurement:

'66 Ford Mustang (used). Acquired from Jo Ann's dad after our marriage in 1974, I failed to recognize this classy sauterne gold beauty as a classic. My tunnel vision saw limited trunk size that did not lend itself to hauling voluminous quantities of fishing gear.

'67 Chevy Chevelle (used). As Dad and Uncle Ben (both previous owners) used to growl regarding the marine blue bomber, "It's got guts." When seated behind the wheel, as a blessing and a curse, its lack of power steering and power brakes resulted in a great workout. This vehicle is also remembered for carrying the multi-day stench resulting from an unfortunate incident involving a skunk's ill-timed attempt to cross the road as we motored, in the pre-dawn, to a fishing outing on the Chain O' Lakes.

'75 Chevy Nova (new). Burgundy with black vinyl interior, this two-door coupe was the first new car after our marriage.

'75 Plymouth Duster (used). It liked hot, dry weather, true to its color name: Sahara beige. It often refused to start (or died when it did) in cool, damp weather. Jesus Chrysler!

'80 Chevy Chevette (new). Sporty black over gold paint job, raised white lettering on tires, and 74 horses. Can you say glue factory?

'80 Ford Granada Station Wagon (used). This gray wagon turned my mood gray, almost living up to the Ford acronym, *F*ix *O*r *R*epair *D*aily.

'82 Ford Escort (used). Periodic transmission issues plagued this little red rogue frequently escorted to the dealership. It was our last experiment with a Ford—another four letter word that starts with "f."

'85 Chevy Celebrity (new). Back to GM with this light sage, midsize sedan. Great trunk capacity!

'86 Dodge Aries (used). Got almost 100,000 miles out this ice blue K-Car before we put it on ice.

'90 Buick Le Sabre (used). My father-in-law's hand-me down, this torch red 'tank' ran to 140,000.

'92 Chevy Cavalier (used). On Easter Sunday, 2002, returning Eddie to college after spring break, this turquoise 10-year-old workhorse kept us injury-free, accordioned as the fourth vehicle in a six-car pileup while stopped in traffic on I-80/94. (We were rear-ended by a pickup truck that was rear-ended by a semi.)

'92 Chevy Lumina (used). Previously owned by Dad, this garnet red hand-me-down reliably ran to 130,000 miles over 14 years.

'99 Chevy Malibu (new). If you wanted to feel every pebble in the road, this was the car for you. Traded toward the '02 Saturn.

'00 Saturn SL2 (new). Dependable and fuel efficient. Became Eddie's upon graduation.

'02 Saturn SL2 (new). Consistent 32 mpg and 100K on original brakes, Jo Ann loved this silver compact like no other.

'06 Saab 9-3 SportCombi (a "Svedish station vagon") (new). Fusion blue, generous cargo area, comfy, and turbo-fun to drive. First car with leather and heated seats, keeping the blood in my rear end circulating in cold weather. (Traded in three months before Saab went out of business in 2011.)

'08 Chevy Malibu hybrid (new). The imperial blue 'Bu was purchased pre-GM bankruptcy, post-model year in '09. With manufacturer and government rebates, they almost paid me to take it.

'11 Hyundai Santa Fe (new). Cargo area the size of the Grand Canyon, this mineral gray midsize SUV easily accommodates my continuously-expanding angler accoutrements.

And, best for last, there were many before and some after but none that will ever compare:
'92 Oldsmobile Cutlass Cruiser Station Wagon (new). A flame will always burn for this special, flame red metallic set of wheels purchased new on June 30, 1992. With a "Standard Vehicle Price" of $13,860, a Value Options

Package, and a number of other upgrades, the final sticker price, including a $500 Destination Charge, totaled $18,254. Yes, that's a lot of (1992) dollars but no, that's not what we paid. I don't recall the final price—Larry Faul Oldsmobile, like many car dealers located in Schaumburg, offered significant discounts to locally employed Motorolans.

For the better part of two decades, the Cutlass wagon, with IFISH 44 Illinois license plates affixed front and rear, transported friends and family to numerous lakes and rivers Midwest and Canada. Her dark maple red interior lent an ear to eager fishermen conversing on the subject of lures and strategies as we traveled to the location of our next quest. On return journeys, she cradled weary warriors in restful slumber after absorbing debriefings of what worked and what didn't, how the big one was caught or (more often) got away, and return plans to create the next chapter of memories.

As Ms. Cutlass celebrated her twelfth birthday in 2004, the Oldsmobile brand closed its doors after 107 years of vehicle manufacture. Badged with a proud heritage, this bump in the road did not deter her. I faithfully maintained my 'lass with recommended fluid and filter changes and a more in-depth annual checkup by Bill, my trusted mechanic. With his therapeutic oversight, she continuously provided unwavering service: always starting, running smoothly, and taking me safely from every "here" to every "there," to and from fishing holes near and far. Don't hold it against me, but I sometimes showed my appreciation with a gentle pat to her dashboard. Jo Ann, aware and accepting of the fondness for my longtime friend, joked that the wagon should serve as my burial vessel for the ride to the great beyond.

As I reached age 57, she turned 17. Together almost half my driving life, time began taking a toll—on both of us. As we traveled, in tandem, down life's highway, rust spots bubbled her fenders and doors, much like the random liver spots now speckling areas of my face, hands, and arms. She developed some squeaks and creaks, like the hints of arthritis in my fingers, neck, and knees. A black-ice minor fender-bender required eye-work via a headlight replacement, occurring shortly after my cataract procedures and the subsequent repair of a partially detached retina.

The health of her components continued their decline. The telltale broken-glass death-rattle of the catalytic converter muffled into the passenger compartment. Her demeanor hinted that a tune up, brakes, and exhaust system would soon be needed. The power window on the driver's side became temperamental, refusing to raise after being lowered, necessitating opening the door when paying a toll or using my keycard when entering the parking lot at work. Another area of rust, where the roof met the windshield, allowed rainwater into the header, the moisture dripping onto my hand as I held the steering wheel.

I struggled with the issues of her failing health. In a difficult and emotionally charged decision, I exercised the Vehicle Health Care Power of Attorney. On April 30, 2009, with 162,262 ticks on her odometer, I bade a tearful farewell to my loyal friend.

~~~~~

Stones - Fishing for Fossils

Fishing in the creek, hunting frogs, a World Series triumph, building a thatched hut, winning World War II—they could all appear on our "before age ten" resumé of summertime activities at Uncle Ben and Aunt Irene's Grayslake homestead. Oh, and one more.

Heads down, concentration intense while on all fours near the single-car detached garage, Larry and I inched along the semi-circular driveway "paved" with gravel. Numbering in the tens of thousands, we scoured the stones that ranged in size from dimes to quarters, invigorated by the possibility of finding "hard" evidence of life from millions of years ago.

We "imagined" one of Uncle Ben's empty wooden cigar boxes as a fossil finder. One of us would sweep it, to and fro, inches above the stones, snapping the lid up and down. When the frequency increased, like a Geiger counter nearing uranium, our in-depth search would begin. Completely manual and non-scientific, the "cigar box divining rod" possessed the power of a Ouija Board, paranormally leading us to successful finds. (Yes, random search would have produced the same results, and we knew that, but this was the fun way.)

To find the prehistoric impression of a seashell or a fossilized fragment of a leaf or insect sparked excitement, much like a Cubs victory or catching a fish. Our finds tossed into the box, portions of the days to follow were spent examining and reexamining our bedrock booty scavenged from the days when dinosaurs thundered the Earth.

Dormant through most of the year, and most years since, the rock-search impulse still surfaces when Jo Ann and I vacation. My interest no longer fossil-related (though finding one would certainly be a welcome bonus), I'm not a "rock hound" per se. I can't categorize sedimentary, metamorphic, and igneous specimens. My interest in collected samples is simple: intriguing shape, color, composition, or texture. Many years ago, I built a tabletop fountain with some of these interesting finds. Larger examples occupy places of prominence in our garden. Smaller ones line my desk beneath the computer monitor, while others function as stands for some of the small carved eagles in my modest collection. All of these stones serve as reminders of happy times at memorable locations near and far: Wisconsin, Iowa, Michigan, Arizona, North Carolina, Tennessee, South Dakota, Montana, Wyoming, Alaska, Hawaii, Ontario, Alberta, British Columbia, and the Yukon, among others.

After a 25-year absence, Jo Ann and I returned to the shores of Lake Superior along Michigan's Upper Peninsula. Whitefish Point, Big Bay, and Copper Harbor provided prime perusing for my plucking pastime.

In the standard sequence of events, we hike a trail, typically forested. Tree roots crisscross the woodland floor, stair-steps leading to a sandy lakeshore location. There, a boulder or large piece of driftwood provides a place to sit, rest, and enjoy whatever the lake may offer that day. Often, white caps rise from the deep blue, curling and folding as they reach the shallows before crashing ashore. A cool north wind sustains the rhythmic rush, refreshing body and soul. A minute into the relaxation, Jo Ann unlocks my invisible collar with the words, "Go ahead..."

Released to fetch, I bolt from our perch, my singular focus silencing the waves and becalming the breeze. On all fours, reminiscent of childhood days on the Grayslake driveway, my head swivels and eyes dart about, this search's fervor accelerated by the constraint of time. Leave no stone unturned! See them all—nay, too many to see in the seemingly limitless sea! Oh, the pressure in today's game of "comb the rocks - beat the clock" and the fear of leaving the Holy Grail undiscovered!

My hands sieve the pebbles mortared with soft sand, turning, rubbing, tossing, probing, separating, scrutinizing, all in search of the special nuggets that call to me above the others. Unique, each tells a story of formation molded by the forces of Mother Nature over millions of years.

Time to return, I'll cull my find to the two or three most prized and show them to my wife. She smiles, happy that I'm happy. Like when she nets one of my fish. At this moment, and those, all's right with the world.

Part Six

Dad and Mom
December 1944
Matron of Honor – Mom's sister, Irene
Best Man – Dad's brother Joe

~~~~~

But angling alone is not a health-retaining and health-giving pastime. It is a medicine to the mind as well as to the body; and unlike too many of the pleasures of life, it scatters no seeds from which the nettle of remorse may grow to sting the conscience or drive sunshine from the heart. Like the unclouded friendships of youth, it leaves only joyous memories.
—George Dawson
Pleasures of Angling with Rod & Reel for Trout and Salmon, 1876

Dad

    The third child among a mix of four boys and three girls, Dad was born of Polish immigrant parents in 1918. The building that housed the flat of his childhood adjoined a junkyard on the major thoroughfare of Elston Avenue, in the Chicago neighborhood known as the Near North Side. As the oldest son, he would often lead his brothers Wally, Lenny, and Joe on jaunts to the nearby railroad tracks where they would collect pieces of coal that had rolled off hopper cars, the precious nuggets used to heat their residence during blustery Chicago winters.

In his early teens, with the Great Depression in full swing, demands for his family's needs necessitated he quit high school after the tenth grade. He worked odd jobs, among them loading and unloading 50-pound bags of flour on a delivery truck. He later toiled as a leather cutter at a factory where his mother, Angeline, and older sister, Helen, were also employed. All his earnings turned over to his father, he received a $1 weekly allowance in return.

At age 20, he was introduced to the girl he would later wed by her young uncle, one of his group of buddies who would congregate on evenings and weekends under the roofed entryway of the Gianni & Hilgart stained glass factory near the intersection of Blackhawk and Noble Streets. Mom was sweet 16 when their relationship began, smitten to a swoon by the good looks of the slender young man with blond hair and blue eyes. They dated regularly over the next several years, a typical Saturday night enjoyed at the Crown Theatre near Division and Ashland Streets, the movie's 10-cent ticket doable on Dad's meager allowance. Unable to afford chocolates or flowers, he would bring her a package of Fan Tan gum upon arriving for each date. On rare occasions, they would head over to the Congress Theatre on Milwaukee Avenue to attend a movie, or for a few pennies more, a vaudeville show.

The Japanese attack on Pearl Harbor changed the lives of most Americans, including the two young lovebirds from Chicago. Drafted into the Army in May of 1942 at age 23, Dad's draft card listed his height at 5' 7½" and weight at 145 pounds. He served in the 5th Army, 53rd Signal Battalion, and during the course of his service was promoted from private to the rank of Technician 5th class. Overseas for thirty-five months, twenty-six of those in combat, he earned the European-African-Middle Eastern Theatre ribbon with one Silver and two Bronze Battle Stars. Three amphibious assaults were included among seven Campaigns: Algeria-French Morocco, Tunisia, Sicily, Naples-Foggia, Rome-Arno, North Apennines, and Po Valley. He religiously mailed home all but $6 of his $66 per month military salary.

Weary from the travails of over two and one-half years of war, he was furloughed in December 1944 and looked forward to returning stateside to marry the love of his life. The journey back to the States included 14 days of heaving discomfort in the bowels of the *Henry Gibbons*, as the army transport ship inched westward across the Atlantic. With little time for formal wedding preparations, Mom borrowed her wedding dress from her matron of honor and younger sister, Irene, who had married one month earlier. Dad's youngest brother, Joe, witnessed as best man.

While on furlough, soldiers hailing from the Chicago area were required to check-in weekly at Fort Sheridan, the Army facility located north of the city on the shore of Lake Michigan. On February 18, 1945, Dad made the call to his new bride that orders dictated an immediate return to his unit, with no opportunity for a face-to-face goodbye. He participated in the final campaigns leading to the German surrender in Italy on May 2. V-E Day, ending the war in Europe, occurred six days later on May 8, 1945.

After logging 3½ years of wartime service and being honorably discharged in September 1945, Dad worked several factory jobs, cutting leather football helmets and baseball gloves for sporting goods manufacturers Riddell and Wilson, and ice skates at F.W. Planert & Sons. No longer a craft, cutting leather now involved the precarious and drudging effort of operating a machine in an assembly line environment. Brief jobless periods also sprinkled the post-war years.

In 1947, elated with the arrival of his first child, daughter Nancy, the proud papa was often seen pushing his pride and joy through the neighborhood streets in her stroller. My birth followed five years later.

From the mid-1950s into the 1960s, he found steady employment at Wheeler Protective Apparel. The tasks and working conditions much the same as his previous jobs, the primary difference was the material being cut—asbestos—for the manufacture of firefighter apparel. From the mid-60s until his retirement in 1982, Dad worked as a clerk for the U.S. Postal Service, sorting international-bound and -received mail at the postal facility housed at Chicago's O'Hare International Airport.

~ ~ ~ ~ ~

Fathers who fish and later introduce their children to the sport can take credit for the joys it bestows upon their offspring. Or, depending on their demeanor and method of teaching, unpleasant and frustration-filled memories can source from the parental instructor. Favorable experiences lay the groundwork for a pleasant pastime to last a lifetime. Fishless hours watching a bobber under a mandate of silence can steer a youngster toward a sport such as golf, where the only interaction with water involves the challenge to keep their Titleist out of it.

For those of us born with "I'd rather be fishing" molecules threaded through our DNA, the number and size of the catch is of no (okay, maybe a little) consequence. Although catching fish always satisfies, the anticipation of the day, thrill of the hunt, and time spent together can also imprint the day as a success.

With regard to my Dad and fishing, his brother-in-law, my Uncle Ben, introduced him to the sport circa 1950. Although I can't say for certain, part of the allure may have involved the ability to quaff a beverage during the interludes when panfish in the Grayslake-area lakes showed no interest in the worms they were soaking. My reason for believing this revolves around the lifelong observation of Dad and my Uncle, kindred spirits who loved their spirits, sharing quality time with their buddies-in-a-bottle, Jim Beam, Old Grand-Dad, and the brothers Ernest and Julio Gallo.

Viewing fishing more as a pleasant pastime than a high stakes game of masculine bravado, Dad wasn't terribly accomplished as a fisherman, and he would be the first to tell you so. But he sure loved to do it, with or without the spirits. The enjoyment of time on the water and the hope of catching a big fish don't have to be mutually exclusive events.

Now well into his 70s, Dad had yet to catch the elusive musky. In line with life's natural order, age dictating the evolution of role reversal wherein the parent becomes the child, I gradually assumed responsibility for planning our trips, reserving accommodations, and when on the water, playing the role of guide: picking the lake and spots to fish, making sure his equipment was in good repair, and tying his knots and untangling the line in his reel from the occasional "bird's nest." Dad was more than accepting of these gradual changes and, as the years went on, welcomed them. In the 1990s, I'm certain Dad caught more and bigger fish on our excursions to Emerald Lake than all his previous fishing years combined. He always looked forward to those weekend trips.

Reflections from the Lake

This day, like most others of the workweek, awakened ordinary. Unlike them, however, it traveled a path to the comfort of a simple yet special conclusion.

I've trained myself to shower every morning whether I need one or not. Today's version of that task completed, I've dressed for work—business casual—for an all-day meeting. Outside at 6:15 a.m. to retrieve the newspaper, the July 19 air hangs warm and heavy, draping a dewy sweat on the windows and siding of the house. Moisture also coats the ten-year-old ice-blue '86 Dodge Aries parked in the driveway, causing it to look as if it's beginning to melt. The heat and humidity does not bode well for the weekend fishing trip scheduled with Dad, who will be celebrating his 78th birthday in a few months. Though our time on the water may be limited, maybe this will be the weekend when he catches his first muskellunge, the fierce fighting "fish of 10,000 casts."

I won't bore you with the details of the business meeting other than to describe it as tolerable, measured by my ability to stay awake for the duration, and made more so by concluding 15 minutes ahead of schedule. I've been to quite a few of these in my two-plus decades on the job and remain strikingly successful at managing to keep my head from exploding.

After exiting the building, a northerly breeze greets me. Refreshing, it has swept away the stifling morning humidity. On the ride home, the radio reports a temperature 10 degrees cooler than the morning. My hands slide along the steering wheel, stopping at the 10- and 2-o'clock position with a "thumbs up" that acknowledges the positive weather change.

Always early "just in case," Dad has been waiting at our Bloomingdale home since mid-afternoon, anxiously anticipating my return that signals the start of our weekend getaway. As I pull into the driveway, he's seated on a lawn chair just inside the garage door opening. His brown imitation-leather suitcase rests beside him on the concrete floor. I've taken to storing his fishing equipment, as the last couple of years the only trips he makes are with me. I pop the trunk so he can load his articles while I head inside for a quick change of clothes from business casual to almost hobo. My favorite fishing garb consists of a white T-shirt imprinted with a walleye (my lucky shirt for catching bass, go figure) and a pair of no-name denim jeans, the bottom, back edge of both legs frayed into strings, the knees worn to the thinness of velum paper.

Loaded with cooler, two parts luggage, and twenty-two parts fishing paraphernalia, Dad and I take to the highway in the old Dodge dotted with rust spots in varying sizes of pocket change. On this typically busy route, the lack of traffic surprises me, particularly during rush hour on a Friday evening. Halfway to the cabin, we catch a quick meal at McDonald's. I remark how nice it would be to score a quick million dollars in their Olympic Games promotion. Not today (big surprise...): free burger if the women's fencing team secures a medal. Dad mentions how a worker at the bowling alley he frequents won $16,000 on an Illinois lotto game. "We're not lucky like that. We have to work hard for everything we get." I nod in agreement, knowing he's referring to a lifetime of demanding jobs that he and Mom worked for meager wages, but I also consider how his statement applies when we're on the water fishing, though the latter is clearly a labor of love.

An hour further down the road, the sun slips behind a bank of clouds. A crevice at its midpoint funnels "glory" beams that light distant trees, barns, and farm houses scattered across the hills of the rolling countryside. That pastoral scene tempers the anticipation of what the weekend of fishing might bring. As they always do on trips like this, the last miles of the road run long, if not in real time, certainly on my traveler's internal clock. The trusty, rusty Dodge negotiates the final twists and turns of the yellow-striped asphalt road leading to our destination.

Upon arrival, I open the cottage windows to clear out the summer stuffiness and suggest we sit on the back porch while awaiting the cool down. Twice the width of the patio doors by which it is accessed, the porch accommodates a charcoal grill, a two-foot-square knee-high table and a couple of green plastic patio chairs.

After easing into one of them, I reach into the cooler, my fingers swimming through smooth chunks of marble-size ice. Cold aluminum the next sensation to the touch, I grab a can of Coke and hand it to Dad. He no longer partakes of alcoholic beverages, as a long list of medications are part of his daily regimen. He's had to deal with more than his fair share of serious health issues in the last couple of years: surgery to clear a carotid artery blockage, a triple bypass, and when that one didn't take properly, a quadruple bypass. To his credit, none of them dampened his positive outlook on life.

In spite of an "impressive" list of bodily breakdowns of my own, a cholesterol-reducing pill is my only ongoing prescription drug. Unwilling to let one tiny white tablet stand in the way of mildly mind-numbing refreshment, I plunge my hand back into the Coleman and grab a Leinenkugel longneck. I've long since bid adieu to the days when a flask of blackberry brandy in the boat was as integral a part of the fishing experience as rods, reels, and lures. (I eventually learned that a 70-proof elixir mixed with sharp hooks could make *me* the catch of the day.)

In the world of quality conversation time, boat talk is good, but porch talk is better—no chance of interruption by the strike of an inconsiderate fish. Dad fingers the ring on top of the Coke can, a slow pull causing the distinctive "pop" as thin metal separates, the can belching carbonated bubbles. He begins the conversation: "Last time I saw you with a Leinie was when we went up to Janaczek's place on Lake Namakagon in Cable. When *was* that?"

A swig of beer to aid my thought process, I reply, "Mid-70s, about 20 years ago. I had graduated from NIU, and you still had the '67 Chevelle."

"That was a long way to go for three stinking crappies," Dad says, the long-ago disappointment still an annoying sore spot. "Janaczek was a nice guy, but he sure didn't take care of his cabins. And he wasn't any help putting us on fish, either."

"Dad, Dad, how quickly you forget. It was *only* 20 years ago that he took us to his honey hole that second evening, guiding us to those three crappies. In fact, we would have had four if not for his ripping hookset on the last fish. I'll never forget the sight of his hook flying out of the water with the white circle of crappie lips hanging from it."

Dad chuckles, finishing the recollection of the scene. "My chunky friend looked like he was setting the hook on Moby Dick. Almost tumbled out of the boat, too."

Intertwined in the fabric of our lives, sports, not only the participatory fishing but spectator like baseball, football, basketball, and hockey, provide fodder for chats. Dad brings the Coke can to his mouth and draws a few sips, followed by a satisfying smack of tongue and lips. "Do you think we'll ever see the Cubs win a World Series?"

Running all the words in the sentence together, I reply, "Let me think about that for a second, NO."

Dad comments, "With the last one in 1908, the law of averages should be in our favor. And like Jack Brickhouse says, 'Any team can have a bad century.'"

After a gulp of Leinie, I continue, "I have to admit that I started getting tired of investing three hour chunks of my life with no payback in the never-ending disappointment of Cubs losses. Then the '94 strike was the last straw—at least as far as Major League baseball goes. I still love baseball. I love the game. I think I always will. But I'd just as soon watch Little Leaguers just play for the pure joy of it. The millionaire players and millionaire owners, the 'haves' and the 'have mores' can go scratch."

"Wow, you can really hold a grudge."

"I can. But I didn't hold one against you, at least not more than a second or two, when you didn't let me run onto the field at Wrigley after the Cardwell no-hitter. I think that game was our Cubs 'World Series.'"

Dad smiles and nods his head in agreement. "I had just gotten back from overseas when the Cubs lost to the Tigers in the '45 Series. I didn't get to see any of the games, but your Uncle Ben and I made up for it the next summer. Don't tell your mother, but he and I would sneak over to Wrigley now and then to take in a game when we were supposed to be looking for jobs."

The last vestige of light giving way to dusk, the green-yellow glow of fireflies begins flickering about, the flashing dots burning rich against the shadow of junipers and oaks that line the top of the ridge at the back of the property. Their randomness matches the choice of conversation topics. Dad asks, "How's Eddie's job? Is he making any money at it?"

"The golf store he works for just bumped him 35 cents to $5.60 an hour. What they don't know is that he likes it there so much he'd probably pay *them* to work there."

"That's good. It's important to like what you're doing. They can see he's a good kid—and a good worker. You and Jo Ann have done a real nice job raising him. And he can really hit a golf ball. He did good when I took him to the driving range."

"Yeah, he's gotten a lot better. His high school coach said it was the biggest improvement he's ever seen in a player from one year to the next."

After another sip from the iconic red can, Dad continues, "I really enjoy it when the three of us play pinochle. Three Ed's are better than one, you know."

He often rolls out that corny line, to which I always reply, "Very *punny*, Dad." Eddie and I look forward to our card games as well. For whatever reason, perhaps an unavoidable function of his sandpapery, "pork sausage" fingers, Dad always encounters difficulty when it's his turn to deal. No matter how careful, he ends up a card short or one too many, requiring each of us to count and shift a card from one of us to another. As far as the game itself, I consider myself a pretty fair player, having learned by logging many hours across the table from Uncle Stanley, but he and Dad clearly rank as grandmasters.

Card games contested at family get-togethers that celebrated holidays, birthdays, Baptisms, First Holy Communions, and Confirmations remain strong as childhood memories. Some combination of Dad, Uncle Ben, Uncle Rich, Uncle Stanley, Grandpa Ben, and Uncle Bill would belly-up to the kitchen table or a card table set up in the living room. The game of choice either pinochle or its half-sister, "66" (with similar rules but played with half a pinochle deck), each player (except Dad, who gave up smoking in the mid-1950s) puffed away on a cigar or cigarette, a gray haze filling the rooms of the small house or flat hosting the party. I can still see Dad securing a trick, his left hand plucking a card from the neatly fanned set in his right hand, raising it to ear level, and rifling it to the table with a distinctive "slap."

Dad making a point to cigar-smoking Uncle Stanley.
Grandpa Ben (left) and Uncle Rich (right) watch the goings-on.

The liquor always flowed freely, a highball—whiskey mixed with seltzer water or ginger ale—the choice of most players. The games completed, the men would often vanish for an hour or two, making their way to one of the local watering holes: The Country Club on Ashland Avenue, Miska's on Western, or creatively named, The Tavern, on the corner of Leavitt and Charleston.

The direction of my thoughts apparently matching Dad's stream of consciousness, his next words bring us back to the old neighborhood. "You know, sometimes timing is everything." He pauses for a moment then asks a question without waiting for a reply. "You were still pretty little, but do you remember when the boiler went up in flames when we lived on Dickens? I was having a belt with Mr. Podgornik at The Tavern when a fire truck rumbles by, the siren blaring and lights flashing. I didn't think much of it, but used it as a call to head for home. When I got to the alley, the fire truck is next to the house, firemen running around like a bunch of chickens with their heads cut off. I hear your mother screaming 'My husband's down there, my husband's down there!' I guess she thought I was working in the basement. Probably because I told her that's where I'd be.

"I hightail it into the yard, where she's trying to get through the door into the basement as a fireman is struggling to restrain her. I run up to them with an 'It's okay, I'm here!' She breaks free from the fireman and wraps me in a big hug. A 'thank God you're safe' gives her time to smell my breath. As she wipes away a tear, the hug gets undone and she puts her hands on her hips, stern expression and tone of her voice asking a question that she already knew the answer to: 'And just where the hell were you?'

"This whole mess catches me off guard, and the best I can come up with is 'Podgornik needed to talk to me about joining his bowling team.' I felt guilty as hell. But we *were* talking bowling. Luckily, there was no major damage to the house. But there was a big chill for a couple of days, and rightfully so, but eventually things smoothed out."

Like most married couples, Mom and Dad had their occasional arguments. Although overhearing a verbal joust was always uncomfortable and outward expressions of affection like hugs, kisses, and "I love yous" few and far between, I never sensed any cracks in the foundation of my parent's relationship. Underneath their non-touchy-feely exterior, there was never any question of their loyalty and love. I noticed they always kissed goodbye when Dad and I would be leaving on fishing trips that included one or more overnights.

Dad's mention of bowling in the story of the basement fire brought back yet another early childhood memory. He used the sounds of bowling to soothe my psyche during violent thunderstorms, explaining the wall-shaking, rolling rumble of thunder as "St. Peter's bowling again," and the crack of lightning as, "Another strike!"

Dad loves to bowl as much as he loves to fish. When we lived on Dickens he bowled regularly at the Congress Lanes, located on the second floor of a building on Milwaukee Avenue between The Congress Theatre and Bargain Town, the spacious children's toy store and forerunner of Toys "R" Us.

Before I was old enough to handle a bowling ball, I'd sit on the bench behind the scoring desk, wide-eyed, taking in the sights and sounds occurring helter-skelter across multiple lanes: the brightly lit pins at the end of polished wood alleys; the thump and heavy roll of 16-pound balls along the thin planks; the crack and crash of pins. Dad's quick, five-step approach wasn't graceful but wasn't awkward either. As he'd slide his right foot parallel to the foul line, his effortless, southpaw backswing and follow through would send the black Brunswick gently hooking toward its intended target between the first and second pins. On shots to pick up a spare, as the ball was making contact, he'd slide his left foot behind the heel of his right, providing the body English to nudge a pin in the direction of others needing to be knocked down.

When my back went bad in '92, my days of bowling, racquetball, and golf came to an end. With bowling it was just as well. Although fairly coordinated for most athletic endeavors, I never achieved a significant level of proficiency (as evidenced by my lowest lifetime average among the Fabulous Maretti Brothers) as some number of the white, standing-at-attention soldiers with red neckties remained undisturbed at the end of most frames. For whatever reason, I couldn't implement Dad's frequent advice, "Loft it out there," "Watch your mark," and "Follow through, shake hands with the head pin."

As evening darkness takes further hold, I empty my bottle with two hearty gulps, then step inside the patio door and flick on a lamp. Upon returning to my chair, I'm pleased that the action produced the desired effect, the backlit shades on the windows illuminating the porch with the softness of a nightlight.

Dad did not stir during the execution of my brief chore, still staring ahead, apparently lost in thought. With only a bit of sag in his jowls, he looks good for 78. Thin but not frail, he's nearer the 145 pounds at the time of his military induction than his potbelly peak of middle age, the time when young boys see their dads as the biggest and strongest men in the world. I never saw the blond hair of his youth, familiar only with the sandy brown of his adult life. Only recently have hints of gray begun to appear. He's always had a measure of a receding hairline, but by and large, he's still the proud owner of an almost-full head of hair. The bridge of his nondescript nose supports the large, plastic, amber color eyeglass frames that recall the style of the 1970s, reminding me of another of Dad's oft-shared catch phrases: "When you find something you like, stick with it."

Snapping back to the now without a prompt, Dad drains the last drops of Coke, squeezes the can into an hourglass, and hands it to me. As I toss it into the cooler, he declines my offer of another. I grab a second Leinie. While Dad's last monologue took me to bowling, the interlude obviously absorbed him in thoughts of his wife of 52 years. "Your mother's a good woman. We wouldn't have what we do if it wasn't for her. Every week I'd hand her my measly paycheck, and she'd take care of it from there. I don't know how she did it all—working, paying the bills, taking care of the house, taking care of us, and Busia, and Stashu, and Francey."

As is his way, Dad never took any credit for all he did for his in-laws over the years. Always Johnny-on-the-spot with toolbox in hand, he'd perform any repairs needed at Busia's small flat on Noble Street. Uncle Rich, who lived with her, never learned to drive, had a bad shoulder, and lacked the knowledge of basic home fixes. When we moved to Niles, and after Uncle Rich married Aunt Dee, Busia, Auntie Fran, and Uncle Stanley occupied the flats on Dickens virtually rent-free for some 20 years. To keep the house in good repair, Dad would frequently make the 25-mile round trip when it would have been much simpler and saved a lot of money and aggravation to just sell it. Because Mom never learned to drive, the burden of caring for his aging in-laws—trips to doctors, hospitals, nursing homes, picking up food, prescriptions, and life's other necessities—fell on Dad's shoulders. He always completed them without question or complaint.

I'm surprised and pleased with Dad's chattiness this evening, our conversations usually more brief than extended. His train of thought still on the subject of Mom, the time machine jettisons back a few more years. "When I was in the service, your mother sent me a package once a month. The guys would gather 'round, knowing there would be a bunch of goodies in there. There was always a log of salami, candy, Lucky Strikes. She even got me socks and underwear when I asked for them. She wrote me a letter every day. I don't know how she found stuff to write about, but she always did."

Night creeping its chill, Dad rubs his hands together and then intertwines his fingers before resting them on his lap. The letters and packages from Mom trigger thoughts of other wartime memories. "When our unit was in Italy, I heard that my friend Skonie's company was in the area. Things were quiet for a day or two, and I was so homesick that I asked my staff sergeant if I could swing back to pay him a visit. He said no, that we might be moving out soon. I thought he was giving me a line of bull, so a little while later I grabbed a jeep and took off. Well, I never found Skonie, and when I got back that evening my unit was gone. Talk about a helpless feeling.... I scrambled and finally caught up. My buddies had covered for me, packing up my gear and pup tent, so the sergeant never found out. Or never let on that he did."

Shifting in his chair, as if still uncomfortable in spite of the 50 years separating the incident from the thought, Dad reflects, "The military doesn't look kindly on AWOLs. That was drilled into us, like a lot of other things. I never considered the risk ... or the consequences. When you've been away from home two straight years and your life's on the line every day, you don't always think things through."

Like most veterans, Dad never spoke much about the war, but tonight for whatever reason, the vault opened for a further peek into those hellish days...

...losing souvenir-seeking buddies to booby-traps during the North African campaign.

...a last minute change during the invasion of Sicily, pulled from one landing craft to another, the original one hit by an enemy shell and destroyed, leaving no survivors.

...while in Italy, having the "distinction" of being addressed by General George Patton during an impromptu stop to review his battle-weary unit—"Where's your leggings, soldier?"

...on the Allied advance north to Rome, multiple assaults in the Battle of Monte Cassino, fired upon by the Germans as well as being mistakenly strafed by "friendly fire" from U.S. warplanes.

...fighting a dug-in enemy through the rugged terrain of the North Apennine Mountains, mules used to carry supplies across narrow passages inaccessible by vehicles, torrential spring and fall rains spawning swollen streams that washed out roads and bridges, trudging through shin-deep mud.

...brothers Lenny, Wally, and Joe—all served, all survived.

*Dad, looking exhausted after the Battle of Monte Cassino
January – May 1944*

    Back from memories unpleasant to haunting, Dad ends his soliloquy with a "typically Dad" shift to the light side. "After we liberated Rome, we had an audience with Pope Pius XII at the Vatican. I got to kiss his ring. Under the circumstances, next best thing to kissing your Mom, I guess. Good thing General Clark was our commander. If Patton was there, the tough old buzzard might have expected the Pope to kiss *his* ring, if not his ass." His words catch me off guard; I struggle to keep the mouthful of Leinie that just passed my lips from spraying all over my best-bad clothes.

    Stars and planets speckle the sky, brilliant diamonds becoming more so as their backdrop darkens. Away from the city lights and only a sliver of a crescent moon not disturbing tonight's celestial show, the oval-shaped haze of the Milky Way shines like few others I've ever witnessed. I tell Dad of shooting stars I'd seen here on a special night several years ago and mention that if we stay outside long enough, we might catch a glimpse of one. "Good chance to make a wish," I offer.

Apparently talked out and feeling chilled, Dad replies, "Time to turn in. It's getting pretty nippy out here—just like the April night I drove your mother to the hospital the day before you were born." Slowly rising from his chair, he says, "You can stay out, and if you see any shooting stars, wish a musky for me. And one for yourself, too. Yours can even be bigger."

We are awake, dressed, sipping cups of coffee, and munching on raspberry sweet rolls. No alarm clock set, the days of needing to be on the water before the crack of dawn have passed both of us by. Besides, in my experience, this lake willingly shares its bounty during daytime fishing efforts. The radio reminds us that today celebrates the 27th anniversary of the lunar landing by Apollo 11. Perhaps a small lake in Illinois will be the site of history on a more personal level this July 20—Dad catching his first musky.

With the passage of yesterday's front, the morning dawns cool. Breaks in the clouds hint the blue sky behind them. A perfectly placed keyhole opening allows the sun to produce another magnificent "glory," similar to the one seen last evening. Silence fills the car, a function of our anticipation amping up with each passing minute. A rafter of wild turkeys mill about an open field near the entrance to the marina.

After loading the boat and settling into our seats, my Crestliner eases past the "no wake" buoys at the outside edge of the docking area. The trolling motor glides us across the shallow weed flat. I've rigged two spinning rods for Dad—one with a "cranapple" color Rat-L-Trap and the other a Cubby-blue plastic worm imbedded with silver flakes. Fifty yards past the buoys the water deepens and the weeds thin to more "fishable" clumps. The motor speed reduced to low, today's adventure begins. Dad, seated in the bow, picks up the rod with the worm and makes his first cast. I stand in the stern, pitching a "tequila sunrise" color Rat-L-Trap with my bait-casting equipment. Ten minutes pass without a bite. Each day on the water starts with a clean slate; until the first fish tugs, the discomforting seeds of doubt regarding location, technique, and lure selection sprout and grow.

Those doubts evaporate as Dad rears back, setting the hook. Steadily reeling, the tip of his rod bounces in a sustained rhythm. Still unseen as it approaches the boat, the fish runs beneath it, typically the sign of a specimen of better size. Dad maintains pressure as the struggle plays out, prevailing as a 17-inch bass, a nice 3-pounder, comes to net.

Minutes later, the scene repeats, though with more dimension and intensity. Its bend more pronounced, the front half of his rod bows heavily to longer, deeper throbs. Some 20 feet away, the unseen adversary rises in the water column and makes a run parallel to the boat. The reel's drag sings its mechanical tune. Could this be the one? Another bull rush, this time in the opposite direction, allows a glimpse of the fish's elongated form, its sides painted with vertical striping.

My adrenaline output doubles as I alert Dad, "It's a musky!" I ready the net as the fight continues, calmly doling out advice that gives no hint of the nervousness coursing my body: "Don't give him any slack … rod tip up, keep a tight line … don't reel if he's pulling drag…" On the edge of the seat and absorbed in the moment, I'm pretty sure Dad isn't hearing a word I'm saying.

Each time the fish turns or runs I hold my breath, hoping the thin, leaderless 8-pound test monofilament line will not cross the jagged teeth that will easily slice it. Anxious seconds become minutes that feel like hours. His straining arms tight to his body, Dad continues to coax the fish of his dreams toward the boat. The gap narrows. Yards become feet become inches. Victory but a net-length away, the musky refuses to concede, a quick flex bolting its powerful body deep and out of sight beneath the boat. I shudder, knowing the longer the struggle continues, the more opportunity the fish has to regain its freedom; the longer the struggle continues, the greater the disappointment if the fish swims free.

Less drag pulled from the reel than the earlier runs tells me the musky is tiring. Both fish and fisherman seem ready for the battle's last gasp. Dad labors with the final cranks of the reel handle while lifting the rod with slow, steady pressure. The musky comes into view and is guided into the waiting net.

Overwhelmed by relief both physical and mental, Dad slumps back in his chair, a deep breath exhaling the slain ghost of muskellunge-catching virginity. With the fish secure in the net and still in the water, I extend a hand to Dad. I can't tell (and don't care) whose hand trembles more, as smiles beam to the movement of a hearty handshake.

It takes me a few moments to free the two small hooks imbedded at the outside edge of the musky's mouth. "Beauty, Dad."

Unhooked, I slide the fish out of the net and into the boat, measure it at 33 inches, and hand it off to Dad with a quick primer on the proper hold. I ready the camera to preserve this special moment, framing the shot through the viewfinder. Dad stands, holding his prize possession. The vertically-striped tiger musky stretches at a 45-degree angle, head in the upper left, tail to the lower right. Dad's zipped lifejacket covers most of his navy blue Chicago Bears jacket, two rows of orange trim stripes circling each sleeve matching the color of his Surf detergent baseball cap. Behind those plastic rim glasses his eyes do not meet the camera, but gaze down at the object of hope fulfilled. A subtle smile whispers a wordless, "Finally…" Click. A push of the shutter button captures the moment. Perfect.

That first musky proved to be the stepping stone, or keeping with the Apollo 11 theme, "launching pad" for further musky fishing accomplishments by Dad in 1996 and beyond. At an August outing on Emerald Lake, my cousin Bill joined us. The bass fishing excellent, each of us scored numerous largemouth. As if moved by a sixth sense, Dad had just put down his rod rigged with a plastic worm. He verbalized the change, "Let's give the Rat-L-Trap a try…" At mid-retrieve of his first cast, a savage strike nearly ripped the rod out of his hand. He triumphed in that monumental struggle as well, landing a magnificent 42-inch tiger musky. And on October 26, his fishing season closed out with two more. The larger, at 33 inches, grabbed a Rat-L-Trap on the second cast after he changed out the lure for a gray and black "Smokey Joe" color. Hunch? Instinct? Luck? Don't know. Don't care. Doesn't matter. Just more great photos for Dad to share with the guys at the bowling alley.

~ ~ ~ ~ ~

In the spring of 1999, Dad experienced more chest pains that required extensive testing. Fortunately, no major problems loomed, but at age 80, adjustments to his fishing methods would be needed. Lobbing a plastic worm and slowly retrieving it remained in the repertoire, but "burning" (the fast retrieve of) a Rat-L-Trap, the method used to catch most of his muskies, was no longer an option.

On a mid-June outing, Dad and I witnessed a man and his teenage son troll-up two 40-inch-plus muskies on Emerald Lake. While fighting the fish they shouted for assistance, hoping we could provide a net. We eased over to furnish them with same, enabling the successful landing of both fish. Also advising us that they had forgotten a camera, I snapped a few photos with my Polaroid. During the course of providing these "up close and personal" services, I noticed the unlikely method of their success. Obviously not targeting muskies, their rigs consisted of small, crawdad pattern Rapala Shad Raps, tight-wiggling crankbaits attached to leaderless, monofilament line on spinning set ups. Their catches of these "accidental" muskies matched our own when using similar gear as we casted for bass.

On the water the next morning at 9 a.m., the sun had already broken through the clouds. The temperature on its way to the 80s, high humidity also thickened the air. After every dozen-or-so casts with the plastic worm, I noticed Dad taking a break, flexing his fingers.

Only a half hour in, he offered a suggestion. "Want to try trolling?"

I had filed yesterday's observation in my bag of possibilities but didn't think we'd need to draw on it quite so early in the day. "Sure, we can do that," knowing it would be easier on Dad to just sit back and hold onto the rod as we cruised likely areas.

I re-rigged Dad's rod with a small brown and gold Shad Rap, one that's been in my tackle box (seeing limited use) since its original issue some 15 years ago. Underway for less than a minute with the trolling motor at full speed, Dad's rod doubled over as he shouted, "I'm snagged!"

I immediately slowed down, turned, and headed in the direction of the snag as Dad reeled in with the pace of the boat. I shut off the motor as the line neared perpendicular, then took hold of it in an attempt to pull it free from the obstruction. As I began applying pressure, the snag, with a fair amount of weight behind it, began to move. Next, the unmistakable feeling of headshakes transmitted through the line. "Dad, I think your snag may be a musky!"

After a slow release of my grip to keep tension on the line back to Dad's rod, I scurried for the net while Dad played the fish. Conveniently close to the boat as a result of our previous movement, a relatively short engagement played out before a 36-incher came to net, only one hook of the small back treble in the corner of the fish's mouth.

Unhooked, measured, and photographed, the post-release ritual followed: rinse slimed areas including net (I love the smell of musky-musk in the morning); put camera away; return net to proper location; inspect knot and line for fraying; check lure and hooks for damage. After I flipped the switch to turn on the motor and reposition the boat, Dad swiveled around in his seat to make a cast to begin our next trolling run. I noticed his intention to cast off of "my side" and caught him on the backswing. "Whoa, Dad, throw it off the other side." The direction correction acknowledged, he made the cast and engaged his reel.

As soon as the boat's speed had taken the bow out of his line (that motion causing the lure to speed up and dive), Dad called out, "I think I got one!" His inclusion of the word "think" hedged his bet, not wanting to take a chance on repeating the miscalculation of the "snag." I stopped the motor and looked over my shoulder to see his outstretched arms struggling to keep control of his rod, now bent in the shape of a boomerang. "Round 1" of another bout underway, this fish fought with the intensity and insanity of few others I've ever seen, regardless of size or species. This duel lasted an exhausting five to ten minutes before the muskellunge, another three-footer, came to rest in the bottom of the net. It signaled another victory for the wearied but pleased fisherman and our newly borrowed method. Rewind and replay post-catch procedure.

We're back in business and recuperating in the throes of a ten-minute respite when Dad shouts, "Got another one!" Music to my ears, the words triggered a repeat of actions, today a pleasant, broken record: motor off, fast and furious reel-in, prepare the net, rein in my rapidly beating heart. The magnitude and duration of this encounter somewhere between the first musky and the second, I assumed this one to be of similar size. Wrong. Buoyantly wrong.

Dad, seated during this bout as he was the others, did not see the fish as the tussle see-sawed toward and away from the boat. I, however, caught a glimpse of a musky significantly longer and thicker than the others. Not wanting to add to the pressure of the day's third battle royale, I kept the information to myself but silently mouthed words (something like) "Holy guacamole, that's one *big* fish!" One eye on Dad, I'm thinking that between this fish and the cumulative effect of the earlier tug-o-wars he must surely be experiencing some level of fatigue. No evidence backs the thought; again engrossed in the moment, adrenaline overcomes all.

Dad's confidence and technique aided by previous successes, he maneuvered the aquatic titan toward the net—I silently questioned whether it has the capacity to hold her. Now partially in, the lure fell free as the fish thrashed. With writhing, violent swats of her tail she began edging backwards, the rear portion of her body backing out beyond the net frame. Quickly thrusting the handle to Dad, I grabbed and lifted the hoop, using my free hand to stuff the back half of the escaping musky back into the rubberized netting.

Dropping the net back into the water with the fish secured, I readied the camera and then reached down to bring her into the boat. Well-fed with a thick belly, inch by inch by inch she just kept coming and coming and coming...

"Dad, look at the size of this thing!" I held her next to the tape measure affixed inside the hull—"43 inches!"

Still seated, Dad unzipped his life jacket and adjusted his purple Winona State University (alma mater of granddaughter Jennifer) baseball cap as he awaited the hand-off. I presented her with the care of passing a newborn infant. His first words since we landed the fish, Dad asked, "How much do you think she weighs?"

"At least 5 pounds more than your bowling ball—over 20 pounds for sure!"

After a quick dry of my hands (on a blue hand-towel imprinted with bowling pins and the words "Crying Towel" that Dad had given to me many years ago), I grabbed the camera.

Dad's head slightly tilted and his torso leaning ever-so-slightly forward, the idyllic pose contrasted sharply to the commotion that played out just minutes ago. All his previous muskies building to this crescendo, the crown jewel of his fishing life was solidly in his grasp. His relaxed smile of satisfaction said, "This is the one I've been waiting for…"

~ ~ ~ ~ ~

Dad was diagnosed with cancer of the kidney in December, 2001. Its removal and months of chemotherapy could not stop the spread of the disease, metastasizing to the liver and causing anemia and cardiac failure. He died at 11:58 p.m. on September 18, 2002, at 84 years of age. The pinochle game in heaven with Uncle Stanley, Uncle Rich, and Uncle Bill must have been starting at midnight.

Ol' Lefty was as down-to-earth as they come. Anyone searching for a reason not to like him would have to dig deep and likely coming up empty. Loved by family and friends, he possessed an easy-going nature, engaging smile, and subtle sense of humor. Life circumstances negated his opportunity for extended formal education, yet he took pride with a breadth of knowledge spanning many subjects, frequently tossing out questions of trivia about this or that. A devoted son, husband, father, brother, and son-in-law, he worked hard all his life as a laborer, never making much money, but with Mom watching the purse strings we never lacked for life's essentials. He gave freely of himself, of his time—that being perhaps his greatest gift. Content with his station in life, he was unassuming and uncomplicated—a simple man who fully enjoyed life's simple pleasures.

Dad's visitation and burial were on Saturday, September 21, the day of the Emerald Lake fishing tournament. A gorgeous day with calm air, shining sun, and the thermometer touching 60, it reminded me of many early autumn days we shared on the lake. The day before, Mom, Nancy, Jo Ann, and I assembled the collages of photos for display at the funeral home. The ladies put together their board in short order while I worked solo on the "important" one, the fishing pictures. As I flipped through my photos, I contemplated every one in which Dad appeared, picking it up, placing it, then picking it up again, moving it to another place, picking it up again, seeking some kind of perfection, or at least logical sequence to the puzzle that lay before me.

With the viewing of each picture I entered the way-back machine, lovingly transported to happy and carefree times: Kipling Island in Canada, Lake Winnibigoshish in Minnesota, Little St. Germain and Dam Lakes in Wisconsin, Lake Erie in Ohio, and the Chain O' Lakes and Emerald Lake in Illinois. Bullheads, sunfish, crappie, perch, bass, walleye, northern pike, muskellunge. I could feel our boat rocking vigorously in October's waves. I could hear the drops of a spring rain slapping against our opaque parkas. I could feel a soft southwesterly breeze nudge us across a weedy bay. I could smell the earthworms just plucked from the moist dirt of our Hills Brothers coffee can. I could feel my grip tighten on the cool aluminum of the net handle, watching with eager anticipation as Dad, with lightweight equipment, dueled the heavyweight fish of a lifetime.

Jo Ann saw me struggling with my task and suggested a simple, random approach to the photo placement. Her words returned me to the moment, and I proceeded based on her input. When I came to the photo of the last fish Dad caught, I showed it to Nancy. Like most of the other "Kodak moments" spanning the past 40-plus years, I have a distinct recollection of the particulars.

The sun had just dipped behind the western treeline on a pleasant, early September day of 2001. We were trolling an Emerald Lake shoreline, a firetiger Shad Rap attached to Dad's line. I saw the tip of Dad's rod bobbing lightly, beyond what the tightly wobbling lure might account for, and suggested he might have a fish on. I slowed the motor as he reeled in a 13-inch walleye. Though not a typical photo opportunity, I felt compelled to snap a picture. It was the last outing of the weekend, and most likely the last time I'd get out with Dad in '01. We'd be heading home in the morning, and I remember clearly having the thought that Dad had really slowed down over the past year, and one never knows what the future may hold. Looking at the picture, Nancy said, "Oh, look at Dad, look at how happy he was—that picture just says it all!" We cried. Just as I am now as I write this. I'll miss you, Dad.

~~~~~

Cousin Larry dedicated his 2002 Symposium letter to Dad's memory:

> I think this is more a special remembrance than a dedication. My letter this year is not much in the way of stirring information, vivid and moving drama, or great philosophic moments, so perhaps dedicating a quiet year, a stable year to my Uncle Ed is fitting.
>
> I have not one "bad" memory of my Uncle. I can't recall a time or moment when I feared him, when I found him not to be genuine, and good. I think he had the quality of integrity, which to me means he was the same on the outside as the inside; I could count on him to be steady. He was a loving father and much a father to me when I spent time at his house. He did not council me, but gave me an example of gentleness and friendship. I felt welcomed around him. I never felt the sting of criticism from him, but rather acceptance—that I was okay. How did he manage that?
>
> I couldn't write all the scenes I remember where he appears in the story of my life, not in less than hundreds of pages—family gatherings, playing catch with Ed and me, taking us to the Forest Preserve, at the card table, at the Scrabble board, fishing comrade, teacher, eating and drinking with us, coming to NIU and taking me with his family to dinner, always reaching a hand out in a welcoming grasp when I'd take Mom and Dad to visit, or they'd come out to Grayslake in the late years of retirement. His lifeblood flows through the veins of my own life—totally integrated.
>
> I often thought of him as the more pleasant and easygoing companion of my high-strung father when we'd all get together. My father: Fred Flintstone; Uncle Ed: Barney Rubble; my father: Ralph Cramden; Uncle Ed: Ed Norton. But such comparisons don't do him justice, though they speak to the way I sometimes saw him—through a child's eyes, which is the way I can't help but see him, because he will always be older, wiser, more seasoned, experienced, always my uncle, my godfather, a man who possessed the most elusive and valuable quality, "Goodness," one of my favorite persons of all time.

~ ~ ~ ~ ~

Whatever is raucous, dissonant, clanging, and distracting in the city disappears in fishing country. Edges soften. Decibels decline.... Colors blend ... leaves flutter, grasses bend, trees sway, water glides, and the world is at once still and vibrant. Call it nature's embrace that soft context of leaf and sky, stone and water in which, if we pause to reflect upon our space and time, we feel a more natural fit. Like summer rain falling on dry land, the effect of nature on the soul is nothing if not healing.... This gentle embrace holds and soothes our angler.... If he is lucky, he might not only catch a fish, but find himself.
—Paul Quinnett, *Pavlov's Trout*

With everything that went on with Dad in 2002, trips to Emerald Lake were few and far between. I invited him for an outing in May, but he wasn't feeling up to it. It was also the year that rough times befell the lake. In early June, an 11-inch rainfall spawned a flood that ripped out the docks and tossed every boat, helter skelter, into the lake, some above, some below the water. With the cover remaining solidly in place, my Crestliner survived the havoc, with only a few scratches marring the hull. So significant the lake's tumult, it did not reopen for fishing until August.

After Dad's passing in September, a free Saturday opened up in October. I asked Larry then Rich then Terry then Chuck then Ben then Art then Mike then Tom if they could join me. All were unavailable. I made the trip solo. As I cruised and casted the lake, the memories of Dad's catches, spot by spot, flooded back. It became clear that I was meant to make that trip alone.

Part Seven
Fishing for the Meaning of Life

Fishermen should be the easiest men to convince to commence the search for the soul, because fishing is nothing but the pursuit of the elusive.... What was a fisherman but an untransmuted seeker?
—David James Duncan, *The River Why*

The Symposiums

"Cousin Larry dedicated his 2002 Symposium Letter to Dad's memory." Symposium Letter—hmmm, what's that again? In the experience of life, we've trolled quite a distance since the inception of the revered ritual.

As a refresher, before departure from NIU, *"We vowed to keep the venerable tradition of the Symposium alive ... formalizing a process to retain open lines of communication. Beginning late in the inaugural year of 1973, we agreed to compose and send a letter annually, each member to the others. A gathering to discuss the written offerings would follow a short time thereafter, to take place in an insular venue reminiscent of the original meetings."*

The odds of fulfilling such a bold plan, in spite of best intentions, classified it as a long shot. Liken it to any four individuals collectively honoring—for a lifetime—an interdependent New Year's resolution. Following our undergraduate years, although further academic aspirations and career choices took us in varied directions intellectually, geographically, and socially, I'm pleased to report that our council of four remained true to the commitment made 40 years prior. We beat the odds. At least, so far.

I, as the unofficial Symposium keeper of the records (a stat-man of the words...), maintain a complete set of the 1973-to-present letters, the accumulation bulging the seams of seven oversized binders. Individual letters have varied in length from one page to eighty-five. The letter media itself peepholes a four-decade time capsule: handwritten and duplicated on a copy machine; typewritten via manual and electric machines, carbon-papered for copies; word-processed via computer and hard copies run on dot-matrix, ink jet, and most recently, laser printers.

Before too long, the annual letters largely abandoned esoteric topics and began to journalize the twists and turns and ups and downs and triumphs and defeats and joys and sorrows chronicling the lives of four anything-but-nondescript guys hailing from the heart of the Midwest. The pages, often filled with a healthy dose of drama from these "days of our lives," would do proud the television soap opera of the same name. With form and content carte blanche, the letters have also served as vehicles for creative outlet: mostly prose, an occasional poem, and on singular occasions, a soundtrack accompaniment and a VHS video production.

An annual photo, two actually, became part of the pre-Symposium agenda beginning in 1994. With our council of four aligned side by side, the first snapshot records us facing the camera in a standard pose. In the second, our gazes angle skyward with thoughtful and more serious expressions that befit our contemplation of the mysteries of the universe. Or that squirrel scampering along nearby tree branches.

Elected annually, a "Symposiarchos" hosts the event and assumes responsibility for communicating and coordinating the letter mailing and meeting dates to the "Symposiaziens." The "Archos" also arranges for the venue, and provides food and wine for the lengthy gathering, which on average lasts ten hours. The Symposiarchos, identified in the photos as the individual holding a member-carved "talking stick" (talking not required) also adds a feather (found in the wild, not plucked from a living creature) to the top of the stick each year.

Prior to the commencement of each Symposium, Council members may submit trinkets, photos, documents, clothing, and any other miscellaneous memorabilia they deem significant to their life and times. After Council review (approval for submission not required), said items find a new home in each individual's multi-gallon size, color-coded Rubbermaid bin, each personal and historical collection of "stuff" referred to as the "Tub o' Archives." The Symposium and its ceremony are revered, but we are not above poking fun at ourselves.

A small fetish of carved green onyx, the "Tiki," occupies a place of honor as it observes every Symposium. In the early years, competitions such as a chess tournament would take place, the Tiki traveling with the victor until the following year.

I speculate that when the final member of the Symposium Council passes from this earth (dies), the Tiki will begin to glow, as a burning ember. The heat and setting-sun-orange light will gradually increase in intensity, radiating in all directions. The thousands of candlelit hours absorbed at the sacred Symposiums will consume it, and in a silent "explosion" of light and color transcending matter, time, and space, the collective ideas, words, and thoughts of all Symposiums past will jettison to the farthest reaches of the universe, bringing perfect knowledge and peace to all living things.

Or not.

Long before J.K. Rowling brought her mystical cast of *Harry Potter* characters to life, the magical aura surrounding the Symposiums led the Council members to bestow the titles of "Wizard of..." to each of its members: Words (Chuck), Wonder (Larry), World (me), and Whether/Weather (Terry). While our Council lacks the mystery of the Masons and the showmanship of the Shriners, remember that the television shows of our childhoods included *The Honeymooners*, featuring a Grand High Exalted Mystic Ruler of the Royal Order of Raccoons, and *The Flintstones*, with the Loyal Order of Water Buffaloes Lodge No. 26. At least we stopped short of purchasing pointed, star-studded Merlin headwear, unlike Ralph and Ed with their coonskin caps, Fred and Barney with water buffalo fedoras, and the tasseled, ornately decorated fezzes of the Shriners.

Unwritten bylaws provide the framework to guide us on organizational questions and issues large and small. Members of the Council invoke them as necessary to make a point, defend a position, or define an undefined point of order. You may ask, "How can 'unwritten' bylaws provide such guidance?" Precisely.

Unfortunately, it is these very unwritten bylaws (and the potential threat of unenforceable sanctions imbedded therein) that precludes me from painting a rich-in-detail picture of an actual Symposium gathering. Some Council members might say I've already said (written) too much. Most of our friends, co-workers, wives, and other family members seem fascinated by the concept and ritual of the Symposium and are impressed with its longevity. Special and unique, the fabric of the Symposium and its written record integrates many threads, among them enthusiasm, anxiety, hope, disgust, appreciation, guilt, gratitude, grief, pride, regret, optimism, depression, love (and loves), pity, self-pity, happiness, frustration, and humor. And binding them all? The powerful fervor of friendship. And a couple of bottles of wine.

The Symposium Council – Chuck, me, Larry, and Terry.

Contemplating the universe – or a squirrel.

As we approached the 20-year mark after college graduation, the tradition of Symposiums with annual letters and gatherings continued to endure. For several years in the early 1990s, toward the goal of generating additional discussion, the Symposium Council injected a breath of fresh air into its standard procedure with an initiative whereby each member posed a specified number of questions to one or all of the members on a predetermined date, to be answered in that year's Symposium letter.

Larry posed this question to me for response in my 1992 Symposium letter:

> *Let's imagine you did not awake from the anesthetic on the day of your back surgery. Instead, you went into cardiac arrest and then onto "The Big Chill." You awake, a conscious spirit, and learn through some appropriate media that there is a God, a heaven, and a hell. Hell is an eternity of pain many times worse than the stab in your back, hip and leg before the surgery. Heaven is pure bliss—something like being twenty-one, landing a 40-pound musky, and being drunk on Bols Strawberry without the nausea. The catch is, you have to write an essay justifying your existence, the one you just had on earth through July 1992, summarizing your contributions, the lives you affected positively and why, where you might have failed, and how you have reconciled yourself to that failure. Eternity rides on the essay. Please write it.*

I'll spare you the full breadth of my response, but in answer to "the lives you affected positively and why" part, I presented quotes from my best and closest friends, words that my fellow Symposium Council members had written about me, in Symposium Letters past.

From Chuck, February 4, 1984:

My friendship with Ed is meaningful—far more than most. He, I think, believes in my creative potential and has, indeed, inspired creativity in me. And our friendship has always been entertaining.

Ed, you—as has been stated time and time again—are the steady, conservative one. With solid roots and convictions, you live what appears (and I have no reason to doubt otherwise) a full and peacefully content existence.

You wrote boldly of friendship, need and love in your 1982 Symposium letter. We, the other members of the Symposium Council, seem to pay lip service to the "importance" of our friendships, but fail to fully tap this vital and invaluable human resource. Well, from my standpoint, and as unapparent as it often may seem, I greatly value your friendship, equally feel the need, and share the love.

From Larry, April 18, 1985:

I don't have enough paper to put down everything that comes to mind when you say "Ed." Without Ed, my whole life is different.... There's no separating Ed from my life. It's like denying having parents.

What is he now to me?

Part of me, part of my past. Part of the present. I know that some people are really envious that I have had something like that. It's like Lennon and McCartney: no matter what happens in the future there's no denying that they were the best. I had the best friendship ever, no one can say that—and it's something no one else gets a piece of—it is a fact. So, he's part of me—period. As to what I think of him, well, I think he's a good father. He represents a positive form of survival in today's world. Unless he's been lying these last few years, he seems pretty content. That's success. He's successful. He hasn't won a Nobel Prize but he's accomplished a lot just having his life in order. So I think pretty highly of him. He has his obsession—fishing—and I understand obsessions. His life works. He's got a fine wife and a good kid—for him I think he can ride that out for a long time without regret. So there's not much else to say.

From Terry, January 23, 1991:

It's been a great, fun time spending life with Ed.

~ ~ ~ ~ ~

At a Loss

Most people who know me would likely disagree or at least find it hard to believe: There's a chunk of my personality stamped with the words, "I'm shy." Why? Don't know. Though an above average student in my grammar school years, perhaps Sister Sarastine's method of correcting wrong answers with a swat of her hand catapulted me to more than a few moments of mouth-frozen-shut timidity. With a little bit of smarts and a big case of lockjaw in the school years that followed the third-grade trauma, my ultra-reserved demeanor, when in the company of adults, often drew the comment, "Still waters run deep." Fooled them, though I did like the water-related idiom.

Fish catching excluded, I've generally kept the outward expression of my emotional cards close to the vest: "cool, shy, and sensitive," as my Psychometric Affiliates report noted. I also tempered life's highs and lows, guiding them toward a balanced center point.

One of those lows occurred in 1983, when Jo Ann twice suffered miscarriages while expecting our second child. Though the "why" will always remain an unknown, Mother Nature must have had her reasons. Jo Ann and I processed our sadness, our grief, in a similar manner, dealing with it privately, silently. Even now, in the midst of typing thousands of words, adequate description of our misfortune fails me. The passing of time only softens the scar of sadness. Such loss never fully heals. Most often lingering beneath the level of consciousness, it still surfaces on occasion, evoking thoughts of what might have been.

~ ~ ~ ~ ~

On to Happy Days

Eddie filled our years with joy.

I recall any number of scenes embodying the homespun simplicity of Norman Rockwell illustrations, one in particular indelibly etched:

Upon returning home from work one evening, my view into the kitchen framed the thigh-high 15-month-old dressed in a brown and orange flannel shirt tucked into brown corduroy pants. Intently occupied with one of his toys, he did not see me enter. During the day, Jo Ann had taken him for his first haircut. With the hair that previously curled over his ears and at the base of his neck now gone, the sweet, innocent, and unforgettable image before me announced he'd crossed the threshold from baby to little boy.

As a three-year old, and continuing into the years that followed, he took a liking to board games—Chutes and Ladders and Candy Land early on. Outdoors he enjoyed a spin or two around the local putt-putt golf course, always followed by a soft serve ice cream cone. Oh, and lest I forget, we began outings to the local fishing holes: the Chain O' Lakes, the park pond near the house, and Emerald Lake. At age four, we trolled up his first fish, a six-inch white bass from The Chain's Lake Marie. It might as well have been a 60-inch musky as far as *my* reaction. Though "cool" on the outside, I held my breath with heart racing as his tiny hands forced the reel handle, eventually bringing the prize to the boat.

Eddie's first – a "fighting white" bass from The Chain.

Like his dexterity and concentration with the putter during mini golf, he similarly handled fishing rods and reels, executing casts without backlashes and exhibiting good focus and coordination when setting the hook on a nibbling bluegill or bass. As father and guide, I planned trips that would put the odds of catching fish in our favor, cognizant of the time of year, weather forecast, locations, and methods that might best ensure success. Jo Ann packed our Playmate cooler with snacks, fruit, and juice boxes. We caught fish with regularity—almost always, actually. Also aware of the fleeting nature of a child's attention span, I never forced the issue by overstaying our welcome, calling it a day when the antsy-factor appeared.

On a sunny spring day, we were invited to fish a private pond near the Crystal Lake home of a Motorola co-worker, Darwin. Eddie landed his fair share of the catch and amazed us with an ongoing tally of the bluegill, sunfish, and crappie, by species, by fisherman, as each fish was caught. Perhaps a statistician's occupation was in *his* future.

In the summer of that same year, a group of The Fabulous Maretti Brothers, wives, dads, and sons vacationed at Dam Lake in northern Wisconsin. Eddie and Terry's son, Jeff, both scored their first northern pike on that trip. Eddie also connected with his first walleye, which I found proudly centered on the kitchen table upon returning to the cabin after securing and unloading the boat.

Several years later, he won a rod and reel in a writing contest, the prize award letter as follows:

> *Dear Eddie:*
>
> *Your creative and unique writing skills have won you first place in the Fish Story Contest sponsored by Eagle Claw fishing tackle for the age category of five to ten.*
>
> *As a first place winner, you will be receiving an Eagle Claw top-of-the-line Fishin' Hole spinning rod with matching Gray Eagle Reel.*
>
> *Thank you for participating in our contest and enjoy fishing with Eagle Claw products. They make "fish stories" a reality.*
>
> *Sincerely,*
> *Gene Wilson, Marketing Manager*

The winning entry:

> The Walleye
>
> Walleye, walleye in the river
> For dinner I'll have you with liver.
> Here I am above your fishing hole
> With my favorite fishing pole.
> Please Mr. Walleye come up for my bait
> Don't make me sit and wait.
> Here I am in this nice day in May
> Waiting for you to swim my way.
> And if you are not too small
> I'll mount you on my bedroom wall.

That's my boy!

The water you touch in a river is the last of that which has passed, and the first of that which is coming; thus it is with time.
—Leonardo da Vinci

Goodbye, Old Friends

Art

Now retired for a number of years, this winter was the last straw—Art had had enough. The combination of snow and cold during the winter of 2013-2014 tormented as the most brutal in memory. Two were snowier, two were colder, but this one packed frigid temperatures, wind chills, and precipitation in one nasty, season-long haymaker. Snow totaled 82 inches, more than double the 35-inch average. Low temperatures below zero occurred on 26 days. Lake Michigan was 90% covered with ice. Art upped his lifelong Illinois roots, moving to the sunny, warm climes of Las Vegas.

No one can fill the void of his nonstop one-liners delivered at NIU football games, during a game of Risk, or just sitting around shooting the breeze. He said he'll fly back for an occasional Maretti Brothers get-together. I hope he's true to his word. We'll see.

Art "branching out" with a Chain O' Lakes catch circa 1978.

Douglas Hall to be Demolished

So read the title of a *Northern Star* online article posted Wednesday, March 26, 2014. The article continued, in part:

> Before the fall semester, Douglas Hall will be demolished and students will have to look to other residence halls for housing. The closing of Douglas Hall is a part of NIU President Doug Baker's Master Plan Thesis, designed to create a new campus, said NIU spokesman Paul Palian.
>
> Bill Nicklas, vice president of Public Safety and Community Relations, said Douglas' furniture will be salvaged and the hall demolished prior to the 2014-2015 academic year and Lucinda Drive will be extended to provide easier access and navigation.
>
> "Douglas Hall is one of the original 1960's large residence halls," Nicklas said. "It's not inviting. And it's old."

Old. Indeed. So too, Bill, are many of us who lived within its walls, calling it home during those years of learning both inside and outside the classroom. Sad, the bulldozing, but alas, time marches on. Perhaps no longer inviting, Bill, I know there was no place *as* inviting as D-2 those many years ago. I won't forget.

(And to ensure I won't forget [mental capacity issues previously noted], I scavenged an exquisite fragment of exterior concrete from the partially razed D-2 wing of the residence hall, the 50-year-old masonry nugget viewed daily from its place of prominence on my desk.)

Douglas Hall demolition – the memories won't be bulldozed.

Motorola 1309 Building Succumbs to the Wrecking Ball

From the *Daily Herald,* Tuesday, June 24, 2014

> Last September, Zurich American announced it would move out of its Zurich Towers in Schaumburg in favor of an energy-efficient, state-of-the-art building that would be constructed on 38.8 acres of unused land on the Motorola Solutions campus. Schaumburg officials approved the plan in February, and Motorola's so-called Parts Building at 1309 E. Algonquin Road, which had been unused in recent years, was demolished for the project.

~ ~ ~ ~ ~

Ernie Banks
January 31, 1931 – January 23, 2015

The 1959 Topps baseball card listed his height at 6"1" and weight at 170 pounds. He corralled his second consecutive MVP that year, playing shortstop for a team unable to finish above .500 in either of those campaigns. The first negro Chicago Cubs player, his 19-year career spanned 1953 to 1971. All 512 home runs were launched in a Cubs uniform.

Playing in the only major league ballpark without lights, his ever-present smile lit Wrigley Field like the summer sun. In spite of a Hall of Fame career, he never played in a post-season game. And like every Cubs fan still alive, he never saw his beloved Cubs win a World Series.

Rest in Peace, #14, "Mr. Cub."

"It's a beautiful day for a ballgame. Let's play two!"

He seems to regard angling as an amusement in which to pass the time pleasantly, rather than as a craft to be closely studied.
—W. Earl Hodgson

Retirement

Questions from the Swans, Others, or Self (S.O.S.):

S.O.S.: "So, how's that retirement thing going? What have you been doing? What's on the agenda going forward?"

E.L.P.: "Sleep. I've been catching up on sleep—35 years' worth. How sweet to forever bury that 5 a.m. wake-up and luxuriate atop the Serta until 7 a.m., give or take half an hour. No more struggling to stay awake through the 9 p.m. news, either. I'm burning the other end of that candle to 10:30 p.m., and once in a while, 11."

S.O.S.: "Don't overexert yourself."

E.L.P.: "And on many an afternoon, I'll float into a nap."

S.O.S.: "Like Georg and Yortuk Festruck from the old *Saturday Night Live* skits, you are one 'wild and crazy guy.' What else you got?"

E.L.P.: "Reading."

S.O.S.: "Something other than the Bass Pro Shop and Cabela's catalogs?"

E.L.P.: "Yeah, those, but the newspaper, too. I've always read the daily newspaper. And magazines like *Musky Hunter*, *Fishing Facts*, and more recently, *AARP*. But books? Not so much. In a good year, I might have finished one. Or at least started one. The plan was to change that."

S.O.S.: "Very noble. How's it working out?"

E.L.P.: "Many years before our retirement, Jo Ann purchased and presented me with a novel, Ernest Hemingway's *The Old Man and the Sea*. Published in 1952, the year of my birth (there's that fishy connection again), she inscribed it as follows:

> *Dear Ed,*
> *I wanted to purchase the first novel for your retirement library. I thought about it for a long time and settled on this selection—I hope you will enjoy it. Also, please remember that it is given to you with much love from the person who very much looks forward to spending our "golden years" together.*
> *With all my love, now and forever,*
> *Jo Ann*

"I surmise she chose that book envisioning her fisherman-spouse aging into the title role. And she knew I'd be less intimidated by the large font filling only 117 pages, many of those illustrated with drawings."

S.O.S.: "So, did you read it?"

E.L.P.: "Indeed I did. But I'm not pleased to report that shortly thereafter, I reverted to my minimalistic pre-retirement level of reading."

S.O.S.: "So if you're not reading, what do you do with all that time?"

E.L.P.: "Get up. Have a cup of coffee. Read the *Daily Herald*. (Yes, sad to admit, I've reached the age that compels me to peruse the obituaries, partially for reassurance that I'm not in them.) Eat a bowl of cereal. Take a shower. Get dressed. (Proud to say my pants size hasn't changed since college—still 36 x 32.) Check and respond to e-mails, including extensive deliberation before sending the daily chess move to Chuck. Take a walk. Get the mail. Pay the bills. By then, it's lunchtime.

"In the afternoon, assuming Jo Ann, I, or Mom (she's in her 90s now, with living quarters in our house) don't have a test, appointment, or follow up with our respective general practitioner, rheumatologist, pulmonologist, cardiologist, nephrologist, proctologist, neurologist, ophthalmologist, retina specialist, orthopedist, physical therapist, audiologist, dermatologist, E.N.T. specialist, or dentist, or have some yard work or shopping to do, I try to get some writing done until dinner time. Afterward, depending on the day of the week, the television goes on for the first time. Shows that might be viewed include *Seinfeld* re-runs, *Antiques Roadshow*, *Deadliest Catch*, *American Pickers*, or *Pawn Stars*. After that, if it's not too late, it's back to writing or maybe selling some stuff on eBay. Like several dozen lures never scarred by a musky's canines, the lures that had me mumbling after their first usage, 'Why the hell did I ever buy this?'

"If the season is right, I'm treated to Blackhawks hockey. Retirement's been well-timed in that regard. No issue staying up for the late-start West Coast games that end around midnight. I bought a 46-inch (by the way, an inch longer than my biggest musky) high-definition television and didn't miss a game during the 2009-10 Stanley Cup season, nor any game since. After ending the 49-year drought since Hull and Mikita brought home The Cup in '61, imagine my delight when Toews, Kane, and a revamped supporting cast repeated in '13. And unbelievably, again in '15."

S.O.S.: "We're happy for you. Really, we are. No TV during the day?"

E.L.P.: "Nope."

S.O.S.: "The *Days of our Lives*, *Maury*, and *Dr. Phil* sponsors won't be happy to hear that. Okay, let's move on. Don't you and Jo Ann get on each other's nerves?"

E.L.P.: "Interesting. It's a question asked by a lot of people."

S.O.S.: "Inquiring minds want to know, perhaps to glimpse their own future."

E.L.P.: "We do a lot together and a fair amount apart. If nothing else is going on, Jo Ann usually reads or works on her crafts. I write. I don't know if our marriage flies in the face of the ordinary, but we rarely fight—rarely fought. Maybe once every couple of years we'd have a disagreement on something that brought our voices to a raised level, but that's about it. Few, far between, and of short duration, I don't think there's ever been a night when we went to sleep angry at each other."

S.O.S.: "Lucky you."

E.L.P.: "Truly. Our preferences on house duties nicely mesh, too. She does the "inside" stuff—the cooking, housecleaning, and laundry. I manage our finances and handle the "outside" tasks: yard work, garden, garage, house exterior, and cars. We both do volunteer work for the Kishwaukee Health Care System Hospice, though Jo Ann does the lion's share. She also hand-crafts greeting cards for Operation Write Home, their mission: 'Helping heroes keep in touch with home.' The organization forwards the holiday and general themed cards to soldiers stationed overseas, who sign and send them to their loved ones at home.

"And we babysit our grandson, Matthew, on Thursdays and Fridays as well as other days or evenings as needed. Although rising at 5 a.m. parallels the old working days, the wakeup has a different feel—probably something to do with looking forward to the day's activities, a labor of love."

S.O.S.: "Hmmm ... busy, busy. Can you even find time to go to the bathroom?"

E.L.P.: "That 'Depends.'"

S.O.S.: "You rarely miss an opportunity, do you?"

E.L.P.: "I just *go* with the *flow*..."

S.O.S.: "Well played."

E.L.P.: "Thank you. And by the way, it really is a slow flow. The pace to get things done is more relaxed, but the days still fly by. Andy Rooney's analogy rings true: 'Life is like a roll of toilet paper. The closer it gets to the end, the faster it goes.' And my Uncle Joe brought the point home in another way. His son Phil and I were sitting across the table from him at his 85th birthday party when he deadpanned, 'You know, you guys looked a lot younger 40 years ago.'"

S.O.S.: (finishing a chuckle...) "Ah, the Piotrowski humor runs deep and Sahara-dry.... Your mention of a party takes me to another thought. It seems like you were a pretty social guy, with a wide array of relationships—Motorolans, the Fabulous Maretti Brothers, The Club, your cousins and other fishing friends. Do you miss the frequent contact? Do you stay in touch?"

E.L.P.: "I'll begin my answer with my Motorola farewell e-mail":

> *To my co-workers, associates, and friends,*
>
> *Last week marked the 35th anniversary of my employment with Motorola. To celebrate the occasion, I will be retiring on Friday, December 11th. As you might expect, such a major decision was not an easy one, but the list of things to do and enjoy outside the formal work environment is long, and I have decided now is the time to dig into it.*
>
> *While a book is made of paper and binding and ink, I prefer to think of it as the story it contains. Likewise, as corporations consist of brick and mortar, brands, and products, I view them in terms of people and the relationships that are established, develop, and prosper over time. In the story of my working career, each of you played a role in one or more of the chapters.*
>
> *I thank you all for your help, counsel, and friendship over these many years. It is, without doubt, the most valued and rewarding aspect of my years with Motorola and is what I will miss the most. I wish you all the best.*
>
> *Ed*

S.O.S.: "So you played the overused 'I won't miss the work, but I will miss the people' card in your retirement ta-ta?"

E.L.P.: "Yes. I wrote it. And I said it. And I meant it. I probably average a luncheon per month with those still employed or since retired.

"Larry and I meet for breakfast at the IHOP in McHenry every six weeks or so. There's an occasional get together with various members of The Fabulous Maretti Brothers. Competitive events have become less physically taxing with the passing of years: the beanbag-toss game some know as "cornhole," casting a hookless plug into a bucket, pinochle, and, always, a game of Risk. Of course, Art's departure to Las Vegas may be the final chapter on all things Maretti. The ties with my web of fishing partners remain strong, even though actual time on the water has dwindled."

S.O.S.: "In a life flush with fishing, we find that odd. Seems like it should be just the opposite. Does that bother you?"

E.L.P.: "No. I'm content that I've had a life well fished. I still enjoy the annual sojourn to Canada to hunt the elusive muskellunge and travel to Emerald Lake, on occasion, to bass fish. Besides that, when is there time?"

S.O.S.: "If you don't mind, we'll ask the questions. Aren't retirees supposed to have all the time in the world? You're not painting a pretty picture for the workers-in-waiting."

E.L.P.: "Working folks don't want to hear how busy a retiree is. And I don't blame them. Oh, and speaking of painting, there'll be some of that in my future, and not just with Dutch Boy and Sherwin Williams. I've dabbled in watercolors, you know."

S.O.S.: "Yes, we heard something about that. How did it go?"

E.L.P.: "I think some relatives and friends might have preferred I paint their houses rather than do paintings *of* them."

S.O.S.: Most of your days seem filled with taking care of basic 'life stuff,' necessary but mundane. Are you okay with that? How are you feeling about yourself? Satisfied? Other than catching a giant musky, any stones still left unturned?"

E.L.P.: "Why don't you run a few more questions together so I don't remember any of them? I'm easily confused these days, you know."

S.O.S.: "Sorry. We forget that your declining mental state tracks with your physical deterioration. Let's just go with this: You mentioned that you write on some afternoons and evenings. What's that all about?"

E.L.P.: "Yes. I want to create. I need to create. Creativity leads to the ultimate realization of personal fulfillment, the pinnacle of the human experience. After sex, that is."

S.O.S.: "So, like your watercolors, writing is another outlet for creative foreplay. What type of writing are you doing? *Penthouse* letters?"

E.L.P.: "No, I have bigger fish to fry. I'm working on a memoir-style autobiography. Rather than waiting for my life to flash before my eyes in the moments preceding the definitive 'dirt nap,' I'm enjoying documenting my recollections. It's a pleasant, leisurely cruise. Its working title is *The Project*."

S.O.S.: "Very creative."

E.L.P.: "I'm guessing you've heard the comment from British-American author and journalist, Christopher Hitchens: "Everyone has a book inside them."

S.O.S.: "We have. But are *you* aware of his complete statement? 'Look, everyone has a book inside them ... which is where I think it should, in most cases, remain.'"

E.L.P.: "S.O.S., you're starting to grate on me, like a fish scaler. I must go now. Got to get back to my writing."

S.O.S.: "Whatever floats your boat. Until next time...."

Part Eight
Sunset and Another Dawn – Fishing for Serenity

Being close to the things your true heart loves is the surest source of joy, whether family, friends or fishing.
—Paul Quinnett, *Fishing Lessons*

Calm Waters

Our sweet grandchild, Matthew, measured 20-inches and weighed 6½-pounds at birth. Like his dad, and his father before him, he sized favorably to a largemouth bass that most anglers would be proud to catch...

His birth added the role of "grandpa" to my bio. That moniker officially classifies me as old, though most who know me would argue my ongoing parade of physical maladies began my movement into that category decades ago.

Insightful comments from my Symposium compatriots did not disappoint:

Larry: "That should keep you busy for, oh, the next 18 years or so..."

Terry (two weeks post-announcement): "How are you doing on changing diapers? If you haven't done it yet, start. You will need the practice. Just about the time Matthew gets out of them, you will start wearing them. And then you can change your own."

Chuck: "...a star piercing the Northern Sky ... winds calling forth the Song of Mariah ... a spirit surges from the Force Within ... Voila! ... Grandpa Ed will be on hand to ensure Matthew's casts will be Straight and True."

Since his birth, Jo Ann and I babysit him two days per week. I'm not pleased to report that during his first year he likely developed a tin ear as a result of my crooning the tarantella as I swung him through the air prior to each bottle feeding. I believe the excitement coursing through his body, evidenced by legs flailing and flapping, relates to the Pavlovian reflex recognizing an upcoming meal rather than exuberant enjoyment of the off-key melody.

Since he began walking at the 14-month mark, the little dynamo has been wearing out the carpets. And in his world, the only thing better than roving the rooms of the house is rambling in the out-of-doors.

On any given day, the move into sunshine and fresh air can't come soon enough. Just the mention of the word "outside" sends him racing to the laundry room where he grabs his pint-size Velcro-fastened sneakers. Resolute strides bring him to the second-floor staircase where he sits down and attempts to put them on himself. His dexterity not far enough advanced, the task completes with help from Grandma or Grandpa. (Good practice for me: It can't be long before the shoes I wear go Velcro.) Next, it's "Go get your hat," sending him to the bin containing his Lightning McQueen baseball cap. Unassisted, he positions the cap atop his head. He's ready to go.

He chases and pops the bubbles Jo Ann swirls through the air. We play catch: I roll a tennis ball to him and he throws it back, remarkably accurate for a tyke and equally comfortable with either arm. (A cost-conscious major league club will, one day, appreciate his "two for the price of one" skill.) He whacks an emptied plastic spool of fishing line, a makeshift puck, with a just-right-for-his-size hockey stick. On some days we stroller him to the park where he enjoys time on the toddler-friendly playground equipment.

Many things he says or does make us laugh. Certain noises, certain words, certain actions make him laugh. His giggles—innocent, genuine, infectious—amplify our joy. Those treasured moments now top my revised list of "favorite things."

He swings his toy golf club at the plastic balls—one yellow, one purple, one blue. We've been working on color recognition for a couple of weeks now.

"Matthew, what color is this golf ball?"

"Bee-yoo."

"No, it's yellow."

"Yay-yo."

"That's right—yellow!"

"What color is *this* ball?"

"Bee-yoo."

"No, it's purple."

"Pur-puh."

"Good job, purple!"

"What color is this ball, Matthew?"

"Bee-yoo."

"Yes, blue! What a bright boy you are!"

When inclement weather denies outdoor activities we'll drive to an indoor shopping mall for a change of scenery and the opportunity to stretch our legs. Or perhaps a trip to a local retailer, where pet department tanks filled with goldfish and colorful tropical fish capture his attention.

Not long after he turned 18-months of age, we ventured to the local outdoors-outfitters store. Near the center of the main floor and adjacent to an extensive exhibit of wild animal mounts in a natural setting, dimly lit aquariums line both sides of a walkway through a faux cave. Specimens that roam nearby lakes, largemouth and smallmouth bass, crappie, bluegill, catfish, gar, carp, northern pike, and muskellunge inhabit the tanks. Matthew enjoyed watching the "fishies" as much, I believe, as his subsequent unfettered advance through the aisles displaying thousands of colorful lures and other fishing equipment.

He uncannily slowed upon reaching the children's gear. Then, as if respectful of an altar, dropped to his knees in front of a shelf containing plastic tackle boxes, their red bottoms and yellow tops decorated with the Pixar *Cars* theme. He displayed a demeanor intense and focused, as an angler trying to determine the exact instant to set the hook on a walleye nibbling on a jig and minnow. Right arm finally reaching forward, his tiny fingers snagged the handle of the closest one. The prize firmly in his grasp, he labored to his feet and resumed his march through the store for the better part of 15 minutes with the box solidly in tow. Yes, I bought it for him *and* had the good fortune to find a matching child's life vest on our way to the checkout.

Matthew also loves to read books, or more accurate to his tender age, sit attentively on my lap looking at the pictures and words as I read them to him. His extensive library, filling a number of storage crates, puts my two-shelf (one of those filled with fishing books) lifetime library to shame. A Sesame Street Play-a-Song title, *Elmo's Piano*, ranks among his favorites. Pressing any of the nine buttons, coded with musical instruments, plays four bars of notes of classic children's tunes, among them, "The Wheels on the Bus," "Head, Shoulders, Knees and Toes," and "Here We Go 'Round the Mulberry Bush." The button Matthew pushes most frequently, however, floats the notes to "Row, Row, Row Your Boat." I always sing the words to him:

> *Row, row, row your boat,*
> *Gently down the stream,*
> *Merrily, merrily, merrily, merrily,*
> *Life is but a dream.*

Matthew grins. My mind snaps a photo: the smile, exposing the almost-full upper row of baby teeth; a button nose and plump cheeks; the soft down of blond hair; large blue eyes the color of a lake, pure.

I wonder if he'll be ready to go fishing next year. If not, perhaps the year after. I know bluegills-in-waiting swim the local ponds. Years down the road, I envision grandfather and grandson fishing Emerald Lake, and in the evening we'll relax on a cabin porch, sip a soda, and chat about whatever comes to mind.

An hour after lunch, Jo Ann puts him down for his afternoon nap. When she returns, I'll take a nap, too.

With book in hand, she leans against the couch's armrest, legs outstretched across half the cushions. Sofa pillow beneath my head and resting on her thigh, I lay fully reclined with feet dangling, as if off the edge of a pier.

Eyes closed I take a deep breath and drift into a smile…

Row, row, row your boat,
Gently down the stream,
Merrily, merrily, merrily, merrily,
Life is but a dream,
Life is but a dream, , ,
Life is but a dream, , , , , ,

~ ~ ~ ~ ~

No life is so happy and so pleasant as the well-governed angler.
—Izaak Walton

~~~~~ Fin ~~~~~
(As in the fish's...)

From the Author

My grandson, Matthew, is one of approximately 15 million Americans, almost half of those children, who suffer from severe, life-threatening food allergies.

Ten percent of the net proceeds from each copy of this book will be donated to FARE (Food Allergy Research and Education), the world's leading organization dedicated to finding a cure and making the world safe for individuals afflicted with this serious disorder.

~~~~~~~

If you've enjoyed reading this book, please consider going to **Amazon.com** to rate and review it. If you haven't, well, let's just keep it our little secret...

In either case, please feel free to send me comments via email at ifish44.ep@gmail.com -- I'd love to hear from you!

Thanks!